HOLT MATHEMATICS

HOLT, RINEHART AND WINSTON, PUBLISHERS
New York • Toronto • Mexico City • London • Sydney • Tokyo

4

AUTHORS

Eugene D. Nichols
Robert O. Lawton Distinguished Professor
  of Mathematics Education
Florida State University
Tallahassee, Florida

Paul A. Anderson
Former Elementary School Teacher
Instructor of Elementary Mathematics
University of Nevada
Las Vegas, Nevada

Francis M. Fennell
Associate Professor of Education
Director of Mathematics Clinic
Western Maryland College
Westminster, Maryland

Frances Flournoy
Professor of Elementary Education
University of Texas
Austin, Texas

Sylvia A. Hoffman
Resource Consultant in Mathematics
Illinois State Board of Education
State of Illinois

Robert Kalin
Professor of Mathematics Education
Florida State University
Tallahassee, Florida

John Schluep
Emeritus Professor of Mathematics
State University of New York
Adjunct in Mathematics
Hartwick College
Oneonta, New York

Leonard Simon
Former Mathematics Teacher and
  Assistant Director of Curriculum Development
New York City Board of Education
New York, New York

COMPUTER CONSULTANT

Frank M. Trunzo
Mathematics Curriculum Coordinator and
  Director of Lower School Computer Program
Mathematics Teacher
Germantown Academy
Fort Washington, Pennsylvania

Copyright © 1985 by
Holt, Rinehart and Winston, Publishers
All rights reserved
Printed in the United States of America

ISBN 0-03-064208-6

01234 069 10987654

Art and photo credits appear on page 420.

Cover design by Carole Anson.

Cover photos: TL, Stan Pantovic/Photo
Researchers; **TR,** HRW photo by **Russell Dian;**
BL, HRW photo by **James Gilmour; BR,** Janeart
Ltd/Image Bank.

TABLE OF CONTENTS

1 ADDITION AND SUBTRACTION FACTS

Addition	2
Bright Ideas	4
Midchapter Review/Something Extra (Calculator Activities)	6
Computer	7
Subtraction	8
Fact Tricks	10
Problem-Solving Skills/Choosing an Operation	12
Skills Review/Something Extra (Non-Routine Problems)	14
Related Sentences	15
Using Related Sentences	16
Computer	17
Number Patterns	18
Problem-Solving Applications/Career	20
Chapter Review	21
Chapter Test	22
Skills Check	23

2 NUMERATION

Writing Numerals	26
Place Value/Skills Review	28
Thousands	30
Millions	32
Midchapter Review/Skills Review	34
Number Names	35
Roman Numerals/Something Extra (Non-Routine Problems)	36
Problem-Solving Skills/Choosing the Correct Number Sentence	38
Comparing Numbers	40
Rounding Numbers	42
Rounding Thousands	44
Skills Review	45
Problem-Solving Applications/ Reading a Chart	46
Chapter Review	47
Chapter Test	48
Skills Check	49

3 ADDITION

Computer	52
Adding Tens and Ones	53
Column Addition	54
Adding Tens	56
Adding Hundreds	58
Adding Thousands	60
Adding More Thousands	62
Midchapter Review/Something Extra (Calculator Activities)	64
Comparing	65
Problem-Solving Skills/Writing the Correct Number Sentence	66
Money	68
Adding Money	70
Skills Review/Something Extra (Non-Routine Problems)	71
Estimating Sums	72
Problem-Solving Applications/Career	74
Chapter Review	75
Chapter Test	76
Skills Check	77

4 SUBTRACTION

Computer	80
Checking Subtraction	81
Subtracting Tens	82
Subtracting Hundreds	84
Subtracting Thousands	86
Zeros in Subtraction	88
Midchapter Review/Something Extra (Non-Routine Problems)	90
Flowcharts	91
Problem-Solving Skills/Using Four Steps	92
Skills Review/Something Extra (Non-Routine Problem)	94
Subtracting Money	95
Making Change	96
Estimating Differences	98
Problem-Solving Applications/ Estimating Differences	100
Chapter Review	101
Chapter Test	102
Skills Check	103

5 MULTIPLICATION AND DIVISION FACTS

Multiplication	106
Zero	108
One	109
Two	110
Even and Odd	111
Three and Four	112
Five and Six	114
Seven and Eight	116
Nine	117
Skills Review/Computer	118
Midchapter Review/Something Extra (Non-Routine Problem)	119
Grouping Property	120
Multiplication-Addition Property	121
Problem-Solving Skills/Is the Answer Reasonable?	122
Division	124
Dividing by 1, 2, and 3	126
Computer	127
Related Sentences	128
Skills Review	129
Dividing by 4, 5, and 6	130
Dividing by 7, 8, and 9/Something Extra (Calculator Activity)	132
Multiples and Factors/Something Extra (Activity)	134
Problem-Solving Applications/ Career	136
Chapter Review	137
Chapter Test	138
Skills Check	139

6 MEASUREMENT

Centimeters	142	Time Earlier and Later	160
Centimeters, Meters, Kilometers	144	Writing the Date	162
Changing Units of Measure	146	Skills Review/Something Extra	
Liter and Milliliter	147	(Non-Routine Problem)	163
Units of Mass	148	Measuring in the Customary System	164
Measuring Temperature	150	Length in the Customary System	166
Midchapter Review/Something Extra		Liquid Measure in the Customary	
(Non-Routine Problem)	152	System	167
Skills Review	153	Weight in the Customary System	168
Computer	154	Fahrenheit Temperature	169
Problem-Solving Skills/Writing a		Problem-Solving Applications	170
Number Sentence	156	Chapter Review	171
Time	158	Chapter Test	172
		Skills Check	173

7 MULTIPLICATION

Computer	176	Estimating Products	190
Tens, Hundreds, and Thousands	177	Special Products	192
Multiplying Tens	178	Multiplying by Multiples of 10/	
Multiplying Hundreds	180	Something Extra	
Multiplying Thousands	182	(Non-Routine Problem)	194
Multiplying Money	184	Multiplying 2-digit Numbers	196
Midchapter Review/Something Extra		Multiplying Larger Numbers	198
(Calculator Activities)	186	Problem-Solving Applications/	
Skills Review/Something Extra		Career	200
(Non-Routine Problems)	187	Chapter Review	201
Problem-Solving Skills/Choosing a		Chapter Test	202
Number Sentence	188	Skills Check	203

8 DIVISION

		Computer	223
Computer	206	Problem-Solving Skills/Two-Step	
Special Quotients	207	Problems	224
Remainders	208	Dividing by Multiples of 10	226
2-Digit Quotients	210	More Dividing by Multiples of 10	228
More 2-Digit Quotients	212	Dividing Money	230
3-Digit Quotients	214	Skills Review	231
More 3-Digit Quotients	216	Time	232
Zeros in the Quotient	218	Two-Digit Division	234
Midchapter Review/Something Extra		Computer	235
(Non-Routine Problems)	220	Problem-Solving Applications	236
Skills Review/Something Extra		Chapter Review	237
(Non-Routine Problems)	221	Chapter Test	238
Averages	222	Skills Check	239

9 FRACTIONS

Fractions 242
More on Fractions 244
Equal Fractions 246
Lists of Equal Fractions 248
Finding Equal Fractions 250
Midchapter Review/Something Extra
　(Non-Routine Problems) 252
Checking for Equal Fractions 253
Problem-Solving Skills/Finding a
　Hidden Step 254
Finding a Fraction of a Number 256
Ratios as Fractions 257
Skills Review/Something Extra
　(Non-Routine Problems) 258
Comparing Fractions 259
More Comparing 260
Fractions and One 262
Fractions as Division 263
Mixed Numbers 264
Problem-Solving Applications/
　Career 266
Chapter Review 267
Chapter Test 268
Skills Check 269

10 ADD AND SUBTRACT FRACTIONS

Adding Fractions 272
Sums 1 and Greater than 1 274
Different Denominators 276
Adding Mixed Numbers 278
Midchapter Review/Something Extra
　(Calculator Activities) 280
Skills Review/Something Extra
　(Non-Routine Problems) 281
Problem-Solving Skills/Identifying
　Extra Information 282
Subtracting Fractions 284
Different Denominators 286
Subtracting Mixed Numbers 288
Decimals-Tenths/Computer 290
Decimals-Hundredths 292
Adding Decimals 294
Subtracting Decimals 295
Problem-Solving Applications/Using
　Fractions and Decimals 296
Chapter Review 297
Chapter Test 298
Skills Check 299

11 GEOMETRY

Points, Line Segments, and Lines 302
Angles/Something Extra
　(Non-Routine Problems) 304
Circles/Skills Review 306
Polygons 308
Triangles, Rectangles, and Squares 310
Midchapter Review/Something Extra
　(Non-Routine Problems) 312
Computer 313
Symmetry 314
Perimeter 316
Something Extra (Calculator
　Activity) 317
Activities with Area/Skills Review 318
Finding Area by Multiplying 320
Problem-Solving Skills/Using
　Pictures or Diagrams 322
Solid Figures 324
Volume 326
Problem-Solving Applications/
　Finding the Better Buy 328
Chapter Review 329
Chapter Test 330
Skills Check 331

12 GRAPHS AND PROBABILITY

Pictographs 334
Bar Graphs 336
Circle Graphs 338
Midchapter Review 340
Skills Review/Something Extra
  (Non-Routine Problems) 341
Problem-Solving Skills/Is There
  Enough Information? 342
Graphing Ordered Pairs 344

Probability/Something Extra
  (Calculator Activity) 346
More Probability 348
Problem-Solving Applications/
  Customary Measure 350
Chapter Review 351
Chapter Test 352
Skills Check 353

Computer Literacy 354
Addition Table 366
Multiplication Table 367
Extra Practice 368

Table of Measures 394
Glossary and Symbol List 395
Answers to the Learning Stage 400
Index 413

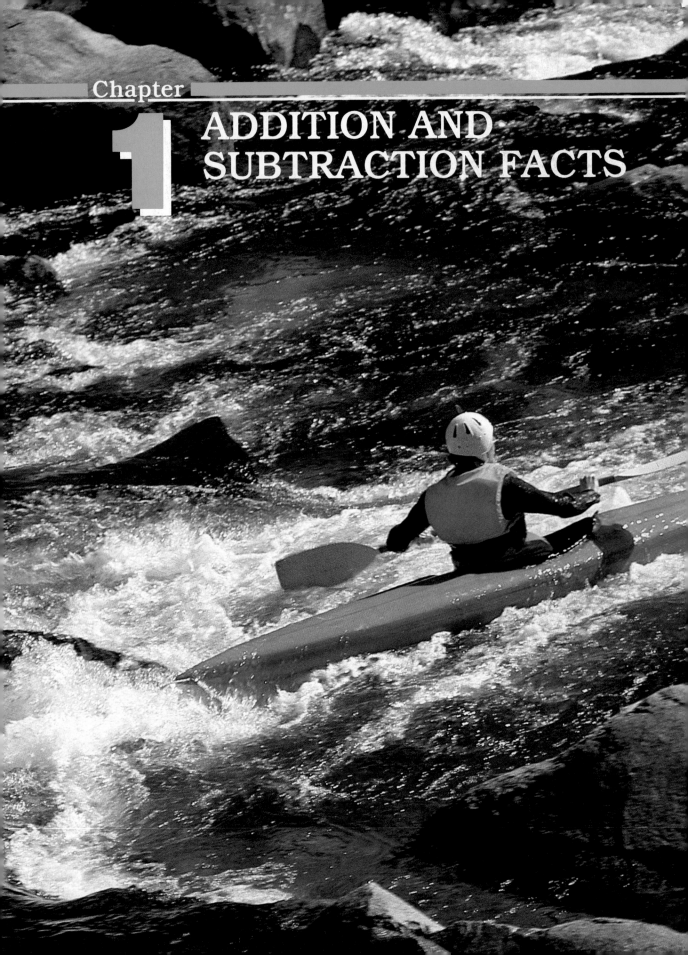

1 ADDITION AND SUBTRACTION FACTS

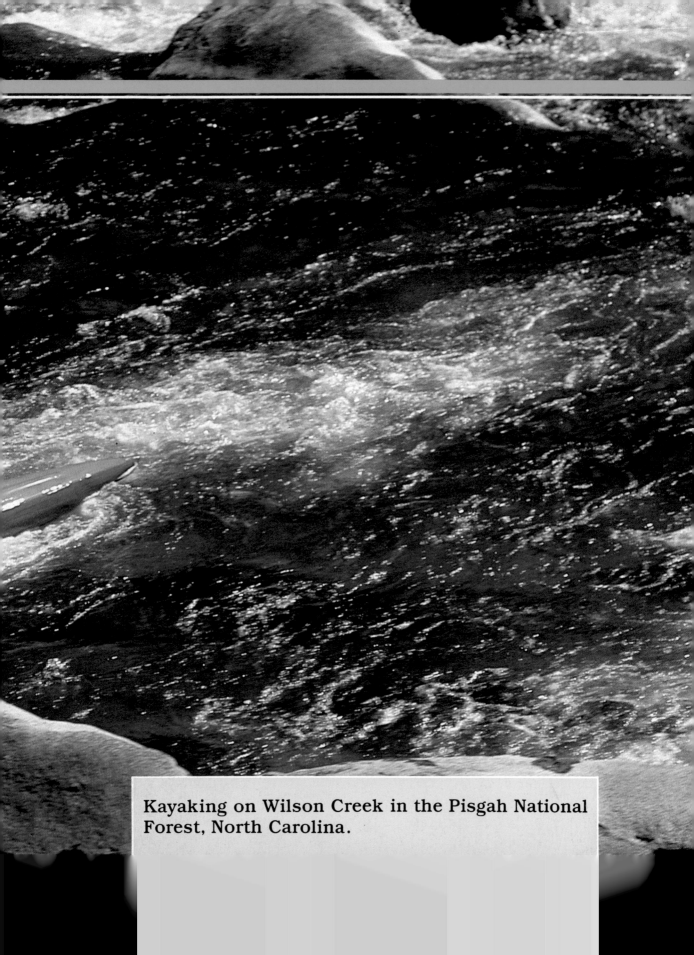

Kayaking on Wilson Creek in the Pisgah National Forest, North Carolina.

ADDITION

Addition is joining groups together.

$$\begin{array}{r} 3 \\ + 2 \\ \hline 5 \end{array}$$ ← addends
← sum

$$3 + 2 = 5$$
↑   ↑   ↑
addends   sum

Study and Learn

A. Complete.

   1. Draw a picture to show $5 + 6$.

   2. $5 + 6 = $ __?__

   3. What are the addends?

   4. What is the sum?

B. Complete.

   5. Draw a picture to show $6 + 5$.

   6. $6 + 5 = $ __?__

▶ $5 + 6 = 11$ and $6 + 5 = 11$, so the order of the addends does not change the sum.

▶ When adding 0 and a number, the sum is that number.

C. Add.

   7. $\quad \begin{array}{r} 4 \\ + 5 \\ \hline \end{array} \quad \begin{array}{r} 5 \\ + 4 \\ \hline \end{array}$
   8. $\quad \begin{array}{r} 3 \\ + 7 \\ \hline \end{array} \quad \begin{array}{r} 7 \\ + 3 \\ \hline \end{array}$
   9. $\quad \begin{array}{r} 7 \\ + 0 \\ \hline \end{array} \quad \begin{array}{r} 0 \\ + 7 \\ \hline \end{array}$

Practice

Add.

1. $1 + 9$ 2. $3 + 6$ 3. $4 + 5$ 4. $3 + 8$ 5. $9 + 3$

6. $\begin{array}{r} 0 \\ + 0 \\ \hline \end{array}$ 7. $\begin{array}{r} 3 \\ + 0 \\ \hline \end{array}$ 8. $\begin{array}{r} 0 \\ + 3 \\ \hline \end{array}$ 9. $\begin{array}{r} 1 \\ + 1 \\ \hline \end{array}$ 10. $\begin{array}{r} 9 \\ + 1 \\ \hline \end{array}$

11. $\begin{array}{r} 2 \\ + 2 \\ \hline \end{array}$ 12. $\begin{array}{r} 8 \\ + 2 \\ \hline \end{array}$ 13. $\begin{array}{r} 2 \\ + 8 \\ \hline \end{array}$ 14. $\begin{array}{r} 3 \\ + 3 \\ \hline \end{array}$ 15. $\begin{array}{r} 6 \\ + 3 \\ \hline \end{array}$

16. $\begin{array}{r} 4 \\ + 4 \\ \hline \end{array}$ 17. $\begin{array}{r} 7 \\ + 4 \\ \hline \end{array}$ 18. $\begin{array}{r} 4 \\ + 7 \\ \hline \end{array}$ 19. $\begin{array}{r} 6 \\ + 4 \\ \hline \end{array}$ 20. $\begin{array}{r} 4 \\ + 8 \\ \hline \end{array}$

21. $\begin{array}{r} 5 \\ + 5 \\ \hline \end{array}$ 22. $\begin{array}{r} 9 \\ + 5 \\ \hline \end{array}$ 23. $\begin{array}{r} 5 \\ + 9 \\ \hline \end{array}$ 24. $\begin{array}{r} 8 \\ + 5 \\ \hline \end{array}$ 25. $\begin{array}{r} 5 \\ + 7 \\ \hline \end{array}$

26. $\begin{array}{r} 6 \\ + 6 \\ \hline \end{array}$ 27. $\begin{array}{r} 6 \\ + 7 \\ \hline \end{array}$ 28. $\begin{array}{r} 7 \\ + 6 \\ \hline \end{array}$ 29. $\begin{array}{r} 6 \\ + 8 \\ \hline \end{array}$ 30. $\begin{array}{r} 8 \\ + 6 \\ \hline \end{array}$

31. $\begin{array}{r} 7 \\ + 7 \\ \hline \end{array}$ 32. $\begin{array}{r} 8 \\ + 7 \\ \hline \end{array}$ 33. $\begin{array}{r} 7 \\ + 8 \\ \hline \end{array}$ 34. $\begin{array}{r} 9 \\ + 7 \\ \hline \end{array}$ 35. $\begin{array}{r} 7 \\ + 9 \\ \hline \end{array}$

36. $\begin{array}{r} 8 \\ + 8 \\ \hline \end{array}$ 37. $\begin{array}{r} 8 \\ + 9 \\ \hline \end{array}$ 38. $\begin{array}{r} 9 \\ + 8 \\ \hline \end{array}$ 39. $\begin{array}{r} 8 \\ + 3 \\ \hline \end{array}$ 40. $\begin{array}{r} 5 \\ + 8 \\ \hline \end{array}$

41. $\begin{array}{r} 9 \\ + 9 \\ \hline \end{array}$ 42. $\begin{array}{r} 9 \\ + 6 \\ \hline \end{array}$ 43. $\begin{array}{r} 6 \\ + 9 \\ \hline \end{array}$ 44. $\begin{array}{r} 9 \\ + 2 \\ \hline \end{array}$ 45. $\begin{array}{r} 0 \\ + 9 \\ \hline \end{array}$

Solve Problems

46. 6 skaters
6 skating instructors
How many people
in all?

47. Pam skated 3 laps.
Sue skated 5 laps.
How many laps
skated in all?

BRIGHT IDEAS

Here are some ways to help you find addition facts.
Think of doubles.

6	Think:
+ 7	6 + 6 and
13	1 more

8	Think:
+ 7	7 + 7 and
15	1 more

5	Think:
+ 7	5 + 5 and
12	2 more

Study and Learn

A. Add. Think of doubles.

1.   4
   + 5

2.   7
   + 8

3.   5
   + 6

4.   6
   + 8

5.   7
   + 9

> Making a 10 can also help to find a fact.
>
> 7   Think:
> + 5   7 + 3 = 10 and 2 more
> 12
>
> 8   Think:
> + 5   8 + 2 and 3 more
> 13

B. Add. Think of tens.

6.   8
   + 3

7.   5
   + 6

8.   7
   + 4

9.   4
   + 8

10.   3
   + 9

> Here's a special trick for adding 9's.
>
> 7 ← Subtract 1 from 7. Get 6.
> + 9 ← Add 1 to 9. Get 10.
> 16 ← Add 6 + 10. Get 16.

C. Add. Remember 9's.

11.   8
   + 9

12.   6
   + 9

13.   9
   + 3

14.   9
   + 5

15.   2
   + 9

Practice

Add. Remember the addition tricks.

1. 8
  + 8

2. 6
  + 6

3. 9
  + 9

4. 7
  + 7

5. 5
  + 5

6. 4
  + 4

7. 8
  + 9

8. 6
  + 7

9. 6
  + 5

10. 8
  + 7

11. 5
  + 6

12. 5
  + 7

13. 1
  + 9

14. 8
  + 2

15. 3
  + 7

16. 6
  + 4

17. 4
  + 6

18. 7
  + 3

19. 9
  + 2

20. 3
  + 8

21. 7
  + 5

22. 9
  + 3

23. 8
  + 4

24. 7
  + 4

25. 9
  + 8

26. 9
  + 7

27. 6
  + 9

28. 5
  + 9

29. 9
  + 4

30. 4
  + 9

31. 6
  + 8

32. 3
  + 4

33. 2
  + 5

34. 6
  + 2

35. 4
  + 8

36. 4
  + 7

37. 2
  + 3

38. 8
  + 6

39. 7
  + 9

40. 5
  + 8

41. 6
  + 3

42. 4
  + 5

43. 9
  + 0

44. 7
  + 2

45. 4
  + 0

46. 7
  + 6

47. 0
  + 5

48. 8
  + 5

Midchapter Review

Add. *(2)*

1. 6 + 6	**2.** 9 + 7	**3.** 7 + 9	**4.** 7 + 5	**5.** 8 + 8	**6.** 6 + 5
7. 7 + 6	**8.** 8 + 7	**9.** 2 + 8	**10.** 9 + 8	**11.** 7 + 3	**12.** 9 + 6

Something Extra
Calculator Activities

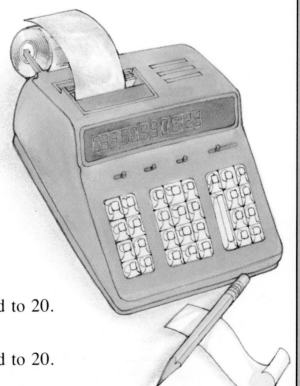

Look at the keys on a calculator.

1. Pick 3 different numbers that add to 20.

2. Pick 4 different numbers that add to 20.

3. Pick 5 different numbers that add to 20.

4. Pick 4 same numbers that add to 20.

5. Pick 5 same numbers that add to 20.

6. What is the sum of all the numbers shown?

COMPUTER—HOW IT WORKS

Input 8	→	Compute 8 + 5	→	Output 13

You enter information into the computer.

The computer works on the information.

The computer gives the answer.

Write the outputs.

1. 9	Input + 3	?
2. 7	Input + 9	?
3. 6	Input + 5	?
4. 8	Input + 7	?
5. 3	Input + 8	?
6. 5	Input + 6	?
7. 9	Input + 6	?
★ **8.** 18	Input + 93	?
★ **9.** 275	Input + 70	?
★ **10.** 462	Input + 815	?

7

SUBTRACTION

▶ Subtraction can be thought of as taking away part of a group.

Had 9 cents
Spent 4 cents
How much is left?

$9 - 4 = 5$ $\begin{array}{r} 9 \\ -\ 4 \\ \hline 5 \end{array}$

↑
difference →

There are 5 cents left.

Study and Learn

▶ Subtraction may also be thought of as comparing.

A. Look at the picture.

  1. How many dimes?

  2. How many nickels?

  3. How many more dimes than nickels?

  4. $6 - 3 = \underline{\quad ? \quad}$

B. Subtract.

  5. $9 - 3$ **6.** $12 - 4$ **7.** $14 - 6$ **8.** $8 - 5$ **9.** $7 - 4$

  10. $\begin{array}{r} 10 \\ -\ 6 \\ \hline \end{array}$ **11.** $\begin{array}{r} 12 \\ -\ 3 \\ \hline \end{array}$ **12.** $\begin{array}{r} 14 \\ -\ 9 \\ \hline \end{array}$ **13.** $\begin{array}{r} 18 \\ -\ 9 \\ \hline \end{array}$ **14.** $\begin{array}{r} 16 \\ -\ 8 \\ \hline \end{array}$

  15. $\begin{array}{r} 12 \\ -\ 7 \\ \hline \end{array}$ **16.** $\begin{array}{r} 11 \\ -\ 3 \\ \hline \end{array}$ **17.** $\begin{array}{r} 14 \\ -\ 5 \\ \hline \end{array}$ **18.** $\begin{array}{r} 10 \\ -\ 3 \\ \hline \end{array}$ **19.** $\begin{array}{r} 15 \\ -\ 6 \\ \hline \end{array}$

Practice

Subtract.

1. $10 - 1$ **2.** $12 - 3$ **3.** $13 - 4$ **4.** $9 - 9$ **5.** $9 - 5$

6. $\begin{array}{r} 0 \\ -\ 0 \\ \hline \end{array}$ **7.** $\begin{array}{r} 8 \\ -\ 0 \\ \hline \end{array}$ **8.** $\begin{array}{r} 6 \\ -\ 0 \\ \hline \end{array}$ **9.** $\begin{array}{r} 1 \\ -\ 1 \\ \hline \end{array}$ **10.** $\begin{array}{r} 7 \\ -\ 1 \\ \hline \end{array}$

11. $\begin{array}{r} 2 \\ -\ 2 \\ \hline \end{array}$ **12.** $\begin{array}{r} 6 \\ -\ 2 \\ \hline \end{array}$ **13.** $\begin{array}{r} 11 \\ -\ 2 \\ \hline \end{array}$ **14.** $\begin{array}{r} 3 \\ -\ 3 \\ \hline \end{array}$ **15.** $\begin{array}{r} 10 \\ -\ 3 \\ \hline \end{array}$

16. $\begin{array}{r} 4 \\ -\ 4 \\ \hline \end{array}$ **17.** $\begin{array}{r} 7 \\ -\ 4 \\ \hline \end{array}$ **18.** $\begin{array}{r} 10 \\ -\ 4 \\ \hline \end{array}$ **19.** $\begin{array}{r} 12 \\ -\ 4 \\ \hline \end{array}$ **20.** $\begin{array}{r} 11 \\ -\ 4 \\ \hline \end{array}$

21. $\begin{array}{r} 5 \\ -\ 5 \\ \hline \end{array}$ **22.** $\begin{array}{r} 14 \\ -\ 5 \\ \hline \end{array}$ **23.** $\begin{array}{r} 10 \\ -\ 5 \\ \hline \end{array}$ **24.** $\begin{array}{r} 13 \\ -\ 5 \\ \hline \end{array}$ **25.** $\begin{array}{r} 11 \\ -\ 5 \\ \hline \end{array}$

26. $\begin{array}{r} 6 \\ -\ 6 \\ \hline \end{array}$ **27.** $\begin{array}{r} 12 \\ -\ 6 \\ \hline \end{array}$ **28.** $\begin{array}{r} 10 \\ -\ 6 \\ \hline \end{array}$ **29.** $\begin{array}{r} 13 \\ -\ 6 \\ \hline \end{array}$ **30.** $\begin{array}{r} 15 \\ -\ 6 \\ \hline \end{array}$

31. $\begin{array}{r} 7 \\ -\ 7 \\ \hline \end{array}$ **32.** $\begin{array}{r} 10 \\ -\ 7 \\ \hline \end{array}$ **33.** $\begin{array}{r} 14 \\ -\ 7 \\ \hline \end{array}$ **34.** $\begin{array}{r} 16 \\ -\ 7 \\ \hline \end{array}$ **35.** $\begin{array}{r} 11 \\ -\ 7 \\ \hline \end{array}$

36. $\begin{array}{r} 8 \\ -\ 8 \\ \hline \end{array}$ **37.** $\begin{array}{r} 16 \\ -\ 8 \\ \hline \end{array}$ **38.** $\begin{array}{r} 15 \\ -\ 8 \\ \hline \end{array}$ **39.** $\begin{array}{r} 17 \\ -\ 8 \\ \hline \end{array}$ **40.** $\begin{array}{r} 10 \\ -\ 8 \\ \hline \end{array}$

41. $\begin{array}{r} 16 \\ -\ 9 \\ \hline \end{array}$ **42.** $\begin{array}{r} 10 \\ -\ 9 \\ \hline \end{array}$ **43.** $\begin{array}{r} 18 \\ -\ 9 \\ \hline \end{array}$ **44.** $\begin{array}{r} 15 \\ -\ 9 \\ \hline \end{array}$ **45.** $\begin{array}{r} 13 \\ -\ 9 \\ \hline \end{array}$

Solve Problems

46. 7 brown wallets
4 black wallets
How many more
brown wallets?

47. 8 dime wrappers
3 nickel wrappers
How many more
dime wrappers?

FACT TRICKS

Here are some tricks for subtraction facts.

This is a trick for subtracting 9's.

Think: Think: Think:
1 2 ← Add 1 here.   1 6 ← Add 1 here.   1 4 ← Add 1 here.
− 9   2 + 1 = 3   − 9   − 9
  3 ← Answer 3   7 ← Answer 7   5 ← Answer 5

Study and Learn

A. Subtract. Remember 9's.

| **1.** | 13 − 9 | **2.** | 17 − 9 | **3.** | 15 − 9 | **4.** | 10 − 9 | **5.** | 18 − 9 | **6.** | 11 − 9 |

These are special subtraction tricks.

1 3   1 5   When the bottom digit is 1 more than
− 4 − 6   the top digit, the answer is always 9.
  9   9

B. Which have 9 for the answer?

| **7.** | 12 − 3 | **8.** | 18 − 9 | **9.** | 11 − 2 | **10.** | 17 − 8 | **11.** | 13 − 6 | **12.** | 13 − 4 |

10

Practice

Subtract. Remember the subtraction tricks.

1. 13 − 8	**2.** 7 − 7	**3.** 8 − 3	**4.** 3 − 0	**5.** 9 − 5	**6.** 10 − 7
7. 16 − 9	**8.** 14 − 9	**9.** 18 − 9	**10.** 15 − 9	**11.** 17 − 9	**12.** 13 − 9
13. 11 − 2	**14.** 10 − 1	**15.** 17 − 8	**16.** 16 − 7	**17.** 14 − 5	**18.** 13 − 4
19. 3 − 3	**20.** 11 − 9	**21.** 15 − 6	**22.** 10 − 5	**23.** 9 − 7	**24.** 6 − 0
25. 5 − 2	**26.** 3 − 2	**27.** 15 − 8	**28.** 11 − 8	**29.** 12 − 8	**30.** 11 − 4
31. 7 − 4	**32.** 9 − 3	**33.** 8 − 7	**34.** 5 − 1	**35.** 6 − 3	**36.** 8 − 4
37. 10 − 9	**38.** 9 − 9	**39.** 11 − 5	**40.** 10 − 2	**41.** 14 − 8	**42.** 12 − 9
43. 13 − 8	**44.** 10 − 3	**45.** 13 − 7	**46.** 12 − 7	**47.** 11 − 6	**48.** 11 − 3

Solve Problems

49. There were 17 words on a very difficult spelling test. Sue spelled 9 right. How many did she spell wrong?

50. The final baseball score was Tigers 14, Angels 5. By how many runs did the Tigers win?

Problem-Solving Skills
Choosing an Operation

5 hours to Los Angeles
2 hours to San Diego
How many hours in all?

Think:

1. What is asked? ──────────→ How many in all?

2. Do you add or subtract? ──────→ Add.

▶ To find how many in all, add.

Study and Learn

A. Complete.

18 hours to Dallas
9 hours to Little Rock
How many more hours to Dallas?

1. What is asked?

2. Do you add or subtract?

▶ To find how many more, subtract.
▶ To find how many are left, subtract.

B. Which operation would you use? Write + or − .

3. 7 small cars
6 large cars
How many in all?

4. 14 trucks
8 leave
How many are left?

Practice

Which operation would you use? Write + or − .

1. 4 hours to Harrisburg
   11 hours to Pittsburgh
   How many more hours to
   Pittsburgh?

2. 8 speed limit signs
   9 destination signs
   How many signs in all?

3. 2 drawbridges
   5 toll bridges
   How many bridges in all?

4. 7 hours to Boise
   15 hours to Phoenix
   How many more hours to
   Phoenix?

5. 6 hours to Boston
   12 hours to Raleigh
   How many hours in all?

6. 8 cities
   3 towns
   How many more cities?

7. 17 gallons of gas
   8 gallons used
   How many gallons left?

8. Spent $3 for oil
   Bought a map for $2
   How much was spent?

9. Had $9 to spend on gas
   Spent $4
   How much is left?

10. Traveled 9 hours
    Traveled 6 hours
    How many hours traveled?

Skills Review

Add. *(2)*

1. $\begin{array}{r} 0 \\ +1 \\ \hline \end{array}$	**2.** $\begin{array}{r} 1 \\ +3 \\ \hline \end{array}$	**3.** $\begin{array}{r} 7 \\ +3 \\ \hline \end{array}$	**4.** $\begin{array}{r} 4 \\ +4 \\ \hline \end{array}$	**5.** $\begin{array}{r} 5 \\ +2 \\ \hline \end{array}$

6. $\begin{array}{r} 3 \\ +1 \\ \hline \end{array}$	**7.** $\begin{array}{r} 4 \\ +5 \\ \hline \end{array}$	**8.** $\begin{array}{r} 2 \\ +8 \\ \hline \end{array}$	**9.** $\begin{array}{r} 4 \\ +2 \\ \hline \end{array}$	**10.** $\begin{array}{r} 6 \\ +4 \\ \hline \end{array}$

11. $\begin{array}{r} 9 \\ +4 \\ \hline \end{array}$	**12.** $\begin{array}{r} 2 \\ +9 \\ \hline \end{array}$	**13.** $\begin{array}{r} 6 \\ +6 \\ \hline \end{array}$	**14.** $\begin{array}{r} 5 \\ +9 \\ \hline \end{array}$	**15.** $\begin{array}{r} 8 \\ +6 \\ \hline \end{array}$	**16.** $\begin{array}{r} 5 \\ +6 \\ \hline \end{array}$	**17.** $\begin{array}{r} 7 \\ +8 \\ \hline \end{array}$

18. $\begin{array}{r} 3 \\ +9 \\ \hline \end{array}$	**19.** $\begin{array}{r} 8 \\ +5 \\ \hline \end{array}$	**20.** $\begin{array}{r} 6 \\ +9 \\ \hline \end{array}$	**21.** $\begin{array}{r} 4 \\ +7 \\ \hline \end{array}$	**22.** $\begin{array}{r} 7 \\ +6 \\ \hline \end{array}$	**23.** $\begin{array}{r} 8 \\ +9 \\ \hline \end{array}$	**24.** $\begin{array}{r} 4 \\ +8 \\ \hline \end{array}$

Subtract. *(8)*

25. $\begin{array}{r} 2 \\ -1 \\ \hline \end{array}$	**26.** $\begin{array}{r} 3 \\ -0 \\ \hline \end{array}$	**27.** $\begin{array}{r} 5 \\ -2 \\ \hline \end{array}$	**28.** $\begin{array}{r} 4 \\ -1 \\ \hline \end{array}$	**29.** $\begin{array}{r} 6 \\ -2 \\ \hline \end{array}$	**30.** $\begin{array}{r} 7 \\ -4 \\ \hline \end{array}$	**31.** $\begin{array}{r} 10 \\ -6 \\ \hline \end{array}$

32. $\begin{array}{r} 3 \\ -2 \\ \hline \end{array}$	**33.** $\begin{array}{r} 9 \\ -5 \\ \hline \end{array}$	**34.** $\begin{array}{r} 10 \\ -3 \\ \hline \end{array}$	**35.** $\begin{array}{r} 8 \\ -6 \\ \hline \end{array}$	**36.** $\begin{array}{r} 4 \\ -4 \\ \hline \end{array}$	**37.** $\begin{array}{r} 8 \\ -4 \\ \hline \end{array}$	**38.** $\begin{array}{r} 5 \\ -4 \\ \hline \end{array}$

39. $\begin{array}{r} 11 \\ -6 \\ \hline \end{array}$	**40.** $\begin{array}{r} 13 \\ -4 \\ \hline \end{array}$	**41.** $\begin{array}{r} 15 \\ -7 \\ \hline \end{array}$	**42.** $\begin{array}{r} 17 \\ -8 \\ \hline \end{array}$	**43.** $\begin{array}{r} 18 \\ -9 \\ \hline \end{array}$	**44.** $\begin{array}{r} 16 \\ -8 \\ \hline \end{array}$	**45.** $\begin{array}{r} 12 \\ -9 \\ \hline \end{array}$

46. $\begin{array}{r} 14 \\ -9 \\ \hline \end{array}$	**47.** $\begin{array}{r} 12 \\ -3 \\ \hline \end{array}$	**48.** $\begin{array}{r} 16 \\ -9 \\ \hline \end{array}$	**49.** $\begin{array}{r} 14 \\ -5 \\ \hline \end{array}$	**50.** $\begin{array}{r} 15 \\ -8 \\ \hline \end{array}$	**51.** $\begin{array}{r} 13 \\ -6 \\ \hline \end{array}$	**52.** $\begin{array}{r} 11 \\ -4 \\ \hline \end{array}$

Something Extra
Non-Routine Problems

Solve.

1. $9 + 7 = 8 + \square$

2. $10 - 3 = 12 - \square$

3. $\square - 3 = 4 + 2$

4. $11 - \square = 6 + 5$

RELATED SENTENCES

Here are four related sentences
for 8, 6, and 14.

$$8 + 6 = 14$$

$$6 + 8 = 14$$

$$14 - 8 = 6$$

$$14 - 6 = 8$$

Study and Learn

A. Complete.

1. $9 + 6 = 15$
$6 + 9 = \square$
$15 - 6 = \square$
$15 - \square = 6$

2. $13 - 6 = 7$
$\square + 6 = \triangle$
$\square - 7 = \triangle$
$6 + \square = \triangle$

3. $7 + 8 = \square$
$8 + \triangle = \square$
$15 - \square = 7$
$\triangle - \square = 8$

B. Write four related sentences for each.

4. 3, 7, 10   **5.** 16, 9, 7   **6.** 8, 0, 8   **7.** 4, 7, 3

Practice

Write four related sentences for each.

1. 4, 5, 9   **2.** 3, 9, 12   **3.** 11, 8, 3   **4.** 13, 8, 5

5. 9, 8, 17   **6.** 8, 6, 14   **7.** 10, 4, 6   **8.** 12, 5, 7

15

USING RELATED SENTENCES

Donna has 8¢.
A pencil costs 15¢.

How much more does
Donna need?

$8 + \square = 15$

Choose the related sentence that fits.

$15 - 8 = \square$

$15 - 8 = 7$

$8 + \square = 15$
$\square + 8 = 15$
$15 - 8 = \square$
$15 - \square = 8$

Donna needs 7 cents.

Study and Learn

A. Solve. Use the related sentence that fits.

1. $\square + 9 = 16$

$\square + 9 = 16$
$9 + \square = 16$
$16 - 9 = \square$
$16 - \square = 9$

2. $8 + \square = 17$

$8 + \square = 17$
$\square + 8 = 17$
$17 - 8 = \square$
$17 - \square = 8$

B. Solve.

3. $6 + \square = 12$

4. $7 + \square = 13$

5. $\square + 8 = 9$

6. $\square + 4 = 11$

7. $6 + \square = 15$

8. $\square + 2 = 10$

Practice

Solve.

1. $5 + \square = 9$

2. $7 + \square = 12$

3. $\square + 3 = 10$

4. $\square + 6 = 8$

5. $6 + \square = 14$

6. $\square + 9 = 10$

7. $\square + 5 = 13$

8. $2 + \square = 11$

9. $9 + \square = 15$

10. $\square + 8 = 16$

11. $\square + 9 = 14$

12. $8 + \square = 17$

★**13.** $8 = \square + 4$

★**14.** $7 = 3 + \square$

★**15.** $13 = \square + 6$

COMPUTER—AS A CALCULATOR

A computer can be used as a calculator. Follow the directions given here, and you will be able to make the computer add or subtract.

A. To add 8 and 5, you tell the computer: **PRINT 8 + 5**

The computer output will be 13.

How would you tell the computer to do these? Write the computer input and output for each.

1. 6 + 7   **2.** 9 + 5   **3.** 8 + 3   **4.** 4 + 7

B. To subtract 8 from 14, you tell the computer: **PRINT 14 − 8**

The computer output will be 6.

How would you tell the computer to do these? Write the computer input and output for each.

5. 18 − 9   **6.** 16 − 7   **7.** 17 − 8   **8.** 15 − 6

★ **C.** You can have the computer add and subtract large numbers. You must type in each number without a comma.

To add 3,413 and 4,352 tell the computer: **PRINT 3413 + 4352**

The computer output will be 7765.

How would you tell the computer to do these? Write the computer input and output for each.

9. 2,304 + 4,293   **10.** 8,385 − 5,052

11. 1,312 + 2,434 + 4,121   **12.** 4,938 − 1,924

H A N D S   O N

You can check your answers on the computer. Press [RETURN] after you type each line. Always use the <u>number</u> 0 or Ø for zero.

NUMBER PATTERNS

Maureen and Paul are playing What's the Rule.

Paul says	Maureen answers
6 ——————→	13
3 ——————→	10
9 ——————→	16
0 ——————→	7

Maureen's rule is **add 7.**

Study and Learn

A. Look at this game.

Ronald says	6	9	5	12	13	7	8	14
Kristine answers	1	4	0	7				

    1. What's the rule?

    2. Complete the game.

B. Look at this pattern.

    4, 7, 10, 13, __?__, __?__, __?__, __?__, __?__, __?__

    3. Are the numbers increasing or decreasing?

    4. By how much are they increasing?

    5. Complete the pattern.

Practice

Find the rule to complete.

1.	Philip says	6	1	8	9	7	5	3	0	2	4
	Stephanie answers	14	9	16							
2.	Meryl says	15	10	8	14	12	13	16	7	9	11
	Reiko answers	8	3								
3.	Juanita says	13	15	9	11	18	12	17	10	16	14
	Eduardo answers	4	6	0							

Complete the patterns.

4. 39, 36, 33, 30, __?__, __?__, __?__, __?__, __?__

5. 3, 5, 7, 9, __?__, __?__, __?__, __?__, __?__

6. 9, 14, 19, 24, __?__, __?__, __?__, __?__, __?__

7. 26, 24, 22, 20, __?__, __?__, __?__, __?__, __?__

8. 7, 11, 15, 19, __?__, __?__, __?__, __?__, __?__

9. 3, 12, 21, 30, __?__, __?__, __?__, __?__, __?__

★ **10.** 1, 2, 4, 7, 11, __?__, __?__, __?__, __?__, __?__

★ **11.** 31, 30, 28, 25, 21, __?__, __?__, __?__

★ **12.** 6, 8, 12, 18, 26, __?__, __?__, __?__, __?__

★ **13.** 1, 2, 3, 5, 8, __?__, __?__, __?__, __?__

★ **14.** 3, 5, 9, 17, 33, __?__, __?__, __?__, __?__

Problem-Solving Applications

Career

Solve.

1. There are 7 jets and 6 helicopters at the airport. How many aircraft in all? [HINT: $7 + 6 = \underline{}$]

2. There were 8 planes on the field. 3 took off. How many were left?

3. There were 11 planes in the air. 7 landed. How many are still in the air?

4. 6 planes landed. 4 more are landing. How many planes are there in all?

5. There were 11 air controllers. 6 went to lunch. How many were left?

★ 6. There are 6 planes on the ground. 3 more land and 4 take off. How many are now on the ground?

Chapter Review

Add. *(2)*

1. 8
    + 0

2. 9
    + 7

3. 3
    + 8

4. 6
    + 6

5. 4
    + 7

6. 9
    + 9

7. 3
    + 6

8. 8
    + 7

9. 3
    + 5

10. 7
     + 6

Subtract. *(8)*

11. 7
     − 5

12. 8
     − 0

13. 9
     − 9

14. 10
     − 6

15. 12
     − 7

16. 14
     − 9

17. 16
     − 7

18. 17
     − 9

19. 15
     − 8

20. 13
     − 7

Write four related sentences. *(15)*

21. 9, 16, 7

Complete the patterns. *(18)*

22. 3, 7, 11, 15, _?_, _?_, _?_, _?_, _?_

23. 27, 25, 23, 21, _?_, _?_, _?_, _?_, _?_

Which operation would you use? Write + or − . *(12)*

24. There were 8 jars of red paint. There were 12 jars of blue paint. How many more blue jars than red jars?

Solve. *(20)*

25. There were 9 doves. 7 doves flew away. How many doves were left?

Chapter Test

Add. *(2)*

1.	6	**2.**	8	**3.**	3	**4.**	7	**5.**	8
	+ 0		+ 6		+ 8		+ 1		+ 7

6.	4	**7.**	5	**8.**	8	**9.**	9	**10.**	6
	+ 3		+ 6		+ 3		+ 8		+ 6

Subtract. *(8)*

11.	18	**12.**	16	**13.**	14	**14.**	12	**15.**	10
	− 9		− 8		− 6		− 9		− 7

16.	6	**17.**	4	**18.**	13	**19.**	15	**20.**	17
	− 6		− 0		− 8		− 9		− 8

Write four related sentences. *(15)*

21. 7, 11, 4

Complete the patterns. *(18)*

22. 32, 29, 26, 23, __?__, __?__, __?__, __?__

23. 5, 8, 11, 14, __?__, __?__, __?__, __?__

Which operation would you use? Write + or − . *(12)*

24. There were 8 small paint brushes. There were 6 large paint brushes. How many paint brushes in all?

Solve. *(20)*

25. Joan had 16 cents. She spent 7 cents. How much did she have left?

Skills Check

1.

$$\begin{array}{r} 5 \\ 7 \\ 4 \\ + 6 \end{array}$$

A	B	C	D
19	22	23	32

2.

$$138 + 641 = \underline{}$$

E	F	G	H
750	769	779	797

3.

$$\begin{array}{r} 29 \\ + 15 \end{array}$$

A	B	C	D
44	46	54	65

4.

$$\begin{array}{r} 263 \\ + 119 \end{array}$$

E	F	G	H
371	382	484	570

5.

$$\begin{array}{r} 421 \\ 303 \\ + 245 \end{array}$$

A	B	C	D
861	960	969	988

6.

$$9 + 8 = \underline{}$$

E	F	G	H
17	18	21	27

7.

$$\begin{array}{r} 6 \\ + 7 \end{array}$$

A	B	C	D
10	12	13	15

8.

$$\begin{array}{r} 14 \\ - 7 \end{array}$$

E	F	G	H
6	7	9	21

9.

$$16 - 9 = \underline{}$$

A	B	C	D
3	5	6	7

10.

$$\begin{array}{r} 58 \\ - 27 \end{array}$$

E	F	G	H
16	21	22	31

11.

$$\begin{array}{r} 525 \\ - 106 \end{array}$$

A	B	C	D
328	419	421	631

12.

$$\begin{array}{r} 337 \\ - 245 \end{array}$$

E	F	G	H
64	72	81	92

23

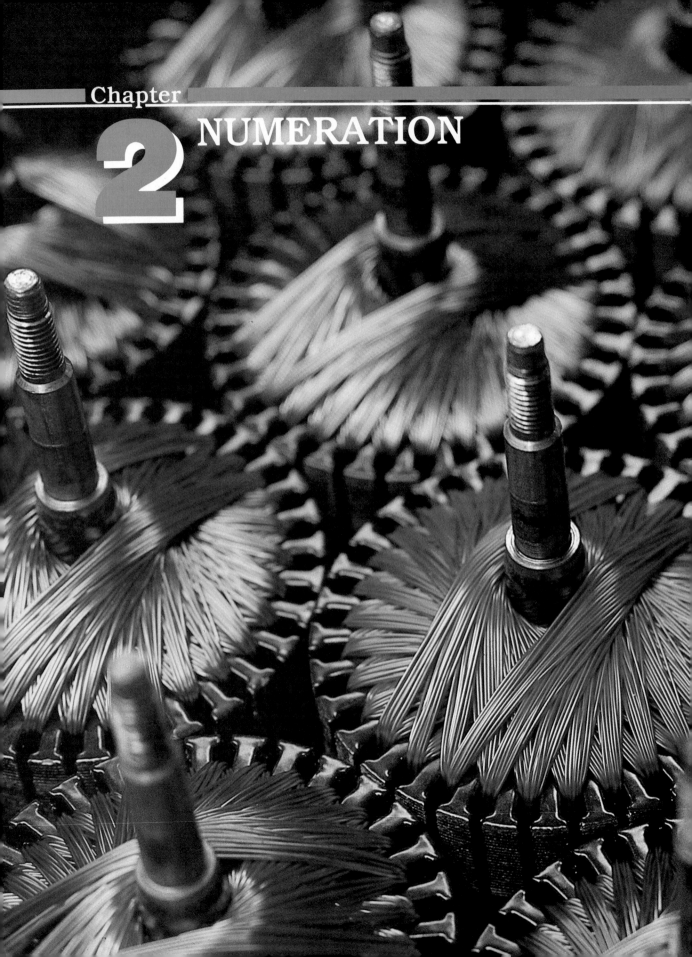

Armatures help produce electrical or mechanical power.

WRITING NUMERALS

Expanded Numeral	Standard Numeral
300 + 40 + 5	345
6 hundreds, 0 tens, and 7 ones	607
4,000 + 600 + 70 + 5	4,675
8 thousands, 9 hundreds, 7 tens, and 0 ones	8,970

Word Name	Write
Eighty-seven	87
Nine hundred three	903
Six thousand, forty-seven	6,047

Study and Learn

A. Write standard numerals.

1. 4 tens and 8 ones

2. 500 + 70 + 6

3. 7 hundred, 2 tens, and 1 one

4. 8,000 + 900 + 70

5. 8 thousands, 6 hundreds, 0 tens, and 4 ones

B. Write standard numerals.

6. Seventy-six

7. Ninety

8. Six hundred thirty-four

9. Five hundred twelve

10. Five thousand, six hundred fifty-four

11. Eight thousand, eight hundred eight

C. Write word names.

12. 33 **13.** 80 **14.** 767 **15.** 4,500 **16.** 1,201

Practice

Write standard numerals.

1. 10 + 6   **2.** 40 + 9   **3.** 3 tens and 2 ones

4. 6 hundreds, 8 tens, and 4 ones   **5.** 700 + 90 + 3

6. 6,000 + 300 + 20 + 1   **7.** 2,000 + 400 + 10 + 7

8. 8 thousands, 9 hundreds, 1 ten, and 8 ones

Write standard numerals.

9. Fifteen   **10.** Seventy-five

11. Seven hundred   **12.** Three hundred twelve

13. One hundred ten   **14.** Eight hundred eighty

15. Eight thousand, eighty-nine   **16.** Three thousand

17. Five thousand, sixty-four   **18.** Six thousand, one hundred

19. Four thousand, seven hundred fifty-three

20. Six thousand, one hundred eighty-six

★ **21.** Thirty-five thousand

★ **22.** Nine hundred thousand

Write word names.

23. 16   **24.** 61   **25.** 746   **26.** 674   **27.** 605

28. 1,234   **29.** 8,604   ★ **30.** 19,058   ★ **31.** 29,003

PLACE VALUE

A place-value plan is used to write numbers. Example: 1,235.

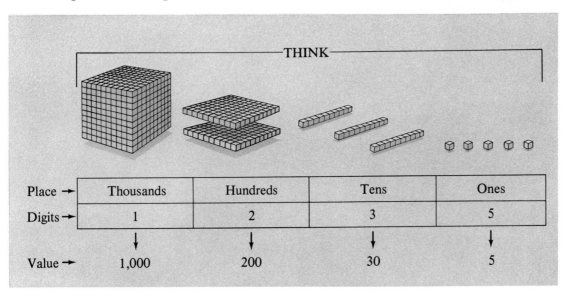

Place →	Thousands	Hundreds	Tens	Ones
Digits →	1	2	3	5
Value →	1,000	200	30	5

Study and Learn

A. Look at the number 5,379.

    1. Which digit is in the hundreds place?

    2. Which digit is in the tens place?

B. In which place is each underlined digit?

    3. 4<u>7</u>9   **4.** <u>5</u>86   **5.** 61<u>9</u>   **6.** 4<u>0</u>1   **7.** 12<u>3</u>

    8. 5,04<u>4</u>   **9.** <u>6</u>,000   **10.** 8,2<u>8</u>1   **11.** 9,<u>4</u>07   **12.** <u>2</u>,671

C. What is the value of each underlined digit?

    Example   <u>5</u>,379   5,000

    13. <u>2</u>89   **14.** <u>8</u>61   **15.** 17<u>7</u>   **16.** 9,<u>4</u>76   **17.** 1,7<u>3</u>4

    18. 1,00<u>9</u>   **19.** <u>8</u>,760   **20.** 4,<u>5</u>69   **21.** 7,0<u>4</u>8   **22.** 3,12<u>9</u>

Practice

In which place is each underlined digit?

1. 7̲64

2. 67̲8

3. 8̲00

4. 777̲

5. 30̲1

6. 3,865̲

7. 5,0̲00

8. 7̲,219

9. 4,36̲9

10. 6̲,781

11. 4,987̲

12. 6,7̲80

13. 5,21̲0

14. 9̲,635

15. 8,62̲4

16. 49̲8

17. 8,9̲44

18. 9̲,843

19. 896̲

★ **20.** 2̲3,748

What is the value of each underlined digit?

21. 2̲00

22. 37̲8

23. 909̲

24. 83̲1

25. 4̲62

26. 6,079̲

27. 7̲,580

28. 8,9̲41

29. 9̲,072

30. 2,174̲

31. 2,376̲

32. 6,7̲32

33. 7,32̲6

34. 3̲,267

35. 1,2̲97

36. 8̲89

37. 9,81̲4

38. 8̲,049

39. 265̲

★ **40.** 7̲4,679

Skills Review

Add. *(2)*

1. 8 + 2

2. 6 + 0

3. 2 + 4

4. 7 + 3

5. 4 + 5

6. 6 + 3

7. 2 + 5

8. 2 + 6

9. 4 + 6

10. 3 + 3

11. 6 + 8

12. 5 + 8

13. 7 + 9

14. 5 + 6

15. 9 + 2

16. 8 + 7

17. 9 + 5

18. 7 + 6

19. 9 + 1

20. 9 + 8

21. 9 + 9

22. 4 + 7

23. 3 + 9

24. 8 + 3

25. 5 + 9

26. 7 + 7

27. 4 + 8

28. 7 + 5

29. 6 + 7

30. 6 + 6

31. 8 + 6

THOUSANDS

There are thousands of stars in the universe.
This place-value chart shows the first 6 places.

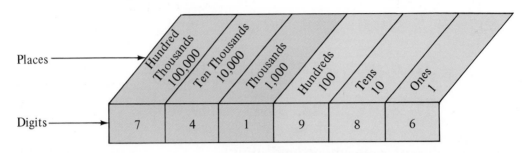

The digit 4 is in the ten thousands place.
It has the value of 40,000.

Study and Learn

A. In 8<u>5</u>2,394 the digit 5 has the value of 50,000.

   1. What is the value of the digit 8?

   2. What is the value of the digit 2?

B. What is the value of each underlined digit?

   3. <u>9</u>6,281   **4.** 8<u>7</u>,364   **5.** 69,8<u>6</u>1

   6. 1<u>2</u>8,407   **7.** <u>7</u>02,207   **8.** 307,<u>9</u>64

> The standard numeral for
> 600,000 + 50,000 + 3,000 + 500 + 70 + 7 is 653,577.

C. Write standard numerals.

   9. 300,000 + 50,000 + 9,000 + 600 + 40 + 7

   10. 50,000 + 4,000 + 800 + 70 + 0

D. Write standard numerals.

   Example   368 thousand, 496   368,496

   11. 47 thousand, 276   **12.** 705 thousand, 670

   13. 38 thousand   **14.** 706 thousand, 7

Practice

What is the value of each underlined digit?

   1. 4<u>9</u>,286   **2.** 6<u>8</u>2,947   **3.** <u>3</u>08,705

   4. 498,<u>2</u>07   **5.** 97,2<u>8</u>8   **6.** 44,44<u>4</u>

   7. 9<u>8</u>3,389   **8.** <u>6</u>0,064   **9.** <u>8</u>79,486

   10. 38<u>7</u>,496   **11.** <u>7</u>47,477   **12.** 6<u>7</u>1,047

Write standard numerals.

   13. 30,000 + 9,000 + 400 + 30 + 8

   14. 500,000 + 70,000 + 3,000 + 900 + 80 + 3

   15. 900,000 + 0 + 4,000 + 0 + 40 + 0

   16. 700,000 + 80,000 + 5,000 + 0 + 0 + 0

   17. 34 thousand, 276   **18.** 384 thousand, 300

   19. 586 thousand, 75   **20.** 39 thousand, 7

★ Write short word names.

   Example   100,001   100 thousand, 1

   21. 321,123   **22.** 498,075   **23.** 698,007

MILLIONS

This place-value chart shows millions.

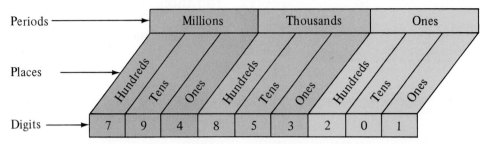

The digit 9 is in the millions period. It is in the 10 millions place.

Study and Learn

A. Look at the chart.

   1. What place is just left of the 100 thousands place?

   2. What place is just left of the 1 millions place?

   3. What place is just left of the 10 millions place?

> 794,853,201 is read as 794 million, 853 thousand, 201.

B. Read these.

   4. 76,285,101   **5.** 497,286,105   **6.** 8,764,491

> The standard numeral for 768 million, 25 thousand, 7 is 768,025,007. Commas are used to separate the periods.

C. Write standard numerals.

   7. 29 million, 348 thousand, 768   **8.** 900 million

   9. 9 million, 9 thousand, 9   **10.** 42 million, 750

Practice

In which place is each underlined digit?

1. <u>8</u>,795,281 **2.** 4,<u>2</u>98,765 **3.** 1,36<u>7</u>,201

4. <u>4</u>9,287,341 **5.** 49<u>7</u>,286,000 **6.** <u>9</u>24,876,035

7. 173,<u>0</u>07,073 **8.** 64<u>2</u>,000,001 ★**9.** <u>1</u>,329,465,780

Write standard numerals.

10. 7 million, 7 **11.** 7 million, 7 thousand

12. 438 million, 696 **13.** 438 million, 696 thousand

14. 398 million, 297 thousand, 698

15. 42 million, 205 thousand, 310

16. 4 million, 707 thousand, 4

17. 70 million, 70 thousand, 70

18. 500 million, 50 thousand, 5

19. 945 million, 1 thousand

★Write short word names.

20. 9,476,487 **21.** 74,285,076 **22.** 78,000,000

23. 9,000,000 **24.** 428,706,949 **25.** 349,349,349

26. A movie cost $3,287,000 to make.

33

Midchapter Review

Write standard numerals. *(26, 30, 32)*

1. 80 + 7

2. 3 hundreds, 0 tens, and 4 ones

3. 8 thousands, 0 hundreds, 5 tens, and 6 ones

4. 700 + 40 + 2

5. Nine thousand, eight hundred fifty

6. 40,000 + 3,000 + 500 + 60 + 7

7. 328 thousand, 704

8. 80 million, 85 thousand, 50

Write word names. *(26)*

9. 36

10. 749

11. 6,370

In which place is each underlined digit? *(28, 30, 32)*

12. 6<u>3</u>1

13. <u>4</u>,978

14. <u>7</u>65,903

15. 2<u>3</u>,000,350

What is the value of each underlined digit? *(28, 30)*

16. <u>3</u>,920

17. 8<u>6</u>,495

18. <u>4</u>27,306

Skills Review

Subtract. *(8)*

1. 5
    − 2

2. 9
    − 3

3. 8
    − 3

4. 7
    − 5

5. 9
    − 4

6. 10
    − 6

7. 11
    − 9

8. 12
    − 6

9. 15
    − 7

10. 16
     − 8

11. 17
     − 9

12. 16
     − 9

13. 11
     − 8

14. 12
     − 4

15. 14
     − 6

16. 13
     − 8

17. 15
     − 6

NUMBER NAMES

5 + 4	4 + 4	16 − 7	10 − 4	5 + 3	13 − 8
6 + 2	2 + 7	10 − 3	11 − 3	15 − 7	12 − 3
12 − 5	10 − 6	13 − 4	15 − 9	9 + 3	11 − 4
9 − 3	4 + 3	12 − 4	15 − 8	10 − 1	10 − 2
8 + 1	14 − 5	2 + 4	16 − 8	6 + 1	9 + 0

Study and Learn

Numbers have many names.

1. There are nine names for the number nine above.
   Find and list them.

2. Write eight names for the number eight.

3. Write six names for the number seven.

4. Write four names for the number six.

ROMAN NUMERALS

The Romans used different numerals.

Roman Numerals	I	V	X	L	C
Our Numerals	1	5	10	50	100

Our numerals can be written for Roman numerals.

	XXIII
Steps	X X I I I
Write our numerals below.	10 + 10 + 1 + 1 + 1
Add.	23

Study and Learn

A. Write our numerals.

1. VII   **2.** XXVII   **3.** XVI   **4.** CLXVI

> The Romans used subtraction in some special cases.
>
> IV is 5 − 1, or 4.   XL is 50 − 10, or 40.

B. Write our numerals for these special cases.

5. IX   **6.** XC

> You use the special cases this way.
>
> | **Steps** | CCCXLIX |
> |---|---|
> | Circle special cases. | C   C   C   (XL)   (IX) |
> | Write our numerals. | 100 + 100 + 100 + 40 + 9 |
> | Add. | 349 |

C. Write our numerals.

7. XXIX   **8.** XLVII   **9.** XLIX   **10.** CCCXCIV

D. Write Roman numerals.

Example   324 is CCC + XX + IV, or CCCXXIV

11. 75   **12.** 43   **13.** 239   **14.** 344

Practice

Write our numerals.

1. CLXVI   **2.** CCXXII   **3.** LV   **4.** XIX

5. CCLIV   **6.** XLVII   **7.** CXC   **8.** CCXXXIII

Write Roman numerals.

9. 12   **10.** 9   **11.** 95   **12.** 239

13. 101   **14.** 348   **15.** 65   ★**16.** 500

★**17.** You have encyclopedia volumes VIII and XI. Your friend has the two volumes in between yours. What volumes does your friend have?

Something Extra
Non-Routine Problems

Complete each pattern.

1. A, 3, B, 5, C, 7, _?_, _?_, _?_, _?_

2. 9, L, 12, M, 15, N, _?_, _?_, _?_, _?_

3. A, 1, C, 2, E, 3, _?_, _?_, _?_, _?_

4. F, 10, E, 8, D, 6, _?_, _?_, _?_, _?_

5. Z, 4, Y, 8, X, 12, _?_, _?_, _?_, _?_

Problem-Solving Skills
Choosing the Correct Number Sentence

There were 13 dinosaurs.
Six of them walked away.
How many are left?

Think:

What is asked? ———————→ How many are left?

What is given? ———————→ 13 dinosaurs, 6 walked away.

Do you add or subtract? ——→ Subtract.

This number sentence fits the problem.

$$13 \quad - \quad 6 \quad = \quad \underline{\quad ? \quad}$$

dinosaurs   walk away   how many are left

Study and Learn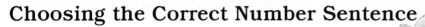

A. A Tyrannosaurus Rex is 15 meters from head to tail.
A Stegosaurus is 6 meters from head to tail.
How many more meters is the Tyrannosaurus?

  1. What is asked?

  2. What is given?

  3. Do you add or subtract?

  4. Which number sentence fits the problem?
    $15 + 6 = \underline{\;?\;}$ $15 - 6 = \underline{\;?\;}$ $24 + 6 = \underline{\;?\;}$

B. Which number sentence fits the problem?

5. 9 Stegosaurus
8 Brontosaurus
How many in all?

$9 - 8 = \underline{\quad?\quad}$
$9 + 8 = \underline{\quad?\quad}$
$9 - 1 = \underline{\quad?\quad}$

6. 75 kilograms of food
48 kilograms were eaten.
How many kilograms are left?

$75 - 48 = \underline{\quad?\quad}$
$75 + 48 = \underline{\quad?\quad}$
$48 - 27 = \underline{\quad?\quad}$

Practice

Which number sentence fits the problem?

1. A Diplodocus is 28 meters from head to tail.
A Brontosaurus is 25 meters from head to tail.
How many meters in all?

$28 - 25 = \underline{\quad?\quad}$ $28 + 25 = \underline{\quad?\quad}$ $28 - 3 = \underline{\quad?\quad}$

2. A Diplodocus is 8 meters from head to shoulder.
A Stegosaurus is 1 meter from head to shoulder.
How many more meters is the Diplodocus?

$8 + 1 = \underline{\quad?\quad}$ $9 - 8 = \underline{\quad?\quad}$ $8 - 1 = \underline{\quad?\quad}$

3. A Brontosaurus is 5 meters from head to shoulder.
A Tyrannosaurus Rex is 2 meters from head to shoulder.
How many meters in all?

$5 - 2 = \underline{\quad?\quad}$ $7 - 5 = \underline{\quad?\quad}$ $5 + 2 = \underline{\quad?\quad}$

COMPARING NUMBERS

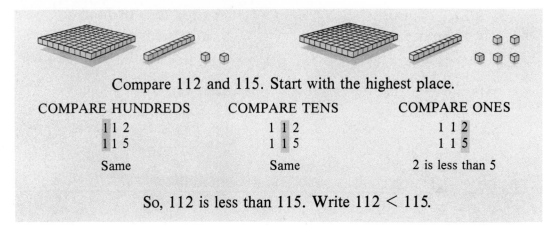

Compare 112 and 115. Start with the highest place.

COMPARE HUNDREDS	COMPARE TENS	COMPARE ONES
1 1 2	1 1 2	1 1 2
1 1 5	1 1 5	1 1 5
Same	Same	2 is less than 5

So, 112 is less than 115. Write 112 < 115.

Compare 7,635 and 7,629.

The thousands are the same.   7,635 and 7,629

The hundreds are the same.   7,635 and 7,629

The tens are different.   7,635 and 7,629

3 is greater than 2, so 7,635 > 7,629.   7,635 ≡ 7,629.
                                                    >

Study and Learn

A. Compare. Replace ≡ with >, <, or =.

   1. 75 ≡ 74   **2.** 369 ≡ 379   **3.** 782 ≡ 782

   4. 6,231 ≡ 6,230   **5.** 4,286 ≡ 4,386

B. Compare 32,614 and 32,785.

   6. Are the ten thousands the same?

   7. Are the thousands the same?

   8. Are the hundreds the same?

   9. Complete. 6 ≡ 7 so, 32,614 ≡ 32,785.

C. Compare. Use > or <.

10. 37,621 ≡ 57,621   **11.** 46,729 ≡ 45,971

12. 44,662 ≡ 44,650   **13.** 34,528 ≡ 34,529

Practice

Compare. Use >, <, or =.

1. 37 ≡ 41   **2.** 77 ≡ 76   **3.** 162 ≡ 262

4. 786 ≡ 708   **5.** 198 ≡ 197   **6.** 641 ≡ 651

7. 3,799 ≡ 3,799   **8.** 1,700 ≡ 1,701

9. 4,499 ≡ 5,000   **10.** 1,298 ≡ 1,892

11. 5,040 ≡ 5,039   **12.** 9,001 ≡ 9,000

13. 36,498 ≡ 36,497   **14.** 49,487 ≡ 49,598

15. 66,641 ≡ 66,598   **16.** 79,486 ≡ 79,486

17. 87,624 ≡ 90,099   **18.** 94,200 ≡ 93,898

19. 83 ≡ 38   **20.** 374 ≡ 374

21. 3,942 ≡ 3,888   **22.** 26,479 ≡ 26,500

23. 63,071 ≡ 63,071   **24.** 4,288 ≡ 4,289

25. 798 ≡ 897   **26.** 38,136 ≡ 40,000

★**27.** 724,785 ≡ 724,765   ★**28.** 469,746 ≡ 470,000

Solve Problems

29. There are 12 children on one tug-of-war team and 15 on the other. Which is the greater number?

30. The newspaper reported that there were 36,248 people at the Astro's game on Friday. There were 36,842 people at the game on Saturday. On which day did the Astro's have the larger crowd?

ROUNDING NUMBERS

A rounded number tells *about* how many.
Round 37 to the nearest ten.

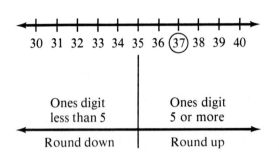

37 is between 30 and 40.
37 is closer to 40 than 30.
37 rounded to the nearest
ten is 40.

35 is in the middle. Middle
numbers are always rounded up.

▶ To round to the nearest ten, look at the ones place.

Round 32.

Less than 5, so
round down to 30.

Round 35.

5 or more, so round
up to 40.

Study and Learn

A. Round each to the nearest ten.

1. 24   **2.** 43   **3.** 65   **4.** 12   **5.** 89

▶ To round to the nearest hundred, look at the tens place.

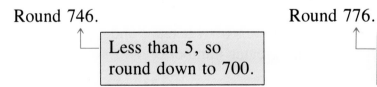

Round 746.

Less than 5, so
round down to 700.

Round 776.

5 or more, so
round up to 800.

B. Round each to the nearest hundred.

6. 329   **7.** 472   **8.** 936   **9.** 250   **10.** 887

▶ Rounding to the nearest dollar is like rounding to the nearest hundred.

Round $6.24.   Round $6.84.

| Less than 5, so round down to $6.00. |

| 5 or more, so round up to $7.00. |

C. Round each to the nearest dollar.

11. $3.89   **12.** $5.25   **13.** $8.50   **14.** $4.09   **15.** $7.88

Practice

Round each to the nearest ten.

1. 11   **2.** 15   **3.** 19   **4.** 22   **5.** 26

6. 33   **7.** 44   **8.** 55   **9.** 66   **10.** 77

Round each to the nearest hundred.

11. 109   **12.** 901   **13.** 190   **14.** 910   **15.** 119

16. 746   **17.** 751   **18.** 350   **19.** 670   **20.** 921

Round each to the nearest dollar.

21. $1.42   **22.** $2.74   **23.** $6.50   **24.** $1.75   **25.** $8.19

26. $3.48   **27.** $4.86   **28.** $5.28   **29.** $6.79   **30.** $7.36

★ Round each to the nearest ten.

31. 732   **32.** 492   **33.** 98   **34.** 495

Solve Problems

35. 515 students watched the air show. About how many students were there?

36. 28 teachers saw the show. About how many saw the show?

ROUNDING THOUSANDS

▶ To round to the nearest thousand, look at the hundreds place.

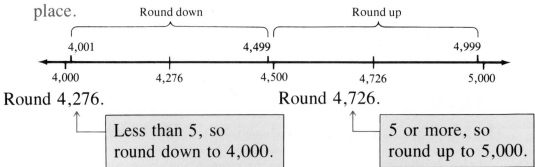

Round 4,276.

Less than 5, so round down to 4,000.

Round 4,726.

5 or more, so round up to 5,000.

Study and Learn

A. Round each to the nearest thousand.

1. 7,286   **2.** 5,904   **3.** 3,586   **4.** 1,500   **5.** 8,797

6. 1,287   **7.** 2,500   **8.** 3,978   **9.** 6,433   **10.** 7,724

Practice

Round each to the nearest thousand.

1. 4,123   **2.** 3,424   **3.** 7,649   **4.** 8,976   **5.** 7,287

6. 2,823   **7.** 6,107   **8.** 7,500   **9.** 7,198   **10.** 7,918

★**11.** 25,500   ★**12.** 63,098   ★**13.** 19,905   ★**14.** 39,785

Solve Problems

15. Mount Vesuvius in Italy is 4,190 feet high. About how many feet high is that?

16. A mountain climber got to within 3,970 feet of the top of Mount Everest. About how many feet from the top was the climber?

Skills Review

Add or subtract. *(2, 8)*

1. 8 $+\,2$	**2.** 5 $+\,7$	**3.** 9 $-\,9$	**4.** 8 $+\,3$	**5.** 15 $-\,8$
6. 17 $-\,8$	**7.** 5 $+\,6$	**8.** 11 $-\,5$	**9.** 17 $-\,9$	**10.** 12 $-\,4$

11. 2 $+\,5$	**12.** 9 $+\,5$	**13.** 7 $+\,4$	**14.** 7 $+\,7$	**15.** 12 $-\,7$	**16.** 9 $+\,8$	**17.** 13 $-\,5$
18. 7 $+\,1$	**19.** 13 $-\,9$	**20.** 18 $-\,9$	**21.** 10 $-\,7$	**22.** 9 $+\,1$	**23.** 9 $-\,3$	**24.** 8 $-\,5$
25. 7 $-\,5$	**26.** 15 $-\,7$	**27.** 6 $+\,4$	**28.** 10 $-\,2$	**29.** 16 $-\,7$	**30.** 11 $-\,8$	**31.** 6 $+\,6$
32. 9 $+\,6$	**33.** 8 $+\,1$	**34.** 9 $+\,0$	**35.** 8 $+\,8$	**36.** 9 $+\,4$	**37.** 8 $+\,5$	**38.** 13 $-\,8$
39. 12 $-\,3$	**40.** 14 $-\,7$	**41.** 9 $-\,7$	**42.** 11 $-\,2$	**43.** 4 $+\,6$	**44.** 5 $+\,9$	**45.** 16 $-\,9$
46. 4 $+\,8$	**47.** 8 $-\,2$	**48.** 10 $-\,4$	**49.** 5 $+\,3$	**50.** 7 $-\,6$	**51.** 14 $-\,9$	**52.** 9 $+\,9$
53. 4 $+\,9$	**54.** 14 $-\,8$	**55.** 7 $+\,6$	**56.** 16 $-\,8$	**57.** 9 $+\,7$	**58.** 15 $-\,9$	**59.** 7 $+\,8$
60. 7 $+\,3$	**61.** 6 $+\,8$	**62.** 15 $-\,6$	**63.** 13 $-\,7$	**64.** 7 $+\,9$	**65.** 13 $-\,4$	**66.** 10 $-\,9$
67. 8 $+\,6$	**68.** 13 $-\,6$	**69.** 6 $+\,7$	**70.** 8 $+\,7$	**71.** 14 $-\,5$	**72.** 12 $-\,9$	**73.** 8 $+\,9$
74. 10 $-\,5$	**75.** 8 $+\,4$	**76.** 12 $-\,6$	**77.** 6 $+\,9$	**78.** 14 $-\,6$	**79.** 6 $+\,5$	**80.** 5 $+\,8$

Problem-Solving Applications

Reading a Chart

PLANETS	DAYS TO ORBIT SUN	HOURS TO ROTATE	NUMBER OF MOONS
Mercury	88 days	1,416 h	0
Venus	225 days	5,832 h	0
Earth	365 days	24 h	1
Uranus	30,660 days	11 h	5

Look at the chart above.

1. How many hours does it take the Earth to rotate?

2. Which takes longer to orbit, Uranus or Earth?

3. Does Mercury take fewer days to orbit the sun than Venus?

4. Which planet takes the most number of hours to rotate?

5. Which planet has more moons, Earth or Uranus?

★**6.** How much longer does it take Venus to rotate than Mercury?

Chapter Review

Write standard numerals. *(26, 30, 32)*

1. Five thousand, three hundred sixty-four

2. 8 thousands, 9 hundreds, 0 tens, and 5 ones

3. 600,000 + 70,000 + 8,000 + 900 + 80 + 4

4. 245 million, 350 thousand, 10

What is the value of each underlined digit? *(28, 30)*

5. 9̲87   **6.** 2̲,478   **7.** 4̲9,276   **8.** 5̲79,148

Write our numerals. *(36)*

9. XVII   **10.** CXLIX   **11.** XXVI   **12.** CCXCII

Compare. Use >, <, or =. *(40)*

13. 962 ≡ 962   **14.** 64 ≡ 84   **15.** 37,901 ≡ 36,901

16. Round 37 to the nearest ten. *(42)*

17. Round $4.19 to the nearest dollar. *(42)*

18. Round 7,849 to the nearest thousand. *(44)*

19. Which number sentence fits the problem? *(38)*

36 brown sweaters
23 green sweaters
How many in all? $36 - 23 = \underline{\ ?\ }$ $36 + 23 = \underline{\ ?\ }$ $59 - 23 = \underline{\ ?\ }$

20. Solve. *(46)*

On which day were the most fiction books checked out?

Library Check-outs

Day	Fiction	Nonfiction
Monday	36	83
Tuesday	62	59

Chapter Test

Write standard numerals. *(26, 30, 32)*

1. Nine thousand, six hundred fourteen

2. 9 thousands, 8 hundreds, 4 tens, and 0 ones

3. 400,000 + 30,000 + 9,000 + 800 + 10 + 6

4. 463 million, 227 thousand, 115

What is the value of each underlined digit? *(28, 30)*

5. 9,487   6. 49,107   7. 875,398   8. 498,764

Write Roman numerals. *(36)*

9. 34   10. 76   11. 142   12. 369

Compare. Use >, <, or =. *(40)*

13. 78 ▤ 87   14. 3,941 ▤ 3,859   15. 48,741 ▤ 48,741

16. Round 742 to the nearest hundred. *(42)*

17. Round $4.30 to the nearest dollar. *(42)*

18. Round 7,514 to the nearest thousand. *(44)*

19. Which number sentence fits the problem? *(38)*

    6 polar bears
    2 grizzly bears
    How many more polar bears? $6 + 2 = \underline{?}$ $8 - 6 = \underline{?}$ $6 - 2 = \underline{?}$

20. Solve. *(46)*

    On which day were there more boys than girls at the park?

Children at Park

Day	Boys	Girls
Wednesday	126	149
Thursday	174	168

Skills Check

1. What is another way to write 300 + 60 + 2?

   A 263   B 326

   C 362   D 632

2. What is another way to write 4,000 + 200 + 90 + 1?

   E 1,291   F 4,029

   G 4,129   H 4,291

3. What is the standard numeral for fifty-three?

   A 35   B 53

   C 153   D 503

4. Find the second bird.

   E   F   G   H

5. What is 29 rounded to the nearest ten?

   A 20   B 25

   C 30   D 40

6. Compare.
   876 ▤ 867

   E >   F =

   G <   H +

7. What is the value of the underlined digit?

   <u>8</u>25

   A 8   B 80

   C 82   D 800

8. What time is it?

   E 7:25   F 7:35

   G 7:40   H 8:25

3 ADDITION

The Grand Coulee Dam is on the Columbia River in Washington State.

COMPUTER—AN EARLY MACHINE

Blaise Pascal was just 19 years old in 1642. He lived in France. He wanted an easy way to add long columns of numbers. So, Pascal invented the first mechanical computer. His machine was called the Pascaline.

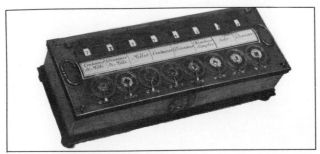

A. The Pascaline had eight dials. Each dial had the numbers 0 to 9 on it. Each dial stood for a place value from hundredths (on the right) to hundred thousands (on the left).

B. Each dial was connected to a gear. When any dial made a complete turn, the dial to its left moved up one number.

C. Here is how to add 18 + 3 on the Pascaline.

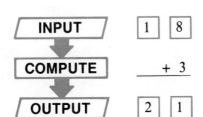

| INPUT | 1 | 8 |

| COMPUTE | + 3 |

| OUTPUT | 2 | 1 |

1. Turn the tens dial to 1 and the ones dial to 8.

2. Turn the ones dial three spaces.

3. The answer is shown in the "windows" above the tens and ones dial.

D. Suppose the ones dial is moved 8 spaces. What numbers would you see above these Pascaline dials?

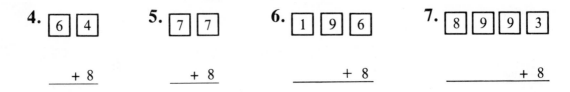

4. 6 4
   + 8

5. 7 7
   + 8

6. 1 9 6
   + 8

7. 8 9 9 3
   + 8

ADDING TENS AND ONES

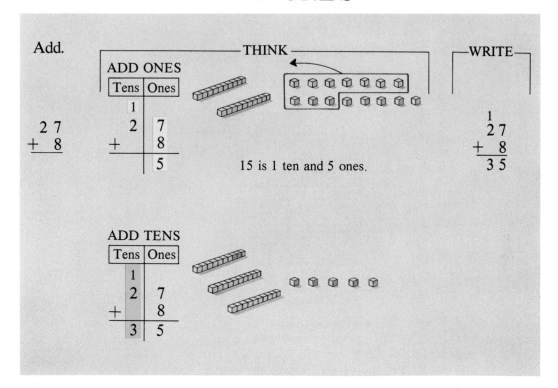

Add.

ADD ONES

Tens	Ones
1	
2	7
+	8
	5

27
+ 8

THINK

15 is 1 ten and 5 ones.

WRITE

1
27
+ 8
35

ADD TENS

Tens	Ones
1	
2	7
+	8
3	5

Study and Learn

A. Add.

1.	**2.**	**3.**	**4.**	**5.**
76	37	83	19	24
+ 3	+ 1	+ 8	+ 7	+ 6

Practice

Add.

1.	**2.**	**3.**	**4.**	**5.**
26	63	40	68	72
+ 2	+ 5	+ 8	+ 4	+ 8

6.	**7.**	**8.**
43	92	58
+ 9	+ 5	+ 9

★ **9.** 36 + □ = 41

53

COLUMN ADDITION

Barbara, Linda, and Gene added 8 + 4 + 2 + 2.

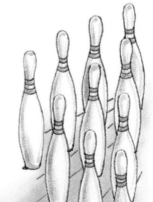

Barbara

$$
\begin{array}{l}
8 \\
4 \\
2 \\
+\,2
\end{array}
\quad
\begin{array}{l}
12 \\
14 \\
16
\end{array}
$$

Linda

$$
\begin{array}{l}
8 \\
4 \\
2 \\
+\,2
\end{array}
\quad
\begin{array}{l}
16 \\
8 \\
4
\end{array}
$$

Gene

$$
\begin{array}{l}
8 \\
4 \\
2 \\
+\,2
\end{array}
\quad
\begin{array}{l}
10 \\
6
\end{array}
\quad 16
$$

Study and Learn

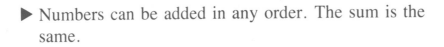

A. Look at the addition examples above.

    1. Barbara added down. What is her sum?

    2. Linda added up. What is her sum?

    3. Gene looked for tens. What is his sum?

▶ Numbers can be added in any order. The sum is the same.

B. Find the sums. Add any two numbers first.

    4. 7 + 5 + 3   **5.** 6 + 4 + 7   **6.** 9 + 2 + 1 + 8

C. Add.

7.	**8.**	**9.**	**10.**	**11.**	**12.**
4	7	5	4	9	6
2	3	4	2	7	8
+ 6	5	5	5	3	3
	+ 4	3	+ 2	+ 2	2
		+ 6			+ 4

Practice

Add.

1. 4 + 7 + 3   **2.** 9 + 1 + 8

3. 3 + 6 + 4 + 9   **4.** 7 + 6 + 5 + 4 + 3

5. 4 2 + 6	**6.** 7 3 + 6	**7.** 5 4 + 5	**8.** 8 6 + 4	**9.** 9 8 + 7	**10.** 3 4 + 5

11. 7 2 8 + 1	**12.** 6 4 9 + 8	**13.** 8 3 7 + 4	**14.** 6 8 3 + 7	**15.** 9 8 7 + 6	**16.** 5 6 7 + 8

17. 4 2 9 6 + 8	**18.** 4 8 2 3 + 3	**19.** 6 5 7 4 + 3	**20.** 8 9 0 1 + 2	**21.** 4 5 6 7 + 8	**22.** 9 8 7 6 + 5

23. 3 2 + 7	**24.** 4 8 7 + 5	**25.** 6 2 4 + 9	**26.** 7 4 3 6 + 5	**27.** 9 9 9 + 9	★**28.** 8 8 8 8 8 + 8

Solve Problems

29. Anil went bowling. He scored 8 pins, 7 pins, 5 pins, 6 pins, and 8 pins in the first five frames. How many pins did Anil score in all?

ADDING TENS

One day Carol sold 27 angelfish and 16 guppies at the pet shop. How many fish did she sell in all?

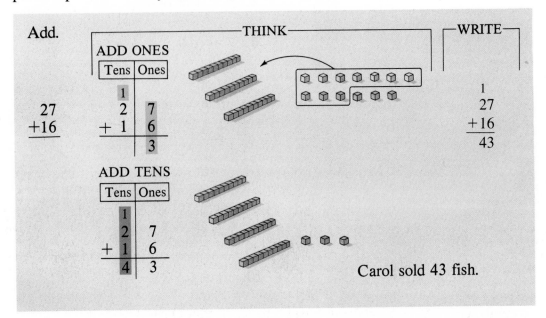

Add.

ADD ONES

Tens	Ones
1	
2	7
+ 1	6
	3

27
+16

THINK

WRITE

1
27
+16
43

ADD TENS

Tens	Ones
1	
2	7
+ 1	6
4	3

Carol sold 43 fish.

Study and Learn

A. Find 49 + 78 + 37 + 50. Complete.

1. Add ones. 9 + 8 + 7 + 0 = __?__

2. How is 24 written? __?__

3. Add tens. 2 + 4 + 7 + 3 + 5 = __?__

4. What is the sum?

WRITE

2
49
78
37
+ 50
214

B. Add.

5.	6.	7.	8.	9.
21	76	49	62	90
+ 37	+ 16	12	58	39
		+ 93	25	42
			+ 4	+ 19

Practice

Add.

1. 74 + 13	**2.** 61 + 24	**3.** 56 + 62	**4.** 61 + 95	**5.** 87 + 60
6. 15 + 18	**7.** 27 + 49	**8.** 48 + 37	**9.** 24 + 36	**10.** 73 + 17
11. 94 + 87	**12.** 58 + 63	**13.** 62 + 98	**14.** 57 + 43	**15.** 87 + 19
16. 15 16 + 17	**17.** 42 38 + 71	**18.** 56 28 + 35	**19.** 34 63 + 5	**20.** 17 8 + 9
21. 59 60 74 + 85	**22.** 51 62 73 + 84	**23.** 19 47 18 + 36	**24.** 47 56 29 + 7	**25.** 76 29 9 + 8
26. 21 + 48	**27.** 19 72 + 26	**28.** 46 25 75 + 13	**29.** 42 58 21 + 8	**30.** 68 75 + 9

31. 86 + 94

32. 32 + 6 + 21

33. 75 + 18 + 23 + 6

★ **34.** 13 + 16 + □ = 99

Solve Problems

35. 27 parakeets
 18 parrots
 How many birds in all?

36. 36 gray mice, 42 white mice, and 19 black mice
 How many mice in all?

ADDING HUNDREDS

It was helmet day at the baseball game. There were 798 boys and 874 girls at the game. How many children in all?

Add 798 + 874.

Step 1	Step 2	Step 3
ADD ONES	ADD TENS	ADD HUNDREDS
1	1 1	1 1
798	798	798
+ 874	+ 874	+ 874
2	72	1,672

12 is 1 ten and 2 ones

There were 1,672 children.

Study and Learn

A. Complete.

	1.	2.	3.	4.	5.
	746	1 579	493	428	946
	+ 123	+ 618	+ 274	+ 75	+ 8
	9	7			

B. Find 476 + 874 + 166. Complete.

6. Add ones. 6 + 4 + 6 = ___?___

7. Add tens. 1 + 7 + 7 + 6 = ___?___

8. Add hundreds. 2 + 4 + 8 + 1 = ___?___

9. What is the sum?

WRITE

```
  2 1
  4 7 6
  8 7 4
+ 1 6 6
-------
1,5 1 6
```

C. Add.

10.	11.	12.	13.	14.
326	419	380	598	489
241	207	141	747	538
+ 312	+ 324	283	986	27
		+ 192	+ 487	+ 5

Practice

Add.

1. 345
   + 254

2. 641
   + 123

3. 724
   + 435

4. 870
   + 908

5. 753
   + 14

6. 428
   + 354

7. 714
   + 828

8. 591
   + 683

9. 874
   + 934

10. 878
    + 19

11. 789
    + 486

12. 487
    + 943

13. 875
    + 249

14. 648
    + 556

15. 497
    + 46

16. 427
    398
    + 568

17. 884
    675
    + 498

18. 826
    749
    + 827

19. 749
    648
    + 27

20. 198
    35
    + 5

21. 487
    298
    148
    + 374

22. 987
    746
    894
    + 681

23. 555
    706
    607
    + 491

24. 374
    286
    28
    + 7

25. 849
    38
    5
    + 4

26. 421
    + 374

27. 726
    478
    + 137

28. 624
    + 819

29. 976
    248
    + 97

30. 473
    + 937

31. 628
    476
    921
    + 807

32. 629
    + 876

33. 964
    875
    197
    + 48

34. 417
    94
    649
    + 7

★35. 7,384
    6,946
    8,741
    + 5,099

Solve Problems

36. 498 red banners
    279 blue banners
    104 yellow banners
    How many banners in all?

37. 721 orange drinks sold
    526 grape drinks sold
    394 lemonade drinks sold
    How many drinks sold in all?

ADDING THOUSANDS

Treeland Park has 9,877 black oak trees and 5,476 white oak trees. How many oak trees are there in all?

Add 9,877 + 5,476.

Step 1	Step 2	Step 3	Step 4
ADD ONES	ADD TENS	ADD HUNDREDS	ADD THOUSANDS
$\begin{array}{r} 1 \\ 9,877 \\ +5,476 \\ \hline 3 \end{array}$	$\begin{array}{r} 11 \\ 9,877 \\ +5,476 \\ \hline 53 \end{array}$	$\begin{array}{r} 111 \\ 9,877 \\ +5,476 \\ \hline 353 \end{array}$	$\begin{array}{r} 111 \\ 9,877 \\ +5,476 \\ \hline 15,353 \end{array}$

There are 15,353 oak trees in all.

Study and Learn

A. Complete.

1. $\begin{array}{r} 7,614 \\ +8,125 \\ \hline 39 \end{array}$
2. $\begin{array}{r} 1 \\ 3,928 \\ +5,048 \\ \hline 6 \end{array}$
3. $\begin{array}{r} 4,678 \\ +9,186 \\ \hline \end{array}$
4. $\begin{array}{r} 5,387 \\ +6,941 \\ \hline \end{array}$

B. Find 27,376 + 38,265. Complete.

5. Add ones. 6 + 5 = ___?___

6. Add tens. 1 + 7 + 6 = ___?___

7. Add hundreds. 1 + 3 + 2 = ___?___

8. Complete the addition.

WRITE
$\begin{array}{r} 11 \\ 27,376 \\ +38,265 \\ \hline 641 \end{array}$

C. Add.

9. $\begin{array}{r} 79,251 \\ +52,967 \\ \hline \end{array}$
10. $\begin{array}{r} 27,614 \\ +18,128 \\ \hline \end{array}$
11. $\begin{array}{r} 52,409 \\ +19,842 \\ \hline \end{array}$
12. $\begin{array}{r} 75,387 \\ +16,945 \\ \hline \end{array}$

Practice

Add.

1. 7,046 + 1,732	**2.** 6,140 + 3,247	**3.** 8,241 + 1,743	**4.** 7,080 + 4,904
5. 3,289 + 3,604	**6.** 2,881 + 7,094	**7.** 6,241 + 1,938	**8.** 8,274 + 9,608
9. 7,284 + 9,378	**10.** 1,798 + 4,875	**11.** 9,876 + 6,789	**12.** 8,704 + 1,887
13. 15,746 + 22,150	**14.** 37,294 + 61,782	**15.** 36,287 + 13,508	**16.** 47,042 + 64,825
17. 39,642 + 48,185	**18.** 87,249 + 61,187	**19.** 38,764 + 98,847	**20.** 49,687 + 93,179
21. 8,204 + 1,742	**22.** 4,737 + 1,148	**23.** 7,698 + 8,704	**24.** 24,698 + 18,406
25. 32,876 + 48,095	**26.** 3,284 + 9,198	★ **27.** 374,298 + 984,187	★ **28.** 675,248 + 248,578

Solve Problems

29. Hatch's Orchard has 4,782 orange trees and 3,648 grapefruit trees. How many trees are in the orchard?

30. A forest service replanted 27,476 acres of new trees last year. It plans to replant 19,726 acres this year. How many acres will have been replanted in these two years?

● **31.** The Nelsons had 11,497 trees on their first farm. They had 10,948 trees on their second farm. On which farm did they have more trees?

ADDING MORE THOUSANDS

A bird sanctuary had
2,744 pheasants, 3,764 quails,
and 1,805 ducks. How many
birds were there in all?

Add 2,744 + 3,764 + 1,805.

Step 1	Step 2	Step 3	Step 4
ADD ONES	ADD TENS	ADD HUNDREDS	ADD THOUSANDS

```
    1         1 1        2 1 1       2 1 1
 2,744      2,744      2,744       2,744
 3,764      3,764      3,764       3,764
+1,805     +1,805     +1,805      +1,805
─────      ─────      ─────       ─────
     3         13        313       8,313
```

There were 8,313 birds.

Study and Learn

A. Find 7,296 + 3,074 + 9,275. Complete.

    1. Add ones. 6 + 4 + 5 = ___?___

    2. Add tens. 1 + 9 + 7 + 7 = ___?___

    3. Add hundreds. 2 + 2 + 0 + 2 = ___?___

    4. Add thousands. 7 + 3 + 9 = ___?___

```
   WRITE
     2 1
   7,296
   3,074
 + 9,275
 ───────
  19,645
```

B. Add.

5.	**6.**	**7.**	**8.**
6,214	6,247	8,888	8,298
7,147	9,041	7,777	4,785
+ 3,326	+ 3,880	+ 6,666	+ 486

Practice

Add.

1.	1,241 2,420 + 3,008	**2.**	6,284 2,141 + 7,083	**3.**	9,047 8,126 + 7,118	**4.**	3,871 4,804 + 6,713	**5.**	8,200 3,947 + 812
6.	4,748 6,291 + 8,850	**7.**	9,428 8,704 + 6,917	**8.**	8,014 6,189 + 3,348	**9.**	9,876 5,432 + 4,710	**10.**	8,654 901 + 719
11.	7,864 2,985 + 3,876	**12.**	4,298 6,874 + 7,807	**13.**	6,295 7,386 + 9,789	**14.**	4,217 8,999 + 3,846	**15.**	7,285 9,846 + 728
16.	3,784 6,000 + 1,211	**17.**	4,287 3,090 + 8,172	**18.**	6,284 7,149 + 6,048	**19.**	8,743 9,685 + 3,049	**20.**	6,041 8,917 + 5,809
21.	2,743 6,287 + 9,403	**22.**	8,476 127 + 37	**★ 23.**	12,486 19,407 + 26,815	**★ 24.**	89,746 78,198 + 81,150		

Solve Problems

25. Feather Park has 1,426 geese, 808 sparrows, and 214 partridges. How many birds in all?

26. The birdwatchers counted 1,111 swallows, 726 crows, and 272 woodpeckers. How many birds altogether?

● **27.** Hillside Park has 16 ducks. Seven are ducklings. How many ducks are fully grown?

Midchapter Review

Add.

1.   47
(53)   + 8

2.   6
(54)   7
     3
     4
   + 1

3.   46
(56)   32
     19
   + 7

4.   49
(56)   + 59

5.   672
(58)   + 399

6.   463
(58)   847
     312
   + 103

7.   3,609
(60)   + 4,897

8.   1,764
(60)   + 3,805

9.   36,128
(60)   + 42,186

10.   8,726
(62)   4,504
   + 9,618

11.   7,284
(62)   3,107
   + 9,209

12.   6,285
(62)   8,749
   + 3,718

Something Extra
Calculator Activities

Complete these chain reactions.

1.   7 → 14 → + 898 → + 9,001
   + 7   + 97   10,010
    14

2.   876 → + 3,829 → + 9,736 → + 85,062
   + 497   100,000

3.   2,222 → + 4,444 → + 8,888 → + 17,776
   + 2,222   35,552

COMPARING

Compare. Use $=$, $>$, or $<$ for $6 + 7 \equiv 9 + 5$.

Sentence $\longrightarrow$ $6 + 7 \equiv 9 + 5$
Do work $\longrightarrow$ $13 \equiv 14$ $\qquad$ $6 + 7 = 13; 9 + 5 = 14$
Compare $\longrightarrow$ $13 < 14$ $\qquad$ 13 is less than 14.

Study and Learn

A. Compare. Use $=$, $>$, or $<$ for $16 - 9 \equiv 4 + 2$.

1. Subtract. $16 - 9 = \underline{\quad?\quad}$ $\qquad$ $7 \equiv 6$

2. Add. $4 + 2 = \underline{\quad?\quad}$ $\qquad$ $7 > 6$

3. Compare. 7 is greater than 6. Which symbol is used?

B. Compare. Use $=$, $>$, or $<$.

4. $8 + 4 \equiv 3 + 9$ $\qquad$ 5. $15 - 9 \equiv 16 - 8$

6. $8 + 6 \equiv 10 - 2$ $\qquad$ 7. $17 - 8 \equiv 4 + 5$

Practice

Compare. Use $=$, $>$, or $<$.

1. $4 + 7 \equiv 3 + 9$ $\qquad$ 2. $6 + 4 \equiv 5 + 5$

3. $14 - 7 \equiv 15 - 9$ $\qquad$ 4. $17 - 9 \equiv 10 - 2$

5. $4 + 5 \equiv 13 - 4$ $\qquad$ 6. $18 - 9 \equiv 11 - 3$

7. $14 - 6 \equiv 5 + 4$ $\qquad$ 8. $12 - 4 \equiv 8 + 2$

9. $9 + 8 \equiv 7 + 6$ $\qquad$ 10. $13 - 7 \equiv 13 - 6$

★11. $6 + 5 + 4 \equiv 7 + 3 + 5$ $\qquad$ ★12. $3 + 4 + 5 + 6 \equiv 9 + 8$

Problem-Solving Skills

Writing the Correct Number Sentence

The Middle City Post Office sold 2,147 regular stamps. It also sold 368 special stamps. How many stamps were sold in all?

Think:

What is asked? ⟶ How many in all?
What is given? ⟶ 2,147 regular stamps, 368 special stamps
Do you add or subtract? ⟶ Add.

This number sentence fits the problem.

$$2{,}147 \quad + \quad 368 \quad = \quad \underline{\quad ? \quad}$$

↑   ↑   ↑

regular stamps   special stamps   how many in all

Study and Learn

A. Elaine Goldman delivered 738 letters on Monday. She delivered 85 letters on Tuesday and 24 on Wednesday. How many did she deliver in all?

   1. What is asked?

   2. What is given?

   3. Do you add or subtract?

   4. Write a number sentence that fits the problem.

B. Write the number sentence that fits the problem.

   5. 85 mail carriers
       15 sorters
       How many more mail carriers?

   6. 362 letters
       138 post cards
       How many in all?

Practice

Write the number sentence that fits the problem.

1. Earl Jackson delivered 73 letters.
   He also delivered 14 packages.
   How many more letters did he deliver?

2. 14 magazines were delivered on Monday.
   12 were delivered on Tuesday and 8 on
   Wednesday. How many were delivered in all?

3. There were 26 workers. 8 workers left
   for lunch. How many were left working?

4. 28 people drive trucks on the day shift.
   14 people drive trucks on the night shift.
   How many drivers are there altogether?

5. There are 360 homes getting mail today on
   Mr. Rivera's mail route. He has delivered
   mail to 186 homes. How many more
   deliveries must he make?

6. The westside mail route has 195 houses and
   235 stores. How many places in all?

7. Mrs. Riley has 377 deliveries on her mail
   route. How many deliveries does she make
   in 3 days?

MONEY

WORD NAME	MONEY NOTATION
Six cents	6¢ or $0.06
Seventy-three cents	73¢ or $0.73
Six dollars	$6 or $6.00
Seventy-three dollars	$73 or $73.00
Five dollars and fifteen cents	$5.15
Fourteen dollars and three cents	$14.03

Study and Learn

A. Write each in two ways.

1. Forty-four cents
2. Twelve cents
3. Fifty cents
4. One cent
5. Ten dollars
6. Two dollars
7. Sixty-five dollars
8. Ninety-nine dollars

B. Write, using the $ sign.

Example   Two dollars and twelve cents is written $2.12.

9. Five dollars and eighty-one cents
10. Twenty-nine dollars and six cents
11. Seventy dollars and seventy cents
12. Ten dollars and one cent

C. Write word names.

13. 82¢   14. $0.14   15. $0.90   16. $44.00   17. $32.10

Practice

Write each two ways.

1. Ninety-four cents

2. Thirteen cents

3. Four cents

4. Eighteen cents

5. Three dollars

6. Sixteen dollars

7. Thirty-three dollars

8. Forty-one dollars

Write, using the $ sign.

9. One dollar and fifty cents

10. Five dollars and twenty-five cents

11. Eleven dollars and eleven cents

12. Twenty-eight dollars and sixty-five cents

13. Eighty-nine dollars and one cent

14. Sixty dollars and sixty cents

Write word names.

15. $0.17

16. $0.80

17. 24¢

18. 95¢

19. $3.00

20. $80.00

21. $71.03

22. $27.38

Solve Problems

23. A large box of crayons costs $1.35. Write the word name for the cost of the crayons.

★ **24.** Billy has 2 quarters, 3 dimes and 4 pennies. He needs ninety-two cents to buy a whistle. Does he have enough money?

ADDING MONEY

Add. $7.68 + $4.95 + $0.27

ADD	PLACE MONEY NOTATION
$ 7.68	$ 7.68
4.95	4.95
+ 0.27	+ 0.27
12 90	$12.90

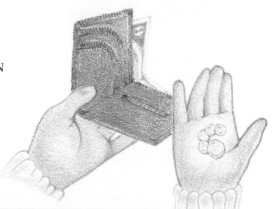

Study and Learn

A. Complete.

1. $ 0.37
  + 0.29
  ——
  66

2. $ 7.28
  + 6.39
  ——
  7

3. $ 9.65
  + 0.87

4. $ 3.84
  2.97
  + 6.24

B. Add.

5. $ 0.97
  + 0.86

6. $ 19.46
  + 27.32

7. $ 38.75
  + 8.66

8. $ 1.98
  6.74
  + 0.78

Practice

Add.

1. $ 0.73
  + 0.25

2. $ 0.96
  + 0.48

3. $ 1.28
  + 3.75

4. $ 12.97
  + 24.68

5. $ 0.47
  0.96
  + 0.08

6. $ 7.98
  6.25
  + 4.74

7. $ 18.47
  17.76
  + 38.06

8. $ 42.87
  9.56
  + 0.98

9. $ 6.94
  + 7.21

10. $ 8.15
  0.47
  + 2.68

11. $ 34.27
  9.48
  + 7.96

12. $ 18.95
  + 0.07

Skills Review

Write standard numerals. *(26, 30)*

1. 760 thousand, 801

2. 30,000 + 5,000 + 700 + 90 + 0

3. 4 thousands, 3 hundreds, 0 tens, and 6 ones

What is the value of each underlined digit? *(28, 30)*

4. <u>7</u>,264   **5.** <u>1</u>9,848   **6.** <u>4</u>12,684   **7.** 78,9<u>4</u>1

Compare. Use =, >, or <. *(40)*

8. 47 ≣ 74   **9.** 968 ≣ 968   **10.** 7,214 ≣ 7,124

Round to the nearest ten. *(42)*

11. 48   **12.** 84   **13.** 65   **14.** 19

Round to the nearest hundred.

15. 378   **16.** 873   **17.** 738   **18.** 450

Round to the nearest dollar.

19. $2.89   **20.** $9.28   **21.** $8.98   **22.** $1.50

Something Extra
Non-Routine Problems

Complete the patterns.

1. 0, 6, 12, 18, 24, __?__, __?__, __?__

2. 1, 4, 2, 5, 3, 6, __?__, __?__

3. 1, 4, 3, 2, 5, 4, 3, 6, __?__, __?__

ESTIMATING SUMS

Estimate 87 + 31 + 25.
Sums are estimated by:

1. Rounding the addends

2. Adding the rounded addends

ROUND ADDENDS	ADD
87 → 90	90
31 → 30	30
25 → 30	+ 30
	150

Study and Learn

A. Estimate. Round to the nearest ten.

1. 42	2. 78	3. 43	4. 62	5. 55
+ 31	+ 45	+ 77	74	94
			+ 36	+ 39

B. Estimate 746 + 358 + 298.
Round to the nearest hundred.

6. Round 746.

7. Round 358.

8. Round 298.

9. What is the estimated sum?

EXACT	ROUNDED
746	700
358	400
+ 298	+ 300
	1,400

C. Estimate $8.95 + $6.04.
Round to the nearest dollar.

10. Round $8.95.

11. Round $6.04.

12. What is the estimated sum?

EXACT	ROUNDED
$ 8.95	$ 9.00
+ 6.04	+ 6.00
	$15.00

D. Estimate the sums.

13. 91	14. 757	15. $ 3.76	16. 895	17. $ 1.98
+ 86	+ 184	+ 4.88	318	8.77
			+ 789	+ 3.29

Practice

Estimate the sums. Round to the nearest ten.

1.	56	**2.**	38	**3.**	92	**4.**	34	**5.**	73
	+ 55		+ 47		+ 81		49		29
							+ 27		+ 38

Estimate the sums. Round to the nearest hundred.

6.	426	**7.**	724	**8.**	892	**9.**	421	**10.**	749
	+ 537		+ 816		+ 347		648		851
							+ 726		+ 415

Estimate the sums. Round to the nearest dollar.

11.	$ 4.98	**12.**	$ 6.12	**13.**	$ 9.05	**14.**	$ 8.21	**15.**	$ 4.88
	+ 6.85		+ 7.25		+ 4.89		4.85		6.99
							+ 1.97		+ 2.14

Estimate the sums.

16.	87	**17.**	678	**18.**	$ 5.25	**19.**	754	**20.**	$ 2.17
	53		+ 214		6.50		629		3.14
	+ 46				+ 8.25		+ 534		+ 8.75

21.	$ 1.75	**22.**	498	**23.**	$ 4.75	★ **24.**	3,565	★ **25.**	$ 89.97
	2.99		376		+ 8.39		2,584		+ 72.21
	+ 0.98		+ 701				+ 4,113		

Estimate to solve.

26. 644 passengers Monday
576 passengers Tuesday
About how many in all?

27. $8.65 to York
$4.51 to Coatsville
About how much in all?

73

Problem-Solving Applications

Career

Estimate to solve.

1. 33 prescriptions on Friday
   48 on Saturday
   About how many in all?
   [HINT: 30 + 50 = __?__]

2. Spent $2.16 today.
   Spent $8.93 yesterday.
   About how much in all?

3. 113 cartons delivered Monday
   107 cartons delivered Tuesday
   About how many in all?

4. 106 customers Thursday
   198 customers Friday
   About how many in all?

5. $2.65 for shampoo
   $1.09 for cotton
   $1.25 for bandages
   About how much in all?

6. Worked 23 days in May and
   16 days in June.
   About how many days in
   all?

Chapter Review

Add.

1.   87   **2.**   4   **3.**   87   **4.**   878   **5.**   976   **6.**   7,273
(53) + 6 *(54)*   2 *(56)*   25 *(58)* 724 *(58)* + 218 *(60)* + 9,419
              6   + 38   327
              3   + 149
          + 5

7.   24,678   **8.**   9,764   **9.** $ 0.34   **10.** $ 42.16
(60) + 39,880   *(62)*   3,018   *(70)* + 0.28   *(70)*   28.44
                 + 6,241   + 72.98

Write, using a $ sign. *(68)*

11. Twenty-two dollars and fourteen cents

12. Fifty dollars and fifty cents

13. Twelve dollars

Estimate the sums. *(72)*

14.   59   **15.**   38   **16.**   287   **17.** $ 7.98   **18.** $ 1.50
    + 71   76   831   + 6.10   2.12
            + 12   + 505   + 3.87

Write the number sentence that fits the problem. *(66)*

19. There were 36 daffodils and 23 tulips.
How many flowers were there in all?

Estimate to solve. *(74)*

20. Jack spent $8.75 for gas and $1.35 for motor oil.
About how much did he spend in all?

Chapter Test

Add.

1. 89 **2.** 3 **3.** 63 **4.** 874 **5.** 784 **6.** 2,847
(53) + 6 *(54)* 2 *(56)* 37 *(58)* 219 *(58)* + 698 *(60)* + 3,196
                        8   + 19   360
                        4   + 194
                      + 6

7. 64,388 **8.** 3,785 **9.** $ 73.87 **10.** $ 63.25
(60) + 91,734 *(62)* 1,248 *(70)* + 9.41 *(70)* 18.20
                       + 4,735   + 87.55

Write, using a $ sign. *(68)*

11. Sixteen dollars and seventy-four cents

12. Forty dollars and five cents

13. Sixty dollars

Estimate the sums. *(72)*

14. 55 **15.** 87 **16.** 685 **17.** 389 **18.** $ 2.50
      + 32   23   + 716   498   3.75
                + 49   + 525   + 1.22

Write the number sentence that fits the problem. *(66)*

19. There were 30 sports magazines and 12 fashion magazines.
How many more sports magazines were there?

Estimate to solve. *(74)*

20. There were 270 passengers going to Chicago and 317
passengers going to Atlanta. About how many passengers in all?

Skills Check

1. Cindy bought crayons for $0.39 and drawing paper for $0.62. How much did she spend?

   A $0.90   B $1.01

   C $1.12   D $1.40

2. There are 29 cars in parking lot A and 43 cars in parking lot B. About how many cars are there in all?

   E 60   F 65

   G 70   H 80

3. How many minutes are there in 2 hours?

   A 30   B 60

   C 100   D 120

4. What is the value of three nickels and two dimes?

   E 15¢   F 32¢

   G 25¢   H 35¢

5. Bob weighed 150 lbs last week. This week he weighs 146 lbs. How much weight did he lose?

   A 4 lbs   B 5 lbs

   C 6 lbs   D 296 lbs

6. Ray spent $1.09 for lunch. He gave the cashier $1.25. How much change should he receive?

   E $0.06   F $0.16

   G $0.20   H $2.34

7. Sharon wanted to buy a pair of shoes. She went to the store and chose a pair she liked. What did she do next?

   A Went home.   B Tried them on.

   C Paid for them.   D Took a bus.

8. Don earns $2.50 an hour washing cars. How much does he earn in 2 hours?

   E $4.00   F $4.50

   G $5.00   H $5.50

4 SUBTRACTION

The Kohlbrand Bridge spans the Seine River in France.

COMPUTER—STORE AND SHOW

You can store numbers in the computer's memory. Each storage place has an address so that you are able to find the numbers again. Sometimes letters of the alphabet are used instead of numbers.

A. To store a number, use the LET command.
To store 12 in place A, tell the computer: **LET A = 12**.
To store 19 in place M, tell the computer: **LET M = 19**.

B. To make the computer show what is stored in its memory, use the **PRINT** command.

To show what is in A, tell the computer: **PRINT A**.
The computer will show 12 because 12 is stored in A.

C. You can also make the computer do arithmetic with stored numbers.

Suppose you tell the computer: **PRINT M − A**.
The computer subtracts the number in A from the number in M. Then, it shows the answer 7, because $19 − 12 = 7$.

D. Suppose you want to store the number 14 in A and the number 7 in B. What input will you give the computer?

Write the outputs for the following inputs.

1. PRINT A.   **2. PRINT A − 6.**   **3. PRINT A − B.**

H A N D S   O N

You can check your work for exercises **1–3** on the computer. Type your **LET** command from **D** above. Then type each **PRINT** command from **1–3** above. Remember to press $\boxed{\text{RETURN}}$ after each command.

CHECKING SUBTRACTION

Check subtraction by adding. Two forms are shown.

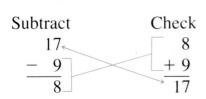

Study and Learn

A. Subtract and check.

1. 10 − 3	**2.** 8 − 8	**3.** 14 − 7	**4.** 13 − 6	**5.** 5 − 0	**6.** 16 − 8

Practice

Subtract and check.

1. 11 − 3	**2.** 9 − 7	**3.** 18 − 9	**4.** 16 − 8	**5.** 7 − 1	**6.** 4 − 3
7. 12 − 5	**8.** 7 − 7	**9.** 3 − 0	**10.** 6 − 5	**11.** 9 − 4	**12.** 10 − 1
13. 7 − 4	**14.** 12 − 9	**15.** 16 − 7	**16.** 14 − 6	**17.** 16 − 9	**18.** 14 − 6

Solve Problems

★ **19.** There was a total of 15 runs scored in the baseball game between the Rangers and the Yankees. The Rangers scored 8 runs. What was the score of the game?

★ **20.** There were 5 runs scored in the next game between the Rangers and the Yankees. The Yankees won by 3 runs. What was the score of the game?

SUBTRACTING TENS

Ms. Jackson's classroom library has 33 adventure books.
Her students are reading 17 of them. How many books are left?

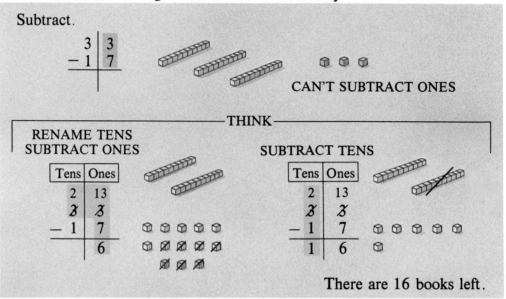

Subtract.

$$\begin{array}{r} 3\ \ 3 \\ -\ 1\ \ 7 \end{array}$$

CAN'T SUBTRACT ONES

THINK

RENAME TENS
SUBTRACT ONES

Tens	Ones
2	13
3̶	3̶
− 1	7
	6

SUBTRACT TENS

Tens	Ones
2	13
3̶	3̶
− 1	7
1	6

There are 16 books left.

Study and Learn

A. Find 74 − 23. Complete.

WRITE

1. Subtract ones. 4 − 3 = ___?___
2. Subtract tens. 7 − 2 = ___?___
3. What is the difference?

$$\begin{array}{r} 74 \\ -\ 23 \\ \hline 51 \end{array}$$

B. Complete.

4.
$$\begin{array}{r} 97 \\ -\ 7 \\ \hline 0 \end{array}$$

5.
$$\begin{array}{r} {}^{2\ 11}3\!\!/1 \\ -\ 4 \\ \hline 7 \end{array}$$

6.
$$\begin{array}{r} 57 \\ -\ 8 \end{array}$$

7.
$$\begin{array}{r} 90 \\ -\ 14 \end{array}$$

8.
$$\begin{array}{r} 42 \\ -\ 26 \end{array}$$

C. Subtract.

9.
$$\begin{array}{r} 36 \\ -\ 14 \end{array}$$

10.
$$\begin{array}{r} 86 \\ -\ 25 \end{array}$$

11.
$$\begin{array}{r} 27 \\ -\ 8 \end{array}$$

12.
$$\begin{array}{r} 86 \\ -\ 28 \end{array}$$

13.
$$\begin{array}{r} 37 \\ -\ 18 \end{array}$$

Practice

Subtract.

1.	55	2.	73	3.	47	4.	16	5.	86
	− 3		− 1		− 7		− 4		− 5

6.	39	7.	58	8.	74	9.	86	10.	57
	− 16		− 21		− 22		− 23		− 40

11.	75	12.	84	13.	51	14.	33	15.	42
	− 8		− 6		− 6		− 9		− 8

16.	97	17.	74	18.	52	19.	86	20.	45
	− 28		− 17		− 23		− 78		− 37

21.	58	22.	70	23.	47	24.	80	25.	90
	− 29		− 37		− 28		− 74		− 19

26.	48	27.	79	28.	19	29.	42	30.	75
	− 12		− 49		− 3		− 13		− 26

31. $74 - 8 = \square$ ★ **32.** $95 - \square = 12$

Solve Problems

33. Jennifer's book has 82 pages. She has read 26 pages. How many pages does she have left to read?

34. Jim's book has 68 pages. Mike's book has 96 pages. How many fewer pages are in Jim's book?

● **35.** Jackie's first book had 78 pages. Her second book had 84 pages. She read both books. How many pages did she read?

83

SUBTRACTING HUNDREDS

Subtract 658 − 193.

Step 1	Step 2	Step 3	Step 4
SUBTRACT ONES	CAN'T SUBTRACT TENS	RENAME HUNDREDS SUBTRACT TENS	SUBTRACT HUNDREDS

$$
\begin{array}{r} 658 \\ -193 \\ \hline 5 \end{array}
\qquad
\begin{array}{r} 658 \\ -193 \\ \hline 5 \end{array}
\qquad
\begin{array}{r} {}^{5}6{}^{15}58 \\ -193 \\ \hline 65 \end{array}
\qquad
\begin{array}{r} {}^{5}6{}^{15}58 \\ -193 \\ \hline 465 \end{array}
$$

Study and Learn

A. Find. 724 − 378. Complete.

WRITE

$$
\begin{array}{r} {}^{6}\;{}^{11}\cancel{1}{}^{14} \\ \cancel{7}\,\cancel{2}\,\cancel{4} \\ -378 \\ \hline 346 \end{array}
$$

    1. Rename tens and subtract ones.
14 − 8 = _?_

    2. Rename hundreds and subtract tens.
11 − 7 = _?_

    3. Subtract hundreds. 6 − 3 = _?_

    4. What is the difference?

B. Complete.

	5.	**6.**	**7.**	**8.**	**9.**
	457	⁶¹⁴ 77̶4̶	426	376	924
	− 140	− 68	− 189	− 369	− 79
	7	6			

C. Subtract.

	10.	**11.**	**12.**	**13.**	**14.**
	684	678	424	386	249
	− 91	− 249	− 107	− 379	− 182

Practice

Subtract.

1. 837 − 720	**2.** 743 − 121	**3.** 826 − 4	**4.** 948 − 42	**5.** 355 − 41
6. 316 − 191	**7.** 541 − 370	**8.** 840 − 708	**9.** 354 − 118	**10.** 425 − 381
11. 760 − 2	**12.** 391 − 8	**13.** 756 − 92	**14.** 335 − 81	**15.** 774 − 65
16. 943 − 658	**17.** 876 − 199	**18.** 720 − 659	**19.** 456 − 387	**20.** 555 − 486
21. 987 − 89	**22.** 411 − 29	**23.** 726 − 89	**24.** 110 − 86	**25.** 320 − 91
26. 378 − 125	**27.** 840 − 30	**28.** 417 − 233	**29.** 920 − 806	**30.** 473 − 469

★ **31.** $387 - \square = 364$ ★ **32.** $120 - \square = 96$

Solve Problems

33. There are 138 students in the fourth grade. 79 are boys. How many are girls?

34. Madison School has 736 students. Harrison School has 812 students. How many more students go to the Harrison School?

● **35.** Which is more? $826 - 237$ or $426 + 198$

85

SUBTRACTING THOUSANDS

Subtract 5,217 − 3,659.

Step 1 SUBTRACT ONES	Step 2 SUBTRACT TENS	Step 3 SUBTRACT HUNDREDS	Step 4 SUBTRACT THOUSANDS
0 17 5,2 1 7 − 3,6 5 9 8	10 1 0 17 5,2 1 7 − 3,6 5 9 5 8	1 1 10 4 1 0 17 5,2 1 7 − 3,6 5 9 5 5 8	1 1 10 4 1 0 17 5,2 1 7 − 3,6 5 9 1,5 5 8

Study and Learn

A. Complete.

1. $\begin{array}{r} 3\,11 \\ 7,2\,4\,1 \\ -\,6,0\,1\,9 \\ \hline 2 \end{array}$

2. $\begin{array}{r} 3\,11 \\ 8,4\,1\,6 \\ -\,3,0\,3\,1 \\ \hline 5 \end{array}$

3. $\begin{array}{r} 9,198 \\ -\,6,684 \\ \hline \end{array}$

4. $\begin{array}{r} 4,241 \\ -\,2,385 \\ \hline \end{array}$

B. Find 37,291 − 19,876. Complete.

WRITE

$\begin{array}{r} 6\ 12\ 8\ 11 \\ 3\,7,2\,9\,1 \\ -\,1\,9,8\,7\,6 \\ \hline 4\ 1\ 5 \end{array}$

5. Rename tens and subtract ones.
   11 − 6 = __?__

6. Subtract tens.
   8 − 7 = __?__

7. Rename thousands and subtract hundreds.
   12 − 8 = __?__

8. Complete. What is the difference?

C. Subtract.

9. $\begin{array}{r} 78,429 \\ -\,46,847 \\ \hline \end{array}$

10. $\begin{array}{r} 99,282 \\ -\,38,995 \\ \hline \end{array}$

11. $\begin{array}{r} 53,785 \\ -\,12,916 \\ \hline \end{array}$

12. $\begin{array}{r} 15,433 \\ -\,14,929 \\ \hline \end{array}$

Practice

Subtract.

1.	7,498 − 3,128	**2.**	4,287 − 3,094	**3.**	3,876 − 1,906	**4.**	2,327 − 1,824
5.	9,083 − 6,245	**6.**	2,724 − 1,897	**7.**	7,746 − 3,981	**8.**	4,294 − 1,897
9.	8,726 − 958	**10.**	5,273 − 987	**11.**	5,241 − 56	**12.**	1,437 − 828
13.	43,297 − 12,054	**14.**	76,148 − 31,803	**15.**	17,286 − 13,475	**16.**	33,127 − 16,015
17.	45,281 − 18,190	**18.**	71,236 − 35,086	**19.**	77,123 − 38,456	**20.**	74,287 − 37,788
21.	13,432 − 2,851	**22.**	19,514 − 3,874	**23.**	16,584 − 7,487	**24.**	51,241 − 156
25.	8,742 − 6,912	26.	8,732 − 3,907	27.	44,731 − 19,080	28.	73,428 − 19,118
29.	8,741 − 3,876	30.	9,422 − 1,730	31.	26,478 − 19,587	★ **32.**	768,417 − 381,949

Solve Problems

33. Harold's grandfather was born in 1936. How old is he now?

34. Harriet's grandmother is now 54 years old. In what year was she born?

ZEROS IN SUBTRACTION

Subtract $700 - 376$.

	Step 1 RENAME HUNDREDS	**Step 2** RENAME TENS	**Step 3** SUBTRACT
CAN'T SUBTRACT ONES CAN'T SUBTRACT TENS		9 6 10 10	9 6 10 10
	6 10		
$\begin{array}{r} 700 \\ -376 \\ \hline \end{array}$	$\begin{array}{r} 700 \\ -376 \\ \hline \end{array}$	$\begin{array}{r} 700 \\ -376 \\ \hline \end{array}$	$\begin{array}{r} 700 \\ -376 \\ \hline 324 \end{array}$

Study and Learn

A. Complete.

1. $\begin{array}{r} \overset{\scriptstyle 9}{\underset{3\ 10\ 10}{400}} \\ -382 \\ \hline \end{array}$
2. $\begin{array}{r} \overset{\scriptstyle 9}{\underset{5\ 10\ 12}{602}} \\ -135 \\ \hline \end{array}$
3. $\begin{array}{r} 500 \\ -137 \\ \hline \end{array}$
4. $\begin{array}{r} 608 \\ -319 \\ \hline \end{array}$
5. $\begin{array}{r} 807 \\ -248 \\ \hline \end{array}$

Larger numbers are subtracted the same way.
Look at these examples.

$\begin{array}{r} \overset{9\ \ 9}{\underset{4\ 10\ 10\ 13}{5{,}003}} \\ -1{,}234 \\ \hline 3{,}769 \end{array}$
$\qquad$
$\begin{array}{r} \overset{9\ \ 9}{\underset{7\ 10\ 10\ 10}{78{,}000}} \\ -26{,}483 \\ \hline 51{,}517 \end{array}$

B. Subtract.

6. $\begin{array}{r} 2{,}000 \\ -1{,}398 \\ \hline \end{array}$
7. $\begin{array}{r} 7{,}003 \\ -2{,}586 \\ \hline \end{array}$
8. $\begin{array}{r} 7{,}076 \\ -5{,}984 \\ \hline \end{array}$
9. $\begin{array}{r} 9{,}020 \\ -4{,}083 \\ \hline \end{array}$

10. $\begin{array}{r} 87{,}700 \\ -43{,}847 \\ \hline \end{array}$
11. $\begin{array}{r} 36{,}030 \\ -22{,}928 \\ \hline \end{array}$
12. $\begin{array}{r} 60{,}500 \\ -39{,}743 \\ \hline \end{array}$
13. $\begin{array}{r} 40{,}806 \\ -32{,}649 \\ \hline \end{array}$

Practice

Subtract.

1. $\begin{array}{r} 400 \\ -\ 226 \\ \hline \end{array}$
2. $\begin{array}{r} 805 \\ -\ 498 \\ \hline \end{array}$
3. $\begin{array}{r} 600 \\ -\ 556 \\ \hline \end{array}$
4. $\begin{array}{r} 506 \\ -\ 338 \\ \hline \end{array}$
5. $\begin{array}{r} 900 \\ -\ 481 \\ \hline \end{array}$

6. $\begin{array}{r} 300 \\ -\ 284 \\ \hline \end{array}$
7. $\begin{array}{r} 800 \\ -\ 483 \\ \hline \end{array}$
8. $\begin{array}{r} 500 \\ -\ 386 \\ \hline \end{array}$
9. $\begin{array}{r} 701 \\ -\ 318 \\ \hline \end{array}$
10. $\begin{array}{r} 407 \\ -\ 159 \\ \hline \end{array}$

11. $\begin{array}{r} 3,000 \\ -\ 2,489 \\ \hline \end{array}$
12. $\begin{array}{r} 4,005 \\ -\ 3,997 \\ \hline \end{array}$
13. $\begin{array}{r} 6,000 \\ -\ 5,946 \\ \hline \end{array}$
14. $\begin{array}{r} 7,004 \\ -\ 6,996 \\ \hline \end{array}$
15. $\begin{array}{r} 4,080 \\ -\ 1,293 \\ \hline \end{array}$

16. $\begin{array}{r} 9,027 \\ -\ 6,598 \\ \hline \end{array}$
17. $\begin{array}{r} 4,300 \\ -\ 1,748 \\ \hline \end{array}$
18. $\begin{array}{r} 9,008 \\ -\ 2,369 \\ \hline \end{array}$
19. $\begin{array}{r} 8,047 \\ -\ 3,048 \\ \hline \end{array}$
20. $\begin{array}{r} 3,000 \\ -\ 2,641 \\ \hline \end{array}$

21. $\begin{array}{r} 7,000 \\ -\ \quad 8 \\ \hline \end{array}$
22. $\begin{array}{r} 5,005 \\ -\ \quad 87 \\ \hline \end{array}$
23. $\begin{array}{r} 2,004 \\ -\ \quad 386 \\ \hline \end{array}$
24. $\begin{array}{r} 9,000 \\ -\ \quad 491 \\ \hline \end{array}$
25. $\begin{array}{r} 3,040 \\ -\ \quad 184 \\ \hline \end{array}$

26. $\begin{array}{r} 30,059 \\ -\ 16,283 \\ \hline \end{array}$
27. $\begin{array}{r} 50,089 \\ -\ 36,715 \\ \hline \end{array}$
28. $\begin{array}{r} 65,007 \\ -\ 28,709 \\ \hline \end{array}$
29. $\begin{array}{r} 53,040 \\ -\ 14,974 \\ \hline \end{array}$

30. $\begin{array}{r} 200 \\ -\ 146 \\ \hline \end{array}$
31. $\begin{array}{r} 72,009 \\ -\ 68,418 \\ \hline \end{array}$
32. $\begin{array}{r} 701 \\ -\ 376 \\ \hline \end{array}$
33. $\begin{array}{r} 8,002 \\ -\ \quad 387 \\ \hline \end{array}$

34. $\begin{array}{r} 5,008 \\ -\ 1,234 \\ \hline \end{array}$
35. $\begin{array}{r} 40,068 \\ -\ 32,781 \\ \hline \end{array}$
36. $\begin{array}{r} 9,030 \\ -\ 1,487 \\ \hline \end{array}$
★ 37. $\begin{array}{r} 104,600 \\ -\ 37,983 \\ \hline \end{array}$

Solve Problems

38. There were 30,366 people at the game. 19,377 were adults. How many were children?

39. North Stadium has 700 seats. Today, 426 people come to see the game. How many seats are empty?

●**40.** The team has traveled 204 miles. They have 186 miles left to travel before they get home. How far is the whole trip home?

Midchapter Review

Subtract.

1. 97 (82) − 36	**2.** 86 (82) − 4	**3.** 78 (82) − 29	**4.** 67 (82) − 8
5. 478 (84) − 435	**6.** 873 (84) − 627	**7.** 970 (84) − 286	**8.** 444 (84) − 99
9. 7,287 (86) − 6,324	**10.** 36,473 (86) − 19,190	**11.** 6,241 (86) − 5,986	**12.** 31,420 (86) − 12,748
13. 600 (88) − 374	**14.** 8,007 (88) − 2,948	**15.** 20,007 (88) − 19,341	**16.** 8,070 (88) − 3,295

Something Extra
Non-Routine Problems

Subtract. Find a pattern for each row. Write three more subtraction examples that follow each pattern.

1. 876   432   210
     − 678   − 234   − 12

2. 5,432   9,876   3,210
     − 2,345   − 6,789   − 123

Find the missing digits.

3. 8,?4?   **4.** 9?,7?1   **5.** 7,???
     − 3,786   − 62,148   − ?,888
     ———   ————   ———
      4,356   ?8,?3?   444

FLOWCHARTS

A flowchart gives directions.
This flowchart shows how to check subtraction.

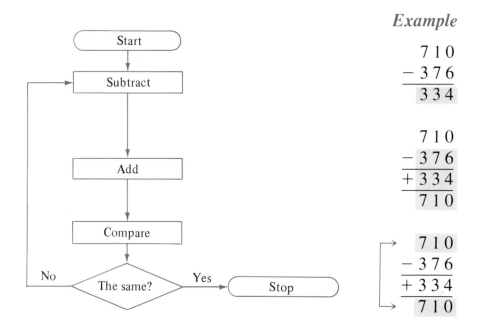

Example

```
  7 1 0
- 3 7 6
  3 3 4
```

```
  7 1 0
- 3 7 6
+ 3 3 4
  7 1 0
```

```
    7 1 0
  - 3 7 6
  + 3 3 4
    7 1 0
```

Study and Learn

A. Use the flowchart above.

    1. Draw the shape that gives a direction.

    2. What should be done if the numbers compared are not the same?

B. Draw a flowchart to show how to sharpen a pencil. Use these steps:
Turn the handle
Stop
Start
Is the pencil sharp?
Put pencil in sharpener
Take out pencil

Problem-Solving Skills
Using Four Steps

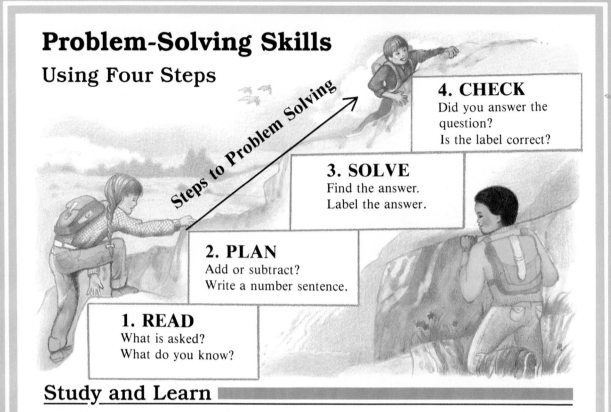

Steps to Problem Solving

4. CHECK
Did you answer the question?
Is the label correct?

3. SOLVE
Find the answer.
Label the answer.

2. PLAN
Add or subtract?
Write a number sentence.

1. READ
What is asked?
What do you know?

Study and Learn

A. 126 students went hiking. 78 of them were wearing hats. How many were not wearing hats?

1. Step 1 **READ** What is asked?

2. Step 2 **PLAN** Write a number sentence.

3. Step 3 **SOLVE** Find the answer and label it.

4. Step 4 **CHECK** Did you check your answer?

B. The students stopped to rest. Around them were 16 large trees and 18 small trees. How many trees were there in all?

5. Step 1 **READ** What is asked?

6. Step 2 **PLAN** Write a number sentence.

7. Step 3 **SOLVE** Find the answer and label it.

8. Step 4 **CHECK** Did you check your answer?

Practice

Use the four steps to solve.

1. The students hiked for 15 minutes. Then they rested. They hiked for another 20 minutes. How many minutes did they hike in all?

2. Amy saw 14 red squirrels and 8 grey squirrels. How many more red squirrels did she see?

3. Jason counted trees. He counted 83 maple trees and 54 oak trees. How many trees did he count in all?

4. There were 126 students. 89 students went berry picking. How many students did not go?

5. Mary Ellen got 17, 24, and 30 correct answers on her first three safety tests. How many correct answers did she have in all?

6. There are 200 total facts in the camping booklet. Bob knows 188 of them. How many more facts does he have left to learn?

7. David has 389 pictures in his book. The book can hold 500 pictures. How many more pictures can David put in the book?

8. Kathy has collected 198 leaves. She needs 52 more to complete her collection. How many leaves will the collection hold?

Skills Review

Add.

1.   41
(53) + 7

2.   96
    + 8

3.   85
(56) + 17

4.   86
    + 27

5.   3
(54)   4
      1
   + 6

6.   8
     2
     6
     1
   + 7

7.   99
(56)   67
   + 88

8.   63
    24
     3
  + 18

9.   431
(58) + 528

10.   847
    + 875

11.   123
    + 804

12.   378
    296
  + 415

13.   748
    291
  + 88

14.   947
    248
     62
  + 941

15.   7,284
(60) + 3,915

16.   6,782
   + 3,949

17.   76,087
   + 39,508

18.   93,714
   + 9,878

19.   41,677
   + 2,579

20.   8,297
(62)   3,748
  + 6,274

21. $ 17.83
     10.21
   + 13.14

Something Extra
Non-Routine Problem

A.   1
      2
   + 3
     6

B.   4
      5
   + 6
   15

C.   7
      8
   + 9
   24

Each of the columns above has a different sum. Move just one addend into another column. Each column should now have the same sum.

SUBTRACTING MONEY

Subtract $9.73 − $6.87.

SUBTRACT	PLACE MONEY NOTATION
16	16
8 ̸6 13	8 ̸6 13
$ 9.7 3	$ 9.7 3
− 6.8 7	− 6.8 7
2 8 6	$ 2.8 6

Study and Learn

A. Complete.

1.
```
    13
  2 3̸ 13
 $ 3.4 3
 − 1.7 8
   6 5
```

2.
```
   6 14
 $ 0.7 4
 − 0.6 9
     5
```

3.
```
     9 9
  3 10̸ 10̸ 10
 $ 4 0.0 0̸
 − 2 3.6 4
```

4.
```
 $ 375.64
 − 278.47
```

B. Subtract.

5. $ 6.03
     − 3.79

6. $ 37.64
     − 19.18

7. $ 50.36
     − 19.87

8. $ 249.00
     − 59.76

Practice

Subtract.

1. $ 8.94
     − 2.65

2. $ 36.15
     − 27.85

3. $ 387.54
     − 79.88

4. $ 684.75
     −   9.84

5. $ 6.00
     − 4.25

6. $ 8.01
     − 3.19

7. $ 40.00
     − 25.78

8. $ 380.56
     − 195.87

9. $ 6.15
     − 1.37

10. $ 28.00
      − 19.06

11. $ 27.49
      − 26.58

12. $ 637.42
      − 274.87

13. $ 6.04
      − 1.43

14. $ 70.07
      − 26.49

★ **15.** $ 3,864.27
        − 1,987.30

★ **16.** $ 4,000.00
        − 1,247.36

95

MAKING CHANGE

Eddie bought a can of tennis balls for $2.19.
He gave the clerk $10.00. Here is the change
he received.

CLERK GIVES	CLERK SAYS
1 penny	$2.20
1 nickel	$2.25
3 quarters	$2.50, $2.75, $3.00
2 one-dollar bills	$4.00, $5.00
1 five-dollar bill	$10.00

Study and Learn

A. Complete.

Betty buys a tennis racquet for $12.65.
She gives the clerk a $20.00 bill.
Complete the list of change.

CLERK GIVES	CLERK SAYS
1 dime	$12.75
1 quarter	$13.00
1. 2  ?	$14.00, $15.00
2. 1 ___?___	$20.00

B. List the change.

3. Ernie buys a tote bag for $7.98.
He gives the clerk a $10.00 bill.

96

Practice

List the change.

1. Agnes buys tennis socks for $6.75.
   She gives the clerk a $10.00 bill.

2. Bob buys sweat bands for $2.98.
   He gives the clerk a $5.00 bill.

3. Paula buys a tennis glove for $4.79.
   She gives the clerk a $10.00 bill.

4. Linda buys sneakers for $13.99.
   She gives the clerk $15.00.

5. Frank buys a warm-up suit for $17.59.
   He gives the clerk a $20.00 bill.

6. Karla buys lunch for $1.93.
   She gives the clerk a $5.00 bill.

7. Carl buys a ticket for 25 cents.
   He gives the ticket seller a $1.00 bill.

★ 8. Fred buys a shirt for $9.99
   and a tie for $3.99. He gives the
   clerk a $20.00 bill.

ESTIMATING DIFFERENCES

Estimate 87 − 38.
To estimate differences:

	ROUND NUMBERS	SUBTRACT
1. Round the numbers.	87 → 90	90
	38 → 40	− 40
2. Subtract the rounded numbers.		50

Study and Learn

A. Estimate. Round to the nearest ten.

1. 75	**2.** 49	**3.** 91	**4.** 67	**5.** 83
− 26	− 28	− 39	− 48	− 44

B. Estimate 908 − 389.
Round to the nearest hundred.

	EXACT	ROUNDED
6. Round 908.	908 ⟶	900
7. Round 389.	− 389 ⟶	− 400
8. What is the estimated difference?		500

C. Estimate $7.25 − $3.34.
Round to the nearest dollar.

	EXACT	ROUNDED
9. Round $7.25.	$ 7.25 ⟶	$ 7.00
10. Round $3.34.	− 3.34 ⟶	− 3.00
		$ 4.00

11. What is the estimated difference?

D. Estimate. Round to the nearest hundred or dollar.

12. $ 8.50	**13.** $ 435	**14.** $ 6.97	**15.** $ 923	**16.** $ 8.34
− 2.75	− 339	− 1.98	− 679	− 2.88

98

Practice

Estimate the differences. Round to the nearest ten.

1. 56
− 41

2. 65
− 26

3. 71
− 32

4. 87
− 48

5. 76
− 27

Estimate the differences. Round to the nearest hundred.

6. 344
− 149

7. 681
− 376

8. 425
− 136

9. 850
− 654

10. 911
− 327

Estimate the differences. Round to the nearest dollar.

11. $ 4.97
− 1.98

12. $ 6.79
− 3.81

13. $ 8.21
− 1.25

14. $ 9.15
− 6.25

15. $ 7.50
− 4.62

Estimate the differences.

16. 91
− 12

17. $ 3.98
− 1.79

18. 48
− 39

19. $ 5.48
− 1.49

20. 887
− 198

21. $ 5.36
− 1.45

22. 69
− 28

23. 825
− 236

★ **24.** 8,587
− 3,398

★ **25.** $28.94
− 12.98

Solve Problems

26. You have a $10.00 bill.
You buy art supplies for $6.98.
About how much change should you receive?

27. 78 students are in art classes.
29 students need paint.
About how many have paint?

99

Problem-Solving Applications

Estimating Differences

This map shows distances in kilometers between some cities of the United States.

1. It is 528 kilometers from New York to Richmond. It is 338 kilometers from New York to Boston. About how much farther is it to Richmond? [HINT: 500 − 300 = _?_ km]

2. It is 819 kilometers from Cincinnati to Richmond. It is 460 kilometers from Cincinnati to Chicago. About how much farther is it to Richmond?

3. It is 790 kilometers from Boise to Helena. It is 683 kilometers from Boise to Reno. About how much farther is it to Helena?

★ 4. About how much farther is it from Nashville to Birmingham than from Birmingham to Atlanta?

Chapter Review

Subtract.

1. (82)	81 − 5	**2.** (84)	428 − 119

1. (82) 81 − 5

2. (84) 428 − 119

3. (84) 784 − 395

4. (86) 6,291 − 4,831

5. (86) 97,358 − 18,183

6. (88) 63,420 − 29,583

7. (88) 700 − 241

8. (88) 6,003 − 1,248

9. (88) 40,002 − 26,487

10. (95) $16.85 − 9.76

11. (95) $48.39 − 19.48

12. (95) $875.47 − 378.29

Estimate the differences. *(98)*

13. 78 − 29

14. 450 − 162

15. $9.38 − 3.49

16. $6.89 − 4.91

List the change. *(96)*

17. Paul bought a gym bag for $15.95.
He gave the clerk a $20.00 bill.

18. Carol bought running shorts for $12.47.
She gave the clerk $15.00.

Solve.

19. There were 36 sports cars and 12 station wagons
(92) at the used-car lot. How many more sports cars
were there?

20. Ms. Copper drove 496 kilometers on Monday and
(100) 420 kilometers on Tuesday. About how many more
kilometers did she drive on Monday?

Chapter Test

Subtract.

1. 84
(82) − 39

2. 422
(84) − 319

3. 724
(84) − 696

4. 86,452
(86) − 39,170

5. 3,240
(86) − 1,876

6. 49,487
(86) − 29,698

7. 302
(88) − 158

8. 9,000
(88) − 2,678

9. 70,007
(88) − 29,278

10. $12.84
(95) − 6.91

11. $72.45
(95) − 18.78

12. $968.27
(95) − 699.49

Estimate the differences. *(98)*

13. 91
− 42

14. $8.50
− 2.61

15. 499
− 199

16. 504
− 287

List the change. *(96)*

17. Jean bought sneakers for $18.69.
She gave the clerk a $20.00 bill.

18. Tom bought a T-shirt for $7.82.
He gave the clerk a $10.00 bill.

Solve.

19. Mr. Arnez sold 120 theater tickets on Monday and
(92) 247 tickets on Wednesday. How many tickets did he
sell in all?

20. There were 368 people in Theater 1. There were 213
(100) people in Theater 2. About how many more people
were in Theater 1?

Skills Check

1.

```
    6
    8
    3
  + 7
```

A 18

B 24

C 36

D 42

2.

```
   35
 + 24
```

E 49

F 55

G 59

H 69

---

3. 127 + 263 = ____?____

A 390

B 392

C 482

D 490

4.

```
   487
 + 365
```

E 722

F 764

G 843

H 852

5.

```
   122
   397
 + 430
```

A 859

B 938

C 949

D 990

6.

```
    7
  + 6
```

E 11

F 13

G 15

H 17

---

7. 9 + 3 = ____?____

A 6

B 11

C 12

D 13

---

8. 8 − 5 = ____?____

E 3

F 4

G 6

H 7

9.

```
   15
 −  7
```

A 4

B 7

C 8

D 9

10.

```
   62
 − 39
```

E 21

F 23

G 33

H 34

11.

```
   538
 − 249
```

A 266

B 279

C 289

D 397

---

12. 373 − 141 = ____?____

E 123

F 224

G 232

H 236

5 MULTIPLICATION AND DIVISION FACTS

A chemical facility in Longview, Texas.

MULTIPLICATION

There are 3 rows of scouts.
Each row has 5 scouts. How
many scouts are there in all?

Addition Sentence: $5 + 5 + 5 = 15$

Multiplication Sentence: $3 \times 5 = 15$ or

$$\begin{array}{r} 5 \\ \times\, 3 \\ \hline 15 \end{array}$$

factors   product   factors $15 \leftarrow$ product

There are 15 scouts in all.

Study and Learn

A. Write the factors. Write the products.

1. $7 \times 6 = 42$ **2.** $8 \times 8 = 64$

3. $\begin{array}{r} 7 \\ \times\, 8 \\ \hline 56 \end{array}$ **4.** $\begin{array}{r} 5 \\ \times\, 7 \\ \hline 35 \end{array}$

B. Write a multiplication sentence for each.

Example $7 + 7 + 7 + 7 = 28$ $4 \times 7 = 28$

5. $9 + 9 = 18$ **6.** $6 + 6 + 6 + 6 + 6 = 30$

7. $8 + 8 + 8 = 24$ **8.** $2 + 2 + 2 + 2 = 8$

C. Write an addition sentence to find the product.

Example $\begin{array}{r} 8 \\ \times\, 2 \\ \hline \end{array}$ $8 + 8 = 16$, so $\begin{array}{r} 8 \\ \times\, 2 \\ \hline 16 \end{array}$

9. $\begin{array}{r} 2 \\ \times\, 3 \\ \hline \end{array}$ **10.** $\begin{array}{r} 3 \\ \times\, 4 \\ \hline \end{array}$ **11.** $\begin{array}{r} 5 \\ \times\, 2 \\ \hline \end{array}$ **12.** $\begin{array}{r} 4 \\ \times\, 2 \\ \hline \end{array}$ **13.** $\begin{array}{r} 6 \\ \times\, 3 \\ \hline \end{array}$ **14.** $\begin{array}{r} 0 \\ \times\, 2 \\ \hline \end{array}$

Products can also be found by drawing arrays.
Find. $3 \times 7 = $ __?__

Show 3 groups of 7.

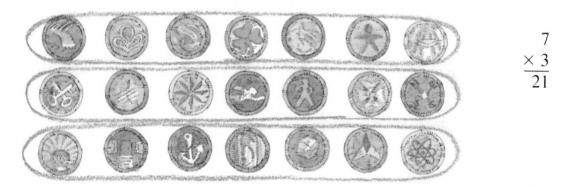

$$\begin{array}{r} 7 \\ \times\ 3 \\ \hline 21 \end{array}$$

D. Draw an array for each. Find each product.

15. $\begin{array}{r} 5 \\ \times\ 3 \\ \hline \end{array}$ 16. $\begin{array}{r} 3 \\ \times\ 5 \\ \hline \end{array}$ 17. $\begin{array}{r} 4 \\ \times\ 6 \\ \hline \end{array}$ 18. $\begin{array}{r} 9 \\ \times\ 6 \\ \hline \end{array}$

Practice

Write a multiplication sentence for each.

1. $9 + 9 + 9 + 9 = 36$ 　　　　2. $6 + 6 + 6 + 6 + 6 = 30$

3. $5 + 5 + 5 + 5 = 20$ 　　　　4. $6 + 6 = 12$

5. $1 + 1 + 1 + 1 + 1 + 1 = 6$ 　　　　6. $0 + 0 + 0 + 0 = 0$

Write an addition sentence to find the product.

7. $\begin{array}{r} 2 \\ \times\ 3 \\ \hline \end{array}$ 8. $\begin{array}{r} 4 \\ \times\ 4 \\ \hline \end{array}$ 9. $\begin{array}{r} 0 \\ \times\ 4 \\ \hline \end{array}$ 10. $\begin{array}{r} 5 \\ \times\ 2 \\ \hline \end{array}$ 11. $\begin{array}{r} 6 \\ \times\ 2 \\ \hline \end{array}$ 12. $\begin{array}{r} 5 \\ \times\ 5 \\ \hline \end{array}$

Draw an array for each. Find each product.

13. $\begin{array}{r} 3 \\ \times\ 9 \\ \hline \end{array}$ 14. $\begin{array}{r} 5 \\ \times\ 3 \\ \hline \end{array}$ 15. $\begin{array}{r} 7 \\ \times\ 2 \\ \hline \end{array}$ 16. $\begin{array}{r} 6 \\ \times\ 4 \\ \hline \end{array}$ 17. $\begin{array}{r} 8 \\ \times\ 3 \\ \hline \end{array}$ 18. $\begin{array}{r} 6 \\ \times\ 6 \\ \hline \end{array}$

ZERO

Find. $3 \times 0 = \underline{\quad ? \quad}$
Think: 3 groups of 0

$$\begin{array}{r} 0 \\ \times\ 3 \\ \hline 0 \end{array} \quad \text{and} \quad \begin{array}{r} 3 \\ \times\ 0 \\ \hline 0 \end{array}$$

Study and Learn

A. Look for a pattern.

$$\begin{array}{r} 0 \\ \times\ 0 \\ \hline 0 \end{array} \quad \begin{array}{r} 0 \\ \times\ 1 \\ \hline 0 \end{array} \quad \begin{array}{r} 0 \\ \times\ 2 \\ \hline 0 \end{array} \quad \begin{array}{r} 0 \\ \times\ 3 \\ \hline 0 \end{array} \quad \begin{array}{r} 0 \\ \times\ 4 \\ \hline 0 \end{array} \qquad \begin{array}{r} 0 \\ \times\ 0 \\ \hline 0 \end{array} \quad \begin{array}{r} 1 \\ \times\ 0 \\ \hline 0 \end{array} \quad \begin{array}{r} 2 \\ \times\ 0 \\ \hline 0 \end{array} \quad \begin{array}{r} 3 \\ \times\ 0 \\ \hline 0 \end{array} \quad \begin{array}{r} 4 \\ \times\ 0 \\ \hline 0 \end{array}$$

1. Is 0 a factor of each?

2. What is the product of each?

▶ When 0 is a factor, the product is 0.

B. Multiply.

3. $\begin{array}{r} 0 \\ \times\ 5 \\ \hline \end{array}$ **4.** $\begin{array}{r} 5 \\ \times\ 0 \\ \hline \end{array}$ **5.** $\begin{array}{r} 0 \\ \times\ 6 \\ \hline \end{array}$ **6.** $\begin{array}{r} 7 \\ \times\ 0 \\ \hline \end{array}$ **7.** $\begin{array}{r} 0 \\ \times\ 8 \\ \hline \end{array}$ **8.** $\begin{array}{r} 9 \\ \times\ 0 \\ \hline \end{array}$

Practice

Multiply.

1. $\begin{array}{r} 0 \\ \times\ 0 \\ \hline \end{array}$ **2.** $\begin{array}{r} 1 \\ \times\ 0 \\ \hline \end{array}$ **3.** $\begin{array}{r} 0 \\ \times\ 2 \\ \hline \end{array}$ **4.** $\begin{array}{r} 7 \\ \times\ 0 \\ \hline \end{array}$ **5.** $\begin{array}{r} 8 \\ \times\ 0 \\ \hline \end{array}$ **6.** $\begin{array}{r} 0 \\ \times\ 9 \\ \hline \end{array}$

7. $\begin{array}{r} 2 \\ \times\ 0 \\ \hline \end{array}$ **8.** $\begin{array}{r} 3 \\ \times\ 0 \\ \hline \end{array}$ **9.** $\begin{array}{r} 0 \\ \times\ 4 \\ \hline \end{array}$ **10.** $\begin{array}{r} 5 \\ \times\ 0 \\ \hline \end{array}$ **11.** $\begin{array}{r} 0 \\ \times\ 6 \\ \hline \end{array}$ ★ **12.** $\begin{array}{r} 36 \\ \times\ 0 \\ \hline \end{array}$

ONE

Find. $3 \times 1 = $ __?__
Think: 3 groups of 1

$$\begin{array}{r} 1 \\ \times\ 3 \\ \hline 3 \end{array}$$

Find. $1 \times 3 = $ __?__
Think: 1 group of 3

$$\begin{array}{r} 3 \\ \times\ 1 \\ \hline 3 \end{array}$$

Study and Learn

A. Look for a pattern.

$$\begin{array}{r} 1 \\ \times\ 1 \\ \hline 1 \end{array} \quad \begin{array}{r} 1 \\ \times\ 2 \\ \hline 2 \end{array} \quad \begin{array}{r} 1 \\ \times\ 3 \\ \hline 3 \end{array} \quad \begin{array}{r} 1 \\ \times\ 4 \\ \hline 4 \end{array} \quad \begin{array}{r} 1 \\ \times\ 5 \\ \hline 5 \end{array} \qquad \begin{array}{r} 1 \\ \times\ 1 \\ \hline 1 \end{array} \quad \begin{array}{r} 2 \\ \times\ 1 \\ \hline 2 \end{array} \quad \begin{array}{r} 3 \\ \times\ 1 \\ \hline 3 \end{array} \quad \begin{array}{r} 4 \\ \times\ 1 \\ \hline 4 \end{array} \quad \begin{array}{r} 5 \\ \times\ 1 \\ \hline 5 \end{array}$$

1. Is 1 a factor of each?

2. What do you notice about the products?

▶ When 1 is a factor, the product is the other factor.

B. Multiply.

3. $\begin{array}{r} 1 \\ \times\ 5 \\ \hline \end{array}$ **4.** $\begin{array}{r} 5 \\ \times\ 1 \\ \hline \end{array}$ **5.** $\begin{array}{r} 1 \\ \times\ 6 \\ \hline \end{array}$ **6.** $\begin{array}{r} 7 \\ \times\ 1 \\ \hline \end{array}$ **7.** $\begin{array}{r} 1 \\ \times\ 8 \\ \hline \end{array}$ **8.** $\begin{array}{r} 9 \\ \times\ 1 \\ \hline \end{array}$

Practice

Multiply.

1. $\begin{array}{r} 1 \\ \times\ 2 \\ \hline \end{array}$ **2.** $\begin{array}{r} 1 \\ \times\ 6 \\ \hline \end{array}$ **3.** $\begin{array}{r} 3 \\ \times\ 1 \\ \hline \end{array}$ **4.** $\begin{array}{r} 1 \\ \times\ 4 \\ \hline \end{array}$ **5.** $\begin{array}{r} 5 \\ \times\ 1 \\ \hline \end{array}$ **6.** $\begin{array}{r} 9 \\ \times\ 1 \\ \hline \end{array}$

7. $\begin{array}{r} 1 \\ \times\ 3 \\ \hline \end{array}$ **8.** $\begin{array}{r} 1 \\ \times\ 1 \\ \hline \end{array}$ **9.** $\begin{array}{r} 1 \\ \times\ 8 \\ \hline \end{array}$ **10.** $\begin{array}{r} 7 \\ \times\ 1 \\ \hline \end{array}$ **11.** $\begin{array}{r} 0 \\ \times\ 1 \\ \hline \end{array}$ ★ **12.** $\begin{array}{r} 28 \\ \times\ \square \\ \hline 28 \end{array}$

TWO

Find. $4 \times 2 = \underline{\quad ?\quad}$
Think: 4 groups of 2

Find. $2 \times 4 = \underline{\quad ?\quad}$
Think: 2 groups of 4

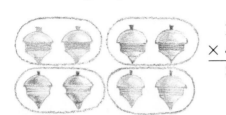

$$\begin{array}{r} 2 \\ \times\ 4 \\ \hline 8 \end{array}$$

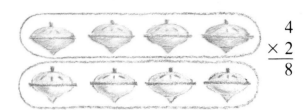

$$\begin{array}{r} 4 \\ \times\ 2 \\ \hline 8 \end{array}$$

Study and Learn

A. Multiply. Look for a pattern in the products.

1.
$$\begin{array}{ccccccccc} 2 & 2 & 2 & 2 & 2 & 2 & 2 & 2 & 2 \\ \times\,1 & \times\,2 & \times\,3 & \times\,4 & \times\,5 & \times\,6 & \times\,7 & \times\,8 & \times\,9 \end{array}$$

2.
$$\begin{array}{ccccccccc} 1 & 2 & 3 & 4 & 5 & 6 & 7 & 8 & 9 \\ \times\,2 & \times\,2 & \times\,2 & \times\,2 & \times\,2 & \times\,2 & \times\,2 & \times\,2 & \times\,2 \end{array}$$

3. What pattern is found in the products?

B. Multiply.

4.
$$\begin{array}{cc} 3 & 2 \\ \times\,2 & \times\,3 \end{array}$$

5.
$$\begin{array}{cc} 7 & 2 \\ \times\,2 & \times\,7 \end{array}$$

6.
$$\begin{array}{cc} 2 & 8 \\ \times\,8 & \times\,2 \end{array}$$

▶ The order of the factors does not change the product.

Practice

Multiply.

1. $\begin{array}{r} 2 \\ \times\,2 \end{array}$ **2.** $\begin{array}{r} 4 \\ \times\,2 \end{array}$ **3.** $\begin{array}{r} 2 \\ \times\,6 \end{array}$ **4.** $\begin{array}{r} 8 \\ \times\,2 \end{array}$ **5.** $\begin{array}{r} 2 \\ \times\,9 \end{array}$ **6.** $\begin{array}{r} 7 \\ \times\,2 \end{array}$

7. $\begin{array}{r} 2 \\ \times\,5 \end{array}$ **8.** $\begin{array}{r} 3 \\ \times\,2 \end{array}$ **9.** $\begin{array}{r} 2 \\ \times\,1 \end{array}$ **10.** $\begin{array}{r} 0 \\ \times\,2 \end{array}$ ★ **11.** $\square \times 2 \times 3 = 24$

EVEN AND ODD

These are even numbers: **0, 2, 4, 6, 8, 10, 12,** . . .

These are odd numbers: **1, 3, 5, 7, 9, 11, 13,** . . .

Study and Learn

A. Write the next five even numbers.

　1. 14, 16, 18, 20, __?__, __?__, __?__, __?__, __?__

　2. Look at the digits in the ones place. Are they even or odd?

B. Write the next five odd numbers.

　3. 15, 17, 19, 21, __?__, __?__, __?__, __?__, __?__

　4. Look at the digits in the ones place. Are they even or odd?

C. Even or odd? Write E or O.

　5. 28 　　　**6.** 37 　　　**7.** 85 　　　**8.** 100 　　　**9.** 325

Practice

Even or odd? Write E or O.

　1. 7 　　　**2.** 16 　　　**3.** 29 　　　**4.** 47 　　　**5.** 60

　6. 221 　　　**7.** 374 　　　**8.** 455 　　　**9.** 554 　　　**10.** 778

　11. 800 　　　**12.** 900 　　　★ **13.** 487,279 　　　★ **14.** 1,111,111,110

THREE AND FOUR

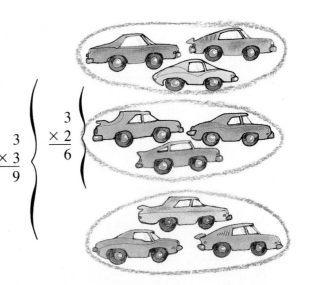

Find. $3 \times 3 = \underline{\ \ ?\ \ }$

You know: $2 \times 3 = 6$
Think: $3 \times 3 = 6 + 3$ more
So, $3 \times 3 = 9$

$$\begin{array}{r} 3 \\ \times\, 3 \\ \hline 9 \end{array}$$

$$\begin{array}{r} 3 \\ \times\, 3 \\ \hline 9 \end{array}$$

$$\begin{array}{r} 3 \\ \times\, 2 \\ \hline 6 \end{array}$$

Study and Learn

A. Multiply. Look for a pattern in the products.

1.
$$\begin{array}{r} 3 \\ \times\, 1 \end{array} \quad \begin{array}{r} 3 \\ \times\, 2 \end{array} \quad \begin{array}{r} 3 \\ \times\, 3 \end{array} \quad \begin{array}{r} 3 \\ \times\, 4 \end{array} \quad \begin{array}{r} 3 \\ \times\, 5 \end{array} \quad \begin{array}{r} 3 \\ \times\, 6 \end{array} \quad \begin{array}{r} 3 \\ \times\, 7 \end{array} \quad \begin{array}{r} 3 \\ \times\, 8 \end{array} \quad \begin{array}{r} 3 \\ \times\, 9 \end{array}$$

2.
$$\begin{array}{r} 1 \\ \times\, 3 \end{array} \quad \begin{array}{r} 2 \\ \times\, 3 \end{array} \quad \begin{array}{r} 3 \\ \times\, 3 \end{array} \quad \begin{array}{r} 4 \\ \times\, 3 \end{array} \quad \begin{array}{r} 5 \\ \times\, 3 \end{array} \quad \begin{array}{r} 6 \\ \times\, 3 \end{array} \quad \begin{array}{r} 7 \\ \times\, 3 \end{array} \quad \begin{array}{r} 8 \\ \times\, 3 \end{array} \quad \begin{array}{r} 9 \\ \times\, 3 \end{array}$$

3. What pattern is found in the products?

B. Multiply. Look for a pattern in the products.

4.
$$\begin{array}{r} 4 \\ \times\, 1 \end{array} \quad \begin{array}{r} 4 \\ \times\, 2 \end{array} \quad \begin{array}{r} 4 \\ \times\, 3 \end{array} \quad \begin{array}{r} 4 \\ \times\, 4 \end{array} \quad \begin{array}{r} 4 \\ \times\, 5 \end{array} \quad \begin{array}{r} 4 \\ \times\, 6 \end{array} \quad \begin{array}{r} 4 \\ \times\, 7 \end{array} \quad \begin{array}{r} 4 \\ \times\, 8 \end{array} \quad \begin{array}{r} 4 \\ \times\, 9 \end{array}$$

5.
$$\begin{array}{r} 1 \\ \times\, 4 \end{array} \quad \begin{array}{r} 2 \\ \times\, 4 \end{array} \quad \begin{array}{r} 3 \\ \times\, 4 \end{array} \quad \begin{array}{r} 4 \\ \times\, 4 \end{array} \quad \begin{array}{r} 5 \\ \times\, 4 \end{array} \quad \begin{array}{r} 6 \\ \times\, 4 \end{array} \quad \begin{array}{r} 7 \\ \times\, 4 \end{array} \quad \begin{array}{r} 8 \\ \times\, 4 \end{array} \quad \begin{array}{r} 9 \\ \times\, 4 \end{array}$$

6. What pattern is found in the products?

C. Multiply.

7. $\begin{array}{r} 4 \\ \times\, 3 \end{array}$ **8.** $\begin{array}{r} 3 \\ \times\, 5 \end{array}$ **9.** $\begin{array}{r} 4 \\ \times\, 6 \end{array}$ **10.** $\begin{array}{r} 7 \\ \times\, 3 \end{array}$ **11.** $\begin{array}{r} 8 \\ \times\, 4 \end{array}$ **12.** $\begin{array}{r} 4 \\ \times\, 4 \end{array}$

Practice

Multiply.

1. 8 × 4	**2.** 9 × 3	**3.** 3 × 2	**4.** 3 × 4	**5.** 1 × 5	**6.** 3 × 3

1. 8 ×4 **2.** 9 ×3 **3.** 3 ×2 **4.** 3 ×4 **5.** 1 ×5 **6.** 3 ×3

7. 9 ×4 **8.** 1 ×8 **9.** 6 ×2 **10.** 8 ×3 **11.** 4 ×4 **12.** 1 ×2

13. 6 ×4 **14.** 0 ×2 **15.** 6 ×3 **16.** 1 ×4 **17.** 1 ×7 **18.** 1 ×3

19. 7 ×2 **20.** 2 ×2 **21.** 5 ×4 **22.** 2 ×4 **23.** 4 ×5 **24.** 1 ×1

25. 4 ×2 **26.** 0 ×4 **27.** 7 ×4 **28.** 7 ×3 **29.** 1 ×6 **30.** 5 ×2

31. 8 ×2 **32.** 1 ×9 **33.** 1 ×3 **34.** 2 ×3 **35.** 9 ×2 **36.** 5 ×3

Solve.

★ **37.** $3 \times 2 \times \square = 24$ ★ **38.** $2 \times 4 \times \square = 16$

Solve Problems

39. 8 boxes
3 race cars in a box
How many race cars in all?

40. 7 race cars in a set
4 sets
How many race cars in all?

FIVE AND SIX

Find. $5 \times 5 = \underline{\quad ? \quad}$

You know: $4 \times 5 = 20$
Think: $\quad 5 \times 5 = 20 + 5$ more
So, $\qquad 5 \times 5 = 25$

$$\begin{array}{r} 5 \\ \times\, 5 \\ \hline 25 \end{array}$$

$$\begin{array}{r} 5 \\ \times\, 5 \\ \hline 25 \end{array} \left\{ \begin{array}{r} 5 \\ \times\, 4 \\ \hline 20 \end{array} \right.$$

Study and Learn

A. Multiply. Look for a pattern in the products.

1.
$$\begin{array}{r} 5 \\ \times\, 1 \\ \hline \end{array} \quad \begin{array}{r} 5 \\ \times\, 2 \\ \hline \end{array} \quad \begin{array}{r} 5 \\ \times\, 3 \\ \hline \end{array} \quad \begin{array}{r} 5 \\ \times\, 4 \\ \hline \end{array} \quad \begin{array}{r} 5 \\ \times\, 5 \\ \hline \end{array} \quad \begin{array}{r} 5 \\ \times\, 6 \\ \hline \end{array} \quad \begin{array}{r} 5 \\ \times\, 7 \\ \hline \end{array} \quad \begin{array}{r} 5 \\ \times\, 8 \\ \hline \end{array} \quad \begin{array}{r} 5 \\ \times\, 9 \\ \hline \end{array}$$

2.
$$\begin{array}{r} 1 \\ \times\, 5 \\ \hline \end{array} \quad \begin{array}{r} 2 \\ \times\, 5 \\ \hline \end{array} \quad \begin{array}{r} 3 \\ \times\, 5 \\ \hline \end{array} \quad \begin{array}{r} 4 \\ \times\, 5 \\ \hline \end{array} \quad \begin{array}{r} 5 \\ \times\, 5 \\ \hline \end{array} \quad \begin{array}{r} 6 \\ \times\, 5 \\ \hline \end{array} \quad \begin{array}{r} 7 \\ \times\, 5 \\ \hline \end{array} \quad \begin{array}{r} 8 \\ \times\, 5 \\ \hline \end{array} \quad \begin{array}{r} 9 \\ \times\, 5 \\ \hline \end{array}$$

3. What pattern is found in the products?

B. Multiply. Look for a pattern in the products.

4.
$$\begin{array}{r} 6 \\ \times\, 1 \\ \hline \end{array} \quad \begin{array}{r} 6 \\ \times\, 2 \\ \hline \end{array} \quad \begin{array}{r} 6 \\ \times\, 3 \\ \hline \end{array} \quad \begin{array}{r} 6 \\ \times\, 4 \\ \hline \end{array} \quad \begin{array}{r} 6 \\ \times\, 5 \\ \hline \end{array} \quad \begin{array}{r} 6 \\ \times\, 6 \\ \hline \end{array} \quad \begin{array}{r} 6 \\ \times\, 7 \\ \hline \end{array} \quad \begin{array}{r} 6 \\ \times\, 8 \\ \hline \end{array} \quad \begin{array}{r} 6 \\ \times\, 9 \\ \hline \end{array}$$

5.
$$\begin{array}{r} 1 \\ \times\, 6 \\ \hline \end{array} \quad \begin{array}{r} 2 \\ \times\, 6 \\ \hline \end{array} \quad \begin{array}{r} 3 \\ \times\, 6 \\ \hline \end{array} \quad \begin{array}{r} 4 \\ \times\, 6 \\ \hline \end{array} \quad \begin{array}{r} 5 \\ \times\, 6 \\ \hline \end{array} \quad \begin{array}{r} 6 \\ \times\, 6 \\ \hline \end{array} \quad \begin{array}{r} 7 \\ \times\, 6 \\ \hline \end{array} \quad \begin{array}{r} 8 \\ \times\, 6 \\ \hline \end{array} \quad \begin{array}{r} 9 \\ \times\, 6 \\ \hline \end{array}$$

6. What pattern is found in the products?

C. Multiply.

7. $\begin{array}{r} 7 \\ \times\, 5 \\ \hline \end{array}$ **8.** $\begin{array}{r} 6 \\ \times\, 7 \\ \hline \end{array}$ **9.** $\begin{array}{r} 5 \\ \times\, 6 \\ \hline \end{array}$ **10.** $\begin{array}{r} 8 \\ \times\, 5 \\ \hline \end{array}$ **11.** $\begin{array}{r} 6 \\ \times\, 8 \\ \hline \end{array}$ **12.** $\begin{array}{r} 9 \\ \times\, 6 \\ \hline \end{array}$

Practice

Multiply.

1.	6 × 4	2.	5 × 1	3.	9 × 4	4.	4 × 4	5.	6 × 2	6.	5 × 8
7.	5 × 9	8.	8 × 4	9.	6 × 1	10.	6 × 5	11.	4 × 3	12.	5 × 0
13.	6 × 9	14.	5 × 7	15.	6 × 8	16.	5 × 2	17.	3 × 4	18.	5 × 4
19.	5 × 0	20.	5 × 3	21.	6 × 3	22.	7 × 4	23.	6 × 4	24.	5 × 5
25.	6 × 7	26.	8 × 3	27.	5 × 6	28.	6 × 0	29.	3 × 7	30.	3 × 3
31.	2 × 4	32.	5 × 3	33.	1 × 4	34.	9 × 3	35.	5 × 1	36.	6 × 6

Solve.

★ **37.** $4 \times 2 \times \square = 40$

★ **38.** $3 \times 2 \times \square = 36$

Solve Problems

39. 5 horseshoes on a ring
7 rings
How many horseshoes?

40. 8 horseshoes on a ring
6 rings
How many horseshoes?

● **41.** Jim threw 8 ringers in
15 horseshoe pitches.
How many times did he
not throw a ringer?

★ **42.** A ringer counts for 2 points.
Jamie threw 4 ringers and
also received 9 points for
being close. How many
points did she receive in all?

SEVEN AND EIGHT

Find. $7 \times 7 = \underline{\ ?\ }$

You know: $6 \times 7 = 42$

Think: $7 \times 7 = 42 + 7$ more

So, $7 \times 7 = 49$

$$\begin{array}{r} 7 \\ \times\ 7 \\ \hline 49 \end{array}$$

$$\begin{array}{r} 7 \\ \times\ 7 \\ \hline 49 \end{array} \qquad \begin{array}{r} 7 \\ \times\ 6 \\ \hline 42 \end{array}$$

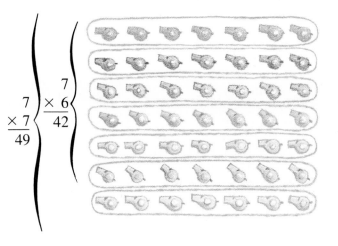

Study and Learn

A. Multiply. Look for a pattern in the products.

1.
$$\begin{array}{ccccccccc} 7 & 7 & 7 & 7 & 7 & 7 & 7 & 7 & 7 \\ \times 1 & \times 2 & \times 3 & \times 4 & \times 5 & \times 6 & \times 7 & \times 8 & \times 9 \end{array}$$

B. Multiply. Look for a pattern in the products.

2.
$$\begin{array}{ccccccccc} 8 & 8 & 8 & 8 & 8 & 8 & 8 & 8 & 8 \\ \times 1 & \times 2 & \times 3 & \times 4 & \times 5 & \times 6 & \times 7 & \times 8 & \times 9 \end{array}$$

C. Multiply.

3. $\begin{array}{r} 7 \\ \times\ 8 \\ \hline \end{array}$ **4.** $\begin{array}{r} 7 \\ \times\ 7 \\ \hline \end{array}$ **5.** $\begin{array}{r} 8 \\ \times\ 9 \\ \hline \end{array}$ **6.** $\begin{array}{r} 8 \\ \times\ 8 \\ \hline \end{array}$ **7.** $\begin{array}{r} 7 \\ \times\ 9 \\ \hline \end{array}$ **8.** $\begin{array}{r} 9 \\ \times\ 8 \\ \hline \end{array}$

Practice

Multiply.

1. $\begin{array}{r} 4 \\ \times\ 3 \\ \hline \end{array}$ **2.** $\begin{array}{r} 5 \\ \times\ 8 \\ \hline \end{array}$ **3.** $\begin{array}{r} 2 \\ \times\ 8 \\ \hline \end{array}$ **4.** $\begin{array}{r} 3 \\ \times\ 3 \\ \hline \end{array}$ **5.** $\begin{array}{r} 8 \\ \times\ 4 \\ \hline \end{array}$ **6.** $\begin{array}{r} 7 \\ \times\ 7 \\ \hline \end{array}$

7. $\begin{array}{r} 5 \\ \times\ 3 \\ \hline \end{array}$ **8.** $\begin{array}{r} 1 \\ \times\ 7 \\ \hline \end{array}$ **9.** $\begin{array}{r} 7 \\ \times\ 6 \\ \hline \end{array}$ **10.** $\begin{array}{r} 8 \\ \times\ 5 \\ \hline \end{array}$ **11.** $\begin{array}{r} 8 \\ \times\ 6 \\ \hline \end{array}$ **12.** $\begin{array}{r} 7 \\ \times\ 5 \\ \hline \end{array}$

★ **13.** $2 \times 4 \times \square = 56$

★ **14.** $3 \times 2 \times \square = 42$

116

NINE

Find. $9 \times 9 = \underline{\quad?\quad}$

You know: $8 \times 9 = 72$
Think: $\quad 9 \times 9 = 72 + 9$
So, $\quad\quad 9 \times 9 = 81$

$$\begin{array}{r} 9 \\ \times\, 9 \\ \hline 81 \end{array}$$

$$\begin{array}{r} 9 \\ \times\, 8 \\ \hline 72 \end{array} \quad \begin{array}{r} 9 \\ \times\, 9 \\ \hline 81 \end{array}$$

Study and Learn

A. Multiply. Look for a pattern in the products.

1.
$\begin{array}{r} 9 \\ \times\, 1 \\ \hline \end{array}$
$\begin{array}{r} 9 \\ \times\, 2 \\ \hline \end{array}$
$\begin{array}{r} 9 \\ \times\, 3 \\ \hline \end{array}$
$\begin{array}{r} 9 \\ \times\, 4 \\ \hline \end{array}$
$\begin{array}{r} 9 \\ \times\, 5 \\ \hline \end{array}$
$\begin{array}{r} 9 \\ \times\, 6 \\ \hline \end{array}$
$\begin{array}{r} 9 \\ \times\, 7 \\ \hline \end{array}$
$\begin{array}{r} 9 \\ \times\, 8 \\ \hline \end{array}$
$\begin{array}{r} 9 \\ \times\, 9 \\ \hline \end{array}$

B. Multiply.

2. $\begin{array}{r} 9 \\ \times\, 2 \\ \hline \end{array}$
3. $\begin{array}{r} 4 \\ \times\, 9 \\ \hline \end{array}$
4. $\begin{array}{r} 9 \\ \times\, 6 \\ \hline \end{array}$
5. $\begin{array}{r} 8 \\ \times\, 9 \\ \hline \end{array}$
6. $\begin{array}{r} 9 \\ \times\, 9 \\ \hline \end{array}$
7. $\begin{array}{r} 7 \\ \times\, 9 \\ \hline \end{array}$

Practice

Multiply.

1. $\begin{array}{r} 0 \\ \times\, 9 \\ \hline \end{array}$
2. $\begin{array}{r} 9 \\ \times\, 9 \\ \hline \end{array}$
3. $\begin{array}{r} 1 \\ \times\, 9 \\ \hline \end{array}$
4. $\begin{array}{r} 8 \\ \times\, 9 \\ \hline \end{array}$
5. $\begin{array}{r} 2 \\ \times\, 9 \\ \hline \end{array}$
6. $\begin{array}{r} 9 \\ \times\, 7 \\ \hline \end{array}$

7. $\begin{array}{r} 9 \\ \times\, 3 \\ \hline \end{array}$
8. $\begin{array}{r} 6 \\ \times\, 9 \\ \hline \end{array}$
9. $\begin{array}{r} 9 \\ \times\, 4 \\ \hline \end{array}$
10. $\begin{array}{r} 9 \\ \times\, 5 \\ \hline \end{array}$
11. $\begin{array}{r} 9 \\ \times\, 8 \\ \hline \end{array}$
12. $\begin{array}{r} 9 \\ \times\, 1 \\ \hline \end{array}$

13. $\begin{array}{r} 4 \\ \times\, 9 \\ \hline \end{array}$
14. $\begin{array}{r} 9 \\ \times\, 2 \\ \hline \end{array}$
15. $\begin{array}{r} 9 \\ \times\, 0 \\ \hline \end{array}$
16. $\begin{array}{r} 7 \\ \times\, 9 \\ \hline \end{array}$
17. $\begin{array}{r} 5 \\ \times\, 9 \\ \hline \end{array}$
★ **18.** $\begin{array}{r} 9 \\ \times\, \square \\ \hline 27 \end{array}$

Skills Review

Subtract.

1. (82)	49 − 24	**2.**	37 − 2	**3.**	86 − 29

4. (84) 879
− 324   **5.** 374
− 203   **6.** 124
− 21

7. 371
− 128   **8.** 952
− 648   **9.** 876
− 94   **10.** 836
− 78   **11.** 224
− 187

12. (86) 7,249
− 6,813   **13.** 74,286
− 19,193   **14.** 2,486
− 1,997   **15.** 73,840
− 69,952   **16.** 61,531
− 42,635

17. (88) 900
− 268   **18.** 507
− 49   **19.** 8,004
− 3,215   **20.** 60,001
− 7,284   **21.** 7,040
− 3,685

22. (95) $ 0.53
− 0.35   **23.** $ 16.82
− 9.47   **24.** $ 74.25
− 36.27   **25.** $ 15.00
− 6.95   **26.** $ 948.16
− 149.38

Computer

The computer uses * as its multiplication sign. To multiply
8 × 6, tell the computer: **PRINT 8 * 6**.
The output will be 48. Write the output for each.

1. PRINT 4 * 2.   **2. PRINT 3 * 8.**   **3. PRINT 5 * 6.**

4. PRINT 6 * 4.   **5. PRINT 8 * 7.**   **6. PRINT 5 * 3.**

Write the input and the computer output for each.

7. 8 × 9   **8.** 8 × 0   **9.** 8 × 8   **10.** 7 × 9

H A N D S O N

You can check your answers on the computer. Remember:
Press [RETURN] after you type. Be sure to use the *number*
0 for zero.

Midchapter Review

Multiply.

1. (108) $\begin{array}{r}3\\ \times 0\end{array}$	**2.** (108) $\begin{array}{r}0\\ \times 8\end{array}$	**3.** (108) $\begin{array}{r}6\\ \times 0\end{array}$	**4.** (109) $\begin{array}{r}1\\ \times 2\end{array}$	**5.** (109) $\begin{array}{r}5\\ \times 1\end{array}$	**6.** (109) $\begin{array}{r}7\\ \times 1\end{array}$
7. (110) $\begin{array}{r}4\\ \times 2\end{array}$	**8.** (110) $\begin{array}{r}8\\ \times 2\end{array}$	**9.** (110) $\begin{array}{r}2\\ \times 5\end{array}$	**10.** (112) $\begin{array}{r}3\\ \times 3\end{array}$	**11.** (112) $\begin{array}{r}3\\ \times 6\end{array}$	**12.** (112) $\begin{array}{r}4\\ \times 9\end{array}$
13. (112) $\begin{array}{r}4\\ \times 6\end{array}$	**14.** (114) $\begin{array}{r}5\\ \times 7\end{array}$	**15.** (114) $\begin{array}{r}6\\ \times 6\end{array}$	**16.** (114) $\begin{array}{r}6\\ \times 8\end{array}$	**17.** (114) $\begin{array}{r}6\\ \times 5\end{array}$	**18.** (116) $\begin{array}{r}7\\ \times 7\end{array}$
19. (116) $\begin{array}{r}8\\ \times 7\end{array}$	**20.** (116) $\begin{array}{r}8\\ \times 5\end{array}$	**21.** (116) $\begin{array}{r}8\\ \times 8\end{array}$	**22.** (117) $\begin{array}{r}9\\ \times 6\end{array}$	**23.** (117) $\begin{array}{r}3\\ \times 9\end{array}$	**24.** (117) $\begin{array}{r}9\\ \times 7\end{array}$

Something Extra
Non-Routine Problems

Which shape comes next in the sequence?

1.  ?

2. ?

3. ?

4. ?

119

GROUPING PROPERTY

Look at the picture.

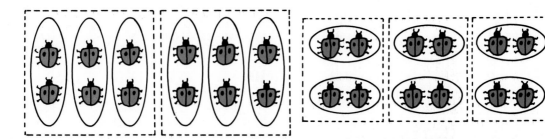

$(3 \times 2) \times 2$

$6 \times 2 = 12$

$3 \times (2 \times 2)$

$3 \times 4 = 12$

$(3 \times 2) \times 2 = 3 \times (2 \times 2)$

▶ Changing the grouping of the factors does not change the product. This is called the **grouping property of multiplication.**

Study and Learn

A. Complete.

1. $(2 \times 3) \times 3 = \underline{}$
$\quad 2 \times (3 \times 3) = \underline{}$

2. $(3 \times 2) \times 4 = \underline{}$
$\quad 3 \times (2 \times 4) = \underline{}$

3. $(2 \times 1) \times 4 = 2 \times (1 \times \underline{})$

4. $(5 \times 1) \times 2 = 5 \times (\underline{} \times 2)$

Practice

Complete.

1. $(4 \times 2) \times 4 = \underline{}$
$\quad 4 \times (2 \times 4) = \underline{}$

2. $(2 \times 1) \times 5 = \underline{}$
$\quad 2 \times (1 \times 5) = \underline{}$

3. $(6 \times 1) \times 2 = 6 \times (1 \times \underline{})$

★ **4.** $7 \times (1 \times 3) = (\underline{} \times \underline{}) \times 3$

120

MULTIPLICATION-ADDITION PROPERTY

2 rows of (3 + 2)   2 rows of 3   2 rows of 2

2 × (3 + 2)   (2 × 3)   +   (2 × 2)

This is the **multiplication-addition** property.

Study and Learn

If you forget a fact, here is a way to find it.

A. Complete.

    1. 6 × 8
       6 × (5 + 3)
       (6 × 5) + (6 × 3)
        30   +   ?
            ?

    2. 6 × 8
       6 × (4 + 4)
       (6 × 4) + (6 × 4)
        ?   +   ?
          ?

    3. What two ways was 8 renamed?

    4. Are the products the same?

B. Complete.

    5. 6 × (4 + 3) = (6 × 4) + (6 × __?__)

    6. 7 × (6 + 1) = (7 × __?__) + (7 × __?__)

    7. 8 × (7 + 2) = (8 × __?__) + (8 × __?__)

    8. 7 × (4 + 3) = (7 × __?__) + (__?__ × __?__)

    9. 3 × (5 + 2) = (__?__ × __?__) + (__?__ × __?__)

★ **10.** 9 × (__?__ + 1) = (9 × 8) + (__?__ × __?__)

121

Problem-Solving Skills

Is the Answer Reasonable?

There were 378 boxcars and 123 flatcars in the railroad yard. How many cars were there in all?

Solve: $378 + 123 = 501$ cars
Estimate to see if the answer is reasonable.

Estimate

$$
\begin{array}{ccc}
378 & \longrightarrow & 400 \\
+\,123 & \longrightarrow & +\,100 \\
\hline
 & & 500
\end{array}
$$

500 is close to 501, so the answer is reasonable.

Study and Learn

A. Complete.

There are 178 wooden boxes ready to be shipped. 303 metal boxes and 110 cardboard boxes will also be shipped. How many boxes will be shipped in all?

SOLVE

$$
\begin{array}{l}
178 \text{ wooden boxes} \\
303 \text{ metal boxes} \\
+\,110 \text{ cardboard boxes} \\
\hline
591 \text{ boxes in all}
\end{array}
$$

   1. What is the estimated sum?

   2. Is the estimated sum close to 591?

   3. Is the answer reasonable?

B. Estimate. Is the answer reasonable?

   4. The railroad has 36 engineers on the first shift. The second shift has 63 engineers. What is the total number of engineers on both shifts?
   Answer: 89 engineers.

Practice

Estimate. Is the answer reasonable?

1. The railroad carried 319 cars and 291 trucks on one train. How many cars and trucks did it carry in all?
Answer: 610 cars and trucks

2. The work crew laid 276 railroad ties on Monday. They laid 350 on Tuesday and 239 on Wednesday. How many ties were laid altogether?
Answer: 765 ties

3. There were 202 cars on the train going west. There were 189 cars on the train going east. What was the total number of cars on both trains?
Answer: 391 cars

4. A passenger train has 3 cars. The first car has 39 passengers. The second car has 51, and the third car has 62. How many passengers are on the train?
Answer: 251 passengers

DIVISION

6 dogs in all
2 groups
How many dogs in each group?

Divide to find the answer.

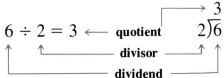

$6 \div 2 = 3 \leftarrow$ quotient
divisor
dividend

There are 3 dogs.

▶ You can show division by drawing arrays.

Study and Learn

A. Look at this array.

1. How many bones in all?

2. How many bones in each group?

3. Divide to find how many groups.
   $8 \div 2 = \underline{\ ?\ }$

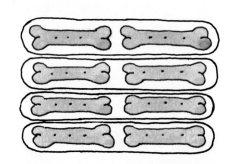

B. Complete.

4.

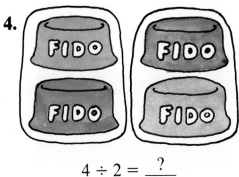

$4 \div 2 = \underline{\ ?\ }$

5.

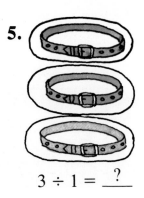

$3 \div 1 = \underline{\ ?\ }$

▶ You can show division by using subtraction.

C. Look at the picture to find 6 ÷ 2.

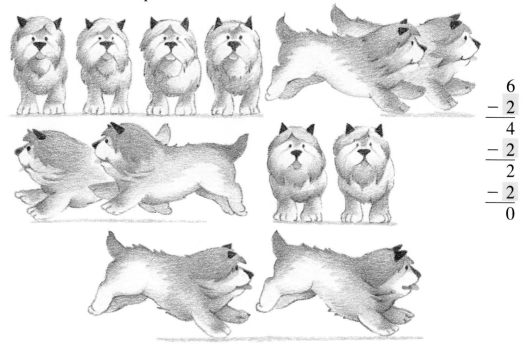

$$\begin{array}{r} 6 \\ -\ 2 \\ \hline 4 \\ -\ 2 \\ \hline 2 \\ -\ 2 \\ \hline 0 \end{array}$$

6. What number is subtracted each time?

7. How many 2's were subtracted?

8. Complete. 6 ÷ 2 = ___?___

Practice

1. Look at the array. How many toys in all?

How many toys in each group?

Divide to find how many groups.

6 ÷ 3 = ___?___

2. How many 3's in 9?

$$\begin{array}{r} 9 \\ -\ 3 \\ \hline 6 \\ -\ 3 \\ \hline 3 \\ -\ 3 \\ \hline 0 \end{array} \text{(1 three)}$$

DIVIDING BY 1, 2, AND 3

Find. $2\overline{)10}$

Think: 10 divided into groups of 2

So, $\overset{5}{2\overline{)10}}$

Check: $5 \times 2 = 10$

Study and Learn

A. Complete.

1.

$1\overline{)6}$

2.

$2\overline{)14}$

3.

$3\overline{)12}$

4.

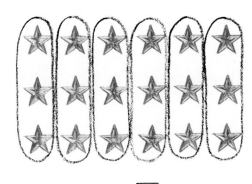

$3\overline{)18}$

B. Divide.

    5. $1\overline{)4}$ **6.** $1\overline{)7}$ **7.** $2\overline{)12}$ **8.** $3\overline{)15}$ **9.** $2\overline{)8}$

   10. $1\overline{)1}$ **11.** $3\overline{)21}$ **12.** $1\overline{)0}$ **13.** $2\overline{)2}$ **14.** $3\overline{)3}$

Practice

Divide.

1. $1\overline{)6}$ 2. $2\overline{)16}$ 3. $2\overline{)6}$ 4. $1\overline{)3}$ 5. $2\overline{)12}$

6. $1\overline{)1}$ 7. $2\overline{)4}$ 8. $2\overline{)18}$ 9. $1\overline{)5}$ 10. $3\overline{)3}$

11. $3\overline{)9}$ 12. $1\overline{)8}$ 13. $3\overline{)12}$ 14. $2\overline{)10}$ 15. $1\overline{)9}$

16. $2\overline{)8}$ 17. $3\overline{)18}$ 18. $1\overline{)2}$ 19. $3\overline{)24}$ 20. $3\overline{)27}$

21. $1\overline{)4}$ 22. $2\overline{)14}$ 23. $3\overline{)6}$ 24. $3\overline{)15}$ 25. $3\overline{)21}$

26. $2\overline{)2}$ 27. $1\overline{)7}$ 28. $1\overline{)1}$ ★ 29. $1\overline{)35,261}$

Solve Problems

30. There are 27 star stickers. There are 9 stickers on each sheet. How many sheets are there?

31. Carl has 16 rainbow stickers. There are 8 stickers on each roll. How many rolls does he have?

Computer

The computer uses / as its division sign.

To divide 18 by 2, tell the computer: **PRINT 18/2.**
The output will be 9.

Write the input and output for these:

1. $10 \div 2$ 2. $18 \div 3$ 3. $3 \div 3$ 4. $9 \div 1$ 5. $27 \div 3$

H A N D S   O N

You can check your answers on the computer. Remember: Press [RETURN] after you type a line.

RELATED SENTENCES

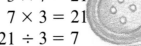

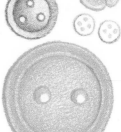

Here are four related sentences for 3, 7, and 21.

$$3 \times 7 = 21$$
$$7 \times 3 = 21$$
$$21 \div 3 = 7$$
$$21 \div 7 = 3$$

Study and Learn

A. Write four related sentences for each.

1. 1, 9, 9   **2.** 2, 3, 6   **3.** 24, 3, 8   **4.** 2, 8, 16

> You can write a related multiplication sentence for a division sentence.
>
> | Division Sentence | Related Multiplication Sentence |
> |---|---|
> | $12 \div 2 = \square$ | $\square \times 2 = 12$ |
> | $27 \div 3 = \square$ | $\square \times 3 = 27$ |

B. Write a related multiplication sentence for each.

5. $6 \div 1 = \square$ **6.** $15 \div 3 = \square$ **7.** $8 \div 2 = \square$

> You can use a related multiplication sentence to help divide.
>
> *Example* $3\overline{)18}$ ⟵ Think: $\square \times 3 = 18$ 6
> $6 \times 3 = 18$, so $3\overline{)18}$

C. Divide. Think of the related multiplication sentence.

8. $2\overline{)10}$ **9.** $1\overline{)7}$ **10.** $2\overline{)14}$ **11.** $2\overline{)12}$ **12.** $3\overline{)12}$

Practice

Write four related sentences for each.

1. 1, 5, 5   **2.** 2, 5, 10   **3.** 3, 5, 15   **4.** 6, 1, 6

5. 2, 14, 7   **6.** 3, 27, 9   **7.** 2, 1, 2   **8.** 18, 3, 6

Write a related multiplication sentence for each.

9. $8 \div 1 = \square$ **10.** $18 \div 2 = \square$ **11.** $9 \div 3 = \square$

12. $4 \div 2 = \square$ **13.** $3 \div 3 = \square$ **14.** $3 \div 1 = \square$

Divide.

15. $1\overline{)4}$ **16.** $2\overline{)8}$ **17.** $3\overline{)12}$ **18.** $2\overline{)16}$ **19.** $1\overline{)7}$

20. $3\overline{)6}$ **21.** $2\overline{)6}$ **22.** $3\overline{)21}$ **23.** $3\overline{)24}$ **24.** $1\overline{)9}$

Skills Review

Multiply. *(108–117)*

1. $\begin{array}{r} 3 \\ \times 0 \\ \hline \end{array}$ **2.** $\begin{array}{r} 7 \\ \times 6 \\ \hline \end{array}$ **3.** $\begin{array}{r} 2 \\ \times 5 \\ \hline \end{array}$ **4.** $\begin{array}{r} 3 \\ \times 4 \\ \hline \end{array}$

5. $\begin{array}{r} 4 \\ \times 6 \\ \hline \end{array}$ **6.** $\begin{array}{r} 4 \\ \times 0 \\ \hline \end{array}$ **7.** $\begin{array}{r} 2 \\ \times 7 \\ \hline \end{array}$ **8.** $\begin{array}{r} 1 \\ \times 2 \\ \hline \end{array}$

9. $\begin{array}{r} 2 \\ \times 2 \\ \hline \end{array}$ **10.** $\begin{array}{r} 3 \\ \times 6 \\ \hline \end{array}$ **11.** $\begin{array}{r} 3 \\ \times 3 \\ \hline \end{array}$ **12.** $\begin{array}{r} 9 \\ \times 9 \\ \hline \end{array}$ **13.** $\begin{array}{r} 6 \\ \times 6 \\ \hline \end{array}$ **14.** $\begin{array}{r} 8 \\ \times 2 \\ \hline \end{array}$

15. $\begin{array}{r} 7 \\ \times 3 \\ \hline \end{array}$ **16.** $\begin{array}{r} 0 \\ \times 9 \\ \hline \end{array}$ **17.** $\begin{array}{r} 1 \\ \times 3 \\ \hline \end{array}$ **18.** $\begin{array}{r} 6 \\ \times 0 \\ \hline \end{array}$ **19.** $\begin{array}{r} 4 \\ \times 7 \\ \hline \end{array}$ **20.** $\begin{array}{r} 8 \\ \times 8 \\ \hline \end{array}$

21. $\begin{array}{r} 8 \\ \times 1 \\ \hline \end{array}$ **22.** $\begin{array}{r} 4 \\ \times 8 \\ \hline \end{array}$ **23.** $\begin{array}{r} 2 \\ \times 3 \\ \hline \end{array}$ **24.** $\begin{array}{r} 3 \\ \times 5 \\ \hline \end{array}$ **25.** $\begin{array}{r} 4 \\ \times 4 \\ \hline \end{array}$ **26.** $\begin{array}{r} 5 \\ \times 0 \\ \hline \end{array}$

DIVIDING BY 4, 5, AND 6

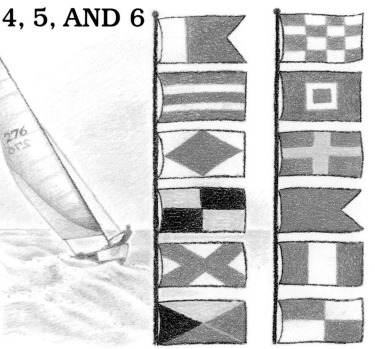

12 flags
6 to a column
How many columns?

Find. $6\overline{)12}$

Think: $\square \times 6 = 12$
$2 \times 6 = 12$

So, $6\overline{)12}^{\,2}$

Study and Learn

A. Find $4\overline{)12}$.

   1. Think: $\square \times 4 = 12$

   2. What is the quotient?

B. Solve.

   3. $5\overline{)30}$ **4.** $6\overline{)30}$ **5.** $4\overline{)28}$
   Think: $\square \times 5 = 30$ Think: $\square \times 6 = 30$ Think: $\square \times 4 = 28$

   6. $4\overline{)0}$ **7.** $6\overline{)6}$ **8.** $5\overline{)25}$
   Think: $\square \times 4 = 0$ Think: $\square \times 6 = 6$ Think: $\square \times 5 = 25$

C. Divide.

   9. $4\overline{)8}$ **10.** $5\overline{)10}$ **11.** $4\overline{)16}$ **12.** $6\overline{)48}$ **13.** $5\overline{)15}$

   14. $5\overline{)0}$ **15.** $4\overline{)4}$ **16.** $6\overline{)18}$ **17.** $4\overline{)36}$ **18.** $6\overline{)54}$

Practice

Divide.

1. $4\overline{)20}$ 2. $6\overline{)30}$ 3. $4\overline{)8}$ 4. $1\overline{)7}$ 5. $5\overline{)5}$

6. $3\overline{)27}$ 7. $5\overline{)10}$ 8. $6\overline{)42}$ 9. $4\overline{)36}$ 10. $6\overline{)12}$

11. $5\overline{)30}$ 12. $4\overline{)4}$ 13. $5\overline{)0}$ 14. $5\overline{)35}$ 15. $2\overline{)18}$

16. $6\overline{)36}$ 17. $3\overline{)24}$ 18. $4\overline{)24}$ 19. $2\overline{)16}$ 20. $3\overline{)6}$

21. $4\overline{)28}$ 22. $5\overline{)40}$ 23. $2\overline{)12}$ 24. $4\overline{)0}$ 25. $6\overline{)6}$

26. $3\overline{)15}$ 27. $4\overline{)32}$ 28. $6\overline{)24}$ 29. $5\overline{)45}$ 30. $3\overline{)9}$

31. $5\overline{)15}$ 32. $4\overline{)16}$ 33. $3\overline{)18}$ 34. $3\overline{)3}$ 35. $6\overline{)48}$

36. $6\overline{)18}$ 37. $5\overline{)25}$ 38. $5\overline{)20}$ 39. $2\overline{)2}$ 40. $1\overline{)5}$

41. $6\overline{)54}$ 42. $4\overline{)12}$ 43. $3\overline{)12}$ 44. $2\overline{)8}$ 45. $3\overline{)0}$

Solve Problems

46. There were 30 flags on the village parade grounds. The flags were in groups of 5 each. How many groups were there?

47. Mrs. Brown's class had 32 students. They were seated in 8 rows. How many students were in each row?

●48. A class had 8 students in a group. There were 2 groups. How many students were there?

DIVIDING BY 7, 8, AND 9

27 buttons
9 on each jacket
How many jackets?

Find. $9\overline{)27}$

Think: $\square \times 9 = 27$
         $3 \times 9 = 27$

So, $9\overline{)27}^{\;3}$

There are 3 jackets.

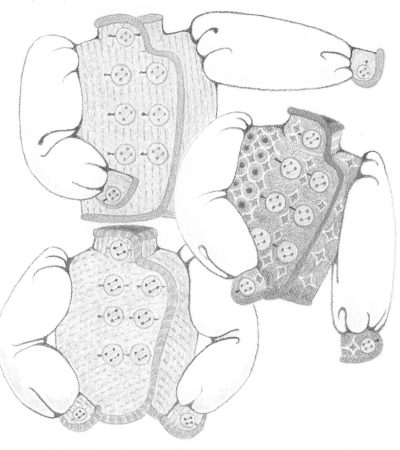

Study and Learn

A. Solve.

  1. $7\overline{)14}$
Think: $\square \times 7 = 14$

  2. $7\overline{)28}$
Think: $\square \times 7 = 28$

  3. $9\overline{)63}$
Think: $\square \times 9 = 63$

  4. $8\overline{)48}$
Think: $\square \times 8 = 48$

  5. $9\overline{)9}$
Think: $\square \times 9 = 9$

  6. $8\overline{)0}$
Think: $\square \times 8 = 0$

B. Divide.

  7. $7\overline{)42}$ **8.** $8\overline{)64}$ **9.** $9\overline{)18}$ **10.** $7\overline{)0}$ **11.** $8\overline{)16}$

  12. $8\overline{)40}$ **13.** $7\overline{)35}$ **14.** $7\overline{)63}$ **15.** $9\overline{)72}$ **16.** $9\overline{)81}$

Practice

Divide.

1. $8\overline{)8}$ 2. $6\overline{)36}$ 3. $7\overline{)35}$ 4. $9\overline{)27}$ 5. $5\overline{)45}$

6. $7\overline{)28}$ 7. $9\overline{)81}$ 8. $8\overline{)32}$ 9. $5\overline{)35}$ 10. $4\overline{)28}$

11. $9\overline{)45}$ 12. $8\overline{)16}$ 13. $4\overline{)36}$ 14. $6\overline{)0}$ 15. $7\overline{)49}$

16. $6\overline{)42}$ 17. $7\overline{)7}$ 18. $9\overline{)63}$ 19. $8\overline{)48}$ 20. $5\overline{)25}$

21. $7\overline{)42}$ 22. $6\overline{)54}$ 23. $8\overline{)24}$ 24. $9\overline{)18}$ 25. $4\overline{)20}$

26. $9\overline{)72}$ 27. $8\overline{)40}$ 28. $4\overline{)32}$ 29. $7\overline{)21}$ 30. $6\overline{)18}$

31. $8\overline{)72}$ 32. $7\overline{)63}$ 33. $5\overline{)40}$ 34. $4\overline{)0}$ 35. $9\overline{)54}$

36. $7\overline{)56}$ 37. $9\overline{)36}$ 38. $6\overline{)48}$ 39. $8\overline{)56}$ 40. $3\overline{)27}$

41. $9\overline{)9}$ 42. $8\overline{)64}$ 43. $7\overline{)14}$ 44. $6\overline{)30}$ 45. $6\overline{)12}$

Solve Problems

46. 40 buttons
8 buttons on each jacket
How many jackets?

47. 56 buttons
7 buttons on each shirt
How many shirts?

Something Extra
Calculator Activity

Estimate which would have the larger answer.
Then check by finding the exact answers.

1. $\begin{array}{r} 87 \\ +\ 34 \end{array}$ or $\begin{array}{r} 64 \\ +\ 48 \end{array}$
2. $\begin{array}{r} 376 \\ +\ 941 \end{array}$ or $\begin{array}{r} 498 \\ +\ 730 \end{array}$
3. $\begin{array}{r} \$\ 6.50 \\ -\ 3.51 \end{array}$ or $\begin{array}{r} \$\ 7.51 \\ -\ 3.50 \end{array}$

MULTIPLES AND FACTORS

The first five multiples of 3 are 3, 6, 9, 12, and 15.
You can find them this way.

$$1 \times 3 = 3$$
$$2 \times 3 = 6$$
$$3 \times 3 = 9$$
$$4 \times 3 = 12$$
$$5 \times 3 = 15$$

Study and Learn

A. List the first five multiples of each.

1. 1   **2.** 2   **3.** 6   **4.** 8

> Is 15 a multiple of 5? Think: $3 \times 5 = 15$
> So, 15 is a multiple of 5.

B. Is the first number a multiple of the second? Write yes or no.

5. 15; 3   **6.** 24; 6   **7.** 12; 5   **8.** 27; 4

> You can find all the factors of a number this way.
>
> For 18,
> $$1 \times 18 = 18$$
> $$2 \times 9 = 18$$
> $$3 \times 6 = 18$$
> $$4 \times \,? = 18$$
> These are not factors. $$5 \times \,? = 18$$
> Stop when a factor repeats. $$6 \times 3 = 18$$
>
> The factors of 18 are 1, 2, 3, 6, 9, and 18.

C. List all the factors of each.

9. 2   **10.** 6   **11.** 9   **12.** 16   **13.** 17

Practice

List the first eight multiples of each.

1. 4   **2.** 5   **3.** 7   **4.** 9   ★ **5.** 10

Is the first number a multiple of the second? Write yes or no.

6. 32; 8   **7.** 32; 4   **8.** 32; 6   **9.** 18; 4   **10.** 49; 7

11. 8; 1   **12.** 13; 2   **13.** 27; 3   **14.** 53; 9   ★ **15.** 100; 10

List all the factors of each.

16. 3   **17.** 4   **18.** 5   **19.** 7   **20.** 8

21. 10   **22.** 11   **23.** 14   **24.** 15   ★ **25.** 48

★ **26.** List the first ten numbers that have exactly two factors.

Something Extra
Activity

$6\overline{)0}$

THINK: $\square \times 6 = 0, 0 \times 6 = 0$, so $6\overline{)0}^{\,0}$.

$0\overline{)9}$

THINK: $\square \times 0 = 9$, so there is no answer.
You cannot divide a number by 0.

Divide. Write no answer for division by zero.

1. $7\overline{)0}$ **2.** $0\overline{)8}$ **3.** $4\overline{)0}$ **4.** $0\overline{)6}$

Problem-Solving Applications
Career

Solve.

1. A shipment of milk cost $37.90. A shipment of fruit cost $40.75. How much did these shipments cost in all? [HINT: $37.90 + $40.75 = ___?___]

2. $642.80 was collected this week. $756.93 was collected last week. How much more was collected last week?

3. $98.15 was collected on Monday. $89.40 was collected on Tuesday. $95.65 was collected on Wednesday. How much was collected in the three days?

4. A shipment of meat cost $85.90. A shipment of vegetables cost $51.95. How much more did the meat cost?

5. 1,625 hot lunches were made this week. 976 hot lunches were made last week. How many more hot lunches were made this week?

Chapter Review

Multiply.

1. 0	**2.** 9	**3.** 2	**4.** 7	**5.** 3
(108) × 8	(109) × 1	(110) × 8	(110) × 2	(112) × 6

6. 7	**7.** 7	**8.** 4	**9.** 5	**10.** 6
(112) × 3	(112) × 4	(112) × 4	(114) × 5	(114) × 6

11. 6	**12.** 7	**13.** 8	**14.** 9	**15.** 9
(114) × 7	(116) × 7	(116) × 8	(117) × 9	(117) × 8

Even or odd? Write E or O. *(111)*

16. 27   **17.** 63   **18.** 726

Divide.

19. 1)9   **20.** 2)14   **21.** 3)21   **22.** 2)18
(126)   *(126)*   *(126)*   *(126)*

23. 6)48   **24.** 5)45   **25.** 4)28   **26.** 4)32
(130)   *(130)*   *(130)*   *(130)*

27. 9)63   **28.** 7)56   **29.** 8)40   **30.** 8)56
(132)   *(132)*   *(132)*   *(132)*

Write four related sentences. *(128)*

31. 4, 9, 36

Estimate. Is the answer reasonable? *(122)*

32. There were 26 forks and 42 knives. How many forks and knives in all? Answer: 58

Solve. *(136)*

33. Spent $1.95 for a brush and $1.69 for shampoo. How much more did the brush cost?

Chapter Test

Multiply.

1. 7		**2.** 3		**3.** 5		**4.** 9		**5.** 7	
(108) × 0		*(109)* × 1		*(110)* × 2		*(110)* × 2		*(112)* × 3	

6. 3		**7.** 6		**8.** 4		**9.** 6		**10.** 4	
(112) × 8		*(112)* × 4		*(112)* × 9		*(114)* × 7		*(114)* × 5	

11. 6		**12.** 8		**13.** 8		**14.** 7		**15.** 9	
(114) × 6		*(116)* × 7		*(116)* × 6		*(117)* × 9		*(117)* × 5	

Even or Odd? Write E or O. *(111)*

16. 96   **17.** 83   **18.** 221

Divide.

19. 2)12   **20.** 1)8   **21.** 3)24   **22.** 2)16
(126)   *(126)*   *(126)*   *(126)*

23. 6)54   **24.** 4)36   **25.** 6)30   **26.** 5)35
(130)   *(130)*   *(130)*   *(130)*

27. 7)28   **28.** 8)48   **29.** 9)54   **30.** 9)81
(132)   *(132)*   *(132)*   *(132)*

Write four related sentences. *(128)*

31. 63, 7, 9

Estimate. Is the answer reasonable? *(122)*

32. There were 61 blue chairs and 33 black chairs.
How many more blue chairs were there? Answer: 28

Solve. *(136)*

33. Spent $3.50 for breakfast and $5.67 for lunch.
How much spent in all?

Skills Check

1. What is the standard numeral for three hundred seventy-six?

   A 306   B 370

   C 376   D 763

2. What is the standard numeral for eight thousand, five hundred thirteen?

   E 5,813   F 8,053

   G 8,503   H 8,513

3. What is the value of the underlined digit?

   $\underline{6},424$

   A 6   B 60

   C 600   D 6,000

4. What is 755 rounded to the nearest hundred?

   E 760   F 800

   G 805   H 855

5. Compare.

   $$2{,}311 \equiv 2{,}113$$

   A >   B +

   C =   D <

6. What time is it?

   E 2:09   F 3:10

   G 3:48   H 3:50

7. What time is it?

   A 8:07   B 2:08

   C 8:02   D 2:40

8. What is another way to write July 8, 1983?

   E 8/7/83   F 7/8/83

   G 6/8/83   H 2/7/83

Chapter

6 MEASUREMENT

A shrimp boat under construction in St. Augustine, Florida.

CENTIMETERS

A **centimeter (cm)** is a unit of length.

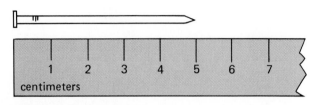

The nail is 5 cm long.

Study and Learn

A. Look at line segment *AB*.

   1. Is it closer to 3 cm or 4 cm?

   2. What is the length to the nearest centimeter?

B. Measure to the nearest centimeter.

   3. 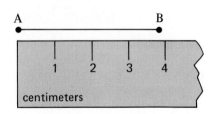   **4.**

   5.

C. Draw line segments with these lengths.

   6. 1 cm   **7.** 3 cm   **8.** 7 cm   **9.** 10 cm

Practice

Measure to the nearest centimeter.

1.
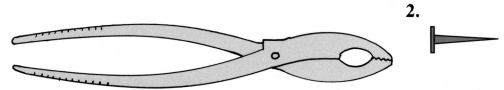

2.

3.
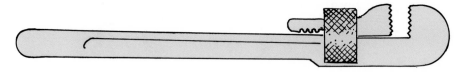

4. •————————————•   **5.** •————————————•

6. •——————————————————————————•

7. •————————————————•   **8.** •————————————•

9. •————————————————————•   **10.** •——————•

11. •————————————————————•

12. •————————————————•   **13.** •————————————•

14. •————————————————————•   **15.** •————•

16. •——————————————————————•

Draw line segments with these lengths.

17. 2 cm   **18.** 5 cm   **19.** 9 cm   **20.** 20 cm

CENTIMETERS, METERS, KILOMETERS

Centimeter (cm), meter (m), and **kilometer (km)** are units of length.

A centimeter is about the width of a small finger.

▶ 1 m = 100 cm
A meter is about the height of a chair.

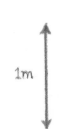

▶ 1 km = 1,000 m
A kilometer is about how far you could walk quickly in 10 minutes.

Study and Learn

A. The centimeter is used for short lengths. The meter is used to measure longer things.

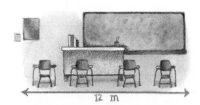

   1. What is the length of the room?

B. The kilometer is used for long distances.

   2. How far is it from Sagebrush to Joshua?

C. Which unit would you use to measure each? Use cm, m, or km.

   3. Length of your book   **4.** Distance around your room

   5. Height of your wall   **6.** Distance to the South Pole

Practice

Which unit would you use to measure each?
Use cm, m, or km.

1. Length of a sparrow

2. Length of a park bench

3. A scout hike

4. Height of a flagpole

5. Height of a house

6. Distance between New York and Chicago

7. Length of a city block

8. Length of a bus

9. Length of a playground

10. Width of a mailbox

11. Height of a tree

12. Length of a butterfly

CHANGING UNITS OF MEASURE

How many centimeters high is this ladder?

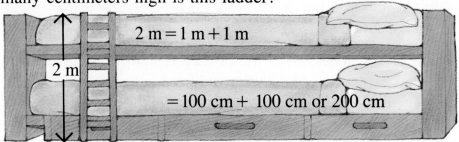

2 m = 1 m + 1 m

2 m

= 100 cm + 100 cm or 200 cm

Study and Learn

A. Complete.

1. 3 m = 1 m + 1 m + 1 m
= 100 cm + 100 cm + 100 cm or __?__ cm

2. 200 cm = 100 cm + 100 cm
= 1 m + 1 m or __?__ m

3. 4 m = __?__ cm   **4.** 600 cm = __?__ m

B. Complete.

5. 2 km = 1 km + 1 km
= 1,000 m + 1,000 m or __?__ m

6. 3,000 m = 1,000 m + 1,000 m + 1,000 m
= 1 km + 1 km + 1 km or __?__ km

7. 5 km = __?__ m   **8.** 8,000 m = __?__ km

Practice

Complete.

1. 6 m = __?__ cm   **2.** 400 cm = __?__ m   **3.** 8 m = __?__ cm

4. 2,000 m = __?__ km   **5.** 6,000 m = __?__ km   **6.** 4 km = __?__ m

★**7.** 13,000 m = __?__ km   ★**8.** 16 km = __?__ m

LITER AND MILLILITER

Liter and **milliliter** are used to measure liquids.

▶ 1 liter **(L)** = 1,000 milliliters **(mL)**

1 liter

10 drops of water are about 1 milliliter.

Study and Learn

A. Complete.

1. 3 L = 1 L + 1 L + 1 L
= 1,000 mL + 1,000 mL + 1,000 mL or __?__ mL

2. 2,000 mL = 1,000 mL + 1,000 mL
= 1 L + 1 L or __?__ L

3. 6 L = __?__ mL   **4.** 9,000 mL = __?__ L

B. Which unit would you use to measure each? Use mL or L.

5. A spoonful of medicine   **6.** A large fishtank

Practice

Complete.

1. 7 L = __?__ mL   **2.** 4 L = __?__ mL   **3.** 3,000 mL = __?__ L
4. 6,000 mL = __?__ L   **5.** 2 L = __?__ mL   ★**6.** 12 L = __?__ mL

Which unit would you use to measure each? Use mL or L.

7. A bottle of perfume   **8.** A bathtub of water

9. A truckload of gasoline   **10.** A tablespoon of vanilla

UNITS OF MASS

Gram (g), kilogram (kg), and **metric ton (t)** are units of mass.

▶ 1,000 g = 1 kg   ▶ 1,000 kg = 1 t

Mass is the amount of matter an object contains.

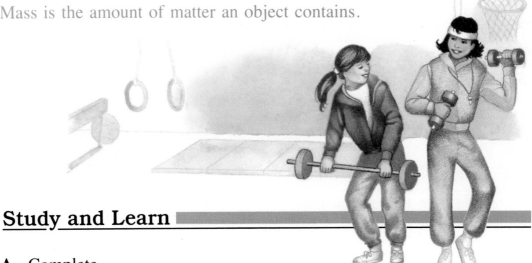

Study and Learn

A. Complete.

   1. 3 kg = 1 kg + 1 kg + 1 kg
          = 1,000 g + 1,000 g + 1,000 g or __?__ g

   2. 2,000 g = 1,000 g + 1,000 g
            = 1 kg + 1 kg or __?__ kg

   3. 4 kg = __?__ g   **4.** 3,000 g = __?__ kg

B. Complete.

   5. 3 t = 1 t + 1 t + 1 t
         = 1,000 kg + 1,000 kg + 1,000 kg or __?__ kg

   6. 2,000 kg = 1,000 kg + 1,000 kg
             = 1 t + 1 t or __?__ t
   7. 4 t = __?__ kg   **8.** 6,000 kg = __?__ t

C. Which unit would you use to measure each?
   Use g, kg, or t.

   9. An elephant   **10.** A hat   **11.** A dog

Practice

Complete.

1. 7 kg = ___?___ g   **2.** 9 t = ___?___ kg   **3.** 4 kg = ___?___ g

4. 8,000 kg = ___?___ t   **5.** 5,000 g = ___?___ kg   **6.** 7,000 kg = ___?___ t

7. 2,000 kg = ___?___ t   **8.** 5 t = ___?___ kg   **9.** 9 kg = ___?___ g

Which unit would you use to measure each?
Use g, kg, or t.

10. A horse   **11.** A feather   **12.** A clown

13. A hat   **14.** A ball   **15.** A scarf

16. A box of popcorn **17.** A lion   **18.** A car

MEASURING TEMPERATURE

A thermometer is used to measure temperature.
The unit of measure is called a **degree** (°).
These thermometers use the **Celsius (C)** scale.

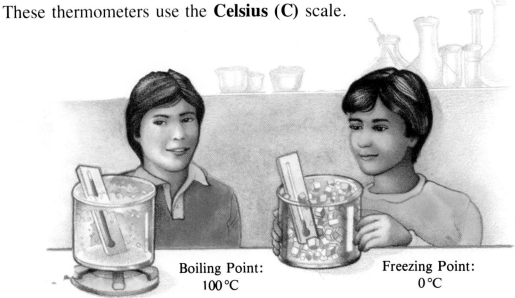

Boiling Point:
100°C

Freezing Point:
0°C

Study and Learn

A. Look at the thermometers above.

   1. At what temperature does water boil?

   2. At what temperature does water freeze?

   3. How many degrees are there between freezing and
      boiling on the Celsius scale?

B. What temperatures are shown?

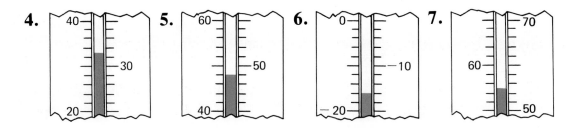

4.   **5.**   **6.**   **7.**

C. Look at the thermometer.

    8. What temperature is shown?

    9. If the temperature rose 7°C,
        what temperature would it be then?

    10. If the temperature fell 4°C,
       what temperature would it be then?

Practice

What temperatures are shown?

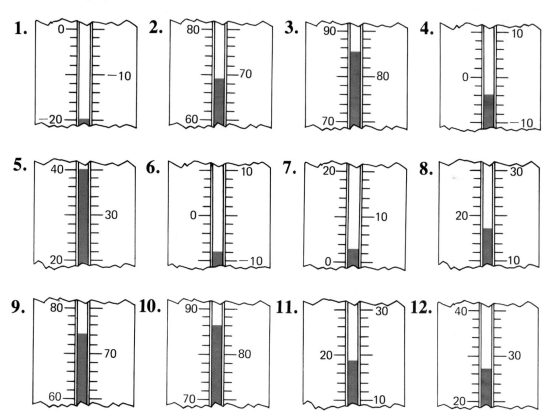

Solve Problems

13. Temperature: Was 14°C.
Rose 9°. Temperature now?

14. Temperature: Was 43°C.
Fell 14°. Temperature now?

Midchapter Review

Measure to the nearest centimeter. *(142)*

1.

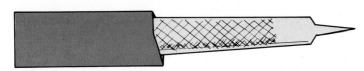

2.

Complete.

3. 700 cm = __?__ m **4.** 6 m = __?__ cm **5.** 3 km = __?__ m
(146)   *(146)*   *(146)*

6. 4,000 m = __?__ km **7.** 3 L = __?__ mL **8.** 2,000 mL = __?__ L
(146)   *(147)*   *(147)*

9. 2,000 kg = __?__ t **10.** 3,000 g = __?__ kg **11.** 4 kg = __?__ g
(148)   *(148)*   *(148)*

What temperatures are shown? *(150)*

12. 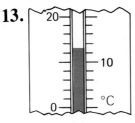 **13.** **14.** 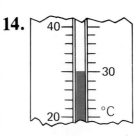 **15.**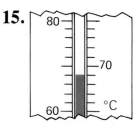

Something Extra
Non-Routine Problem

The digits are 0, 1, 2, 3, 4, 5, 6, 7, 8, and 9. Make up
a correct subtraction problem using all of the digits. No
digit may be used more than once.

$$
\begin{array}{r}
???? \\
- \ ??? \\
\hline
??? \\
\end{array}
$$

Skills Review

Multiply. *(108–117)*

1. $\begin{array}{r} 7 \\ \times 0 \\ \hline \end{array}$	**2.** $\begin{array}{r} 1 \\ \times 1 \\ \hline \end{array}$	**3.** $\begin{array}{r} 0 \\ \times 4 \\ \hline \end{array}$	**4.** $\begin{array}{r} 1 \\ \times 2 \\ \hline \end{array}$	**5.** $\begin{array}{r} 1 \\ \times 4 \\ \hline \end{array}$
6. $\begin{array}{r} 2 \\ \times 0 \\ \hline \end{array}$	**7.** $\begin{array}{r} 1 \\ \times 3 \\ \hline \end{array}$	**8.** $\begin{array}{r} 0 \\ \times 5 \\ \hline \end{array}$	**9.** $\begin{array}{r} 6 \\ \times 1 \\ \hline \end{array}$	**10.** $\begin{array}{r} 0 \\ \times 8 \\ \hline \end{array}$

11. $\begin{array}{r} 1 \\ \times 7 \\ \hline \end{array}$	**12.** $\begin{array}{r} 0 \\ \times 3 \\ \hline \end{array}$	**13.** $\begin{array}{r} 1 \\ \times 9 \\ \hline \end{array}$	**14.** $\begin{array}{r} 9 \\ \times 0 \\ \hline \end{array}$	**15.** $\begin{array}{r} 1 \\ \times 5 \\ \hline \end{array}$	**16.** $\begin{array}{r} 0 \\ \times 0 \\ \hline \end{array}$	**17.** $\begin{array}{r} 6 \\ \times 0 \\ \hline \end{array}$
18. $\begin{array}{r} 2 \\ \times 1 \\ \hline \end{array}$	**19.** $\begin{array}{r} 3 \\ \times 4 \\ \hline \end{array}$	**20.** $\begin{array}{r} 2 \\ \times 5 \\ \hline \end{array}$	**21.** $\begin{array}{r} 4 \\ \times 2 \\ \hline \end{array}$	**22.** $\begin{array}{r} 3 \\ \times 9 \\ \hline \end{array}$	**23.** $\begin{array}{r} 2 \\ \times 4 \\ \hline \end{array}$	**24.** $\begin{array}{r} 2 \\ \times 8 \\ \hline \end{array}$
25. $\begin{array}{r} 3 \\ \times 7 \\ \hline \end{array}$	**26.** $\begin{array}{r} 2 \\ \times 2 \\ \hline \end{array}$	**27.** $\begin{array}{r} 4 \\ \times 7 \\ \hline \end{array}$	**28.** $\begin{array}{r} 4 \\ \times 3 \\ \hline \end{array}$	**29.** $\begin{array}{r} 3 \\ \times 5 \\ \hline \end{array}$	**30.** $\begin{array}{r} 3 \\ \times 8 \\ \hline \end{array}$	**31.** $\begin{array}{r} 4 \\ \times 4 \\ \hline \end{array}$
32. $\begin{array}{r} 2 \\ \times 7 \\ \hline \end{array}$	**33.** $\begin{array}{r} 4 \\ \times 8 \\ \hline \end{array}$	**34.** $\begin{array}{r} 2 \\ \times 3 \\ \hline \end{array}$	**35.** $\begin{array}{r} 3 \\ \times 1 \\ \hline \end{array}$	**36.** $\begin{array}{r} 2 \\ \times 9 \\ \hline \end{array}$	**37.** $\begin{array}{r} 2 \\ \times 6 \\ \hline \end{array}$	**38.** $\begin{array}{r} 4 \\ \times 9 \\ \hline \end{array}$
39. $\begin{array}{r} 3 \\ \times 3 \\ \hline \end{array}$	**40.** $\begin{array}{r} 3 \\ \times 2 \\ \hline \end{array}$	**41.** $\begin{array}{r} 4 \\ \times 5 \\ \hline \end{array}$	**42.** $\begin{array}{r} 3 \\ \times 6 \\ \hline \end{array}$	**43.** $\begin{array}{r} 4 \\ \times 1 \\ \hline \end{array}$	**44.** $\begin{array}{r} 3 \\ \times 0 \\ \hline \end{array}$	**45.** $\begin{array}{r} 4 \\ \times 6 \\ \hline \end{array}$
46. $\begin{array}{r} 5 \\ \times 5 \\ \hline \end{array}$	**47.** $\begin{array}{r} 5 \\ \times 6 \\ \hline \end{array}$	**48.** $\begin{array}{r} 6 \\ \times 3 \\ \hline \end{array}$	**49.** $\begin{array}{r} 6 \\ \times 7 \\ \hline \end{array}$	**50.** $\begin{array}{r} 5 \\ \times 8 \\ \hline \end{array}$	**51.** $\begin{array}{r} 5 \\ \times 1 \\ \hline \end{array}$	**52.** $\begin{array}{r} 5 \\ \times 0 \\ \hline \end{array}$
53. $\begin{array}{r} 7 \\ \times 5 \\ \hline \end{array}$	**54.** $\begin{array}{r} 6 \\ \times 6 \\ \hline \end{array}$	**55.** $\begin{array}{r} 5 \\ \times 4 \\ \hline \end{array}$	**56.** $\begin{array}{r} 5 \\ \times 2 \\ \hline \end{array}$	**57.** $\begin{array}{r} 0 \\ \times 6 \\ \hline \end{array}$	**58.** $\begin{array}{r} 6 \\ \times 2 \\ \hline \end{array}$	**59.** $\begin{array}{r} 5 \\ \times 9 \\ \hline \end{array}$
60. $\begin{array}{r} 7 \\ \times 6 \\ \hline \end{array}$	**61.** $\begin{array}{r} 7 \\ \times 4 \\ \hline \end{array}$	**62.** $\begin{array}{r} 7 \\ \times 8 \\ \hline \end{array}$	**63.** $\begin{array}{r} 8 \\ \times 3 \\ \hline \end{array}$	**64.** $\begin{array}{r} 8 \\ \times 6 \\ \hline \end{array}$	**65.** $\begin{array}{r} 7 \\ \times 7 \\ \hline \end{array}$	**66.** $\begin{array}{r} 8 \\ \times 0 \\ \hline \end{array}$
67. $\begin{array}{r} 7 \\ \times 3 \\ \hline \end{array}$	**68.** $\begin{array}{r} 8 \\ \times 8 \\ \hline \end{array}$	**69.** $\begin{array}{r} 7 \\ \times 9 \\ \hline \end{array}$	**70.** $\begin{array}{r} 8 \\ \times 9 \\ \hline \end{array}$	**71.** $\begin{array}{r} 5 \\ \times 7 \\ \hline \end{array}$	**72.** $\begin{array}{r} 8 \\ \times 7 \\ \hline \end{array}$	**73.** $\begin{array}{r} 7 \\ \times 1 \\ \hline \end{array}$
74. $\begin{array}{r} 9 \\ \times 9 \\ \hline \end{array}$	**75.** $\begin{array}{r} 9 \\ \times 8 \\ \hline \end{array}$	**76.** $\begin{array}{r} 9 \\ \times 6 \\ \hline \end{array}$	**77.** $\begin{array}{r} 9 \\ \times 7 \\ \hline \end{array}$	**78.** $\begin{array}{r} 9 \\ \times 5 \\ \hline \end{array}$	**79.** $\begin{array}{r} 9 \\ \times 1 \\ \hline \end{array}$	**80.** $\begin{array}{r} 9 \\ \times 4 \\ \hline \end{array}$

COMPUTER—PROGRAMS

A program tells the computer what to do. The program must be written in a language that the computer can understand. All the programs in this book are written in the computer language called BASIC.

A BASIC program is a numbered list of commands. The computer carries out the commands in order. It starts with the command that has the smallest number.

Here is how a simple BASIC program looks on a computer screen.

The special LIST command tells the computer to show the program lines.

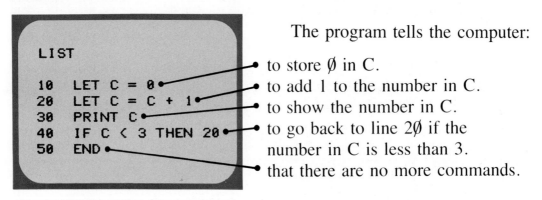

The program tells the computer:

- to store Ø in C.
- to add 1 to the number in C.
- to show the number in C.
- to go back to line 2Ø if the number in C is less than 3.
- that there are no more commands.

Here is what appears on the screen when you run the program.

The special RUN command tells the computer to carry out the program commands.

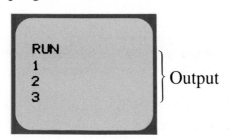

Output

When you first turn on the computer, tell it what number to put in each storage place you are using.

Practice

What is the output of these programs?

1.
```
10  LET A = 14
20  LET B = 3
30  PRINT A X B
40  END
```

2.
```
10  LET E = 15
20  LET F = 3
30  PRINT E / F
40  END
```

3.
```
10  LET P = 18
20  LET Q = 12
30  PRINT P - Q
40  END
```

4.
```
10  LET N = 0
20  LET N = N + 1
30  PRINT N
40  IF N < 10 THEN 20
50  END
```

5.
```
10  LET X = 1
20  LET X = X + 2
30  PRINT X
40  IF X < 11 THEN 20
50  END
```

6.
```
10  LET S = 0
20  LET S = S + 2
30  PRINT S
40  IF S < 10 THEN 20
50  END
```

★**7.** Write a program that puts 10 into F and 3 into L. It should output the product of the numbers.

★**8.** Write a program that makes the computer output the even numbers from 10 to 20. Use an **IF/THEN** command.

You can check your answers on the computer.
Type the program. Press [RETURN] after each line. To make each program run, type **RUN,** and press [RETURN]

Problem-Solving Skills

Writing a Number Sentence

There were 8 bobsled teams.
There were 4 people on each team.
How many people were there in all?

Think:

What is asked? ⟶ How many in all?
What is given? ⟶ 8 teams, 4 people on each team
Do you multiply or divide? ⟶ Multiply

This number sentence fits the problem.

$$8 \quad \times \quad 4 \quad = \quad \underline{\;?\;}$$

teams   people on   people in all
       each team

Study and Learn

A. There are 36 hockey players.
Each team has 6 players.
How many hockey teams are there?

  1. What is asked?

  2. What is given?

  3. Do you multiply or divide?

  4. Write a number sentence that fits the problem.

B. Write the number sentence that fits each problem.

  5. 12 swim teams
       8 swimmers on each team
       How many swimmers in all?

  6. 72 gymnasts
       9 gymnasts on each team
       How many teams?

Practice

Write the number sentence that fits the problem.

1. There were 46 athletes in the kayak event.
   Each kayak seats 2 persons.
   How many kayaks were in the event?

2. The United States basketball team scored
   23 points in each quarter. How many points
   were scored in all 4 quarters?

3. A runner ran 800 meters in 2 minutes.
   She ran the same distance each minute.
   How many meters were run in 1 minute?

4. A soccer team has 11 players.
   How many players are on 6 soccer teams?

5. There are 40 basketball players.
   Each team has 5 players. How many
   teams are there?

6. A relay team has 4 runners. There
   are 7 relay teams. How many runners
   are there?

7. There are 81 baseball players. Each
   team has 9 players. How many baseball
   teams are there?

★8. An athlete swam 800 meters in 8 minutes.
   He swam the same distance each minute.
   How many meters were swum in 2 minutes?

TIME

There are different ways to tell the time.

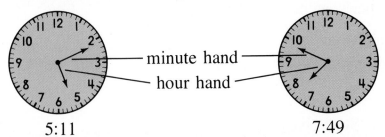

5:11
Read: Five eleven or
11 minutes after 5

7:49
Read: Seven forty-nine or
11 minutes to 8

Study and Learn

A. Complete.

1.

___ : ___

___ minutes after ___

2.

___ : ___

___ minutes to ___

3.

11 : 19

___ : ___

___ minutes after ___

Here are other ways to tell time. Remember that 15 minutes is a quarter hour, and 30 minutes is a half hour.

12 o'clock
12 noon or
12 midnight

8:45
15 minutes to 9
Quarter to 9

4:30
Half past 4
30 minutes after 4

B. Write the time in as many ways as possible.

4.

5.

6.

Practice

Write the time in as many ways as possible.

1.

2.

3.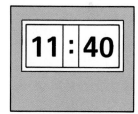

4.

5.

6.

7.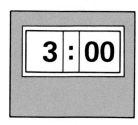

8.

9.

10.

11.

12.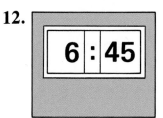

TIME EARLIER AND LATER

Times from midnight up to noon are labeled am.
Times from noon up to midnight are labeled pm.

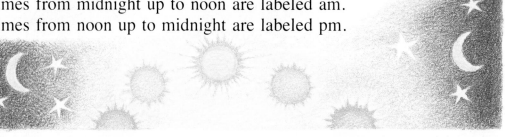

Study and Learn

A. Label each as am or pm.

1. Breakfast: 7:15   **2.** Dinner: 6:30   **3.** Gym: 2:00

You can add time.	
ADD MINUTES	ADD HOURS
3 hours 15 minutes + 2 hours 26 minutes 41 minutes	3 hours 15 minutes + 2 hours 26 minutes 5 hours 41 minutes

B. Add.

4.   6 hours 29 minutes
   + 4 hours 23 minutes

5.   4 hours 25 minutes
   +   15 minutes

You can also subtract time.	
SUBTRACT MINUTES	SUBTRACT HOURS
10 hours 36 minutes − 3 hours 19 minutes 17 minutes	10 hours 36 minutes − 3 hours 19 minutes 7 hours 17 minutes

C. Subtract.

6.   11 hours 50 minutes
   − 5 hours 15 minutes

7.   6 hours 46 minutes
   −   9 minutes

D. Look at the clock.

8. What is the time?

9. What time will it be in 25 minutes?

10. What time will it be in 2 hours?

11. What time will it be in 4 hours and 12 minutes?

12. What time was it 20 minutes ago?

13. What time was it 1 hour and 25 minutes ago?

Practice

Label each as am or pm.

1. Baseball practice: 3:45

2. School starts: 9:00

3. Lunch: 12:30

4. Homework: 5:30

Add.

5.
```
   7 hours  16 minutes
+  4 hours  26 minutes
```

6.
```
   3 hours  42 minutes
+           9 minutes
```

Subtract.

7.
```
   9 hours  42 minutes
−  3 hours  25 minutes
```

8.
```
   6 hours  36 minutes
−  4 hours
```

Look at the clock.

9. What is the time?

10. What time will it be in 2 hours and 10 minutes?

11. What time was it 4 hours and 20 minutes ago?

★12. What time will it be in 35 minutes?

★13. What time was it 35 minutes ago?

WRITING THE DATE

The calendar shows Maureen's birthday.

Word form: September 17, 1975
Numerical form: 9/17/75

The numerical form means:
9th month, 17th day, 1975th year

Study and Learn

Complete.

1. Paul was born October 21, 1976. Write the numerical form for his birthday.

2. Cynthia was born 6/16/77. Write the word form for her birthday.

3. Write the numerical form for the date for the Super Bowl game on January 20th, 1985.

4. If the teams start practice 7 days before the game, on what date do they start practice? Write the word form.

5. What date is the second Monday? Write it in numerical form.

6. What date is ten days after 3/15/86? Write that date in word form.

7. The date is 11/15/86. The homework is due on 11/21/86. How many days until the homework is due?

Skills Review

Divide.

1. $3\overline{)3}$ **2.** $2\overline{)0}$ **3.** $2\overline{)4}$ **4.** $1\overline{)2}$
(126)

5. $2\overline{)10}$ **6.** $1\overline{)1}$ **7.** $3\overline{)6}$ **8.** $3\overline{)15}$

9. $2\overline{)16}$ **10.** $2\overline{)6}$ **11.** $1\overline{)3}$ **12.** $3\overline{)12}$ **13.** $3\overline{)24}$ **14.** $2\overline{)18}$

15. $3\overline{)27}$ **16.** $1\overline{)6}$ **17.** $2\overline{)14}$ **18.** $1\overline{)9}$ **19.** $3\overline{)9}$ **20.** $3\overline{)18}$

21. $4\overline{)8}$ **22.** $6\overline{)12}$ **23.** $6\overline{)54}$ **24.** $5\overline{)30}$ **25.** $6\overline{)48}$ **26.** $4\overline{)36}$
(130)

27. $5\overline{)25}$ **28.** $4\overline{)4}$ **29.** $4\overline{)24}$ **30.** $6\overline{)6}$ **31.** $5\overline{)45}$ **32.** $5\overline{)0}$

33. $5\overline{)20}$ **34.** $6\overline{)36}$ **35.** $5\overline{)5}$ **36.** $6\overline{)18}$ **37.** $4\overline{)32}$ **38.** $6\overline{)24}$

39. $4\overline{)12}$ **40.** $6\overline{)42}$ **41.** $4\overline{)0}$ **42.** $4\overline{)20}$ **43.** $5\overline{)10}$ **44.** $6\overline{)30}$

45. $8\overline{)48}$ **46.** $7\overline{)56}$ **47.** $9\overline{)9}$ **48.** $8\overline{)8}$ **49.** $8\overline{)56}$ **50.** $9\overline{)36}$
(132)

51. $9\overline{)45}$ **52.** $9\overline{)18}$ **53.** $7\overline{)14}$ **54.** $8\overline{)0}$ **55.** $8\overline{)32}$ **56.** $7\overline{)35}$

57. $8\overline{)40}$ **58.** $8\overline{)72}$ **59.** $9\overline{)63}$ **60.** $7\overline{)49}$ **61.** $8\overline{)16}$ **62.** $7\overline{)28}$

63. $9\overline{)27}$ **64.** $7\overline{)42}$ **65.** $7\overline{)7}$ **66.** $9\overline{)54}$ **67.** $8\overline{)64}$ **68.** $7\overline{)63}$

Something Extra
Non-Routine Problem

Copy this triangle. Fill in the circles with 1, 2, 3, 7, 8, and 9 so that the sum on each side is 20. Use each digit only once.

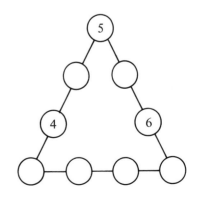

163

LENGTH IN THE CUSTOMARY SYSTEM

These are units of length in the customary system.

inch (in.)   **foot (ft)**   **yard (yd)**   **mile (mi)**

▶ 1 ft = 12 in.   ▶ 1 yd = 36 in.
▶ 1 yd = 3 ft   ▶ 1 mi = 5,280 ft

Study and Learn

A. Complete.

1. 3 ft = 1 ft + 1 ft + 1 ft
     = 12 in. + 12 in. + 12 in. or __?__ in.

2. 2 yd = 1 yd + 1 yd
     = 3 ft + 3 ft or __?__ ft

3. 3 yd = 1 yd + 1 yd + 1 yd
     = 36 in. + 36 in. + 36 in. or __?__ in.

4. 2 mi = 1 mi + 1 mi
     = 5,280 ft + 5,280 ft or __?__ ft

B. Which unit would you use to measure the length of each item? Use in., ft, yd, or mi.

5. A pencil   **6.** A canoe   **7.** A football field

Practice

Complete.

1. 2 ft = __?__ in.   **2.** 4 ft = __?__ in.   **3.** 3 yd = __?__ ft

4. 2 yd = __?__ in.   **5.** 3 mi = __?__ ft   ★ **6.** 5 mi = __?__ ft

Which unit would you use to measure the length of each item? Use in., ft, yd, or mi.

7. A highway   **8.** A bedroom carpet   **9.** A tablecloth

LIQUID MEASURE IN THE CUSTOMARY SYSTEM

Cup, pint (pt), quart (qt), and **gallon (gal)** are units of liquid measure.

▶ 1 pt = 2 cups
▶ 1 qt = 2 pt
▶ 1 gal = 4 qt

Study and Learn

A. Complete.

1. 2 pt = 1 pt + 1 pt
   = 2 cups + 2 cups or __?__ cups

2. 3 qt = 1 qt + 1 qt + 1 qt
   = 2 pt + 2 pt + 2 pt or __?__ pt

3. 3 gal = 1 gal + 1 gal + 1 gal
   = 4 qt + 4 qt + 4 qt or __?__ qt

B. Complete. Use cup, pt, qt, or gal.

4. A glass holds 1 __?__ of milk.

5. Sam's fishtank holds 5 __?__ of water.

Practice

Complete.

1. 3 pt = __?__ cups   **2.** 4 pt = __?__ cups   **3.** 2 qt = __?__ pt

4. 4 qt = __?__ gal   **5.** 2 gal = __?__ qt   ★ **6.** 6 gal = __?__ qt

Complete. Use cup, pt, qt, or gal.

7. Mr. Eng put a __?__ of oil in the car.

8. Mrs. Anderson put 7 __?__ of gas in the car.

WEIGHT IN THE CUSTOMARY SYSTEM

Ounce (oz), pound (lb), and **ton** are units of weight.

▶ 1 lb = 16 oz
▶ 1 ton = 2,000 lb

Study and Learn

A. Complete.

   1. 2 lb = 1 lb + 1 lb
             = 16 oz + 16 oz or __?__ oz

   2. 3 ton = 1 ton + 1 ton + 1 ton
               = 2,000 lb + 2,000 lb + 2,000 lb or __?__ lb

B. Complete. Use oz, lb, or ton.

   3. A letter weighs 1 __?__ .

   4. Tammy bought 2 __?__ of onions.

Practice

Complete.

  1. 3 lb = __?__ oz   **2.** 4 lb = __?__ oz   **3.** 2 ton = __?__ lb

  4. 4 ton = __?__ lb   ★ **5.** 6 lb = __?__ oz   ★ **6.** 32 oz = __?__ lb

Complete. Use oz, lb, or ton.

  7. An apple weighs about 3 __?__ .

  8. An elephant weighs about 3 __?__ .

FAHRENHEIT TEMPERATURE

Temperature can be measured
in degrees **Fahrenheit (°F).**

Study and Learn

A. Look at the thermometer.

   1. What is the freezing point?

   2. What is the boiling point?

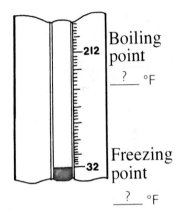

B. What temperatures are shown?

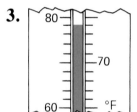 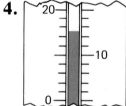 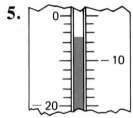 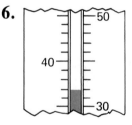

   7. Temperature: Was 60°F. It fell 23°. What is it now?

Practice

What temperatures are shown?

1. 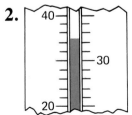 **2.** 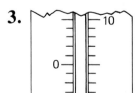 **3.** 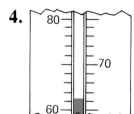 **4.**

   5. Temperature: Was 90°F. It rose 9°. What is it now?

Problem-Solving Applications

Solve.

1. Jessica jumps rope 5 minutes every day. How many minutes does she jump in 7 days? [HINT: $5 \times 7 = \underline{\ ?\ }$]

2. Bob swam 16 laps in 8 minutes. He swam the same distance each minute. How many laps swum in 1 minute?

3. There were 18 children playing basketball. There were 2 basketball teams. How many children were on each team?

4. Andre runs 9 laps every day. How many laps does he run in 9 days?

5. Kay plays 3 games of tennis each week. How many games of tennis does she play in 4 weeks?

Chapter Review

1. Measure to the nearest centimeter. *(142)* •————————•

2. Measure to the nearest $\frac{1}{8}$ inch. *(164)* •————————•

Tell which unit you would use to measure each: km, m, cm.
(144, 147, 148)

3. An elephant

4. A spoon

Complete. *(146, 147, 148)*

5. 8 m = __?__ cm   **6.** 3,000 mL = __?__ L   **7.** 2,000 g = __?__ kg

What temperatures are shown? *(150, 169)*

8.

9.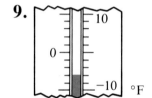

10.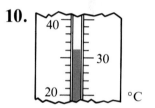

Add or subtract. *(160)*

11.   8 hours 39 minutes
      + 2 hours 20 minutes

12.   11 hours 41 minutes
      −   17 minutes

13. What date is 12 days before 6/23/65? *(162)*

14. What date is 22 days after July 2, 1982? *(162)*

Complete. *(166, 167, 168)*
15. 5 ft = __?__ in.

16. 2 mi = __?__ ft

17. 3 gal = __?__ qt

18. 4 lb = __?__ oz

Write the number sentence.

Solve.

19. There are 9 apples. 3
(156) children share the apples.
How many apples for each
child?

20. Paul runs 2 miles every day.
(170) How many miles does he
run in 14 days?

Chapter Test

1. Measure to the nearest centimeter. *(142)* •————————————————•

2. Measure to the nearest $\frac{1}{8}$ inch. *(164)* •————————•

Tell which unit you would use to measure each: L or mL. *(144, 147, 148)*

3. A bottle of juice

4. An eyedropper

Complete. *(146, 147, 148)*

5. 2 km = __?__ m   **6.** 4 t = __?__ kg   **7.** 5,000 mL = __?__ L

What temperatures are shown? *(150, 169)*

8.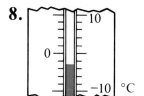

9.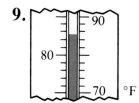

10.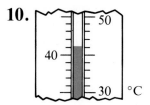

Add or subtract. *(160)*

11.   3 hours 22 minutes
     +   29 minutes

12.   9 hours 54 minutes
     − 4 hours 25 minutes

13. What date is 5 days after 9/9/79? *(162)*

14. What date is 16 days before July 19, 1985? *(162)*

Complete. *(166, 167, 168)*

15. __?__ in. = 2 yd   **16.** 3 yd = __?__ ft

17. 5 pts = __?__ cups   **18.** 3 ton = __?__ lb

Write the number sentence.   Solve.

19. There are 6 eggs in each
(156) carton. There are 5 cartons
of eggs. How many eggs are
there in all?

20. Beth swam 20 laps in 5
(170) minutes. She swam the same
distance each minute. How
many laps swum in 1
minute?

Skills Check

1. Bob earned $4.00 babysitting. He bought a book for $2.69. How much money did he have left?

   A $0.31   B $1.31

   C $2.31   D $6.69

2. 662 people were taking planes to Boston. 229 people were taking trains to Boston About how many people were going to Boston in all?

   E 200   F 400

   G 500   H 900

3. Frank started running at 9:00. What time will it be if he runs for 2 hours and 39 minutes?

   A 11:39   B 11:50

   C 7:39   D 2:39

4. How many hours are there in 180 minutes?

   E 1   F 2

   G 3   H 4

5. What is the value of 1 quarter, 2 nickels, 1 dime, and 3 pennies?

   A $0.38   B $0.45

   C $0.48   D $0.53

6. Denise had a glass of milk and an apple. The milk was 150 calories. The apple was 80 calories. How many calories in all?

   E 70   F 130

   G 220   H 230

7. Which of these units describes a toothbrush?

   A liter   B gram

   C ton   D kilogram

8. How many meters are there in 400 centimeters?

   E 3   F 4

   G 30   H 40

7 MULTIPLICATION

A pipeline carrying natural gas.

COMPUTER—ROBOTS

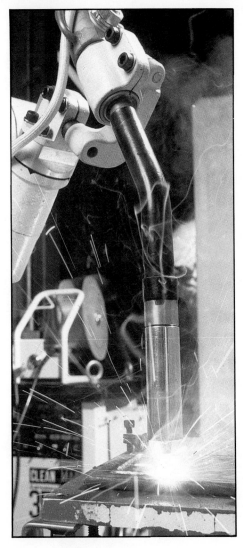

A. A robot is a machine that does a job usually done by a human. Most robots have special shapes and do not look human. A robot can have cameras for eyes or pliers for hands.

B. A robot has a computer for a "brain." The computer is programmed by humans who tell the robot what moves to make. Once it is programmed, a robot can do a job again and again.

C. Computerized robots are used in many factories. Some car makers use robots to lift heavy parts into place and to weld.

D. Robots are sometimes used in difficult places. A robot called Rover will go to Mars in 1986 and will move on the planet's surface. Rover's mechanical arm will scoop up rocks and soil.

It will send information to earth about the rocks and soil it scoops up with its mechanical arm.

TENS, HUNDREDS, AND THOUSANDS

Look for a pattern. Compare the number of zeros in the factors and the products.

$7 \times 10 = 70$ $7 \times 20 = 140$
$7 \times 100 = 700$ $7 \times 200 = 1,400$
$7 \times 1,000 = 7,000$ $7 \times 2,000 = 14,000$

Study and Learn

A. Find 6×400.

   1. How many zeros in the factors?
Put the same number of zeros
in the product.

$$\begin{array}{r} 400 \\ \times\ 6 \\ \hline 2,400 \end{array}$$

   2. Multiply. $6 \times 4 = \underline{\ ?\ }$

   3. Include the zeros. $6 \times 400 = \underline{\ ?\ }$

B. Multiply.

   4. $\begin{array}{r} 20 \\ \times\ 6 \\ \hline \end{array}$ **5.** $\begin{array}{r} 100 \\ \times\ 3 \\ \hline \end{array}$ **6.** $\begin{array}{r} 1,000 \\ \times\ 6 \\ \hline \end{array}$ **7.** $\begin{array}{r} 200 \\ \times\ 8 \\ \hline \end{array}$

Practice

Multiply.

   1. $\begin{array}{r} 10 \\ \times\ 2 \\ \hline \end{array}$ **2.** $\begin{array}{r} 20 \\ \times\ 4 \\ \hline \end{array}$ **3.** $\begin{array}{r} 40 \\ \times\ 8 \\ \hline \end{array}$ **4.** $\begin{array}{r} 10 \\ \times\ 5 \\ \hline \end{array}$ **5.** $\begin{array}{r} 100 \\ \times\ 4 \\ \hline \end{array}$

   6. $\begin{array}{r} 100 \\ \times\ 7 \\ \hline \end{array}$ **7.** $\begin{array}{r} 100 \\ \times\ 9 \\ \hline \end{array}$ **8.** $\begin{array}{r} 200 \\ \times\ 2 \\ \hline \end{array}$ **9.** $\begin{array}{r} 2,000 \\ \times\ 3 \\ \hline \end{array}$ **10.** $\begin{array}{r} 1,000 \\ \times\ 4 \\ \hline \end{array}$

   11. $\begin{array}{r} 1,000 \\ \times\ 9 \\ \hline \end{array}$ **12.** $\begin{array}{r} 4,000 \\ \times\ 2 \\ \hline \end{array}$ **13.** $\begin{array}{r} 1,000 \\ \times\ 7 \\ \hline \end{array}$ ★ **14.** $9 \times 10,000$

MULTIPLYING TENS

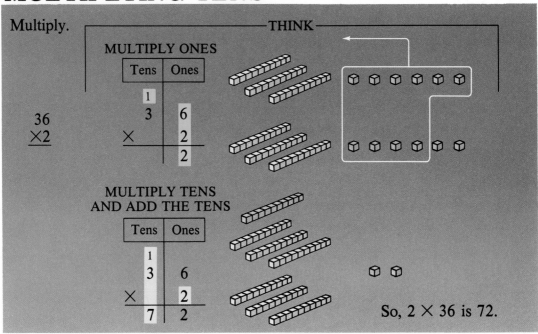

Multiply. ———THINK———

MULTIPLY ONES

Tens	Ones
¹ 3	6
×	2
	2

36
×2

**MULTIPLY TENS
AND ADD THE TENS**

Tens	Ones
¹ 3	6
×	2
7	2

So, 2 × 36 is 72.

Study and Learn

A. Find 7 × 48. Complete.

   1. Multiply ones.

     7 × 8 = _?_

   2. How is 56 written?

   3. Multiply tens.

     7 × 4 tens = _?_ tens

     Add. 28 tens + 5 tens = _?_ tens

   4. What is the product?

WRITE

```
  5
  4 8
× 7
    6
```

```
  5
  4 8
× 7
3 3 6
```

B. Multiply.

5.	**6.**	**7.**	**8.**	**9.**
42	81	43	77	65
× 2	× 9	× 8	× 7	× 8

Practice

Multiply.

1. $\begin{array}{r}32\\ \times\,3\\\hline\end{array}$	**2.** $\begin{array}{r}27\\ \times\,1\\\hline\end{array}$	**3.** $\begin{array}{r}22\\ \times\,4\\\hline\end{array}$	**4.** $\begin{array}{r}21\\ \times\,2\\\hline\end{array}$	**5.** $\begin{array}{r}21\\ \times\,3\\\hline\end{array}$
6. $\begin{array}{r}81\\ \times\,7\\\hline\end{array}$	**7.** $\begin{array}{r}62\\ \times\,3\\\hline\end{array}$	**8.** $\begin{array}{r}84\\ \times\,2\\\hline\end{array}$	**9.** $\begin{array}{r}93\\ \times\,3\\\hline\end{array}$	**10.** $\begin{array}{r}74\\ \times\,2\\\hline\end{array}$
11. $\begin{array}{r}93\\ \times\,2\\\hline\end{array}$	**12.** $\begin{array}{r}67\\ \times\,1\\\hline\end{array}$	**13.** $\begin{array}{r}81\\ \times\,2\\\hline\end{array}$	**14.** $\begin{array}{r}63\\ \times\,3\\\hline\end{array}$	**15.** $\begin{array}{r}22\\ \times\,3\\\hline\end{array}$
16. $\begin{array}{r}63\\ \times\,4\\\hline\end{array}$	**17.** $\begin{array}{r}75\\ \times\,5\\\hline\end{array}$	**18.** $\begin{array}{r}18\\ \times\,3\\\hline\end{array}$	**19.** $\begin{array}{r}27\\ \times\,2\\\hline\end{array}$	**20.** $\begin{array}{r}48\\ \times\,4\\\hline\end{array}$
21. $\begin{array}{r}62\\ \times\,5\\\hline\end{array}$	**22.** $\begin{array}{r}87\\ \times\,3\\\hline\end{array}$	**23.** $\begin{array}{r}94\\ \times\,6\\\hline\end{array}$	**24.** $\begin{array}{r}78\\ \times\,9\\\hline\end{array}$	**25.** $\begin{array}{r}33\\ \times\,7\\\hline\end{array}$
26. $\begin{array}{r}72\\ \times\,5\\\hline\end{array}$	**27.** $\begin{array}{r}63\\ \times\,9\\\hline\end{array}$	**28.** $\begin{array}{r}45\\ \times\,7\\\hline\end{array}$	**29.** $\begin{array}{r}97\\ \times\,9\\\hline\end{array}$	**30.** $\begin{array}{r}35\\ \times\,7\\\hline\end{array}$
31. $\begin{array}{r}42\\ \times\,2\\\hline\end{array}$	**32.** $\begin{array}{r}63\\ \times\,3\\\hline\end{array}$	**33.** $\begin{array}{r}19\\ \times\,3\\\hline\end{array}$	**34.** $\begin{array}{r}24\\ \times\,2\\\hline\end{array}$	**35.** $\begin{array}{r}86\\ \times\,4\\\hline\end{array}$
36. $\begin{array}{r}39\\ \times\,9\\\hline\end{array}$	**37.** $\begin{array}{r}42\\ \times\,3\\\hline\end{array}$	**38.** $\begin{array}{r}86\\ \times\,5\\\hline\end{array}$	★ **39.** $\begin{array}{r}23\\ \times\,\square\\\hline 46\end{array}$	★ **40.** $\begin{array}{r}14\\ \times\,\square\\\hline 70\end{array}$

Solve Problems

41. It takes Jay 9 minutes to walk one lap. How many minutes does it take him to walk 24 laps?

42. Adrian ran one lap in 5 minutes. How many minutes does it take him to run 12 laps?

MULTIPLYING HUNDREDS

Multiply 6 × 739.

Step 1 MULTIPLY ONES	**Step 2** MULTIPLY TENS	**Step 3** MULTIPLY HUNDREDS
5 739 × 6 ―― 4	2 5 739 × 6 ―― 3 4	2 5 739 × 6 ―― 4,4 3 4

Study and Learn

A. Find 8 × 647. Complete.

WRITE

5
647
× 8
――
6

   1. Multiply ones.
      8 × 7 = ___?___

   2. How is 56 written?

3 5
647
× 8
――
76

   3. Multiply tens.
      8 × 4 tens = ___?___ tens
      Add. 32 tens + 5 tens = ___?___ tens

   4. Complete the example.

B. Complete.

| **5.**   ¹
   232
   × 4
   ――
   28 | **6.**   ¹
   319
   × 2
   ――
   8 | **7.** 472
   × 3 | **8.** 748
   × 4 |

C. Multiply.

| **9.** 411
   × 3 | **10.** 618
   × 4 | **11.** 781
   × 7 | **12.** 604
   × 8 |

Practice

Multiply.

1. 312
    × 2

2. 223
    × 3

3. 420
    × 4

4. 611
    × 5

5. 702
    × 4

6. 232
    × 2

7. 747
    × 1

8. 933
    × 3

9. 842
    × 2

10. 621
    × 4

11. 419
    × 3

12. 607
    × 4

13. 883
    × 3

14. 942
    × 4

15. 616
    × 6

16. 981
    × 7

17. 817
    × 4

18. 652
    × 4

19. 804
    × 9

20. 427
    × 3

21. 784
    × 7

22. 649
    × 3

23. 888
    × 2

24. 645
    × 8

25. 327
    × 9

26. 765
    × 4

27. 289
    × 7

28. 356
    × 5

29. 967
    × 8

30. 349
    × 6

31. 410
    × 2

32. 870
    × 3

33. 607
    × 4

34. 829
    × 4

35. 125
    × 8

36. 375
    × 4

37. 491
    × 6

38. 313
    × 3

★ 39.   807
      × □
    4,035

★ 40.   567
      × □
    4,536

Solve Problems

41. A space shuttle traveled at 362 kilometers per hour. It traveled for 3 hours. How many kilometers did it travel in all?

42. A meteor traveled at 986 kilometers per hour. It traveled for 9 hours. How many kilometers did it travel in all?

MULTIPLYING THOUSANDS

Multiply $4 \times 6{,}819$.

Step 1 MULTIPLY ONES	Step 2 MULTIPLY TENS	Step 3 MULTIPLY HUNDREDS	Step 4 MULTIPLY THOUSANDS
$\begin{array}{r} {}^{3} \\ 6{,}8\,1\,9 \\ \times\ 4 \\ \hline 6 \end{array}$	$\begin{array}{r} {}^{3} \\ 6{,}8\,1\,9 \\ \times\ 4 \\ \hline 7\,6 \end{array}$	$\begin{array}{r} {}^{3}\ {}^{3} \\ 6{,}8\,1\,9 \\ \times\ 4 \\ \hline 2\,7\,6 \end{array}$	$\begin{array}{r} {}^{3}\ {}^{3} \\ 6{,}8\,1\,9 \\ \times\ 4 \\ \hline 2\,7{,}2\,7\,6 \end{array}$

Study and Learn

A. Find $4 \times 9{,}123$. Complete.

    1. Multiply ones.
       $4 \times 3 = \underline{\ ?\ }$

    2. Multiply tens.
       4×2 tens $= \underline{\ ?\ }$ tens
       Add. 8 tens + 1 ten $= \underline{\ ?\ }$ tens

    3. Multiply hundreds.
       4×1 hundred $= \underline{\ ?\ }$ hundreds

    4. Complete the example.

WRITE

$\begin{array}{r} {}^{1} \\ 9{,}1\,2\,3 \\ \times\ 4 \\ \hline 2 \end{array}$

$\begin{array}{r} {}^{1} \\ 9{,}1\,2\,3 \\ \times\ 4 \\ \hline 4\,9\,2 \end{array}$

B. Complete.

5. $\begin{array}{r} 4{,}123 \\ \times\ 2 \\ \hline 46 \end{array}$	**6.** $\begin{array}{r} {}^{1} \\ 7{,}123 \\ \times\ 4 \\ \hline 92 \end{array}$	**7.** $\begin{array}{r} {}^{1} \\ 6{,}641 \\ \times\ 4 \\ \hline 64 \end{array}$	**8.** $\begin{array}{r} 9{,}374 \\ \times\ 6 \\ \hline \end{array}$

C. Multiply.

9. $\begin{array}{r} 1{,}230 \\ \times\ 3 \\ \hline \end{array}$	**10.** $\begin{array}{r} 6{,}427 \\ \times\ 2 \\ \hline \end{array}$	**11.** $\begin{array}{r} 8{,}901 \\ \times\ 6 \\ \hline \end{array}$	**12.** $\begin{array}{r} 6{,}457 \\ \times\ 6 \\ \hline \end{array}$

Practice

Multiply.

1. 1,234
 × 2

2. 7,020
 × 4

3. 8,123
 × 3

4. 6,023
 × 2

5. 4,321
 × 3

6. 4,218
 × 3

7. 6,041
 × 7

8. 5,601
 × 8

9. 3,218
 × 4

10. 3,291
 × 3

11. 3,192
 × 2

12. 7,801
 × 8

13. 3,081
 × 7

14. 7,902
 × 3

15. 8,264
 × 2

16. 8,148
 × 5

17. 3,681
 × 7

18. 5,713
 × 4

19. 3,028
 × 9

20. 1,286
 × 3

21. 6,198
 × 4

22. 9,807
 × 4

23. 5,442
 × 4

24. 9,781
 × 8

25. 2,074
 × 4

26. 4,286
 × 8

27. 7,345
 × 3

28. 1,234
 × 9

29. 5,678
 × 4

30. 6,784
 × 6

31. 3,918
 × 7

32. 5,614
 × 4

33. 8,761
 × 7

34. 6,049
 × 8

35. 1,614
 × 3

36. 2,487
 × 2

37. 7,486
 × 6

38. 5,004
 × 8

★ 39. 18,640
 × 9

★ 40. 13,821
 × 9

Solve Problems

41. Each compact car is 1,354 kilograms. There are 5 compact cars on a trailer. How many kilograms is this?

42. Each station wagon is 2,248 kilograms. There are 4 station wagons on a trailer. How many kilograms is this?

MULTIPLYING MONEY

Each rosebush at Walter's Garden Center costs $8.98. Beth bought
6 rosebushes. How much money did she spend?

Multiply 6 × $8.98.

Multiplying money is the same as multiplying whole numbers.

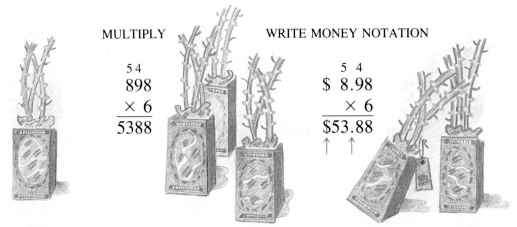

MULTIPLY

```
  5 4
  898
×   6
 5388
```

WRITE MONEY NOTATION

```
  5  4
$ 8.98
×    6
$53.88
  ↑  ↑
```

Study and Learn

A. Write money notation.

1. $0.07	**2.** $3.19	**3.** $24.85	**4.** $86.40
× 5	× 5	× 3	× 9
35	15 95	74 55	777 60

B. Complete.

5. $0.78	**6.** $7.28	**7.** $17.26	**8.** $87.80
× 5	× 3	× 2	× 9
0	4		

C. Multiply.

9. $0.46	**10.** $9.48	**11.** $3.07	**12.** $48.75
× 4	× 5	× 9	× 8

Practice

Multiply.

1. $0.09 × 3	**2.** $0.16 × 4	**3.** $7.48 × 6	**4.** $6.07 × 9	**5.** $2.99 × 4
6. $20.64 × 2	**7.** $51.78 × 6	**8.** $15.80 × 8	**9.** $37.50 × 9	**10.** $70.00 × 6
11. $2.45 × 7	**12.** $55.25 × 3	**13.** $7.95 × 8	★ **14.** $151.86 × 7	★ **15.** $140.50 × 8

Solve Problems

16. Beth wants to buy 4 bags of fertilizer for her lawn. Each bag costs $9.79. How much will 4 bags cost?

17. Walter delivers 8 maple trees to Mrs. Abels. Each maple tree costs $32.50. How much money does Mrs. Abels pay Walter?

● **18.** Mr. Anderson bought an azalea plant for $14.50 and a bag of soil for $3.98. How much money did Mr. Anderson spend?

★ **19.** Bruce paid $24.95 for each of the 4 hemlocks he ordered. He also ordered 3 bags of fertilizer. Each bag cost $12.59. How much money did Bruce spend?

Midchapter Review

Multiply.

1. (177)	10 × 7	**2.** (177)	1,000 × 5	**3.** (178)	41 × 2	**4.** (178)	73 × 3
5. (178)	86 × 4	**6.** (178)	97 × 5	**7.** (180)	614 × 4	**8.** (180)	871 × 9
9. (180)	468 × 5	**10.** (182)	7,148 × 2	**11.** (182)	6,807 × 4	**12.** (182)	3,987 × 5
13. (182)	6,714 × 3	**14.** (184)	$19.36 × 3	**15.** (184)	$0.48 × 7	**16.** (184)	$10.52 × 7

Skills Review

Round to the nearest ten. *(42)*

1. 72   **2.** 38   **3.** 45

Round to the nearest hundred. *(42)*

4. 198   **5.** 412   **6.** 351   **7.** 350   **8.** 349

Round to the nearest dollar. *(42)*

9. $7.65   **10.** $8.47   **11.** $6.50   **12.** $2.49   **13.** $2.51

Add.

14. *(53)*	**15.** *(56)*	**16.** *(58)*	**17.**	**18.** *(60)*
97 + 7	48 + 29	736 + 239	497 + 86	25,287 + 6,948

19. *(56)*	**20.** *(58)*	**21.** *(62)*	**22.** *(70)*	**23.**
87 95 + 46	738 297 + 376	4,287 3,984 + 7,276	$ 6.98 3.47 + 0.98	$ 18.74 19.58 + 7.46

Subtract.

24. *(82)*	**25.**	**26.** *(84)*	**27.**	**28.** *(86)*
73 − 8	87 − 19	476 − 148	712 − 87	4,297 − 3,189

29.	**30.** *(88)*	**31.**	**32.** *(95)*	**33.**
56,287 − 18,198	700 − 268	4,003 − 2,147	$ 9.68 − 1.76	$ 78.74 − 39.86

Something Extra
Non-Routine Problems

What is the next shape and color of each?

1.   ?

2.   ?

187

Problem-Solving Skills
Choosing a Number Sentence

Sound travels 344 meters per second in air.
How far will sound travel in 5 seconds?

PLAN
Which operation should be used? ⟶ Multiplication

Which number sentence fits the problem?

$344 - 5 = \underline{}^{?}$ $344 \div 5 = \underline{}^{?}$ $344 \times 5 = \underline{}^{?}$

The sentence $344 \times 5 = \underline{}^{?}$ fits the problem.

Study and Learn

A. Sound travels 1,450 meters per second in water. How much faster does sound travel in water than air?

   1. PLAN Which operation should be used?

   2. Which number sentence fits the problem?

   $1,450 + 344 = \underline{}^{?}$ $1,450 - 344 = \underline{}^{?}$ $1,450 \div 344 = \underline{}^{?}$

B. Which number sentence fits the problem?

   3. A sound traveled 15,000 meters in 3 seconds. How far did the sound travel in one second?

   $15,000 \times 3 = \underline{}^{?}$ $15,000 \div 3 = \underline{}^{?}$ $15,000 + 3 = \underline{}^{?}$

Practice

Which number sentence fits the problem?

1. Sound travels 1,450 meters per second in water.
   How far will it travel in 4 seconds?

   $1,450 \div 4 =$ __?__ $\qquad 1,450 \times 4 =$ __?__ $\qquad 1,450 - 4 =$ __?__

2. How long would it take a sound to
   travel 1,032 meters in air?

   $1,032 \div 344 =$ __?__ $\quad 1,032 \times 344 =$ __?__ $\quad 1,032 - 344 =$ __?__

3. When a jet plane moves at the speed of sound, it is
   called Mach 1. Mach 1 is equal to 1,238 kilometers per hour.
   If a jet plane travels at Mach 2, which is twice the speed
   of sound, how fast is it moving?

   $1,238 \div 2 =$ __?__ $\qquad 1,238 - 2 =$ __?__ $\qquad 1,238 \times 2 =$ __?__

4. Sound travels 5,000 meters per second in steel and 1,450 meters
   per second in water. How much faster does sound travel in
   steel than in water?

   $5,000 \times 1,450 =$ __?__ $5,000 - 1,450 =$ __?__ $5,000 + 1,450 =$ __?__

ESTIMATING PRODUCTS

Oranges are $0.79 a bag.
About how much would 5 bags cost?

EXACT	ESTIMATED
$0.79	$0.80
× 5	× 5
$3.95	$4.00

The **estimated** cost is $4.00.

Study and Learn

A. Complete.

   1. To estimate 6 × 88, think 6 × 90 = __?__ .

   2. To estimate 4 × $0.71, think 4 × $0.70 = __?__ .

B. Estimate each product. Round the greater factor to the nearest ten or ten cents.

   3. 62   **4.** $0.53   **5.** $0.68   **6.** 25
     × 7   × 6   × 5   × 9

C. Complete.

   7. To estimate 4 × 396, think 4 × 400 = __?__

   8. To estimate 5 × $8.15, think 5 × $8.00 = __?__

D. Estimate each product. Round the greater factor to the nearest hundred or dollar.

   9. 597   **10.** $8.32   **11.** 750   **12.** $3.86
     × 6   × 5   × 3   × 9

   13. $9.26   **14.** 325   **15.** $4.97   **16.** 283
      × 6   × 7   × 5   × 7

Practice

Estimate each product. Round the greater factor to the nearest ten or ten cents.

1. 31
   × 8

2. 73
   × 7

3. $0.38
   × 5

4. $0.41
   × 3

5. 85
   × 4

6. $0.75
   × 4

7. 79
   × 5

8. 62
   × 8

9. $0.39
   × 9

10. $0.48
   × 5

Estimate each product. Round the greater factor to the nearest hundred or dollar.

11. 421
   × 6

12. $8.18
   × 3

13. 894
   × 7

14. $6.89
   × 5

15. 650
   × 7

16. $8.50
   × 8

17. 912
   × 4

18. $8.07
   × 4

19. 388
   × 6

20. $1.98
   × 9

Estimate each product.

21. $0.91
   × 7

22. $8.18
   × 9

23. 814
   × 2

24. $0.22
   × 8

25. 928
   × 4

26. 365
   × 7

27. $0.49
   × 6

28. $3.09
   × 8

29. 788
   × 5

30. $1.75
   × 4

Estimate the cost.

31. 4 kilograms of hamburger

32. 3 kilograms of steak

33. 2 kilograms of hot dogs

★ **34.** $1\frac{1}{2}$ kilograms of chicken

BUTCHER

HAMBURGER $3.98 kg

STEAK $7.11 kg

CHICKEN $3.20 kg

HOT DOGS $2.98 kg

SPECIAL PRODUCTS

Look for a pattern. Compare the number of zeros in the factors and the products.

$80 \times 1 = 80$
$80 \times 10 = 800$
$80 \times 100 = 8,000$

Study and Learn

A. Multiply.

1. 60	**2.** 60	**3.** 40	**4.** 40	**5.** 400
$\times 1$	$\times 10$	$\times 1$	$\times 10$	$\times 10$

Look for a pattern.

$80 \times 2 = 160$
$80 \times 20 = 1,600$
$80 \times 200 = 16,000$

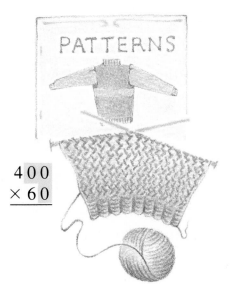

B. Find 60×400.

6. How many zeros in the factors? Put the same number of zeros in the product.

$\begin{array}{r} 400 \\ \times 60 \\ \hline \end{array}$

7. Multiply. $60 \times 400 = \underline{\quad?\quad}$

C. Multiply.

8. 50	**9.** 50	**10.** 90	**11.** 90	**12.** 900
$\times 7$	$\times 70$	$\times 3$	$\times 30$	$\times 30$

13. 400	**14.** 70	**15.** 80	**16.** 20	**17.** 500
$\times 50$	$\times 30$	$\times 50$	$\times 70$	$\times 50$

192

Practice

Multiply.

1. $\begin{array}{r} 70 \\ \times\ 1 \\ \hline \end{array}$

2. $\begin{array}{r} 70 \\ \times\ 10 \\ \hline \end{array}$

3. $\begin{array}{r} 20 \\ \times\ 1 \\ \hline \end{array}$

4. $\begin{array}{r} 20 \\ \times\ 10 \\ \hline \end{array}$

5. $\begin{array}{r} 200 \\ \times\ 10 \\ \hline \end{array}$

6. $\begin{array}{r} 30 \\ \times\ 90 \\ \hline \end{array}$

7. $\begin{array}{r} 60 \\ \times\ 20 \\ \hline \end{array}$

8. $\begin{array}{r} 400 \\ \times\ 70 \\ \hline \end{array}$

9. $\begin{array}{r} 800 \\ \times\ 50 \\ \hline \end{array}$

10. $\begin{array}{r} 400 \\ \times\ 30 \\ \hline \end{array}$

11. $\begin{array}{r} 300 \\ \times\ 90 \\ \hline \end{array}$

12. $\begin{array}{r} 40 \\ \times\ 30 \\ \hline \end{array}$

13. $\begin{array}{r} 50 \\ \times\ 40 \\ \hline \end{array}$

14. $\begin{array}{r} 500 \\ \times\ 30 \\ \hline \end{array}$

15. $\begin{array}{r} 800 \\ \times\ 20 \\ \hline \end{array}$

16. $\begin{array}{r} 50 \\ \times\ 9 \\ \hline \end{array}$

17. $\begin{array}{r} 50 \\ \times\ 90 \\ \hline \end{array}$

18. $\begin{array}{r} 500 \\ \times\ 90 \\ \hline \end{array}$

19. $\begin{array}{r} 400 \\ \times\ 60 \\ \hline \end{array}$

20. $\begin{array}{r} 80 \\ \times\ 70 \\ \hline \end{array}$

21. $\begin{array}{r} 20 \\ \times\ 30 \\ \hline \end{array}$

22. $\begin{array}{r} 800 \\ \times\ 60 \\ \hline \end{array}$

23. $\begin{array}{r} 70 \\ \times\ 90 \\ \hline \end{array}$

24. $\begin{array}{r} 100 \\ \times\ 10 \\ \hline \end{array}$

25. $\begin{array}{r} 60 \\ \times\ 60 \\ \hline \end{array}$

★ Complete.

26. $7 \times \square = 42{,}000$

27. $300 \times \square = 12{,}000$

Solve Problems

28. George hooked a rug. He hooked 5 rows each hour. How many rows in 30 hours?

29. There are 900 pieces of yarn in each package. Kim has 10 packages. How many pieces of yarn in all?

● 30. Jeffrey spends $8.65 on yarn and $2.98 on beads to make a plant hanger. How much money does he spend in all?

★ 31. George used 3 packages of blue beads and 4 packages of green beads. Each package had 12 beads. How many beads did George use?

MULTIPLYING BY MULTIPLES OF 10

Multiply 30 × 47.

Step 1 BRING DOWN THE ZERO	**Step 2** MULTIPLY BY TENS
47 × 3 0 —— 0	2 47 × 3 0 —— 1,4 1 0

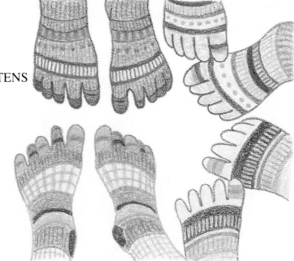

Study and Learn

A. Find 40 × 269. Complete.

   1. Where is the 0 placed?

   2. Multiply by tens.
      4 × 269 = ___?___

   3. What is the product?

WRITE

$$\begin{array}{r} {}^{2\ 3}269 \\ \times\ 4\,0 \\ \hline 1\,0{,}7\,6\,0 \end{array}$$

B. Complete.

	4.	**5.** $6.24	**6.**	**7.** $8.73	**8.** 574
	²78	¹ ³	²64		
	× 30	× 80	× 50	× 90	× 40
	——	——	——		
	40	9.20	0		

C. Multiply.

9. 87	**10.** 94	**11.** 872	**12.** $9.48	**13.** $6.64
× 60	× 30	× 20	× 40	× 50

14. $2.37	**15.** 546	**16.** $8.98	**17.** 39	**18.** $0.62
× 20	× 40	× 30	× 50	× 90

Practice

Multiply.

1. $\begin{array}{r} 36 \\ \times\ 30 \\ \hline \end{array}$ 2. $\begin{array}{r} 47 \\ \times\ 50 \\ \hline \end{array}$ 3. $\begin{array}{r} 68 \\ \times\ 70 \\ \hline \end{array}$ 4. $\begin{array}{r} \$0.91 \\ \times\ 20 \\ \hline \end{array}$ 5. $\begin{array}{r} \$0.85 \\ \times\ 80 \\ \hline \end{array}$

6. $\begin{array}{r} 56 \\ \times\ 50 \\ \hline \end{array}$ 7. $\begin{array}{r} 49 \\ \times\ 40 \\ \hline \end{array}$ 8. $\begin{array}{r} 78 \\ \times\ 60 \\ \hline \end{array}$ 9. $\begin{array}{r} \$0.32 \\ \times\ 20 \\ \hline \end{array}$ 10. $\begin{array}{r} \$0.95 \\ \times\ 70 \\ \hline \end{array}$

11. $\begin{array}{r} 424 \\ \times\ 20 \\ \hline \end{array}$ 12. $\begin{array}{r} 627 \\ \times\ 30 \\ \hline \end{array}$ 13. $\begin{array}{r} 749 \\ \times\ 90 \\ \hline \end{array}$ 14. $\begin{array}{r} \$8.07 \\ \times\ 70 \\ \hline \end{array}$ 15. $\begin{array}{r} \$5.60 \\ \times\ 60 \\ \hline \end{array}$

16. $\begin{array}{r} 294 \\ \times\ 50 \\ \hline \end{array}$ 17. $\begin{array}{r} 678 \\ \times\ 70 \\ \hline \end{array}$ 18. $\begin{array}{r} 831 \\ \times\ 90 \\ \hline \end{array}$ 19. $\begin{array}{r} \$4.54 \\ \times\ 20 \\ \hline \end{array}$ 20. $\begin{array}{r} \$8.96 \\ \times\ 30 \\ \hline \end{array}$

21. $\begin{array}{r} 39 \\ \times\ 40 \\ \hline \end{array}$ 22. $\begin{array}{r} 428 \\ \times\ 20 \\ \hline \end{array}$ 23. $\begin{array}{r} 697 \\ \times\ 10 \\ \hline \end{array}$ 24. $\begin{array}{r} \$0.86 \\ \times\ 50 \\ \hline \end{array}$ 25. $\begin{array}{r} \$0.44 \\ \times\ 70 \\ \hline \end{array}$

26. $\begin{array}{r} 726 \\ \times\ 80 \\ \hline \end{array}$ 27. $\begin{array}{r} 840 \\ \times\ 90 \\ \hline \end{array}$ 28. $\begin{array}{r} 73 \\ \times\ 50 \\ \hline \end{array}$ 29. $\begin{array}{r} \$4.07 \\ \times\ 60 \\ \hline \end{array}$ 30. $\begin{array}{r} \$8.26 \\ \times\ 30 \\ \hline \end{array}$

Solve Problems

31. There are 24 striped scarves in a box. There are 50 boxes. How many scarves are there altogether?

32. Adam's Department Store orders 30 boxes of wool scarves. There are 144 scarves in each box. How many scarves does the store order?

Something Extra
Non-Routine Problem

Unscramble. [Hint: These words are used in mathematics.]

umpltily   rotcaf   enddad   iiidvson   cartstub

dropcut   mus   veslo   dda

MULTIPLYING 2-DIGIT NUMBERS

Multiply 48 × 76.

Step 1	Step 2	Step 3
MULTIPLY BY ONES	MULTIPLY BY TENS	ADD

Step 1

MULTIPLY BY ONES

```
    76
  × 48
   608
```

Step 2

MULTIPLY BY TENS

```
    76
  × 48
   608
  3040
```
↑
Place a zero here.

Step 3

ADD

```
     76
   × 48
    608
 + 3040
  3,648
```

Study and Learn

A. Find 63 × 47. Complete.

1. Multiply by ones.
  3 × 47 = __?__

2. Multiply by tens.
  60 × 47 = __?__

3. Add to find the product.
  141 + 2,820 = __?__

WRITE

```
     2
    47
  × 63
   141
```

```
    47
  × 63
   141
 + 2820
  2,961
```

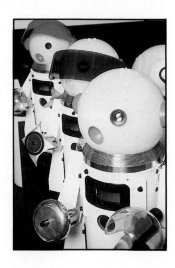

B. Complete.

4.	**5.**	**6.**	**7.**	**8.**
74	96	87	$0.35	$0.46
× 23	× 34	× 56	× 79	× 33
222	384	522		
+ 1 480	0			

C. Multiply.

9.	**10.**	**11.**	**12.**	**13.**
21	75	38	$0.16	$0.44
× 12	× 25	× 27	× 18	× 44

Practice

Multiply.

1. 87
   × 11

2. 24
   × 21

3. 33
   × 13

4. 42
   × 12

5. 31
   × 32

6. 21
   × 27

7. 33
   × 21

8. 44
   × 22

9. 18
   × 11

10. 73
    × 22

11. 97
    × 48

12. 65
    × 23

13. 87
    × 12

14. 25
    × 25

15. 86
    × 68

16. 67
    × 58

17. 56
    × 32

18. 78
    × 52

19. 28
    × 85

20. 68
    × 98

21. $0.49
    × 23

22. $0.73
    × 25

23. $0.48
    × 37

24. $0.65
    × 83

25. $0.18
    × 99

26. 44
    × 22

27. 78
    × 26

28. $0.56
    × 37

29. 19
    × 34

30. $0.89
    × 25

31. $0.56
    × 29

32. 61
    × 48

33. $0.34
    × 22

34. $0.97
    × 65

35. 36
    × 54

Solve Problems

36. There are 36 robots. Each robot has 24 switches. How many switches are there in all?

37. Frank wrote 18 programs for each computer. There are 16 computers. How many programs did Frank write?

38. A standard computer costs $742. The deluxe model costs $1,025. How much more does the deluxe model cost?

39. There are 4 computers for 36 students. How many students should be assigned to each computer?

MULTIPLYING LARGER NUMBERS

Multiply 23 × 789.

Step 1	Step 2	Step 3
MULTIPLY BY ONES	MULTIPLY BY TENS	ADD

$$\begin{array}{r} 789 \\ \times\ 23 \\ \hline 2367 \end{array}$$

$$\begin{array}{r} 789 \\ \times\ 23 \\ \hline 2367 \\ 15780 \end{array}$$

$$\begin{array}{r} 789 \\ \times\ 23 \\ \hline 2367 \\ +\ 15780 \\ \hline 18{,}147 \end{array}$$

Study and Learn

A. Find 45 × 123. Complete.

   1. Multiply by ones.
      5 × 123 = ___?___

   2. Multiply by tens.
      40 × 123 = ___?___

   3. Add to find the product.
      615 + 4,920 = ___?___

WRITE

$$\begin{array}{r} 123 \\ \times\ 45 \\ \hline 615 \end{array}$$

$$\begin{array}{r} 123 \\ \times\ 45 \\ \hline 615 \\ +\ 4920 \\ \hline 5{,}535 \end{array}$$

B. Complete.

4.
$$\begin{array}{r} 723 \\ \times\ 32 \\ \hline 1\,446 \\ +\ 21\,690 \\ \hline \end{array}$$

5.
$$\begin{array}{r} 478 \\ \times\ 21 \\ \hline 478 \\ 0 \\ \hline \end{array}$$

6.
$$\begin{array}{r} 735 \\ \times\ 15 \\ \hline 3\,675 \\ \hline \end{array}$$

7.
$$\begin{array}{r} \$4.82 \\ \times\ 37 \\ \hline \end{array}$$

C. Multiply.

8.
$$\begin{array}{r} 423 \\ \times\ 32 \\ \hline \end{array}$$

9.
$$\begin{array}{r} 724 \\ \times\ 21 \\ \hline \end{array}$$

10.
$$\begin{array}{r} 879 \\ \times\ 45 \\ \hline \end{array}$$

11.
$$\begin{array}{r} \$6.96 \\ \times\ 67 \\ \hline \end{array}$$

Practice

Multiply.

1. $\begin{array}{r} 113 \\ \times\ 23 \\ \hline \end{array}$
2. $\begin{array}{r} 412 \\ \times\ 21 \\ \hline \end{array}$
3. $\begin{array}{r} 613 \\ \times\ 32 \\ \hline \end{array}$
4. $\begin{array}{r} 876 \\ \times\ 11 \\ \hline \end{array}$
5. $\begin{array}{r} 421 \\ \times\ 32 \\ \hline \end{array}$

6. $\begin{array}{r} 104 \\ \times\ 12 \\ \hline \end{array}$
7. $\begin{array}{r} 333 \\ \times\ 22 \\ \hline \end{array}$
8. $\begin{array}{r} 611 \\ \times\ 56 \\ \hline \end{array}$
9. $\begin{array}{r} 912 \\ \times\ 44 \\ \hline \end{array}$
10. $\begin{array}{r} 202 \\ \times\ 34 \\ \hline \end{array}$

11. $\begin{array}{r} 976 \\ \times\ 48 \\ \hline \end{array}$
12. $\begin{array}{r} 891 \\ \times\ 59 \\ \hline \end{array}$
13. $\begin{array}{r} 902 \\ \times\ 68 \\ \hline \end{array}$
14. $\begin{array}{r} 547 \\ \times\ 27 \\ \hline \end{array}$
15. $\begin{array}{r} 644 \\ \times\ 66 \\ \hline \end{array}$

16. $\begin{array}{r} 967 \\ \times\ 27 \\ \hline \end{array}$
17. $\begin{array}{r} 296 \\ \times\ 54 \\ \hline \end{array}$
18. $\begin{array}{r} 388 \\ \times\ 27 \\ \hline \end{array}$
19. $\begin{array}{r} 963 \\ \times\ 94 \\ \hline \end{array}$
20. $\begin{array}{r} 868 \\ \times\ 78 \\ \hline \end{array}$

21. $\begin{array}{r} \$1.87 \\ \times\ 23 \\ \hline \end{array}$
22. $\begin{array}{r} \$4.99 \\ \times\ 32 \\ \hline \end{array}$
23. $\begin{array}{r} \$9.84 \\ \times\ 56 \\ \hline \end{array}$
24. $\begin{array}{r} \$4.75 \\ \times\ 26 \\ \hline \end{array}$
25. $\begin{array}{r} \$7.87 \\ \times\ 19 \\ \hline \end{array}$

26. $\begin{array}{r} \$8.76 \\ \times\ 54 \\ \hline \end{array}$
27. $\begin{array}{r} \$3.98 \\ \times\ 79 \\ \hline \end{array}$
28. $\begin{array}{r} \$8.62 \\ \times\ 96 \\ \hline \end{array}$
29. $\begin{array}{r} \$9.87 \\ \times\ 43 \\ \hline \end{array}$
30. $\begin{array}{r} \$2.88 \\ \times\ 67 \\ \hline \end{array}$

31. $\begin{array}{r} 501 \\ \times\ 34 \\ \hline \end{array}$
32. $\begin{array}{r} 748 \\ \times\ 56 \\ \hline \end{array}$
33. $\begin{array}{r} \$2.45 \\ \times\ 53 \\ \hline \end{array}$
34. $\begin{array}{r} 486 \\ \times\ 75 \\ \hline \end{array}$
35. $\begin{array}{r} \$6.42 \\ \times\ 74 \\ \hline \end{array}$

36. $\begin{array}{r} \$2.27 \\ \times\ 66 \\ \hline \end{array}$
37. $\begin{array}{r} 794 \\ \times\ 59 \\ \hline \end{array}$
38. $\begin{array}{r} \$3.89 \\ \times\ 54 \\ \hline \end{array}$
39. $\begin{array}{r} 223 \\ \times\ 32 \\ \hline \end{array}$
40. $\begin{array}{r} \$1.24 \\ \times\ 22 \\ \hline \end{array}$

Solve Problems

41. Skyline Drive Center contains 12 office buildings. There are 225 people working in each building. How many people work at Skyline Drive Center?

42. There are 144 offices at the Pearson Building. There are 25 people in each office. How many people are in the Pearson Building?

Problem-Solving Applications
Career

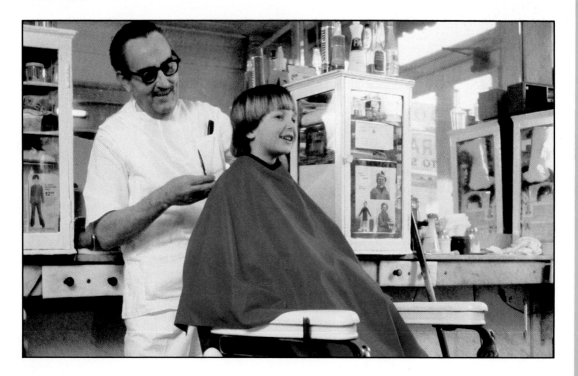

Estimate to solve.

1. Mr. O'Hara can do 16 haircuts a day.
   About how many can he do in 6 days?

2. Mrs. Taber can do 21 haircuts a day.
   She works 5 days a week. About how many
   haircuts does she do in a week?

3. Mr. Osborne sells hair rinse for $1.98 a bottle.
   He sold 8 bottles. About how much did he receive?

4. Mr. Anderson spends $4.95 for a haircut once a month.
   How much does he spend in 6 months?

5. Miss Ortwein pays a helper $3.95 an hour to sweep
   the shop. About how much does she pay for 5 hours' work?

Chapter Review

Multiply.

1. 10	**2.** 1,000	**3.** 82	**4.** 78	**5.** 412
(177) × 9	*(177)* × 6	*(178)* × 4	*(178)* × 6	*(180)* × 3

6. 371	**7.** 3,203	**8.** 7,604	**9.** $1.78	**10.** $43.78
(180) × 5	*(182)* × 3	*(182)* × 9	*(184)* × 8	*(184)* × 6

11. 200	**12.** 80	**13.** 74	**14.** 749	**15.** 64
(192) × 60	*(192)* × 70	*(194)* × 20	*(194)* × 50	*(196)* × 72

16. $0.68	**17.** 48	**18.** 876	**19.** 432	**20.** $2.76
(196) × 45	*(196)* × 66	*(198)* × 13	*(198)* × 64	*(198)* × 78

Estimate each product. *(190)*

21. 21	**22.** 450	**23.** $6.98
× 8	× 7	× 9

Which number sentence fits the problem? *(188)*

24. There are 123 flowers. There are 3 flowers in each vase.
How many flower vases are needed?

$$123 - 3 = \underline{\quad?\quad} \qquad 123 + 3 = \underline{\quad?\quad} \qquad 123 \div 3 = \underline{\quad?\quad}$$

Estimate to solve. *(200)*

25. There are 25 ornaments in each box. There are
7 boxes. About how many ornaments are there in all?

Chapter Test

Multiply.

1. 1,000	**2.** 10	**3.** 91	**4.** 46	**5.** 619
(177) <u>× 7</u>	(177) <u>× 8</u>	(178) <u>× 5</u>	(178) <u>× 7</u>	(180) <u>× 4</u>

6. 793	**7.** 1,243	**8.** 6,798	**9.** $0.86	**10.** $33.95
(180) <u>× 8</u>	(182) <u>× 2</u>	(182) <u>× 5</u>	(184) <u>× 8</u>	(184) <u>× 4</u>

11. 6,000	**12.** 300	**13.** 38	**14.** $6.94	**15.** 79
(192) <u>× 20</u>	(192) <u>× 70</u>	(194) <u>× 90</u>	(194) <u>× 40</u>	(196) <u>× 86</u>

16. $0.94	**17.** 64	**18.** 428	**19.** $6.95	**20.** 694
(196) <u>× 23</u>	(196) <u>× 31</u>	(198) <u>× 27</u>	(198) <u>× 49</u>	(198) <u>× 38</u>

Estimate each product. *(190)*

21. 41	**22.** 137	**23.** $0.88
<u>× 7</u>	<u>× 5</u>	<u>× 6</u>

Which number sentence fits the problem? *(188)*

24. A train ticket cost $1.35. The conductor sold 5 tickets. How much did the tickets cost in all?

$1.35 × 5 = \underline{\quad?\quad}$ $1.35 − 5 = \underline{\quad?\quad}$ $1.35 ÷ 5 = \underline{\quad?\quad}$

Estimate to solve. *(200)*

25. There are 46 rows in a theater. There are 9 people in each row. About how many people are at the theater?

202

Skills Check

1.

$$\begin{array}{r} 329 \\ + 276 \end{array}$$

A 525

B 595

C 605

D 615

2.

$$\begin{array}{r} 403 \\ 311 \\ + 245 \end{array}$$

E 769

F 850

G 948

H 959

3.

$$\begin{array}{r} 243 \\ 225 \\ + 144 \end{array}$$

A 512

B 572

C 602

D 612

4.

$$\begin{array}{r} 724 \\ - 297 \end{array}$$

E 427

F 436

G 455

H 490

5. $6 \times 7 = \underline{}$

A 42

B 49

C 63

D 72

6.

$$\begin{array}{r} 8 \\ \times 4 \end{array}$$

E 24

F 28

G 32

H 48

7.

$$\begin{array}{r} 42 \\ \times 3 \end{array}$$

A 45

B 84

C 126

D 160

8.

$$\begin{array}{r} 213 \\ \times 3 \end{array}$$

E 426

F 639

G 669

H 749

9.

$$\begin{array}{r} 10 \\ \times 3 \end{array}$$

A 3

B 10

C 30

D 300

10. $36 \div 6 = \underline{}$

E 4

F 6

G 7

H 8

11.

$3\overline{)39}$

A 6

B 12

C 13

D 14

12.

$10\overline{)70}$

E 7

F 0.7

G 70

H 700

Sailing off the shore at Newport, Rhode Island.

COMPUTER—GRAPHICS

Computer pictures are called **graphics.** The screen is divided into small blocks. To show a graphic, tell the computer to light up some blocks.

The blocks are named by their column and row numbers. The green block is in column 8, row 4. It is numbered 8,4.

This program tells the computer to draw the lines for tic-tac-toe.

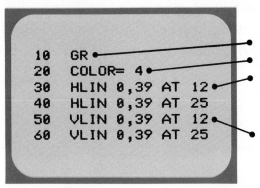

This program tells the computer to

go into graphics.
set the color to dark green.
light a horizontal row of blocks from column 0 to column 39 in row 12.
light a vertical column of blocks from row 0 to row 39 in column 12.

```
10   GR
20   COLOR= 4
30   HLIN 0,39 AT 12
40   HLIN 0,39 AT 25
50   VLIN 0,39 AT 12
60   VLIN 0,39 AT 25
```

Study and Learn

1. What does line 40 make the computer do?

2. What does line 60 make the computer do?

★3. Write a line 35 to make the computer light a horizontal row from column 4 to column 6 in row 3.

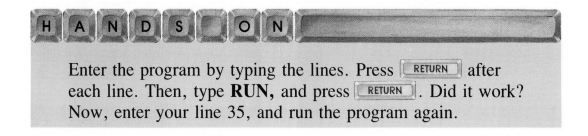

Enter the program by typing the lines. Press ⎡RETURN⎤ after each line. Then, type **RUN,** and press ⎡RETURN⎤. Did it work? Now, enter your line 35, and run the program again.

SPECIAL QUOTIENTS

Look for patterns. Compare zeros in the quotient and dividend.

$$\begin{array}{r} 20 \\ 3\overline{)60} \end{array} \qquad \begin{array}{r} 200 \\ 3\overline{)600} \end{array} \qquad \begin{array}{r} 2,000 \\ 3\overline{)6,000} \end{array}$$

Study and Learn

A. Find $4,000 \div 5$. Complete.

1. Divide. $40 \div 5 = \underline{\ ?\ }$

$$\begin{array}{r} 800 \\ 5\overline{)4,000} \end{array}$$

2. How many zeros are left in the dividend? Put the same number of zeros in the quotient.

3. Check. $800 \times 5 = \underline{\ ?\ }$

B. Divide.

4. $3\overline{)900}$ **5.** $6\overline{)360}$ **6.** $2\overline{)1,200}$ **7.** $4\overline{)2,000}$

Practice

Divide.

1. $2\overline{)40}$ **2.** $4\overline{)80}$ **3.** $3\overline{)120}$ **4.** $5\overline{)150}$ **5.** $9\overline{)270}$

6. $6\overline{)1,800}$ **7.** $5\overline{)1,000}$ **8.** $6\overline{)3,600}$ ★**9.** $3\overline{)120,000}$

Solve Problems

10. Jim bought 3 packages of balloons. There were the same number of balloons in each package. How many balloons were in each package if Jim had 90 balloons?

11. Pat had 140 balloons. She wanted to decorate 7 tables with the same number of balloons. How many balloons did she use to decorate each table?

REMAINDERS

There are 3 steps in division. Use the steps to find $3\overline{)17}$.

Step 1   Estimate

How many 3's in 17?

$3\overline{)17}$

Think: $4 \times 3 = 12$ 15 is the largest
$5 \times 3 = 15$ product less than 17.
$6 \times 3 = 18$ Write **5** in the ones
place.

Step 2   Multiply

$5 \times 3 = 15$

$$\begin{array}{r} 5 \\ 3\overline{)17} \\ 15 \end{array}$$

Step 3   Subtract

$17 - 15 = 2$

$$\begin{array}{r} 5\,r\,2 \\ 3\overline{)\ 17} \\ -15 \\ \hline 2 \end{array}$$

The quotient is 5.
The remainder is 2.

Check

$$\begin{array}{r} 5 \\ \times 3 \\ \hline 15 \\ + 2 \\ \hline 17 \end{array}$$

Study and Learn

A. Divide and check.

1. $3\overline{)8}$ **2.** $8\overline{)19}$ **3.** $6\overline{)17}$ **4.** $4\overline{)27}$ **5.** $8\overline{)44}$

▶ The remainder must always be less than the divisor.

B. Correct if the remainders are too large.

Example

$$\begin{array}{r} 5\,r\,9 \\ 8\overline{)49} \\ -40 \\ \hline 9 \end{array}$$
← Remainder is
too large.
Try 6.

$$\begin{array}{r} 6\,r\,1 \\ 8\overline{)49} \\ -48 \\ \hline 1 \end{array}$$

6. $\overset{6\,r\,5}{4\overline{)29}}$ **7.** $\overset{5\,r\,6}{7\overline{)41}}$ **8.** $\overset{7\,r\,6}{6\overline{)48}}$ **9.** $\overset{7\,r\,10}{7\overline{)59}}$

Practice

Divide.

1. $5\overline{)8}$ 2. $4\overline{)6}$ 3. $3\overline{)8}$ 4. $7\overline{)9}$ 5. $2\overline{)3}$

6. $3\overline{)7}$ 7. $5\overline{)9}$ 8. $8\overline{)9}$ 9. $2\overline{)7}$ 10. $4\overline{)9}$

11. $6\overline{)7}$ 12. $4\overline{)5}$ 13. $2\overline{)9}$ 14. $3\overline{)4}$ 15. $2\overline{)5}$

16. $7\overline{)8}$ 17. $6\overline{)9}$ 18. $5\overline{)6}$ 19. $6\overline{)8}$ 20. $5\overline{)7}$

21. $8\overline{)38}$ 22. $7\overline{)46}$ 23. $8\overline{)21}$ 24. $4\overline{)23}$ 25. $7\overline{)15}$

26. $3\overline{)25}$ 27. $5\overline{)36}$ 28. $9\overline{)20}$ 29. $5\overline{)43}$ 30. $5\overline{)23}$

31. $7\overline{)32}$ 32. $8\overline{)43}$ 33. $6\overline{)22}$ 34. $8\overline{)37}$ 35. $5\overline{)32}$

36. $9\overline{)50}$ 37. $7\overline{)50}$ 38. $9\overline{)24}$ 39. $7\overline{)67}$ 40. $6\overline{)34}$

41. $7\overline{)12}$ 42. $3\overline{)5}$ 43. $4\overline{)7}$ 44. $5\overline{)24}$ 45. $8\overline{)23}$

46. $6\overline{)37}$ 47. $5\overline{)21}$ 48. $8\overline{)46}$ 49. $3\overline{)23}$ 50. $8\overline{)20}$

Solve.

★ 51. $8 \div \square = 2$ ★ 52. $\square \div 2 = 3 \, r \, 1$

Solve Problems

53. There are 9 books.
There are 6 students.
How many books for
each student?
How many books left?

54. Each team has 4 players.
Ten people want to play.
How many teams can be
formed?
How many people will be
substitutes?

2-DIGIT QUOTIENTS

Find $2 \overline{)87}$.

Estimate: How many **2**'s in **8**?
Think: $4 \times 2 = 8$
Write the **4** in the tens place.

$$\begin{array}{r} 4 \\ 2\overline{)87} \\ -8\downarrow \\ \hline 07 \end{array}$$

Multiply: $4 \times 2 = 8$

Subtract: $8 - 8 = 0$
Bring down the 7.

$$\begin{array}{r} 4 \\ 2\overline{)87} \\ 8 \\ \hline 7 \end{array}$$

Repeat the steps.
Estimate: How many **2**'s in **7**?
Think: $\underline{\quad ? \quad} \times 2$ is about 7.
Try **3** in the ones place.

$$\begin{array}{r} 4\,3\,r\,1 \\ 2\overline{)87} \\ 8 \\ \hline 7 \\ -6 \\ \hline 1 \end{array}$$

Multiply: $3 \times 2 = 6$
Subtract: $7 - 6 = 1$
The quotient is 43.
The remainder is 1.

Check
$$\begin{array}{r} 43 \\ \times\, 2 \\ \hline 86 \\ +\, 1 \\ \hline 87 \end{array}$$

Study and Learn

A. Complete.

1. $\begin{array}{r} 22 \\ 3\overline{)66} \\ -6 \\ \hline 6 \end{array}$
2. $\begin{array}{r} 1 \\ 4\overline{)57} \\ -4 \\ \hline 17 \end{array}$
3. $\begin{array}{r} 2 \\ 2\overline{)49} \\ -4 \\ \hline \end{array}$
4. $5\overline{)59}$
5. $6\overline{)84}$

B. Divide.

6. $7\overline{)84}$
7. $6\overline{)74}$
8. $5\overline{)57}$
9. $3\overline{)68}$
10. $2\overline{)97}$

Practice

Divide.

1. $2\overline{)48}$ 2. $3\overline{)39}$ 3. $4\overline{)44}$ 4. $2\overline{)24}$ 5. $3\overline{)36}$

6. $5\overline{)55}$ 7. $4\overline{)84}$ 8. $3\overline{)96}$ 9. $2\overline{)68}$ 10. $6\overline{)66}$

11. $6\overline{)68}$ 12. $7\overline{)79}$ 13. $3\overline{)67}$ 14. $4\overline{)87}$ 15. $2\overline{)63}$

16. $5\overline{)58}$ 17. $3\overline{)94}$ 18. $5\overline{)56}$ 19. $6\overline{)69}$ 20. $2\overline{)87}$

21. $4\overline{)57}$ 22. $6\overline{)73}$ 23. $8\overline{)90}$ 24. $7\overline{)86}$ 25. $3\overline{)88}$

26. $7\overline{)94}$ 27. $5\overline{)67}$ 28. $4\overline{)79}$ 29. $5\overline{)83}$ 30. $8\overline{)94}$

31. $3\overline{)63}$ 32. $2\overline{)84}$ 33. $4\overline{)97}$ 34. $6\overline{)86}$ 35. $4\overline{)86}$

36. $4\overline{)48}$ 37. $3\overline{)66}$ 38. $7\overline{)78}$ 39. $5\overline{)57}$ 40. $6\overline{)84}$

Solve.

★41. $5\overline{)}$ with quotient 11 over $?$

★42. $4\overline{)}$ with quotient 12 over $?$

Solve Problems

43. The teacher has 88 pieces of art paper. 5 students share the paper equally. How many pieces will each student get? How many are left over?

44. The teacher gave out all 88 pieces of art paper. Each student got 8 pieces of paper. How many students got art paper?

MORE 2-DIGIT QUOTIENTS

Find $3\overline{)158}$.

$3\overline{)158}$

Estimate: How many 3's in 1? None

How many 3's in 15?
Write the **5** in the tens place.

$$\begin{array}{r} 5 \\ 3\overline{)158} \\ -15\downarrow \\ \hline 08 \end{array}$$

Multiply: $5 \times 3 = 15$
Subtract: $15 - 15 = 0$
Bring down the 8.

$$\begin{array}{r} 5 \\ 3\overline{)158} \\ 15 \\ \hline 8 \end{array}$$

Repeat the steps.
Estimate: How many 3's in 8?
Think: $\underline{\quad?\quad} \times 3$ is about 8.
Try **2** in the ones place.

$$\begin{array}{r} 5\mathbf{2}\,r2 \\ 3\overline{)158} \\ 15 \\ \hline 8 \\ -6 \\ \hline 2 \end{array}$$

Multiply and **subtract.**

The quotient is 52.
The remainder is 2.
Check: $52 \times 3 = 156$ $156 + 2 = 158$

Study and Learn

A. Find $3\overline{)269}$. Complete.

1. Estimate: How many 3's in 2? $3\overline{)269}$

How many 3's in 26? $3\overline{)269}$

2. Multiply: $8 \times 3 = \underline{\quad?\quad}$

$$\begin{array}{r} 8 \\ 3\overline{)269} \\ -24 \end{array}$$

3. Complete the division.

4. Check.

B. Divide.

5. $4\overline{)168}$ **6.** $2\overline{)168}$ **7.** $5\overline{)158}$ **8.** $3\overline{)134}$

Practice

Divide.

1. $6\overline{)126}$ 2. $5\overline{)105}$ 3. $4\overline{)164}$ 4. $3\overline{)156}$ 5. $2\overline{)148}$

6. $9\overline{)189}$ 7. $3\overline{)159}$ 8. $2\overline{)164}$ 9. $6\overline{)186}$ 10. $3\overline{)129}$

11. $7\overline{)149}$ 12. $4\overline{)167}$ 13. $3\overline{)155}$ 14. $2\overline{)163}$ 15. $7\overline{)148}$

16. $2\overline{)127}$ 17. $8\overline{)169}$ 18. $7\overline{)218}$ 19. $8\overline{)249}$ 20. $5\overline{)206}$

21. $3\overline{)148}$ 22. $6\overline{)139}$ 23. $4\overline{)179}$ 24. $8\overline{)137}$ 25. $2\overline{)113}$

26. $5\overline{)163}$ 27. $4\overline{)195}$ 28. $3\overline{)134}$ 29. $8\overline{)253}$ 30. $9\overline{)192}$

31. $6\overline{)246}$ 32. $4\overline{)173}$ 33. $5\overline{)205}$ 34. $6\overline{)249}$ 35. $7\overline{)147}$

36. $5\overline{)255}$ 37. $7\overline{)287}$ 38. $8\overline{)632}$ 39. $7\overline{)243}$ 40. $8\overline{)168}$

Solve.

★ 41. $672 \div \square = 96$ ★ 42. $249 \div \square = 83$

Solve Problems

43. There are 186 marbles. A team of 6 players wants to share them equally. How many marbles should each player get? How many marbles will be left over?

44. A team of 8 players wants to share 186 marbles. How many marbles should each player get? How many marbles will be left over?

45. A game of checkers costs $5.75. About how much would 8 games cost?

213

3-DIGIT QUOTIENTS

Find $4\overline{)938}$.

Estimate: How many 4's in 9?
Think: __?__ × 4 is about 9.
Try **2** in the hundreds place.

$$
\begin{array}{r}
2 \\
4\overline{)938} \\
-8\downarrow \\
\hline
13
\end{array}
$$

Multiply: 2 × 4 = 8
Subtract: 9 − 8 = 1
Bring down the 3.

$$
\begin{array}{r}
23 \\
4\overline{)938} \\
8 \\
\hline
13
\end{array}
$$

Repeat the steps.
Estimate: How many 4's in 13?
Think: __?__ × 4 is about 13.
Try **3** in the tens place.

$$
\begin{array}{r}
234\,r2 \\
4\overline{)938} \\
8 \\
\hline
13 \\
-12\downarrow \\
\hline
18 \\
-16 \\
\hline
2
\end{array}
$$

Multiply and **subtract.**
Bring down the 8.
Estimate, multiply, and **subtract**
to complete.
The quotient is 234.
The remainder is 2.

Check: 234 × 4 = 936   936 + 2 = 938

Study and Learn

A. Complete.

1.
$$
\begin{array}{r}
13 \\
3\overline{)396} \\
-3 \\
\hline
9
\end{array}
$$

2.
$$
\begin{array}{r}
1 \\
4\overline{)736} \\
-4 \\
\hline
3
\end{array}
$$

3.
$$
\begin{array}{r}
1 \\
6\overline{)921} \\
-6 \\
\hline
\end{array}
$$

4. $5\overline{)587}$

B. Divide.

5. $6\overline{)684}$ **6.** $4\overline{)846}$ **7.** $7\overline{)836}$ **8.** $4\overline{)525}$

Practice

Divide.

1. $6\overline{)684}$ 2. $4\overline{)864}$ 3. $2\overline{)648}$ 4. $3\overline{)936}$ 5. $5\overline{)565}$

6. $3\overline{)423}$ 7. $8\overline{)928}$ 8. $7\overline{)847}$ 9. $8\overline{)968}$ 10. $6\overline{)834}$

11. $3\overline{)687}$ 12. $4\overline{)845}$ 13. $2\overline{)643}$ 14. $5\overline{)582}$ 15. $7\overline{)783}$

16. $3\overline{)958}$ 17. $4\overline{)463}$ 18. $6\overline{)683}$ 19. $8\overline{)987}$ 20. $2\overline{)863}$

21. $3\overline{)784}$ 22. $5\overline{)832}$ 23. $8\overline{)923}$ 24. $6\overline{)847}$ 25. $3\overline{)544}$

26. $5\overline{)692}$ 27. $3\overline{)484}$ 28. $2\overline{)583}$ 29. $4\overline{)982}$ 30. $3\overline{)784}$

31. $3\overline{)639}$ 32. $4\overline{)848}$ 33. $3\overline{)728}$ 34. $4\overline{)928}$ 35. $5\overline{)857}$

36. $2\overline{)842}$ 37. $6\overline{)695}$ 38. $3\overline{)485}$ 39. $5\overline{)556}$ 40. $4\overline{)846}$

★41. $848 \div 4 = \underline{\ ?\ }$ ★42. $326 \div 2 = \underline{\ ?\ }$

Solve Problems

43. Farmer Jones has 648 cattle. She places the same number of cattle into each of 4 pens. How many cattle are in each pen?

44. Jay has 5 shearing bins at his sheep ranch. He divides his 890 sheep equally among the bins. How many sheep are in each bin?

MORE 3-DIGIT QUOTIENTS

Find $3\overline{)1,478}$.

$$3\overline{)1,478}$$

Estimate: How many 3's in 1? None
How many 3's in 14?
Think: __?__ × 3 is about 14.
Try **4** in the hundreds place.

$$\begin{array}{r} 4 \\ 3\overline{)1,478} \\ -12\downarrow \\ \hline 27 \end{array}$$

Multiply and **subtract.**
Bring down the 7.

$$\begin{array}{r} 4 \\ 3\overline{)1,478} \\ 12 \\ \hline 27 \end{array}$$

Repeat the steps.
Estimate: How many 3's in 27?
Write **9** in the tens place.

$$\begin{array}{r} 4\,9\,2\,r2 \\ 3\overline{)1,478} \\ 12 \\ \hline 27 \\ -27\downarrow \\ \hline 8 \\ -6 \\ \hline 2 \end{array}$$

Multiply and **subtract.**
Bring down the 8.
Estimate, multiply, and **subtract**
to complete.
The quotient is 492.
The remainder is 2.

Check: 492 × 3 = 1,476   1,476 + 2 = 1,478

Study and Learn

A. Complete.

1. $\begin{array}{r} 3 \\ 3\overline{)1,165} \\ -9 \\ \hline 26 \end{array}$

2. $\begin{array}{r} 9 \\ 2\overline{)1,847} \\ -18 \\ \hline \end{array}$

3. $6\overline{)3,675}$

4. $5\overline{)4,387}$

B. Divide.

5. $4\overline{)3,687}$

6. $7\overline{)4,979}$

7. $3\overline{)2,214}$

8. $5\overline{)2,674}$

Practice

Divide.

1. $7\overline{)4,977}$ 2. $6\overline{)3,696}$ 3. $8\overline{)2,488}$ 4. $5\overline{)2,595}$

5. $6\overline{)3,744}$ 6. $5\overline{)2,435}$ 7. $9\overline{)2,943}$ 8. $8\overline{)2,528}$

9. $4\overline{)3,678}$ 10. $8\overline{)6,499}$ 11. $7\overline{)4,983}$ 12. $6\overline{)3,682}$

13. $5\overline{)2,563}$ 14. $3\overline{)2,194}$ 15. $6\overline{)3,073}$ 16. $8\overline{)2,497}$

17. $3\overline{)2,572}$ 18. $4\overline{)3,457}$ 19. $8\overline{)3,385}$ 20. $7\overline{)2,355}$

21. $9\overline{)3,751}$ 22. $5\overline{)3,182}$ 23. $6\overline{)3,754}$ 24. $8\overline{)2,852}$

25. $8\overline{)6,488}$ 26. $5\overline{)3,236}$ 27. $4\overline{)1,684}$ 28. $6\overline{)3,685}$

29. $6\overline{)5,493}$ 30. $5\overline{)3,095}$ 31. $4\overline{)3,264}$ 32. $5\overline{)4,369}$

★ 33. $11,486 \div 2 = \underline{\ ?\ }$ ★ 34. $16,843 \div 2 = \underline{\ ?\ }$

Solve Problems

35. A capping machine can cap 6 bottles in one minute. How many minutes does it take to cap 2,562 bottles?

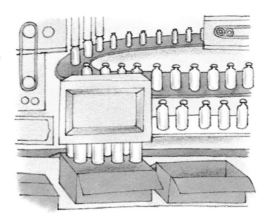

36. A packing machine places 8 bottles in each carton. How many cartons are needed for 2,760 bottles?

217

ZEROS IN THE QUOTIENT

Find $5\overline{)302}$.

$$5\overline{)302}$$

Estimate: How many 5's in 3? None
How many 5's in 30?
Write **6** in the tens place.

$$\begin{array}{r} 6 \\ 5\overline{)302} \\ -30\downarrow \\ \hline 02 \end{array}$$

Multiply and **subtract.**
Bring down the 2.

$$\begin{array}{r} 6\,0\,r2 \\ 5\overline{)302} \\ 30 \\ \hline 2 \end{array}$$

Repeat the steps.
Estimate: How many 5's in 2? None
Write **0** in the ones place.
The quotient is 60.
The remainder is 2.

Check: $60 \times 5 = 300 \qquad 300 + 2 = 302$

Study and Learn

A. Find $7\overline{)719}$.

1. **Estimate:** How many 7's in 7?
   Write __?__ in the hundreds place.

$$\begin{array}{r} 1\,0 \\ 7\overline{)719} \\ -7\downarrow \\ \hline 01 \end{array}$$

2. **Multiply** and **subtract.**
   Bring down the __?__ .

3. **Estimate:** How many 7's in 1?
   Write __?__ in the tens place.

4. Complete the division.

B. Complete.

5.
$$\begin{array}{r} 1 \\ 7\overline{)73} \\ -7 \\ \hline 3 \end{array}$$

6.
$$\begin{array}{r} 7 \\ 7\overline{)496} \\ -49 \\ \hline 6 \end{array}$$

7.
$$\begin{array}{r} 1 \\ 8\overline{)807} \\ -8 \\ \hline \end{array}$$

8. $7\overline{)2,124}$

Practice

Divide.

1. $5)\overline{51}$ 2. $6)\overline{65}$ 3. $4)\overline{82}$ 4. $2)\overline{62}$

5. $6)\overline{361}$ 6. $8)\overline{245}$ 7. $7)\overline{283}$ 8. $8)\overline{642}$

9. $3)\overline{242}$ 10. $7)\overline{216}$ 11. $3)\overline{272}$ 12. $5)\overline{254}$

13. $2)\overline{207}$ 14. $3)\overline{302}$ 15. $4)\overline{831}$ 16. $4)\overline{435}$

17. $2)\overline{625}$ 18. $2)\overline{613}$ 19. $4)\overline{431}$ 20. $2)\overline{601}$

21. $5)\overline{1,507}$ 22. $3)\overline{1,222}$ 23. $6)\overline{3,651}$ 24. $7)\overline{2,151}$

25. $8)\overline{6,442}$ 26. $9)\overline{3,601}$ 27. $7)\overline{2,853}$ 28. $4)\overline{1,631}$

29. $4)\overline{1,642}$ 30. $5)\overline{1,582}$ 31. $6)\overline{3,665}$ 32. $7)\overline{2,172}$

33. $3)\overline{1,561}$ 34. $2)\overline{1,861}$ 35. $4)\overline{2,483}$ 36. $3)\overline{2,792}$

37. $4)\overline{163}$ 38. $5)\overline{2,542}$ 39. $6)\overline{3,664}$ 40. $7)\overline{2,875}$

41. $8)\overline{321}$ 42. $6)\overline{3,643}$ 43. $3)\overline{1,502}$ 44. $4)\overline{83}$

★ 45. $7)\overline{21,634}$ ★ 46. $8)\overline{32,728}$ ★ 47. $6)\overline{36,643}$

Solve Problems

48. There were 433 cars at a car wash.
    There were 8 adults washing cars.
    Each adult washed the same number of cars.
    How many cars did each adult wash?
    How many cars were left to be washed?

Midchapter Review

Divide.

1. $3\overline{)60}$ *(207)*

2. $4\overline{)160}$ *(207)*

3. $2\overline{)20}$ *(207)*

4. $3\overline{)8}$ *(208)*

5. $2\overline{)46}$ *(210)*

6. $4\overline{)63}$ *(210)*

7. $7\overline{)85}$ *(210)*

8. $4\overline{)168}$ *(212)*

9. $3\overline{)154}$ *(212)*

10. $8\overline{)256}$ *(212)*

11. $4\overline{)844}$ *(214)*

12. $6\overline{)684}$ *(214)*

13. $5\overline{)634}$ *(214)*

14. $8\overline{)2,488}$ *(216)*

15. $5\overline{)2,561}$ *(216)*

16. $5\overline{)3,236}$ *(216)*

17. $3\overline{)2,705}$ *(218)*

18. $6\overline{)65}$ *(218)*

19. $4\overline{)1,632}$ *(218)*

20. $9\overline{)8,142}$ *(218)*

Something Extra
Non-Routine Problems

Choose an answer on the right to complete each.

Example   B is to b as P is to __?__.
The answer is p.

l	m	l	p

1. R is to r as T is to __?__.

u	r	t	s

2. A is to C as B is to __?__.

b	D	d	B

3. Z is to ꙅ as C is to __?__.

ꟼ	ꓛ	ꙅ	ꓛ

4. a is to A as b is to __?__.

d	ꓭ	B	b

5. A is to B as C is to __?__.

c	d	C	D

220

Skills Review

Multiply.

1. 100 (177) × 8	**2.** 10 × 5	**3.** 1,000 × 6	**4.** 10 × 9
5. 43 (178) × 2	**6.** 24 × 4	**7.** 46 × 5	**8.** 87 × 6

9. 223 (180) × 3	**10.** 427 × 2	**11.** 634 × 5	**12.** 481 × 6	**13.** 563 × 4
14. 2,043 (182) × 2	**15.** 1,372 × 4	**16.** 3,812 × 3	**17.** 6,743 × 6	**18.** 8,275 × 7
19. $0.42 (184) × 2	**20.** $3.75 × 4	**21.** $29.87 × 6	**22.** 200 (177) × 6	**23.** 40 (192) × 30
24. 32 (196) × 23	**25.** 46 × 21	**26.** 85 × 63	**27.** 47 × 36	**28.** 97 × 38
29. 630 (198) × 23	**30.** 213 × 21	**31.** 769 × 87	**32.** 297 × 62	**33.** 859 (180) × 9

Something Extra
Non-Routine Problems

Change each letter to a number.
All the same letters must be the same number.
All different letters must be different numbers.

1.
```
  A
  A
+ A
----
 BA
```

2.
```
  GO
  GO
  GO
+ GO
----
 TG
```

3.
```
 WX
+ X
----
 XW
```

221

AVERAGES

Jean played 3 games of basketball.
Her **average** points scored was 20.

$$60 \div 3 = 20$$

↑   ↑   ↑

sum of all   number of   average
points   games   points

Game	Points
1	20
2	25
3	15

If she scored 20 points in each game,
her total would have been the same.

$$20 + 20 + 20 = 60$$

Study and Learn

A. Look at John's scores.

Game	Points
1	15
2	20
3	35
4	30

1. What was his highest score?

2. What was his lowest score?

3. Find the sum of all his scores.

4. How many games did he play?

5. Divide the sum by the number of games.
The quotient is the average points scored.

> Find the average by:
>
> • Finding the sum of the numbers
> • Dividing the sum by the number of addends

B. Find the average.

6. 7, 8, 9   **7.** 23, 47, 36, 54   **8.** 278, 246

Practice

Find the average.

1. 8, 4   **2.** 7, 9, 8   **3.** 8, 8, 8, 4

4. 24, 38   **5.** 76, 85, 94   **6.** 48, 76, 32, 100

7. 10, 100   **8.** 70, 70, 60, 60   **9.** 27, 54, 48

Computer

```
10   LET C = 0
20   LET S = 0
30   LET C = C + 1
40   PRINT "ENTER AN ADDEND"
50   INPUT A
60   LET S = S + A
70   PRINT "ANOTHER ADDEND? (Y OR N)"
80   INPUT A$
90   IF A$ = "Y" THEN 30
100  PRINT "THE AVERAGE IS ";S / C
```

This program finds averages.

This program starts by putting 0 in for C and S to clear the storage places. It asks you for an addend (lines 40 and 50). Then it asks if there are any more and loops back to line 30 to keep track of how many addends you entered. After all the addends are entered, it prints the average.

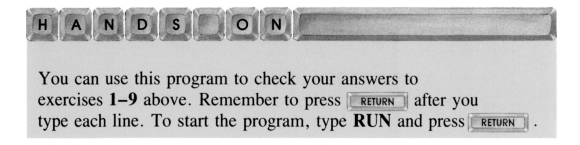

H A N D S   O N

You can use this program to check your answers to exercises **1–9** above. Remember to press RETURN after you type each line. To start the program, type **RUN** and press RETURN .

Problem-Solving Skills

Two-Step Problems

Sometimes it takes two steps to solve a problem.
Elva collects shells. She had 10 shells. She bought
6 more. Then she sold 9. How many shells are left?

What is asked? ———————→ How many shells are left?
What do you know? ———→ Had 10 shells.
                                Bought 6 more shells.
                                Sold 9 shells.
Which operation? ———————→ **Step 1** $10 + 6 = 16$ shells in all.
                                      Step 2 $16 - 9 = 7$ shells left.

There are 7 shells left.

Study and Learn

A. Solve.

David makes model cars. He bought two for $1.97 each,
and another for $2.75. How much did he spend in all?

1. **Step 1** $\$1.97 \times 2 =$ __?__

2. **Step 2** $\$3.94 + \$2.75 =$ __?__

3. David spent __?__ in all.

Practice

Solve.

1. Tom likes to read science fiction books. He has a new book that is 298 pages long. He read 64 pages the first day and 78 pages the second day. How many pages are left to read?

2. Michelle grows vegetables. Her garden had 27 green peppers and 18 red peppers. She gave away a total of 22 peppers. How many peppers are left in her garden now?

3. Kenny collects stamps. He had 3 albums of stamps. Each album had 147 stamps. Then he received another 15 stamps for his birthday. How many stamps does he have in his stamp collection?

4. Beverly paints pictures. She bought 6 jars of paint at $0.75 each and a brush for $1.63. How much did she spend on art supplies?

5. Jamal plays the piano. He practices 1 hour in the morning and 3 hours in the evening. He does this 7 days each week. How many hours does he practice each week?

6. Alfred bought 4 models for $1.75 each. He gave the clerk a $10 bill. How much change should he receive?

DIVIDING BY MULTIPLES OF 10

Find $30\overline{)270}$. **Estimate:** How many 30's in 2? None

$30\overline{)270}$ How many 30's in 27? None

$30\overline{)270}$ How many 30's in 270?
Think: How many 3's in 27?
Write **9** in the ones place.

$$\begin{array}{r} 9 \\ 30\overline{)270} \\ -270 \\ \hline 0 \end{array}$$

Multiply: $9 \times 30 = 270$
Subtract: $270 - 270 = 0$
The quotient is 9.

Study and Learn

A. Find $30\overline{)160}$. Complete.

1. **Estimate:** How many 30's in 160? $30\overline{)160}$
   Think: How many 3's in 16?
   Write 5 in the ones place.

2. **Multiply:** $5 \times 30 = \underline{\ ?\ }$ $\begin{array}{r} 5 \\ 30\overline{)160} \end{array}$
   Subtract to complete.

3. What is the quotient?

4. What is the remainder?

B. Divide.

5. $40\overline{)80}$ 6. $30\overline{)90}$ 7. $70\overline{)350}$ 8. $60\overline{)420}$

9. $20\overline{)70}$ 10. $40\overline{)90}$ 11. $70\overline{)500}$ 12. $90\overline{)100}$

13. $50\overline{)450}$ 14. $80\overline{)480}$ 15. $40\overline{)270}$ 16. $90\overline{)500}$

Practice

Divide.

1. $10\overline{)90}$ 2. $20\overline{)80}$ 3. $30\overline{)60}$ 4. $10\overline{)40}$

5. $30\overline{)90}$ 6. $40\overline{)80}$ 7. $20\overline{)60}$ 8. $10\overline{)50}$

9. $20\overline{)180}$ 10. $30\overline{)120}$ 11. $40\overline{)160}$ 12. $50\overline{)150}$

13. $60\overline{)240}$ 14. $70\overline{)140}$ 15. $80\overline{)160}$ 16. $30\overline{)150}$

17. $20\overline{)90}$ 18. $30\overline{)50}$ 19. $40\overline{)90}$ 20. $50\overline{)70}$

21. $30\overline{)80}$ 22. $20\overline{)50}$ 23. $60\overline{)90}$ 24. $70\overline{)80}$

25. $30\overline{)170}$ 26. $50\overline{)160}$ 27. $40\overline{)190}$ 28. $60\overline{)150}$

29. $70\overline{)160}$ 30. $20\overline{)150}$ 31. $80\overline{)180}$ 32. $30\overline{)130}$

33. $10\overline{)80}$ 34. $30\overline{)70}$ 35. $80\overline{)140}$ 36. $40\overline{)70}$

37. $70\overline{)130}$ 38. $50\overline{)90}$ 39. $60\overline{)590}$ 40. $30\overline{)120}$

Solve.

★ 41. $150 \div \square = 3$ ★ 42. $60 \div \square = 2$

Solve Problems

43. Janice took 100 photos. There were 20 photos on each roll of film. How many rolls of film did she use?

44. Each page of a photo album holds 10 photos. Brett has 50 photos. How many pages does he fill?

● 45. Wayne and Allan went to Mexico. Wayne took 130 pictures. Allan took 50 pictures. How many more pictures did Wayne take?

★ 46. Barbara has 2,800 slides. One tray holds 50 slides. How many trays does she need to hold all of the slides?

MORE DIVIDING BY MULTIPLES OF 10

Find $20\overline{)675}$.

Estimate: How many 20's in 6? None
How many 20's in 67?

$20\overline{)675}$

Think: How many 2's in 6?
Write **3** in the tens place.

$$
\begin{array}{r}
3 \\
20\overline{)675} \\
-60\downarrow \\
\hline
75
\end{array}
$$

Multiply and **subtract.**
Bring down the 5.

$$
\begin{array}{r}
3 \\
20\overline{)675} \\
60 \\
\hline
75
\end{array}
$$

Repeat the steps.
Estimate: How many 20's in 75?
Think: How many 2's in 7?
Try **3** in the ones place.

$$
\begin{array}{r}
33\,r15 \\
20\overline{)675} \\
60 \\
\hline
75 \\
-60 \\
\hline
15
\end{array}
$$

Multiply and **subtract.**
The quotient is 33.
The remainder is 15.

Check: $33 \times 20 = 660$ $\qquad$ $660 + 15 = 675$

Study and Learn

A. Complete.

1. $$
\begin{array}{r}
17 \\
10\overline{)176} \\
-10 \\
\hline
76
\end{array}
$$

2. $$
\begin{array}{r}
2 \\
40\overline{)987} \\
-80 \\
\hline
\end{array}
$$

3. $60\overline{)924}$

4. $90\overline{)999}$

B. Divide.

5. $20\overline{)680}$

6. $30\overline{)747}$

7. $50\overline{)774}$

8. $70\overline{)914}$

Practice

Divide.

1. $10\overline{)360}$
2. $20\overline{)640}$
3. $30\overline{)360}$
4. $20\overline{)480}$

5. $40\overline{)840}$
6. $50\overline{)550}$
7. $10\overline{)490}$
8. $60\overline{)660}$

9. $20\overline{)680}$
10. $30\overline{)960}$
11. $20\overline{)860}$
12. $10\overline{)980}$

13. $30\overline{)946}$
14. $20\overline{)284}$
15. $30\overline{)369}$
16. $50\overline{)554}$

17. $20\overline{)242}$
18. $30\overline{)693}$
19. $50\overline{)560}$
20. $70\overline{)720}$

21. $40\overline{)843}$
22. $60\overline{)670}$
23. $20\overline{)483}$
24. $30\overline{)640}$

25. $20\overline{)420}$
26. $30\overline{)630}$
27. $20\overline{)482}$
28. $30\overline{)930}$

29. $40\overline{)640}$
30. $50\overline{)510}$
31. $20\overline{)381}$
32. $70\overline{)710}$

★ 33. $30\overline{)1,624}$
★ 34. $50\overline{)1,560}$
★ 35. $70\overline{)1,407}$

Solve Problems

36. Hunt's Record Shop receives 640 records. The records are packed 20 to a box. How many boxes of records does the shop receive?

37. Mr. Hunt orders 230 phonograph needles. There are 10 phonograph needles in a case. How many cases does Mr. Hunt order?

DIVIDING MONEY

Divide 5)$7.70

Step 1

DIVIDE

$$
\begin{array}{r}
1\ 54 \\
5)\overline{\$7.70} \\
\underline{-5}\downarrow \\
2\ 7 \\
\underline{-2\ 5} \\
20 \\
\underline{-20} \\
0
\end{array}
$$

Step 2

PLACE MONEY NOTATION

$$
\begin{array}{r}
\$1.54 \\
5)\overline{\$7.70}
\end{array}
$$

Study and Learn

A. Divide.

1. 8)$0.80 → .10

2. 6)$0.78 → .1

3. 2)$2.32 → $1.

4. 3)$7.32

5. 3)$0.36

6. 5)$3.75

7. 7)$2.24

8. 4)$2.80

Practice

Divide.

1. 5)$0.95

2. 7)$0.56

3. 4)$0.32

4. 2)$0.98

5. 7)$6.65

6. 8)$1.52

7. 3)$1.44

8. 5)$1.75

9. 9)$19.53

★ **10.** 20)$18.60

★ **11.** 80)$4.80

Skills Review

Add.

1. 36
(53) + 3

2. 47
(56) + 12

3. 21
+ 49

4. 36
(53) + 8

5. 2
(54) 4
+ 6

6. 3
7
2
+ 3

7. 1
2
4
6
+ 2

8. 36
(56) 24
37
+ 21

9. 47
7
+ 36

10. 371
(58) 212
+ 31

11. 3,297
(60) + 1,863

12. 37,264
+ 13,192

13. $ 14.06
(70) 13.62
+ 12.23

Subtract.

14. 19
(82) − 6

15. 23
− 16

16. 37
− 29

17. 186
(84) − 135

18. 237
− 126

19. 247
− 188

20. 1,368
(86) − 237

21. 2,683
− 1,927

22. 36,427
− 12,384

23. 74,386
− 16,897

24. 306
(88) − 147

25. 2,600
− 387

26. 3,070
− 1,258

27. $ 3.68
(95) − 1.87

28. $ 26.75
− 13.97

Multiply.

29. 100
(177) × 7

30. 10
× 6

31. 1,000
× 5

32. 23
(178) × 3

33. 86
× 4

34. 123
(180) × 2

35. 343
× 4

36. 872
× 3

37. 3,213
(182) × 2

38. 6,813
× 4

39. $1.31
(184) × 4

40. $16.13
× 4

41. 300
(177) × 8

42. 2,000
× 8

43. 80
× 20

44. 44
(196) × 23

45. 62
× 37

46. 126
(198) × 24

47. 331
× 62

48. 203
× 15

TIME

60 seconds = 1 minute   7 days = 1 week

60 minutes = 1 hour   52 weeks = 1 year

24 hours = 1 day   365 days = 1 year

Study and Learn

A. Complete.
   How many seconds in 7 minutes?

   1. 1 minute = __?__ seconds

   2. 7 minutes = 7 × __?__ seconds

   3. 7 minutes = __?__ seconds

> Think: From **larger** unit to **smaller** unit, **multiply.**
> $$\begin{array}{r} 60 \\ \times 7 \\ \hline 420 \end{array}$$

B. Complete. Think larger unit to smaller unit.

   4. 3 hours = __?__ minutes   **5.** 4 days = __?__ hours

   6. 6 weeks = __?__ days   **7.** 3 years = __?__ weeks

   8. 2 years = __?__ days   **9.** 5 minutes = __?__ seconds

C. Complete.
   How many minutes in 480 seconds?

   10. 60 seconds = __?__ minutes

   11. 480 seconds = 480 ÷ __?__ seconds

   12. 480 seconds = __?__ minutes

> Think: From **smaller** unit to **larger** unit, **divide.**
> $$\begin{array}{r} 8 \\ 60)\overline{480} \\ -480 \\ \hline \end{array}$$

D. Complete. Think smaller unit to larger unit.

   13. 120 minutes = __?__ hours   **14.** 35 days = __?__ weeks

Practice

Complete.

1. 3 minutes = _?_ seconds

2. 4 hours = _?_ minutes

3. 3 days = _?_ hours

4. 5 weeks = _?_ days

5. 2 years = _?_ weeks

6. 3 years = _?_ days

7. 300 seconds = _?_ minutes

8. 480 minutes = _?_ hours

9. 28 days = _?_ weeks

10. 42 days = _?_ weeks

11. 7 hours = _?_ minutes

12. 360 seconds = _?_ minutes

13. 49 days = _?_ weeks

14. 2 days = _?_ hours

Solve Problems

15. Which is more, 65 seconds or 1 minute?

16. Which is more, 29 minutes or 1 hour?

17. Which is more, 25 hours or 1 day?

★18. A leap year has 366 days. This occurs every 4 years. 1988 is a leap year. Which is the next leap year?

★19. A decade is 10 years. How many decades in 80 years?

★20. A century is 100 years. How many years in 10 centuries?

★21. A fortnight is 14 days. How many days in 3 fortnights?

TWO-DIGIT DIVISION

Find $32\overline{)98}$. **Estimate:** How many 32's in 98?

Think: How many 3's in 9?

Write **3** in the ones place.

$$\begin{array}{r} 3 \\ 32\overline{)98} \\ 96 \end{array}$$

Multiply: $3 \times 32 = 96$

$$\begin{array}{r} 3 \\ 32\overline{)98} \\ -96 \\ \hline 2 \end{array}$$

Subtract: $98 - 96 = 2$
The quotient is 3.
The remainder is 2.

Check

$$\begin{array}{r} 32 \\ \times\ 3 \\ \hline 96 \\ +\ 2 \\ \hline 98 \end{array}$$

Study and Learn

A. Find $75\overline{)378}$. Complete.

1. Estimate: How many 75's in 37? None $\quad 75\overline{)379}$

How many 75's in 379? $\quad 75\overline{)379}$

Think: How many 7's in 37?
Write 5 in the ones place.

2. Multiply: $5 \times 75 = \underline{\ ?\ }$

$$\begin{array}{r} 5 \\ 75\overline{)379} \\ 375 \end{array}$$

3. Complete the division.

B. Complete.

4. $43\overline{)95}^{\,2}$ **5.** $24\overline{)96}^{\,4}$ **6.** $73\overline{)439}$ **7.** $82\overline{)336}$

C. Divide.

8. $23\overline{)70}$ **9.** $51\overline{)367}$ **10.** $92\overline{)377}$ **11.** $33\overline{)268}$

Practice

Divide.

1. $24\overline{)96}$ 2. $21\overline{)84}$ 3. $21\overline{)36}$ 4. $32\overline{)75}$

5. $34\overline{)170}$ 6. $97\overline{)679}$ 7. $36\overline{)147}$ 8. $41\overline{)128}$

9. $32\overline{)196}$ 10. $22\overline{)198}$ 11. $21\overline{)99}$ 12. $32\overline{)259}$

13. $23\overline{)46}$ 14. $37\overline{)148}$ 15. $31\overline{)279}$ 16. $23\overline{)69}$

Computer

You can use a computer to check answers to division.

For example, consider $32\overline{)135}$ with quotient 4r7.

If the division is correct, then the result of the quotient, 4, times the divisor, 32, plus the remainder, 7, will equal the dividend, 135. Tell the computer: **PRINT 32 * 4 + 7**. The computer output will be 135. Since 135 is the dividend, we know the division is correct.

Write the input to check the results of these division exercises.

1. $46\overline{)152}$ 2. $17\overline{)83}$ 3. $37\overline{)235}$

H A N D S O N

You can use the computer to check your answers to the Practice. Press RETURN after each PRINT statement.

Problem-Solving Applications

Solve.

1. The Chanins decided to insulate their attic. They need 9 rolls of fiberglass. Each roll of fiberglass costs $8.50. How much will it cost to insulate the attic?

2. Car tune-ups help to save fuel. The Ace Garage charges $40 to tune cars. The garage made $480 in car tune-ups. How many cars were tuned?

3. The Marcus family bought 8 storm windows. Each window cost $39.00. What was the total cost for the windows?

4. A store ordered a supply of blankets for $1,248. Each blanket cost the store $8. How many blankets did the store order?

5. Mrs. Shea started a car pool to save gas. There were 4 people in the car pool. Each person gave $1.35 every day for gas. How much money was given each day for gas?

Chapter Review

Divide.

1. $4\overline{)80}$ *(207)*

2. $6\overline{)1,200}$ *(207)*

3. $2\overline{)9}$ *(208)*

4. $9\overline{)80}$ *(208)*

5. $4\overline{)89}$ *(210)*

6. $7\overline{)217}$ *(212)*

7. $6\overline{)787}$ *(214)*

8. $5\overline{)945}$ *(214)*

9. $8\overline{)3,082}$ *(216)*

10. $3\overline{)1,269}$ *(216)*

11. $8\overline{)804}$ *(218)*

12. $6\overline{)3,605}$ *(218)*

13. $40\overline{)165}$ *(226)*

14. $10\overline{)136}$ *(228)*

15. $20\overline{)480}$ *(228)*

16. $3\overline{)\$4.56}$ *(230)*

Divide. *(234)*

17. $31\overline{)96}$

18. $32\overline{)128}$

Find the average. *(222)*

19. 57, 93, 72

20. 85, 100, 76, 83

Complete. *(232)*

21. 4 minutes = __?__ seconds

22. 240 minutes = __?__ hours

23. 21 days = __?__ weeks

Solve.

24. You buy a pen for $2.98 and some paper for $1.75.
(224) You give the clerk a $5.00 bill. How much change
should you receive?

25. Mr. Armstrong filled the car with 9 gallons of gas. Gas
(236) cost $1.25 a gallon. How much did he spend for gas?

Chapter Test

Divide.

1. 2)60
(207)

2. 7)2,100
(207)

3. 6)39
(208)

4. 6)49
(208)

5. 6)87
(210)

6. 6)249
(212)

7. 4)888
(214)

8. 3)674
(214)

9. 6)3,668
(216)

10. 2)1,252
(216)

11. 3)315
(218)

12. 4)437
(218)

13. 20)125
(226)

14. 10)228
(228)

15. 30)630
(228)

16. 2)$24.36
(230)

Divide. *(234)*

17. 21)84

18. 42)258

Find the average. *(222)*

19. 81, 57, 60   **20.** 77, 10, 43, 26

Complete. *(232)*

21. 9 weeks = __?__ days

22. 120 seconds = __?__ minutes

23. 3 days = __?__ hours

Solve.

24. You buy 2 shirts for $7.98 each. Then you buy a
(224) jacket for $26.80. How much do you spend in all?

25. Peggy, Mark, and Lorraine earned $9.00 raking
(236) leaves. They each earned the same amount of money.
How much did they each earn?

Skills Check

1. What is the value of the underlined digit?

    1<u>2</u>,400

A	B	C	D
2	20	200	2,000

2. What is $4.62 rounded to the nearest dollar?

E	F	G	H
$1.00	$4.00	$5.00	$5.50

3. Compare.

    $$\frac{2}{5} \equiv \frac{4}{5}$$

A	B	C	D
+	<	=	>

4. What part of the circle is shaded?

E	F	G	H
$\frac{3}{8}$	$\frac{8}{3}$	$\frac{3}{10}$	$\frac{5}{10}$

5. Which is a rectangle?

    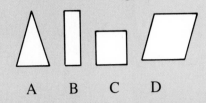

    A   B   C   D

6. Which is a cone?

    E   F   G   H

7. What is the length to the nearest centimeter?

    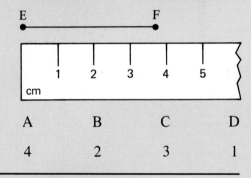

A	B	C	D
4	2	3	1

8. What is the temperature?

    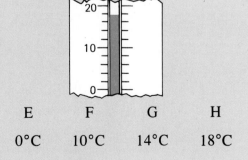

E	F	G	H
0°C	10°C	14°C	18°C

239

9 FRACTIONS

Grapefruits are found by the truckload in Florida.

FRACTIONS

Fractions are used to name parts of things.

	Think	Write	Read
What part is shaded?	1 out of 2	$\frac{1}{2}$	one half
What part is triangles?	2 out of 3	$\frac{2}{3}$	two thirds

Study and Learn

A. Read these fractions.

   1. $\frac{2}{2}$ **2.** $\frac{1}{3}$ **3.** $\frac{4}{6}$ **4.** $\frac{2}{4}$ **5.** $\frac{3}{5}$

▶ $\frac{1}{6}$ ← **Numerator**
    ← **Denominator**

B. Write the numerators.

   6. $\frac{2}{3}$ **7.** $\frac{1}{4}$ **8.** $\frac{5}{4}$ **9.** $\frac{1}{2}$ **10.** $\frac{3}{6}$

C. Write the denominators for items 6–10.

D. Write the fraction for each.

   11. 7 out of 8   **12.** 5 out of 6   **13.** 3 out of 4

E. Write a fraction for the shaded parts.

   14. 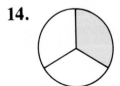   **15.**   **16.**

242

Practice

Write the numerators.

1. $\frac{3}{6}$ **2.** $\frac{1}{8}$ **3.** $\frac{2}{3}$ **4.** $\frac{4}{5}$ **5.** $\frac{2}{2}$

Write the denominators.

6. $\frac{1}{4}$ **7.** $\frac{7}{6}$ **8.** $\frac{3}{5}$ **9.** $\frac{9}{8}$ **10.** $\frac{3}{4}$

Write the fraction for each.

11. 2 out of 5   **12.** 1 out of 4   **13.** 6 out of 8

Write a fraction for the shaded parts.

14. 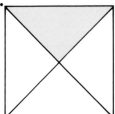   **15.** 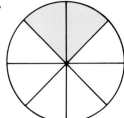   **16.**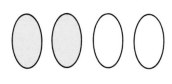

17.    **18.** 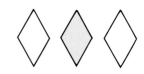   **19.**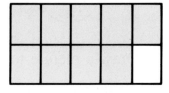

Solve Problems

★ **20.** What part of the jars are missing?

★ **21.** What part of the jars are on the shelf?

243

MORE ON FRACTIONS

Parts of a whole

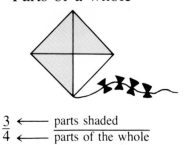

$\dfrac{3}{4}$ ← parts shaded / parts of the whole

Parts of a group

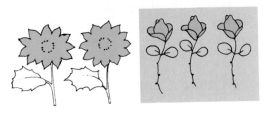

$\dfrac{3}{5}$ ← parts shaded / parts of the group

▶ When fractions name parts of a whole, the parts must be the same size.

▶ When fractions name parts of a group, the parts can be any size or color.

Study and Learn

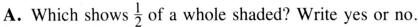

A. Which shows $\frac{1}{2}$ of a whole shaded? Write yes or no.

1.   **2.**    **3.**

B. Draw a picture to show each as part of a whole.

4. $\frac{1}{3}$ **5.** $\frac{1}{4}$ **6.** $\frac{2}{4}$ **7.** $\frac{3}{5}$

C. Which shows $\frac{1}{3}$ of a group shaded? Write yes or no.

8.    **9.**    **10.**

D. Draw a picture to show each as a part of a group.

11. $\frac{2}{3}$ **12.** $\frac{4}{8}$ **13.** $\frac{3}{3}$ **14.** $\frac{1}{6}$

Practice

Which shows $\frac{2}{3}$ of a whole shaded? Write yes or no.

1.   **2.**    **3.**

Draw a picture to show each as a part of a whole.

4. $\frac{2}{2}$ **5.** $\frac{1}{5}$ **6.** $\frac{2}{6}$ **7.** $\frac{7}{10}$

Which shows $\frac{5}{6}$ of a group shaded? Write yes or no.

8.   **9.**   **10.**

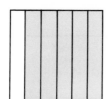      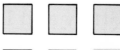

Draw a picture to show each as a part of a group.

11. $\frac{1}{3}$ **12.** $\frac{4}{4}$ **13.** $\frac{3}{8}$ **14.** $\frac{2}{5}$

Solve Problems

15. What part of the umbrella is yellow?

16. What part of the umbrella is green?

17. Write the fraction for 2 parts of the umbrella.

EQUAL FRACTIONS

Look at these rectangles.

$\frac{1}{2}$ of the rectangle is shaded.

$\frac{2}{4}$ of the rectangle is shaded.

$$\frac{1}{2} = \frac{2}{4}$$

▶ Fractions that name the same number are called **equal fractions.**

Study and Learn

A. Which two fractions tell what part is shaded?

1.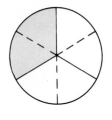

$\frac{1}{4}$ $\frac{2}{6}$ $\frac{1}{3}$

2.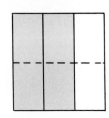

$\frac{2}{6}$ $\frac{4}{6}$ $\frac{2}{3}$

3.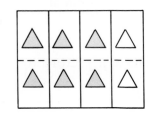

$\frac{3}{4}$ $\frac{6}{8}$ $\frac{1}{4}$

B. Write two equal fractions to tell what part is shaded.

4.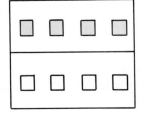

5.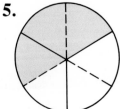

6.

246

Practice

Which two fractions tell what part is shaded?

1.

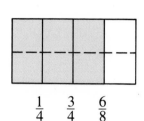

$\frac{1}{4}$ $\frac{3}{4}$ $\frac{6}{8}$

2.

$\frac{4}{6}$ $\frac{2}{6}$ $\frac{2}{3}$

3.

$\frac{6}{9}$ $\frac{2}{3}$ $\frac{1}{3}$

4.

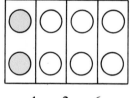

$\frac{1}{4}$ $\frac{2}{8}$ $\frac{6}{8}$

5.

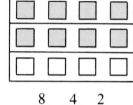

$\frac{8}{12}$ $\frac{4}{12}$ $\frac{2}{3}$

6.

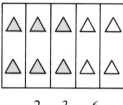

$\frac{2}{5}$ $\frac{3}{5}$ $\frac{6}{10}$

Write two equal fractions to tell what part is shaded.

7.

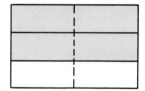

8.

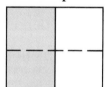

9.

10.

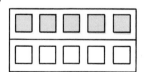

11.

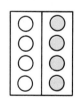

12.

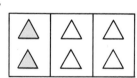

★ Write three equal fractions to tell what part is shaded.

13.

14.

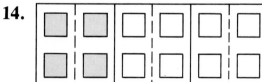

LISTS OF EQUAL FRACTIONS

Here are some equal fractions for $\frac{1}{2}$.

Notice the pattern of the numerators and denominators.

$\frac{1}{2}, \frac{2}{4}, \frac{3}{6}, \frac{4}{8}, \ldots$ means the pattern
goes on forever.

You can also list equal fractions by multiplying.

$$\frac{1 \times 1}{2 \times 1} = \frac{1}{2} \qquad \frac{1 \times 2}{2 \times 2} = \frac{2}{4} \qquad \frac{1 \times 3}{2 \times 3} = \frac{3}{6} \qquad \frac{1 \times 4}{2 \times 4} = \frac{4}{8}$$

Study and Learn

A. Look at these equal fractions.

$\frac{1}{3}, \frac{2}{6}, \frac{3}{9}, \frac{4}{12}, \ldots$

1. What is the pattern of the numerators?

2. What is the pattern of the denominators?

3. List the next three equal fractions.

B. List the next three equal fractions for each.

4. $\frac{1}{4}, \frac{2}{8}, \frac{3}{12}, \frac{4}{16}, \frac{?}{?}, \frac{?}{?}, \frac{?}{?}$

5. $\frac{2}{3}, \frac{4}{6}, \frac{6}{9}, \frac{8}{12}, \frac{?}{?}, \frac{?}{?}, \frac{?}{?}$

C. List the first four equal fractions for $\frac{3}{4}$.

6. $\frac{3 \times 1}{4 \times 1} = \frac{3}{?} \qquad \frac{3 \times 2}{4 \times 2} = \frac{?}{8} \qquad \frac{3 \times 3}{4 \times 3} = \frac{?}{?} \qquad \frac{3 \times 4}{4 \times 4} = \frac{?}{?}$

7. What are the first four equal fractions for $\frac{3}{4}$?

D. List the first four equal fractions for each.

8. $\frac{1}{5}$ 9. $\frac{2}{5}$ 10. $\frac{1}{6}$ 11. $\frac{2}{3}$ 12. $\frac{2}{4}$

Practice

List the next three equal fractions for each.

1. $\frac{1}{7}, \frac{2}{14}, \frac{3}{21}, \frac{4}{28}, \frac{?}{?}, \frac{?}{?}, \frac{?}{?}$

2. $\frac{2}{7}, \frac{4}{14}, \frac{6}{21}, \frac{8}{28}, \frac{?}{?}, \frac{?}{?}, \frac{?}{?}$

3. $\frac{3}{5}, \frac{6}{10}, \frac{9}{15}, \frac{12}{20}, \frac{?}{?}, \frac{?}{?}, \frac{?}{?}$

4. $\frac{3}{10}, \frac{6}{20}, \frac{9}{30}, \frac{12}{40}, \frac{?}{?}, \frac{?}{?}, \frac{?}{?}$

5. $\frac{5}{6}, \frac{10}{12}, \frac{15}{18}, \frac{20}{24}, \frac{?}{?}, \frac{?}{?}, \frac{?}{?}$

6. $\frac{1}{8}, \frac{2}{16}, \frac{3}{24}, \frac{4}{32}, \frac{?}{?}, \frac{?}{?}, \frac{?}{?}$

List the first four equal fractions for each.

7. $\frac{1}{3}$

8. $\frac{2}{3}$

9. $\frac{1}{4}$

10. $\frac{4}{5}$

11. $\frac{5}{6}$

12. $\frac{3}{7}$

13. $\frac{5}{8}$

14. $\frac{1}{10}$

15. $\frac{3}{6}$

16. $\frac{2}{6}$

17. $\frac{2}{4}$

18. $\frac{2}{10}$

19. $\frac{3}{3}$

★ 20. $\frac{24}{36}$

★ 21. $\frac{18}{21}$

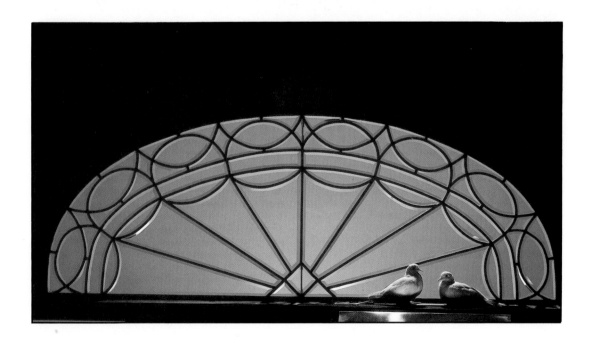

FINDING EQUAL FRACTIONS

Find an equal fraction for $\frac{1}{2}$.

Example $\frac{1}{2} = \frac{?}{8}$

List some equal fractions for $\frac{1}{2}$. $\frac{1}{2}$, $\frac{2}{4}$, $\frac{4}{8}$, $\frac{5}{10}$, . . .

So, $\frac{1}{2} = \frac{4}{8}$.

Study and Learn

A. Complete. $\frac{2}{3} = \frac{?}{12}$

  1. List the equal fractions for $\frac{2}{3}$.

  2. Which fraction has a denominator of 12?

  3. $\frac{2}{3} = \frac{?}{12}$

B. Complete.

  4. $\frac{1}{3} = \frac{?}{9}$ **5.** $\frac{3}{4} = \frac{?}{12}$ **6.** $\frac{1}{4} = \frac{?}{16}$ **7.** $\frac{3}{5} = \frac{?}{10}$

C. Complete. $\frac{1}{2} = \frac{6}{?}$

  8. List the first six equal fractions for $\frac{1}{2}$.

  9. Which fraction has a numerator of 6?

  10. $\frac{1}{2} = \frac{6}{?}$

D. Complete.

  11. $\frac{1}{2} = \frac{2}{?}$ **12.** $\frac{1}{3} = \frac{3}{?}$ **13.** $\frac{2}{3} = \frac{4}{?}$ **14.** $\frac{3}{4} = \frac{9}{?}$

Practice

Complete.

1. $\frac{1}{2} = \frac{?}{4}$

2. $\frac{1}{3} = \frac{?}{12}$

3. $\frac{2}{3} = \frac{?}{9}$

4. $\frac{1}{4} = \frac{?}{8}$

5. $\frac{3}{4} = \frac{?}{8}$

6. $\frac{1}{5} = \frac{?}{10}$

7. $\frac{3}{5} = \frac{?}{15}$

8. $\frac{3}{8} = \frac{?}{24}$

9. $\frac{1}{2} = \frac{6}{?}$

10. $\frac{1}{3} = \frac{4}{?}$

11. $\frac{2}{3} = \frac{6}{?}$

12. $\frac{1}{4} = \frac{3}{?}$

13. $\frac{3}{4} = \frac{6}{?}$

14. $\frac{2}{5} = \frac{4}{?}$

15. $\frac{5}{6} = \frac{10}{?}$

16. $\frac{5}{8} = \frac{15}{?}$

17. $\frac{1}{2} = \frac{?}{10}$

18. $\frac{1}{3} = \frac{6}{?}$

19. $\frac{2}{3} = \frac{10}{?}$

20. $\frac{1}{4} = \frac{5}{?}$

21. $\frac{3}{4} = \frac{15}{?}$

22. $\frac{2}{5} = \frac{?}{10}$

23. $\frac{7}{8} = \frac{?}{16}$

★ 24. $\frac{3}{10} = \frac{?}{100}$

Solve Problems

25. $\frac{1}{3}$ of the eggs are cracked. Is it correct to say $\frac{4}{12}$ of the eggs are cracked?

26. $\frac{3}{4}$ of the pencils have been sharpened. Is it correct to say $\frac{2}{8}$ of the pencils have been sharpened?

27. $\frac{1}{2}$ of the balloons are red. Is it correct to say $\frac{6}{10}$ of the balloons are red?

★ 28. A ball player got 4 hits for every 12 times at bat. Is it correct to say the player got 1 hit for every three times at bat?

★ 29. Sarah roasted $\frac{1}{3}$ of the chestnuts. Jacob roasted $\frac{1}{5}$ of the chestnuts. Did they both roast the same amount?

★ 30. Cindy collected $\frac{1}{5}$ of the logs. Carl collected $\frac{2}{10}$ of the logs. Did they both collect the same amount?

Midchapter Review

Write a fraction for the shaded parts. *(242)*

1.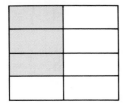

2.

3.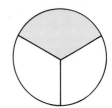

Write two equal fractions to tell what part is shaded. *(246)*

4.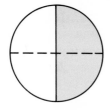

5.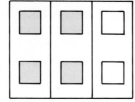

6.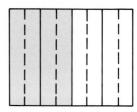

Complete. *(250)*

7. $\frac{2}{3} = \frac{?}{9}$

8. $\frac{1}{3} = \frac{4}{?}$

9. $\frac{2}{5} = \frac{?}{10}$

Something Extra
Non-Routine Problems

Look at the grid.
Write a fraction for each of the following.

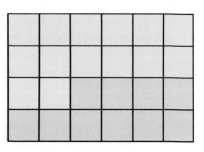

1. ___?___ of the squares are green.

2. ___?___ of the squares are blue.

3. ___?___ of the squares are yellow.

4. ___?___ of the squares are green or blue.

5. ___?___ of the squares are blue or yellow.

CHECKING FOR EQUAL FRACTIONS

Here is a way to find if fractions are equal.
Are $\frac{3}{4}$ and $\frac{6}{8}$ equal fractions?

$$3 \times 8 = 24$$

$$4 \times 6 = 24$$

The products are the same. So, $\frac{3}{4} = \frac{6}{8}$.

Study and Learn

A. Are $\frac{2}{3}$ and $\frac{6}{8}$ equal fractions? Complete.

1. Multiply.
   $2 \times 8 = $ ___?___ and $3 \times 6 = $ ___?___

2. Are the products the same?

3. Are the fractions equal?

B. Are the fractions equal? Write yes or no.

4. $\frac{1}{2}, \frac{5}{10}$
5. $\frac{2}{5}, \frac{6}{10}$
6. $\frac{1}{2}, \frac{3}{8}$
7. $\frac{5}{3}, \frac{10}{6}$

Practice

Are the fractions equal? Write yes or no.

1. $\frac{6}{12}, \frac{1}{2}$
2. $\frac{2}{3}, \frac{4}{6}$
3. $\frac{1}{4}, \frac{2}{10}$
4. $\frac{3}{4}, \frac{9}{12}$

5. $\frac{3}{5}, \frac{9}{12}$
6. $\frac{6}{7}, \frac{6}{7}$
7. $\frac{3}{2}, \frac{9}{6}$
8. $\frac{7}{8}, \frac{6}{7}$

9. $\frac{4}{10}, \frac{2}{5}$
10. $\frac{3}{5}, \frac{6}{9}$
★ 11. $\frac{9}{10}, \frac{18}{100}$
★ 12. $\frac{24}{36}, \frac{12}{18}$

Problem-Solving Skills
Finding a Hidden Step

Sometimes a step is hidden in a word problem.

John will leave for California on June 16th.
He will arrive on July 15th.
How many days will the trip take?

Hidden Step: 30 days in June so, $30 - 16 = 14$
Then: 14 days $+$ 15 days $= 29$ days

John's trip will take 29 days.

Study and Learn

Complete.

A. There are 4 dozen stairs in the monument.
Jimmy walked up 28 stairs.
How many stairs are left to climb?

   1. Hidden Step: 1 dozen $= \underline{\ ?\ }$, so 4 dozen $= \underline{\ ?\ }$

   2. Then: $48 - 28 = \underline{\ ?\ }$

   3. How many stairs left?

B. Solve.

   4. John bought 2 kilograms of cheese.
   He used 250 grams for dinner.
   How much cheese is left?

   5. Sue left for Dallas at 11:00 am.
   She drove for 4 hours.
   What time was it then?

Practice

Solve.

1. Melissa walked 800 meters a day.
   She walked the same distance for 5 days.
   How many kilometers did she walk in all?

2. While camping out, Jerry cooked
   1 kilogram of bacon.
   5 people shared the bacon.
   How many grams of bacon for each?

3. The Celsius thermometer was
   at the freezing point at 6:30 am.
   The temperature rose 12 degrees
   an hour later.
   What was the temperature then?

4. Jackie took 2 dozen snapshots in Arizona.
   She took 6 more snapshots in Texas.
   How many snapshots were taken in all?

5. Adrian's birthday is on January 23rd.
   Nancy's birthday is 10 days after
   Adrian's. What date is Nancy's birthday?

6. A piece of string is 2 feet long. 5 inches
   are cut off. How long is the string now?

7. A roast weighed 2 pounds. During
   cooking, it lost 4 ounces. How much did
   the roast weigh after cooking?

8. The temperature was 48°F.
   It fell to the freezing temperature.
   How many degrees did it fall?

FINDING A FRACTION OF A NUMBER

Look at the picture to find $\frac{1}{2}$ of 6.

Think: Divide 6 by 2.

$6 \div 2 = 3$ So, $\frac{1}{2}$ of 6 = 3.

Study and Learn

A. Complete to find $\frac{1}{3}$ of 6.

1. $6 \div 3 = \underline{\ ?\ }$ **2.** $\frac{1}{3}$ of 6 = $\underline{\ ?\ }$

B. Complete.

3. $\frac{1}{4}$ of 8 = $\underline{\ ?\ }$ **4.** $\frac{1}{3}$ of 12 = $\underline{\ ?\ }$ **5.** $\frac{1}{2}$ of 10 = $\underline{\ ?\ }$

Practice

Complete.

1. $\frac{1}{4}$ of 16 = $\underline{\ ?\ }$ **2.** $\frac{1}{3}$ of 24 = $\underline{\ ?\ }$ **3.** $\frac{1}{5}$ of 25 = $\underline{\ ?\ }$

4. $\frac{1}{2}$ of 18 = $\underline{\ ?\ }$ **5.** $\frac{1}{8}$ of 32 = $\underline{\ ?\ }$ **6.** $\frac{1}{6}$ of 24 = $\underline{\ ?\ }$

7. $\frac{1}{5}$ of 30 = $\underline{\ ?\ }$ **8.** $\frac{1}{7}$ of 21 = $\underline{\ ?\ }$ **9.** $\frac{1}{2}$ of 14 = $\underline{\ ?\ }$

★**10.** $\frac{1}{6}$ of 96 = $\underline{\ ?\ }$ ★**11.** $\frac{1}{10}$ of 100 = $\underline{\ ?\ }$ ★**12.** $\frac{1}{5}$ of 75 = $\underline{\ ?\ }$

Solve Problems

13. There are 12 eggs. Joan cooked $\frac{1}{3}$ of them. How many did she cook?

14. There are 8 slices of bread. Jack toasted $\frac{1}{2}$ of them. How many did he toast?

RATIOS AS FRACTIONS

We use a ratio to compare.
The ratio of squares to circles is 2 to 3.
This can also be written as a fraction.
The ratio of squares to circles is $\frac{2}{3}$.
The ratio of circles to squares is
3 to 2 or $\frac{3}{2}$.

Study and Learn

A. Give the ratio.

   1. Straws to cups is __4__ to __3__ or __?__.

   2. Cups to straws is __?__ to __?__ or __?__.

B. Give the ratio.

   3. pennies to nickels

   4. nickels to pennies

Practice

Give the ratio.

 1. cars to tires

 2. tires to cars

 3. cats to dogs

 4. dogs to cats

★**5.** dogs to animals

★**6.** cats to animals

257

Skills Review

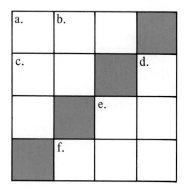

Divide.

1. 4)20
(207)

2. 8)400

3. 9)7,200

4. 5)11
(208)

5. 7)67

6. 3)17

7. 4)88
(210)

8. 2)83

9. 8)248
(212)

10. 7)219

11. 5)161

12. 2)844
(214)

13. 5)671

14. 3)553

15. 6)1,346
(216)

16. 4)1,951

17. 9)1,724

18. 6)302
(218)

19. 7)1,408

20. 3)2,104

21. 8)3,286

22. 20)160
(226)

23. 40)340

24. 30)387
(228)

25. 10)563

26. 50)856

Something Extra
Non-Routine Problems

Copy and complete the puzzle.

Across

a. 89
+ 58

c. 37
+ 29

e. 59
+ 28

f. 64
+ 59

Down

a. 64
39
+ 65

b. 18
13
+ 15

d. 43
46
+ 84

e. 25
18
+ 39

COMPARING FRACTIONS

Compare $\frac{1}{3}$ and $\frac{2}{3}$.

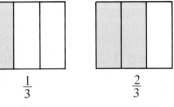

Step 1 Are the denominators the same? yes
Step 2 Compare the numerators.

$1 < 2$, so, $\frac{1}{3} < \frac{2}{3}$.

▶ When the denominators are the same, compare the numerators.

Study and Learn

A. Compare $\frac{4}{7}$ and $\frac{3}{7}$. Use $<$ or $>$ to replace $\equiv$.

  1. Are the denominators the same?

  2. Compare the numerators. $4 \equiv 3$

  3. Complete. $\frac{4}{7} \equiv \frac{3}{7}$

B. Compare. Use $<$ or $>$ to replace $\equiv$.

  4. $\frac{3}{4} \equiv \frac{1}{4}$ **5.** $\frac{7}{8} \equiv \frac{6}{8}$ **6.** $\frac{3}{10} \equiv \frac{7}{10}$ **7.** $\frac{4}{5} \equiv \frac{1}{5}$

Practice

Compare. Use $<$ or $>$ to replace $\equiv$.

1. $\frac{2}{3} \equiv \frac{1}{3}$ **2.** $\frac{2}{4} \equiv \frac{3}{4}$ **3.** $\frac{3}{5} \equiv \frac{4}{5}$ **4.** $\frac{1}{6} \equiv \frac{3}{6}$

5. $\frac{4}{10} \equiv \frac{7}{10}$ **6.** $\frac{3}{8} \equiv \frac{7}{8}$ **7.** $\frac{3}{10} \equiv \frac{1}{10}$ **8.** $\frac{7}{10} \equiv \frac{5}{10}$

9. $\frac{7}{12} \equiv \frac{5}{12}$ **10.** $\frac{2}{4} \equiv \frac{1}{4}$ **11.** $\frac{4}{5} \equiv \frac{1}{5}$ **12.** $\frac{1}{10} \equiv \frac{4}{10}$

13. $\frac{4}{5} \equiv \frac{7}{5}$ **14.** $\frac{6}{8} \equiv \frac{3}{8}$ **15.** $\frac{2}{10} \equiv \frac{8}{10}$ **16.** $\frac{1}{8} \equiv \frac{7}{8}$

MORE COMPARING

Compare $\frac{1}{2}$ and $\frac{1}{3}$.

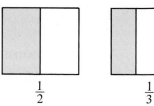

Step 1 Are the denominators the same? no

Step 2 Build lists of equal fractions.

$$\frac{1}{2}, \frac{2}{4}, \boxed{\frac{3}{6}}, \frac{4}{8}, \cdots$$

$$\frac{1}{3}, \boxed{\frac{2}{6}}, \frac{3}{9}, \frac{4}{12}, \cdots$$

Step 3 Find fractions with the same denominators.

$$\frac{1}{2} = \frac{3}{6}, \quad \frac{1}{3} = \frac{2}{6}$$

Step 4 Compare the numerators.

$$3 > 2, \text{ so } \frac{1}{2} > \frac{1}{3}.$$

▶ When the denominators are different, find fractions with the same denominator, then compare.

Study and Learn

A. Compare $\frac{1}{2}$ and $\frac{3}{4}$. Use $>$, $<$, or $=$ to replace $\equiv$.

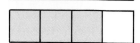

1. Are the denominators the same?

2. Build a list for each fraction.

3. Which fractions have the same denominator?

4. Compare. $\frac{1}{2} \equiv \frac{3}{4}$

B. Compare. Use $>$, $<$, or $=$ to replace $\equiv$.

5. $\frac{1}{2} \equiv \frac{1}{4}$ **6.** $\frac{2}{3} \equiv \frac{3}{4}$ **7.** $\frac{1}{2} \equiv \frac{4}{8}$ **8.** $\frac{2}{5} \equiv \frac{3}{10}$

Practice

Compare. Use $>$, $<$, or $=$ to replace $\equiv$.

1. $\frac{1}{2} \equiv \frac{1}{5}$

2. $\frac{1}{4} \equiv \frac{2}{5}$

3. $\frac{1}{3} \equiv \frac{3}{9}$

4. $\frac{2}{3} \equiv \frac{4}{9}$

5. $\frac{1}{3} \equiv \frac{3}{4}$

6. $\frac{3}{8} \equiv \frac{1}{4}$

7. $\frac{9}{10} \equiv \frac{3}{5}$

8. $\frac{1}{4} \equiv \frac{2}{8}$

9. $\frac{2}{3} \equiv \frac{1}{2}$

10. $\frac{3}{8} \equiv \frac{1}{3}$

11. $\frac{3}{4} \equiv \frac{1}{5}$

12. $\frac{1}{2} \equiv \frac{3}{5}$

13. $\frac{2}{4} \equiv \frac{5}{8}$

14. $\frac{1}{2} \equiv \frac{2}{4}$

15. $\frac{1}{10} \equiv \frac{1}{2}$

16. $\frac{6}{8} \equiv \frac{2}{8}$

17. $\frac{1}{2} \equiv \frac{2}{3}$

18. $\frac{3}{5} \equiv \frac{2}{5}$

19. $\frac{5}{10} \equiv \frac{4}{5}$

20. $\frac{1}{3} \equiv \frac{3}{9}$

Solve Problems

21. Andrew ate $\frac{1}{5}$ of his meatpie. Terry ate $\frac{1}{10}$ of his meatpie. Both meatpies are the same size. Who ate more of his meatpie?

22. Carol ate $\frac{1}{4}$ of a container of potato salad for lunch. Joseph ate $\frac{3}{8}$ of the container of potato salad for dinner. Who ate more of the potato salad?

23. Jerry rides his bicycle to school $\frac{9}{10}$ of the time. Does he ride his bicycle to school more than $\frac{1}{2}$ of the time?

24. Maria makes a hit $\frac{7}{10}$ of the times she bats. Muriel makes a hit $\frac{3}{5}$ of the times she bats. Who is the better hitter?

● 25. There were 32 pineapple slices in a container. Peter ate $\frac{1}{2}$ of the slices. How many pineapple slices were left?

● 26. Altogether, Brian has 75 marbles. He left $\frac{1}{5}$ of them at home. How many marbles did he leave at home?

FRACTIONS AND ONE

Look at this number line.

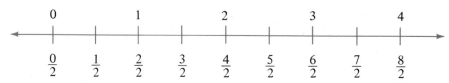

▶ When the numerator is less than the denominator, the fraction is less than 1. $\frac{1}{2} < 1$

▶ When the numerator is equal to the denominator, the fraction equals 1. $\frac{2}{2} = 1$

▶ When the numerator is greater than the denominator, the fraction is greater than 1. $\frac{3}{2} > 1$

Study and Learn

A. Compare. Use $>$, $<$, or $=$ to replace $\equiv$.

1. $\frac{3}{4} \equiv 1$

2. $1 \equiv \frac{4}{4}$

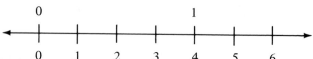

3. $\frac{5}{4} \equiv 1$

Practice

Compare. Use $>$, $<$, or $=$ to replace $\equiv$.

1. $1 \equiv \frac{8}{8}$

2. $1 \equiv \frac{8}{7}$

3. $1 \equiv \frac{7}{8}$

4. $\frac{5}{5} \equiv 1$

5. $\frac{9}{5} \equiv 1$

6. $\frac{4}{7} \equiv 1$

7. $\frac{2}{3} \equiv 1$

8. $\frac{4}{3} \equiv 1$

9. $\frac{7}{12} \equiv 1$

10. $1 \equiv \frac{10}{10}$

★ 11. $\frac{4}{5} \equiv \frac{7}{3}$

★ 12. $\frac{12}{12} \equiv \frac{20}{20}$

FRACTIONS AS DIVISION

The fraction $\frac{1}{2}$ can mean 1 divided by 2.

Fraction	Division
$\frac{1}{2}$	$1 \div 2$ or $2\overline{)1}$
$\frac{5}{3}$	$5 \div 3$ or $3\overline{)5}$

Study and Learn

A. Write a division. Use the $\overline{)}$ form.

1. $\frac{2}{3}$ 2. $\frac{5}{8}$ 3. $\frac{7}{1}$ 4. $\frac{6}{6}$

B. Write a fraction.

5. $5\overline{)4}$ 6. $4\overline{)5}$ 7. $1\overline{)8}$ 8. $8\overline{)1}$

Practice

Write a division. Use the $\overline{)}$ form.

1. $\frac{1}{3}$ 2. $\frac{3}{1}$ 3. $\frac{1}{4}$ 4. $\frac{4}{1}$

Write a fraction.

5. $7\overline{)8}$ 6. $8\overline{)7}$ 7. $4\overline{)3}$ 8. $2\overline{)12}$

Solve Problems

9. There is 1 pineapple to be divided equally between 2 people. How much should each get?

10. There are 2 coconuts to be divided equally among 3 people. How much should each get?

MIXED NUMBERS

For	*Write*	*Say*
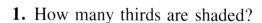	$\frac{1}{2}$	one half
	$\frac{2}{2}$ or 1	two halves or one
	$\frac{3}{2}$ or $1\frac{1}{2}$	three halves or one and one half

Numbers such as $1\frac{1}{2}$, $1\frac{2}{3}$, and $3\frac{4}{5}$ are **mixed numbers.**

Study and Learn

A. Look at the picture. Complete.

    1. How many thirds are shaded?

    2. Write the fraction for the shaded parts.

    3. How many whole pictures are shaded?

    4. What part of the second figure is shaded?

    5. Write the mixed number.

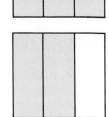

B. Write a fraction for the shaded parts.

  6. 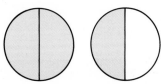   **7.**

C. Write the mixed number for items 6 and 7.

The fraction $\frac{5}{3}$ can be changed to a mixed number by dividing.

$$3 \overline{)\, 5} \quad \begin{array}{l} 1 \end{array}$$

$$\begin{array}{r} 1 \\ 3 \overline{)\, 5} \\ -\ 3 \\ \hline 2 \end{array}$$

Mixed Number

$1\,\frac{2}{3}$

D. Write each as a whole number or mixed number.

8. $\frac{3}{2}$ **9.** $\frac{2}{2}$ **10.** $\frac{9}{7}$ **11.** $\frac{4}{3}$ **12.** $\frac{6}{5}$

Practice

Write a mixed number for the shaded parts.

1. 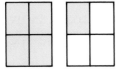   **2.**   **3.**

4. 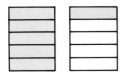   **5.**   **6.**

Write each as a whole number or mixed number.

7. $\frac{7}{5}$ **8.** $\frac{5}{3}$ **9.** $\frac{6}{6}$ **10.** $\frac{9}{8}$ **11.** $\frac{11}{10}$

12. $\frac{5}{4}$ **13.** $\frac{7}{6}$ **14.** $\frac{5}{5}$ **15.** $\frac{7}{4}$ **16.** $\frac{8}{6}$

Solve Problems

★**17.** There are $1\frac{1}{3}$ days until the school play. What fraction is this?

★**18.** Jim finished $1\frac{1}{5}$ of the sets for the play. What fraction is this?

Problem-Solving Applications

Career

Solve.

1. Barry has 24 pages of script to read. He has read $\frac{1}{3}$ of the pages. How many pages has he read?
   (HINT: $24 \div 3 = \underline{\quad ? \quad}$)

2. Amy worked a 45-hour week. $\frac{1}{9}$ of that time was spent on the road. How many hours did she spend on the road?

3. The news broadcast is 30 minutes long. $\frac{1}{6}$ of that time is for commercials. How many minutes are commercials?

4. Pat is on the air for 55 minutes. She talks about sports for $\frac{1}{5}$ of that time. How many minutes does she spend talking about sports?

5. There were 14 announcers. $\frac{1}{2}$ went home. How many went home?

6. Barry is listening to a 60-second tape from the weather bureau. He has listened to $\frac{1}{2}$ of it. How many seconds of the tape has he heard?

★ 7. There were 9 camera people. $\frac{1}{3}$ went to lunch. How many were left?

★ 8. A weather broadcast is 12 minutes long. $\frac{1}{4}$ of it is ready. How many minutes of the broadcast are left to get ready?

Chapter Review

Write two equal fractions to tell what part is shaded. *(246)*

1.

2.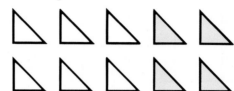

Complete. *(250, 256)*

3. $\frac{3}{4} = \frac{?}{12}$

4. $\frac{2}{3} = \frac{?}{6}$

5. $\frac{1}{5} = \frac{?}{10}$

6. $\frac{3}{5} = \frac{6}{?}$

7. $\frac{1}{3}$ of 9 = _?_

8. $\frac{1}{2}$ of 12 = _?_

9. $\frac{1}{5}$ of 15 = _?_

Compare. Use >, <, or =. *(259, 260, 262)*

10. $\frac{3}{5} \equiv \frac{1}{5}$

11. $\frac{2}{3} \equiv \frac{5}{6}$

12. $\frac{1}{2} \equiv \frac{2}{4}$

13. $\frac{5}{5} \equiv 1$

Give the ratio. *(257)*

14. pencils to pens

15. pens to pencils

Write each as a whole or mixed number. *(264)*

16. $\frac{3}{3}$

17. $\frac{6}{5}$

18. $\frac{5}{3}$

Solve.

19. *(254)* Jan had 3 dozen tennis balls. She used 6 balls. How many did she have left?

20. *(266)* Betty had 20 oranges. She gave $\frac{1}{5}$ of them away. How many oranges did Betty give away?

Chapter Test

Write two equal fractions to tell what part is shaded. *(246)*

1.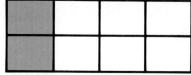

2.

Complete. *(250, 256)*

3. $\frac{1}{2} = \frac{?}{6}$ **4.** $\frac{2}{4} = \frac{?}{8}$ **5.** $\frac{1}{3} = \frac{3}{?}$ **6.** $\frac{2}{6} = \frac{4}{?}$

7. $\frac{1}{2}$ of 16 = ___?___ **8.** $\frac{1}{6}$ of 18 = ___?___ **9.** $\frac{1}{5}$ of 20 = ___?___

Compare. Use >, <, or =. *(259, 260, 262)*

10. $\frac{1}{4} \equiv \frac{3}{4}$ **11.** $\frac{3}{4} \equiv \frac{5}{8}$ **12.** $\frac{4}{4} \equiv 1$ **13.** $\frac{3}{2} \equiv 1$

Give the ratio. *(257)*

14. forks to knives

15. knives to forks

Write each as a whole number or mixed number. *(264)*

16. $\frac{5}{5}$ **17.** $\frac{6}{4}$ **18.** $\frac{3}{2}$

Solve.

19. *(254)* Jane jogged for 15 minutes every day for a week. How many minutes did she jog in a week?

20. *(266)* Ben has 24 jars of paint. $\frac{1}{4}$ of them contain red paint. How many jars contain red paint?

Skills Check

1. A department store waited eight weeks for a delivery of tools. How many months is that?

   A 1 month   B 2 months

   C 3 months   D 4 months

2. Lynn arrived at her aunt's house at 4:30 pm. It took her 1 hour and 30 minutes to get there. At what time did she start?

   E 11:30 am   F 3:00 pm

   G 1:00 pm   H 5:45 pm

3. Ed bought a loaf of bread which had 15 slices. Each slice was 100 calories. How many calories were in the entire loaf?

   A 150   B 650

   C 1,500   D 3,000

4.

Name	Books Read
June	▢ ▢ ▢ ▢ ▢
Chris	▢ ▢
Tina	▢ ▢ ▢

   Each ▢ means 2 books.

   How many books did June read?

   E 5   F 2

   G 6   H 10

5. Ann bought a book for $6.98. She gave the clerk $10.00. What should her change be?

   A $1.20   B $2.02

   C $3.02   D $3.12

6. Paul bought 7,000 mL of apple juice for the scout meeting. How many liters is that?

   E 0.7   F 7

   G 70   H 700

7. Mr. Jonas needed a pipe 36 inches long. How many feet of pipe did he need?

   A 3 ft   B 4 ft

   C 5 ft   D 6 ft

8. What is the perimeter?

   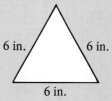

   6 in.   6 in.

   6 in.

   E 6 in.   F 12 in.

   G 18 in.   H 24 in.

10 ADD AND SUBTRACT FRACTIONS

Computer chips hold bits of information.

ADDING FRACTIONS

Add $\frac{1}{6}$ and $\frac{4}{6}$.

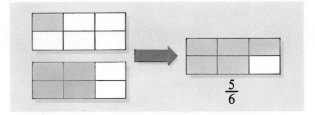

Step 1 Are the denominators the same? yes

Step 2 Add the numerators. $1 + 4 = 5$

Step 3 Use the same denominator.

$$\frac{1}{6} + \frac{4}{6} = \frac{5}{6} \qquad \begin{array}{r} \frac{1}{6} \\ + \frac{4}{6} \\ \hline \frac{5}{6} \end{array}$$

▶ When the denominators are the same, add the numerators.

Study and Learn

A. Complete.

Sandy ate $\frac{1}{3}$ of the apple. Sally also
ate $\frac{1}{3}$. How much was eaten in all?

$\left[\text{Think: } \frac{1}{3} + \frac{1}{3} = \underline{} \right]$

  1. Are the denominators the same?

  2. Add the numerators. Use the same
denominator.

  3. How much was eaten?

B. Add.

4. $\begin{array}{r} \frac{1}{4} \\ + \frac{1}{4} \\ \hline \end{array}$

5. $\begin{array}{r} \frac{3}{7} \\ + \frac{2}{7} \\ \hline \end{array}$

6. $\begin{array}{r} \frac{4}{9} \\ + \frac{3}{9} \\ \hline \end{array}$

7. $\frac{3}{10} + \frac{1}{10}$

272

Practice

Add.

1. $\dfrac{1}{5}$
    $+\dfrac{1}{5}$

2. $\dfrac{1}{6}$
    $+\dfrac{2}{6}$

3. $\dfrac{2}{7}$
    $+\dfrac{2}{7}$

4. $\dfrac{2}{8}$
    $+\dfrac{5}{8}$

5. $\dfrac{6}{9}$
    $+\dfrac{2}{9}$

6. $\dfrac{1}{10}$
    $+\dfrac{7}{10}$

7. $\dfrac{8}{12}$
    $+\dfrac{2}{12}$

8. $\dfrac{3}{5}$
    $+\dfrac{1}{5}$

9. $\dfrac{4}{7}$
    $+\dfrac{2}{7}$

10. $\dfrac{3}{9}$
    $+\dfrac{2}{9}$

11. $\dfrac{3}{8}$
    $+\dfrac{1}{8}$

12. $\dfrac{7}{12}$
    $+\dfrac{4}{12}$

13. $\dfrac{2}{5}$
    $+\dfrac{1}{5}$

14. $\dfrac{4}{9}$
    $+\dfrac{4}{9}$

15. $\dfrac{2}{4}$
    $+\dfrac{1}{4}$

16. $\dfrac{3}{6}$
    $+\dfrac{1}{6}$

17. $\dfrac{1}{9}$
    $+\dfrac{4}{9}$

18. $\dfrac{2}{10}$
    $+\dfrac{6}{10}$

19. $\dfrac{4}{8}$
    $+\dfrac{3}{8}$

20. $\dfrac{3}{9}$
    $+\dfrac{3}{9}$

21. $\dfrac{1}{4}+\dfrac{1}{4}$

22. $\dfrac{1}{5}+\dfrac{3}{5}$

23. $\dfrac{2}{6}+\dfrac{3}{6}$

24. $\dfrac{1}{3}+\dfrac{1}{3}$

25. $\dfrac{3}{8}+\dfrac{2}{8}$

26. $\dfrac{1}{9}+\dfrac{1}{9}$

27. $\dfrac{4}{10}+\dfrac{2}{10}$

★ 28. $\dfrac{7}{12}+\dfrac{2}{12}+\dfrac{3}{12}$

Solve Problems

29. $\dfrac{1}{5}$ of the vendors arrived at 8:00 am. $\dfrac{2}{5}$ of the vendors arrived at 9:00 am. What part of the vendors arrived by 9:00 am?

30. $\dfrac{1}{3}$ of the vendors sold men's clothing. $\dfrac{1}{3}$ of the vendors sold women's clothing. What part of the vendors sold clothing?

● 31. $\dfrac{1}{12}$ of the hats had feathers. $\dfrac{5}{12}$ of the hats had ribbons. Were there more hats with ribbons or feathers?

★ 32. $\dfrac{1}{7}$ of the shirts had stripes, $\dfrac{3}{7}$ had polka dots, and $\dfrac{2}{7}$ had flowers. What part of the shirts had a design?

SUMS 1 AND GREATER THAN 1

$\frac{7}{10}$ of Kim's gas tank was filled.

She added $\frac{3}{10}$ more gasoline to the tank.
What part of the tank was then filled?

$$\begin{array}{r} \frac{7}{10} \\ + \frac{3}{10} \\ \hline \frac{10}{10} \text{ or } 1 \end{array}$$

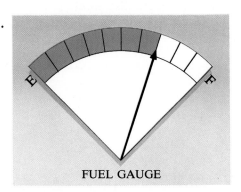

FUEL GAUGE

The tank is full.

▶ When the sum of two fractions is 1 or greater, rename
  the sum as a whole number or mixed number.

Study and Learn

A. Add. Change the sum to a whole number.

1. $\begin{array}{r} \frac{3}{8} \\ + \frac{5}{8} \\ \hline \end{array}$
2. $\begin{array}{r} \frac{3}{6} \\ + \frac{3}{6} \\ \hline \end{array}$
3. $\begin{array}{r} \frac{9}{10} \\ + \frac{1}{10} \\ \hline \end{array}$
4. $\frac{3}{4} + \frac{1}{4}$

> Sometimes the sum is greater than 1. This sum is written as
> a mixed number.
>
> *Example*
> $$\begin{array}{r} \frac{5}{6} \\ + \frac{5}{6} \\ \hline \frac{10}{6} \text{ or } 1\frac{4}{6} \end{array} \longleftarrow \quad \begin{array}{r} 1\frac{4}{6} \\ 6 \overline{)10} \\ -6 \\ \hline 4 \end{array}$$

B. Add. Change the sum to a mixed number.

5. $\begin{array}{r} \frac{5}{9} \\ + \frac{8}{9} \\ \hline \end{array}$
6. $\begin{array}{r} \frac{2}{3} \\ + \frac{2}{3} \\ \hline \end{array}$
7. $\begin{array}{r} \frac{8}{10} \\ + \frac{3}{10} \\ \hline \end{array}$
8. $\frac{5}{8} + \frac{7}{8}$

274

Practice

Add. Change the sum to a whole number or mixed number.

1. $\frac{3}{4}$
   $+\frac{3}{4}$

2. $\frac{4}{6}$
   $+\frac{5}{6}$

3. $\frac{1}{8}$
   $+\frac{7}{8}$

4. $\frac{3}{10}$
   $+\frac{7}{10}$

5. $\frac{4}{5}$
   $+\frac{2}{5}$

6. $\frac{5}{6}$
   $+\frac{3}{6}$

7. $\frac{6}{10}$
   $+\frac{5}{10}$

8. $\frac{3}{10}$
   $+\frac{9}{10}$

9. $\frac{6}{12}$
   $+\frac{8}{12}$

10. $\frac{3}{5}$
    $+\frac{2}{5}$

11. $\frac{2}{3}$
    $+\frac{2}{3}$

12. $\frac{3}{5}$
    $+\frac{4}{5}$

13. $\frac{4}{8}$
    $+\frac{6}{8}$

14. $\frac{2}{6}$
    $+\frac{4}{6}$

15. $\frac{7}{10}$
    $+\frac{8}{10}$

16. $\frac{2}{3}$
    $+\frac{1}{3}$

17. $\frac{2}{4}$
    $+\frac{3}{4}$

18. $\frac{4}{5}$
    $+\frac{1}{5}$

19. $\frac{8}{10}$
    $+\frac{9}{10}$

20. $\frac{7}{9}$
    $+\frac{8}{9}$

21. $\frac{3}{6} + \frac{3}{6}$

22. $\frac{3}{9} + \frac{6}{9}$

23. $\frac{4}{8} + \frac{4}{8}$

24. $\frac{1}{2} + \frac{1}{2}$

25. $\frac{4}{5} + \frac{4}{5}$

26. $\frac{6}{7} + \frac{5}{7}$

★ 27. $\frac{4}{5} + \frac{1}{5} + \frac{3}{5}$

★ 28. $\frac{2}{3} + \frac{2}{3} + \frac{1}{3}$

Solve Problems

29. Willie rode his bicycle $\frac{3}{4}$ hour in the morning. He rode his bicycle $\frac{3}{4}$ hour in the afternoon. How many hours did Willie ride his bicycle?

30. It takes Abe $\frac{1}{2}$ hour to walk to school each morning. It takes him $\frac{1}{2}$ hour to walk home each afternoon. How many hours does it take Abe to walk to and from school each day?

DIFFERENT DENOMINATORS

Add $\frac{1}{2}$ and $\frac{4}{6}$.

Step 1 Are the denominators the same? no

Step 2 List equal fractions for each.

$$\frac{1}{2} \quad : \quad \frac{1}{2}, \quad \frac{2}{4}, \quad \boxed{\frac{3}{6}}, \cdots$$

$$\frac{4}{6} \quad : \quad \boxed{\frac{4}{6}}, \quad \frac{8}{12}, \cdots$$

Step 3 Rewrite the problem using equal fractions with the same denominator.

$$\frac{1}{2} = \frac{3}{6}$$
$$\frac{4}{6} = \frac{4}{6}$$
$$\overline{\frac{7}{6}} = 1\frac{1}{6}$$

Step 4 Add.

So, $\quad \frac{1}{2} + \frac{4}{6} = \frac{7}{6}$ or $1\frac{1}{6}$.

Study and Learn

A. Find $\frac{1}{3} + \frac{1}{4}$.

   1. Are the denominators the same?

   2. List the equal fractions for each.

   3. Complete.

$$\begin{array}{cc} \frac{1}{3} & \frac{?}{12} \\ +\frac{1}{4} & +\frac{?}{12} \\ \hline \end{array}$$

   4. Add.

B. Add.

5. $\begin{array}{r} \frac{1}{2} \\ +\frac{1}{4} \\ \hline \end{array}$

6. $\begin{array}{r} \frac{1}{3} \\ +\frac{1}{6} \\ \hline \end{array}$

7. $\begin{array}{r} \frac{1}{2} \\ +\frac{2}{5} \\ \hline \end{array}$

8. $\frac{3}{8} + \frac{1}{2}$

276

Practice

Add.

1. $\frac{1}{3}$
$+\frac{2}{5}$

2. $\frac{2}{5}$
$+\frac{1}{2}$

3. $\frac{3}{4}$
$+\frac{1}{6}$

4. $\frac{3}{5}$
$+\frac{1}{3}$

5. $\frac{1}{3}$
$+\frac{2}{3}$

6. $\frac{1}{10}$
$+\frac{1}{5}$

7. $\frac{3}{5}$
$+\frac{1}{10}$

8. $\frac{5}{8}$
$+\frac{1}{4}$

9. $\frac{1}{3}$
$+\frac{3}{4}$

10. $\frac{2}{4}$
$+\frac{2}{8}$

11. $\frac{1}{2}$
$+\frac{4}{5}$

12. $\frac{2}{3}$
$+\frac{4}{9}$

13. $\frac{2}{10}$
$+\frac{4}{5}$

14. $\frac{2}{3}$
$+\frac{3}{4}$

15. $\frac{1}{2}$
$+\frac{2}{10}$

16. $\frac{2}{3}$
$+\frac{4}{6}$

17. $\frac{1}{2}$
$+\frac{3}{4}$

18. $\frac{4}{5}$
$+\frac{8}{10}$

19. $\frac{1}{3}$
$+\frac{2}{9}$

20. $\frac{2}{4}$
$+\frac{5}{8}$

21. $\frac{2}{3} + \frac{1}{4}$

22. $\frac{1}{2} + \frac{2}{3}$

23. $\frac{1}{4} + \frac{3}{3}$

24. $\frac{1}{3} + \frac{4}{9}$

25. $\frac{3}{4} + \frac{1}{8}$

26. $\frac{1}{2} + \frac{5}{8}$

★ 27. $\frac{1}{5} + \frac{2}{3} + \frac{3}{5}$

★ 28. $\frac{1}{4} + \frac{3}{8} + \frac{1}{2}$

Solve Problems

29. In the math class, $\frac{1}{3}$ of the students wore red shirts. $\frac{1}{5}$ wore green shirts. What part of the class wore red or green shirts?

30. During the spelling bee contest, $\frac{1}{2}$ of the class was out after the fifth round. An additional $\frac{1}{6}$ of the class was out after the sixth round. What part of the class was out at the end of the sixth round?

ADDING MIXED NUMBERS

There are $1\frac{1}{4}$ bottles of red paint.

There are $2\frac{2}{4}$ bottles of blue paint.

How much paint is there in all?

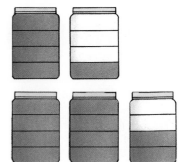

Step 1

ADD FRACTIONS.

$$\begin{array}{r} 1\frac{1}{4} \\ + 2\frac{2}{4} \\ \hline \frac{3}{4} \end{array}$$

Step 2

ADD WHOLE NUMBERS.

$$\begin{array}{r} 1\frac{1}{4} \\ + 2\frac{2}{4} \\ \hline 3\frac{3}{4} \end{array}$$

There are $3\frac{3}{4}$ bottles of paint in all.

Study and Learn

A. Find $4\frac{3}{8} + 5\frac{4}{8}$.

WRITE

1. Add fractions. $\frac{3}{8} + \frac{4}{8} = \frac{?}{?}$

2. Add whole numbers. $4 + 5 = \underline{\quad?\quad}$

3. What is the sum?

$$\begin{array}{r} 4\frac{3}{8} \\ + 5\frac{4}{8} \\ \hline \end{array}$$

B. Add.

4. $\begin{array}{r} 4\frac{1}{3} \\ + 2\frac{1}{3} \\ \hline \end{array}$

5. $\begin{array}{r} 6\frac{3}{5} \\ + 5\frac{1}{5} \\ \hline \end{array}$

6. $\begin{array}{r} 26\frac{2}{7} \\ + 97\frac{3}{7} \\ \hline \end{array}$

7. $\begin{array}{r} 53\frac{1}{10} \\ + 9 \\ \hline \end{array}$

Practice

Add.

1. $4\frac{3}{8}$
  $+\ 5\frac{2}{8}$

2. $7\frac{3}{6}$
  $+\ 8\frac{1}{6}$

3. $7\frac{1}{8}$
  $+\ 9\frac{5}{8}$

4. $3\frac{1}{7}$
  $+\ 5\frac{4}{7}$

5. $6\frac{5}{10}$
  $+\ 5\frac{3}{10}$

6. $5\frac{3}{12}$
  $+\ 7\frac{4}{12}$

7. $9\frac{3}{10}$
  $+\ 8\frac{6}{10}$

8. $4\frac{1}{9}$
  $+\ 4\frac{7}{9}$

9. $8\frac{1}{2}$
  $+\ 9$

10. $37\frac{3}{8}$
  $+\ 42\frac{1}{8}$

11. $16\frac{3}{4}$
  $+\ 7$

12. $37\frac{3}{10}$
  $+\ 96\frac{4}{10}$

13. $52\frac{3}{8}$
  $+\ 69\frac{1}{8}$

14. $37\frac{3}{9}$
  $+\ 49$

15. $74\frac{2}{7}$
  $+\ 96\frac{4}{7}$

16. $35\frac{7}{12}$
  $+\ 86$

17. $8\frac{3}{5}$
  $+\ 6\frac{1}{5}$

18. $20\frac{1}{4}$
  $+\ 8\frac{2}{4}$

19. $7\frac{1}{2}$
  $+\ 9$

20. $83\frac{1}{3}$
  $+\ 9\frac{1}{3}$

21. $6\frac{2}{8}$
  $+\ 10\frac{3}{8}$

22. $29\frac{7}{8}$
  $+\ 16$

★23. $3\frac{2}{3}$
  $+\ 16\frac{2}{3}$

★24. $5\frac{4}{5}$
  $+\ 8\frac{1}{10}$

Solve Problems

25. Henri has $3\frac{1}{8}$ jars of blue paint and $4\frac{6}{8}$ jars of red paint. How many jars of paint does Henri have altogether?

26. Brenda spends $7\frac{1}{2}$ hours working on the design of a mural. She spends 6 hours painting the mural. How much time does Brenda spend on the mural?

Midchapter Review

Add.

1. $\dfrac{1}{4}$
$+\dfrac{1}{4}$
(272)

2. $\dfrac{2}{5}$
$+\dfrac{1}{5}$
(272)

3. $\dfrac{2}{6}$
$+\dfrac{3}{6}$
(272)

4. $\dfrac{6}{8}$
$+\dfrac{5}{8}$
(274)

5. $\dfrac{7}{12}$
$+\dfrac{5}{12}$
(274)

6. $\dfrac{2}{3}$
$+\dfrac{2}{3}$
(274)

7. $\dfrac{3}{7}$
$+\dfrac{4}{7}$
(274)

8. $\dfrac{9}{10}$
$+\dfrac{6}{10}$
(274)

9. $\dfrac{1}{3}$
$+\dfrac{3}{6}$
(276)

10. $\dfrac{3}{4}$
$+\dfrac{1}{12}$
(276)

11. $\dfrac{1}{2}$
$+\dfrac{1}{4}$
(276)

12. $\dfrac{1}{4}$
$+\dfrac{1}{3}$
(276)

13. $\dfrac{2}{5}$
$+\dfrac{8}{10}$
(276)

14. $\dfrac{3}{4}$
$+\dfrac{1}{2}$
(276)

15. $\dfrac{4}{5}$
$+\dfrac{4}{10}$
(276)

16. 3
$+4\dfrac{1}{8}$
(278)

17. $7\dfrac{1}{4}$
$+8\dfrac{2}{4}$
(278)

18. $2\dfrac{1}{10}$
$+9\dfrac{7}{10}$
(278)

19. $7\dfrac{5}{6}$
$+8$
(278)

20. $26\dfrac{3}{12}$
$+87\dfrac{4}{12}$
(278)

Something Extra
Calculator Activities

Use these numbers. 96, 42, 847, 284, 376
Find which two complete these.

1. _?_ + _?_ = 138

2. _?_ + _?_ = 1,223

3. _?_ − _?_ = 188

4. _?_ − _?_ = 563

5. _?_ × _?_ = 4,032

6. _?_ × _?_ = 36,096

Skills Review

Measure to the nearest centimeter. *(142)*

1.

2.

Complete. *(146)*

3. 5 km = ___?___ m   **4.** 3 m = ___?___ cm   **5.** 3,000 m = ___?___ km

Write the time in as many ways as possible. *(158)*

6.    **7.**    **8.**

9. 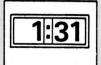   **10.**    **11.**

Something Extra
Non-Routine Problems

Complete each sequence.

1. $\frac{1}{2}, \frac{1}{3}, \frac{1}{4}, \frac{1}{5}, \frac{1}{6}, \frac{?}{?}, \frac{?}{?}, \frac{?}{?}$

2. $\frac{1}{2}, \frac{1}{4}, \frac{1}{6}, \frac{1}{8}, \frac{1}{10}, \frac{?}{?}, \frac{?}{?}, \frac{?}{?}$

3. $\frac{2}{3}, \frac{4}{6}, \frac{6}{9}, \frac{8}{12}, \frac{10}{15}, \frac{?}{?}, \frac{?}{?}, \frac{?}{?}$

Problem-Solving Skills
Identifying Extra Information

Mt. Everest is 8,848 meters above sea level.
Edmund P. Hillary was the first to climb it
in 1953. Junko Tabei climbed it in 1975. How many years
are there between these two years?

$$
\begin{array}{r}
1975 \\
- 1953 \\
\hline
22
\end{array}
$$
There are 22 years between.

It is not necessary to know that Mt. Everest is 8,848 meters
high. This is **extra information.**

Study and Learn

A. The longest fence on earth is a sheep fence in Australia.
It is 2 meters high and 5,532 kilometers long.
It is 6 times longer than the distance from Los Angeles
to the Grand Canyon. How far is it from
Los Angeles to the Grand Canyon?

   1. What information is needed to solve the problem?

   2. What is the extra information?

   3. Solve the problem.

B. Solve. Write the extra information.

   4. Alice Pollock was the oldest author at 102 years of age. Her book was published in 1971. The youngest author was Dorothy Straight at 4 years of age. How much older was Alice Pollock?

   5. The largest jellyfish was found in Massachusetts in 1865. Its body was about 8 feet in diameter. Its tentacles were 245 feet long. How much longer were the tentacles?

Practice

Solve. Write the extra information.

1. Linda Kuerth ate 23 hot dogs in about 3 minutes. Each hot dog weighed 2 ounces. How many hot dogs did she eat in 1 minute?

2. Cynthia Nicholas swam across the English Channel and back in about 20 hours. It was more than 10 hours faster than the previous record. How long did it take her to swim one way?

3. On October 14, 1974, Steve Meltzer ate 96 sausages. He took 6 minutes. How many sausages did he eat in 1 minute?

4. Matthew Webb swam the English Channel one way in 1875. It took him about 22 hours. How many years ago was this?

5. In the 1980 Winter Olympic games, the USA won 12 medals. 6 of the medals were gold, 4 were silver, and 2 were bronze. What part of the total number of medals were silver?

★ **6.** The first spacecraft with passengers to orbit the moon was launched on Dec. 21, 1968. It landed 147 hours later. How many days later did it land?

SUBTRACTING FRACTIONS

Find $\frac{4}{6} - \frac{1}{6}$.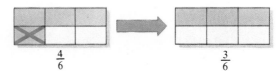

$\frac{4}{6}$ $\frac{3}{6}$

Step 1 Are the denominators the same? yes
Step 2 Subtract the numerators.
Step 3 Use the same denominator.

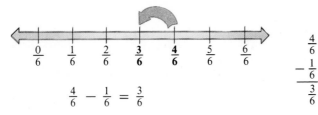

$\frac{4}{6} - \frac{1}{6} = \frac{3}{6}$

$\begin{array}{r} \frac{4}{6} \\ -\frac{1}{6} \\ \hline \frac{3}{6} \end{array}$

▶ When the denominators are the same, subtract the numerators.

Study and Learn

A. Complete.

Judy was given $\frac{2}{3}$ of the packages to deliver. She gave $\frac{1}{3}$ of these to Jamie. What part did Judy have left?

$\left[\text{Think: } \frac{2}{3} - \frac{1}{3} = \underline{\quad?\quad}\right]$

1. Are the denominators the same?

2. Subtract the numerators. Use the same denominator.

3. What part is left?

B. Subtract.

4. $\begin{array}{r} \frac{3}{4} \\ -\frac{1}{4} \\ \hline \end{array}$ **5.** $\begin{array}{r} \frac{8}{9} \\ -\frac{3}{9} \\ \hline \end{array}$ **6.** $\begin{array}{r} \frac{7}{8} \\ -\frac{1}{8} \\ \hline \end{array}$ **7.** $\frac{9}{10} - \frac{1}{10}$

Practice

Subtract.

1. $\frac{3}{5}$ $-\frac{2}{5}$

2. $\frac{7}{10}$ $-\frac{6}{10}$

3. $\frac{8}{9}$ $-\frac{1}{9}$

4. $\frac{9}{10}$ $-\frac{8}{10}$

5. $\frac{8}{12}$ $-\frac{4}{12}$

6. $\frac{3}{4}$ $-\frac{2}{4}$

7. $\frac{4}{5}$ $-\frac{3}{5}$

8. $\frac{7}{8}$ $-\frac{5}{8}$

9. $\frac{4}{9}$ $-\frac{1}{9}$

10. $\frac{2}{5}$ $-\frac{1}{5}$

11. $\frac{3}{6}$ $-\frac{2}{6}$

12. $\frac{4}{8}$ $-\frac{2}{8}$

13. $\frac{2}{4}$ $-\frac{1}{4}$

14. $\frac{5}{9}$ $-\frac{3}{9}$

15. $\frac{7}{8}$ $-\frac{3}{8}$

16. $\frac{5}{10}$ $-\frac{2}{10}$

17. $\frac{2}{7}$ $-\frac{1}{7}$

18. $\frac{6}{12}$ $-\frac{3}{12}$

19. $\frac{4}{5}$ $-\frac{3}{5}$

20. $\frac{3}{10}$ $-\frac{2}{10}$

21. $\frac{4}{5} - \frac{1}{5}$

22. $\frac{5}{6} - \frac{2}{6}$

23. $\frac{6}{7} - \frac{1}{7}$

24. $\frac{3}{8} - \frac{2}{8}$

25. $\frac{6}{9} - \frac{2}{9}$

★ 26. $\frac{4}{12} - \frac{?}{12} = \frac{1}{12}$

★ 27. $\frac{7}{10} - \frac{?}{10} = \frac{5}{10}$

Solve Problems

28. Sue had $\frac{9}{12}$ dozen eggs. She cooked $\frac{3}{12}$ of them for breakfast. What part of a dozen eggs remains?

★ 29. $\frac{7}{10}$ of the packages were wrapped with blue paper. $\frac{2}{10}$ of the packages were wrapped with pink paper. What part of the packages were not wrapped?

DIFFERENT DENOMINATORS

Find $\frac{1}{3} - \frac{2}{9}$.

Step 1 Are the denominators the same? no

Step 2 List equal fractions for each.

$$\frac{1}{3} : \frac{1}{3}, \frac{2}{6}, \boxed{\frac{3}{9}}, \frac{4}{12}, \cdots$$

$$\frac{2}{9} : \boxed{\frac{2}{9}}, \frac{4}{18}, \cdots$$

Step 3 Rewrite the problem using equal fractions with the same denominator.

Step 4 Subtract.

$$\begin{array}{r} \frac{1}{3} = \frac{3}{9} \\ -\frac{2}{9} = \frac{2}{9} \\ \hline \frac{1}{9} \end{array}$$

So, $\frac{1}{3} - \frac{2}{9} = \frac{1}{9}$.

Study and Learn

A. Find $\frac{1}{3} - \frac{1}{4}$.

    1. Are the denominators the same?

    2. List the first four equal fractions for each.

    3. Complete.
$$\begin{array}{cc} \frac{1}{3} & \frac{?}{12} \\ -\frac{1}{4} & -\frac{?}{12} \end{array}$$

    4. Subtract.

B. Subtract.

5. $\quad \begin{array}{r} \frac{1}{2} \\ -\frac{1}{4} \\ \hline \end{array}$
    6. $\quad \begin{array}{r} \frac{5}{6} \\ -\frac{1}{3} \\ \hline \end{array}$
    7. $\quad \begin{array}{r} \frac{2}{3} \\ -\frac{1}{2} \\ \hline \end{array}$
    8. $\frac{7}{8} - \frac{3}{4}$

Practice

Subtract.

1. $\frac{5}{6}$
   $-\frac{1}{2}$

2. $\frac{1}{2}$
   $-\frac{1}{5}$

3. $\frac{3}{8}$
   $-\frac{1}{4}$

4. $\frac{2}{3}$
   $-\frac{1}{4}$

5. $\frac{2}{3}$
   $-\frac{3}{5}$

6. $\frac{3}{10}$
   $-\frac{1}{5}$

7. $\frac{3}{4}$
   $-\frac{1}{6}$

8. $\frac{1}{2}$
   $-\frac{1}{8}$

9. $\frac{1}{2}$
   $-\frac{3}{10}$

10. $\frac{3}{4}$
    $-\frac{1}{2}$

11. $\frac{5}{8}$
    $-\frac{1}{2}$

12. $\frac{2}{3}$
    $-\frac{5}{12}$

13. $\frac{3}{4}$
    $-\frac{7}{12}$

14. $\frac{2}{3}$
    $-\frac{5}{9}$

15. $\frac{3}{4}$
    $-\frac{1}{8}$

16. $\frac{1}{2}$
    $-\frac{1}{3}$

17. $\frac{2}{3}$
    $-\frac{3}{6}$

18. $\frac{8}{12}$
    $-\frac{3}{6}$

19. $\frac{3}{5}$
    $-\frac{1}{2}$

20. $\frac{4}{5}$
    $-\frac{1}{3}$

21. $\frac{7}{8} - \frac{1}{2}$

22. $\frac{3}{4} - \frac{2}{3}$

23. $\frac{4}{5} - \frac{2}{3}$

24. $\frac{7}{8} - \frac{1}{4}$

25. $\frac{1}{2} - \frac{1}{6}$

★ 26. $\frac{3}{8} - \frac{?}{4} = \frac{1}{8}$

★ 27. $\frac{5}{6} - \frac{?}{3} = \frac{3}{6}$

Solve Problems

28. Judy had $\frac{2}{3}$ dozen lemons. She used $\frac{1}{4}$ dozen for a pie. What part of a dozen lemons is left?

29. A pie crust needs $\frac{1}{3}$ cup of flour. Bread needs $\frac{3}{4}$ cup of flour. How much more flour is needed for bread?

● 30. James mixed $\frac{3}{4}$ cup of vinegar with $\frac{1}{2}$ cup of oil for a salad dressing. How much salad dressing did he make?

★ 31. Kevin had $\frac{5}{7}$ quarts of pineapple juice and $\frac{2}{9}$ quarts of orange juice. How much more pineapple juice than orange juice did Kevin have?

SUBTRACTING MIXED NUMBERS

There were $7\frac{3}{4}$ liters of fruit punch.

The students drank $3\frac{1}{4}$ liters.

How many liters were left?

Step 1	Step 2
SUBTRACT FRACTIONS	SUBTRACT WHOLE NUMBERS

$$\begin{array}{r} 7\frac{3}{4} \\ -\ 3\frac{1}{4} \\ \hline \frac{2}{4} \end{array}$$

$$\begin{array}{r} 7\frac{3}{4} \\ -\ 3\frac{1}{4} \\ \hline 4\frac{2}{4} \end{array}$$

There were $4\frac{2}{4}$ liters left.

Study and Learn

A. Find $6\frac{5}{8} - 3\frac{1}{8}$.

                                                    WRITE

1. Subtract fractions. $\frac{5}{8} - \frac{1}{8} = \frac{?}{?}$ $6\frac{5}{8}$

2. Subtract whole numbers. $6 - 3 = \underline{\ ?\ }$ $-\ 3\frac{1}{8}$

3. What is the difference?

B. Subtract.

4. $\begin{array}{r} 4\frac{4}{5} \\ -\ 1\frac{3}{5} \\ \hline \end{array}$ **5.** $\begin{array}{r} 7\frac{9}{10} \\ -\ 4\frac{9}{10} \\ \hline \end{array}$ **6.** $\begin{array}{r} 9\frac{3}{7} \\ -\ 9\frac{1}{7} \\ \hline \end{array}$ **7.** $\begin{array}{r} 28\frac{2}{3} \\ -\ 16 \\ \hline \end{array}$

Practice

Subtract.

1. $9\frac{8}{9}$
   $-3\frac{7}{9}$

2. $4\frac{8}{10}$
   $-3\frac{6}{10}$

3. $8\frac{4}{6}$
   $-2\frac{1}{6}$

4. $5\frac{7}{8}$
   $-1\frac{7}{8}$

5. $16\frac{8}{10}$
   $-9\frac{3}{10}$

6. $17\frac{5}{12}$
   $-9\frac{3}{12}$

7. $15\frac{5}{6}$
   $-9\frac{4}{6}$

8. $18\frac{7}{8}$
   -9

9. $28\frac{7}{12}$
   $-19\frac{3}{12}$

10. $46\frac{7}{9}$
    $-9\frac{3}{9}$

11. $88\frac{6}{10}$
    $-88\frac{1}{10}$

12. $94\frac{5}{8}$
    -89

13. $9\frac{1}{2}$
    $-7\frac{1}{2}$

14. $7\frac{3}{8}$
    $-7\frac{2}{8}$

15. $6\frac{2}{3}$
    -6

16. $7\frac{4}{9}$
    $-7\frac{4}{9}$

17. $9\frac{2}{3}$
    $-2\frac{1}{3}$

18. $13\frac{4}{5}$
    $-7\frac{2}{5}$

19. $7\frac{3}{9}$
    -4

20. $35\frac{7}{8}$
    $-18\frac{5}{8}$

21. $89\frac{9}{10}$
    $-65\frac{6}{10}$

22. $18\frac{5}{6}$
    -7

★ 23. $8\frac{?}{5}$
    $-5\frac{1}{5}$
    $?\frac{2}{5}$

★ 24. $17\frac{?}{9}$
    $-9\frac{3}{9}$
    $?\frac{3}{9}$

Solve Problems

25. The costume party lasted $3\frac{3}{4}$ hours. Tom arrived $1\frac{1}{4}$ hours late. How long was he at the party?

★ 26. Joan had $4\frac{1}{3}$ bags filled with treats. By the end of one week, she had $1\frac{1}{4}$ bags left. How many bags of treats did Joan eat?

DECIMALS—TENTHS

A fraction or mixed number with a denominator of 10
can be written as a decimal.

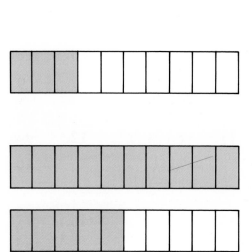

Fraction or Mixed Number	Decimal
$\frac{3}{10}$	0.3
$1\frac{5}{10}$	1.5

0.3 is read three tenths.

1.5 is read one and five tenths.

Study and Learn

A. Read each of these decimals.

   1. 0.1   **2.** 0.9   **3.** 1.8   **4.** 9.7   **5.** 36.4

B. Write a decimal for each.

   6. $\frac{7}{10}$ **7.** $\frac{2}{10}$ **8.** $3\frac{6}{10}$ **9.** $8\frac{1}{10}$ **10.** $21\frac{4}{10}$

C. Write a fraction or mixed number for each.

   11. 0.2   **12.** 0.4   **13.** 3.5   **14.** 7.7   **15.** 46.9

Practice

Write a decimal for each.

1. $\frac{9}{10}$ 2. $\frac{7}{10}$ 3. $\frac{5}{10}$ 4. $\frac{3}{10}$ 5. $\frac{1}{10}$

6. $1\frac{8}{10}$ 7. $2\frac{6}{10}$ 8. $13\frac{4}{10}$ 9. $24\frac{2}{10}$ 10. $5\frac{1}{10}$

Write a fraction or mixed number for each.

11. 0.5   12. 0.2   13. 0.4   14. 0.6   15. 0.8

16. 1.1   17. 2.3   18. 3.5   19. 14.7   20. 34.9

Solve Problems

21. The dash was won with a time of 9.7 seconds. Write a mixed number for this time.

22. The race was run in $22\frac{6}{10}$ seconds. Write a decimal for this time.

Computer

The computer can output a decimal for a fraction. For $\frac{3}{10}$, type: **PRINT 3/10.** The computer output will be .3.
Tell the computer to do these. Write the input and output.

1. $\frac{7}{10}$ 2. $\frac{5}{10}$ 3. $\frac{8}{10}$ ★ 4. $\frac{1}{2}$ ★5. $\frac{4}{5}$

H A N D S   O N

You can check your answers on the computer. Remember: Press [RETURN] after you type a line.

DECIMALS—HUNDREDTHS

Any fraction or mixed number with a denominator of 100 can be shown as a decimal.

		Read as	Fraction or Mixed Number	Decimal
		three hundredths	$\frac{3}{100}$	0.03
		eighty-seven hundredths	$\frac{87}{100}$	0.87
		one and twelve hundredths	$1\frac{12}{100}$	1.12

Study and Learn

A. Write a decimal for the shaded parts.

1.   **2.**   **3.**

B. Read each of these decimals.

4. 0.07   **5.** 0.80   **6.** 0.29   **7.** 4.05   **8.** 26.78

C. Write a fraction or mixed number for each decimal.

9. 0.05   **10.** 0.10   **11.** 0.44   **12.** 7.15   **13.** 46.07

D. Decimals can be shown on a place-value chart.

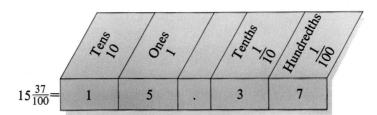

$15\frac{37}{100}=$ | Tens 10 | Ones 1 | . | Tenths $\frac{1}{10}$ | Hundredths $\frac{1}{100}$ |

Write a decimal for each. Use the place-value chart above to help you.

14. three and four hundredths

15. seventeen and ninety-nine hundredths

16. $\frac{8}{100}$ **17.** $\frac{64}{100}$ **18.** $7\frac{9}{100}$ **19.** $58\frac{92}{100}$

Practice

Write a decimal for the shaded parts.

1.   **2.**   **3.**

Write a decimal for each.

4. fifty and nine hundredths   **5.** seventy-four hundredths

6. $\frac{2}{100}$ **7.** $\frac{11}{100}$ **8.** $18\frac{45}{100}$ **9.** $72\frac{6}{100}$

Write a fraction or mixed number for each.

10. 0.03   **11.** 0.71   **12.** 0.88   **13.** 0.16   **14.** 0.09

15. 6.17   **16.** 9.27   **17.** 8.40   **18.** 36.79   **19.** 64.99

ADDING DECIMALS

Add 16.4 + 8.7.

Step 1 Line up the decimal points.
Step 2 Add.
Step 3 Place the decimal point in the answer.

$$
\begin{array}{r}
{\scriptstyle 1\ 1} \\
16.4 \\
+\ \ 8.7 \\
\hline
25.1 \\
\uparrow
\end{array}
$$

Study and Learn

A. Add.

1.	2.	3.	4.	5.
0.5 + 0.4	4.7 + 0.9	7.6 + 4.9	19.8 + 24.7	128.5 + 36.9

Add 1.85 + 2.76. Use the 3 steps.

Example
$$
\begin{array}{r}
{\scriptstyle 1\ 1} \\
1.85 \\
+\ 2.76 \\
\hline
4.61 \\
\uparrow
\end{array}
$$
——Place the decimal point in the answer.

B. Add.

6.	7.	8.	9.	10.
0.04 + 0.19	7.82 + 14.64	18.65 + 23.43	37.24 + 24.89	328.43 + 62.98

Practice

Add.

1.	2.	3.	4.	5.
8.0 + 9.8	4.8 + 6.7	0.98 + 0.74	6.24 + 2.66	725.05 + 11.96

6.	7.	8.	★ 9.	★ 10.
527.18 + 9.87	26.7 + 39.8	37.07 + 49.19	26.3 9.7 + 0.9	42.57 6.29 + 0.98

294

SUBTRACTING DECIMALS

Subtract 9.5 − 3.6.

Step 1 Line up the decimal points.
Step 2 Subtract.
Step 3 Place the decimal point in the answer.

$$
\begin{array}{r}
{}^{8}\,{}^{15}\\
\cancel{9}.\cancel{5}\\
-\ 3.6\\
\hline
5.9\\
\uparrow
\end{array}
$$

Study and Learn

A. Subtract.

1. 0.9 − 0.4	**2.** 8.7 − 1.9	**3.** 17.0 − 8.4	**4.** 36.7 − 36.4	**5.** 170.4 − 82.5

Subtract 9.54 − 3.65. Use the 3 steps.

Example
$$
\begin{array}{r}
{}^{8}\,{}^{14}\,{}^{14}\\
\cancel{9}.\cancel{5}\cancel{4}\\
-\ 3.65\\
\hline
5.89\\
\uparrow
\end{array}
$$
—— Place the decimal point in the answer.

B. Subtract.

6. 0.86 − 0.19	**7.** 2.74 − 1.99	**8.** 19.00 − 3.86	**9.** 43.76 − 28.93	**10.** 203.46 − 0.85

Practice

Subtract.

1. 1.6 − 0.4	**2.** 7.3 − 1.6	**3.** 14.08 − 9.09	**4.** 62.47 − 9.88	**5.** 712.83 − 14.85

6. 60.3 − 18.7	**7.** 96.41 − 45.06	**8.** 175.78 − 82.99	**9.** 72.8 − 14.9	**10.** 15.65 − 8.76

Problem-Solving Applications

Using Fractions and Decimals

Solve.

1. $\frac{1}{2}$ of the pictures are color.

$\frac{1}{4}$ of the pictures are black and white.

How many more pictures are in color?

2. Juanita wrote $\frac{3}{5}$ of a story in June.

She wrote $\frac{1}{5}$ more in July.

How much of the story has she written?

3. $\frac{1}{2}$ of the book has photographs.

$\frac{1}{3}$ of the book has sketches.

The photographs and sketches are what part of the book?

4. Jerry has read 26.4 pages of the book.
There are 73.6 pages left.
How many pages are in the book?

5. Georgia read that the recent world records for the 100-meter dash were 9.95 seconds for men and 10.88 seconds for women. How much faster is the record for men?

Chapter Review

Add.

1. (272)
$$\frac{3}{8} + \frac{4}{8}$$

2. (272)
$$\frac{1}{10} + \frac{7}{10}$$

3. (274)
$$\frac{2}{3} + \frac{2}{3}$$

4. (276)
$$\frac{1}{2} + \frac{3}{8}$$

5. (276)
$$\frac{1}{3} + \frac{3}{4}$$

6. (278)
$$1\frac{2}{5} + 3\frac{1}{5}$$

7. (278)
$$8\frac{1}{2} + 6$$

8. (294)
$$19.7 + 3.8$$

9. (294)
$$4.38 + 6.79$$

Subtract.

10. (284)
$$\frac{3}{5} - \frac{1}{5}$$

11. (284)
$$\frac{4}{10} - \frac{1}{10}$$

12. (286)
$$\frac{1}{2} - \frac{1}{4}$$

13. (286)
$$\frac{7}{8} - \frac{3}{4}$$

14. (286)
$$\frac{3}{5} - \frac{3}{10}$$

15. (288)
$$3\frac{7}{10} - 1\frac{4}{10}$$

16. (288)
$$6\frac{2}{3} - 3$$

17. (295)
$$9.6 - 4.7$$

18. (295)
$$34.12 - 18.27$$

Write a decimal for each. *(290, 292)*

19. $\frac{4}{10}$

20. $8\frac{6}{10}$

21. $\frac{48}{100}$

22. $3\frac{5}{100}$

Write a fraction or mixed number for each. *(290, 292)*

23. 0.7

24. 16.9

25. 0.80

26. 4.97

Solve. Write the extra information.   Solve.

27. (282) 232 people came to the show. The theater held 316 people. 86 people were late. How many people were on time?

28. (296) Anne has 3.5 pitchers of orange juice and 2.5 pitchers of apple juice. How many pitchers of juice are there altogether?

297

Chapter Test

Add.

1. (272)
$$\frac{4}{7} + \frac{1}{7}$$

2. (272)
$$\frac{6}{12} + \frac{5}{12}$$

3. (274)
$$\frac{3}{4} + \frac{2}{4}$$

4. (276)
$$\frac{1}{4} + \frac{5}{8}$$

5. (276)
$$\frac{2}{3} + \frac{1}{2}$$

6. (278)
$$3\frac{1}{5} + 2\frac{2}{5}$$

7. (278)
$$7\frac{2}{3} + 8$$

8. (294)
$$36.7 + 15.6$$

9. (294)
$$9.47 + 6.85$$

Subtract.

10. (284)
$$\frac{4}{7} - \frac{2}{7}$$

11. (284)
$$\frac{6}{9} - \frac{1}{9}$$

12. (286)
$$\frac{3}{4} - \frac{1}{2}$$

13. (286)
$$\frac{7}{10} - \frac{1}{5}$$

14. (286)
$$\frac{1}{2} - \frac{1}{5}$$

15. (288)
$$4\frac{7}{8} - 1\frac{2}{8}$$

16. (288)
$$9\frac{3}{10} - 4$$

17. (295)
$$6.7 - 1.9$$

18. (295)
$$14.83 - 9.95$$

Write a decimal for each. *(290, 292)*

19. $\frac{5}{10}$

20. $7\frac{7}{10}$

21. $\frac{84}{100}$

22. $6\frac{4}{100}$

Write a fraction or mixed number for each. *(290, 292)*

23. 0.8

24. 15.8

25. 0.70

26. 5.83

Solve. Write the extra information.   Solve.

27. (282) 518 people were watching the parade. 178 more people came to watch. 346 people marched in the parade. How many people watched the parade?

28. (296) Andy has 6.25 boxes of nails. He uses 3.00 boxes when he builds a fence. How many boxes of nails does he have left?

Skills Check

1.

$$7 \times 4$$

A 11
B 28
C 32
D 35

2. $3 \times 9 = $ ___?

E 12
F 18
G 21
H 27

3.

$$27 \times 4$$

A 31
B 88
C 108
D 152

4.

$$257 \times 3$$

E 771
F 775
G 857
H 885

5.

$$900 \times 6$$

A 2,700
B 3,600
C 4,500
D 5,400

6.

$$8\overline{)56}$$

E 7
F 8
G 9
H 12

7.

$$7\overline{)49}$$

A 6
B 7
C 8
D 9

8. $54 \div 9 = $ ___?

E 3
F 4
G 6
H 8

9.

$$9\overline{)83}$$

A 4 r 9
B 8 r 2
C 9 r 2
D 18 r 2

10.

$$5\overline{)845}$$

E 169
F 175
G 179
H 196

11.

$$4\overline{)486}$$

A 81 r 2
B 121 r 2
C 131 r 2
D 152 r 1

12.

$$6\overline{)600}$$

E 10
F 60
G 80
H 100

11

GEOMETRY

Solar panels in New Mexico collect energy from the sun.

POINTS, LINE SEGMENTS, AND LINES

▶ A **point** is pictured by a dot. It is named with a capital letter. This is point *B*.

▶ A **line segment** is a straight path between 2 points. This is line segment *AB* or *BA*. It is written $\overline{AB}$ or $\overline{BA}$.

▶ A **line** is a straight path that goes on forever in both directions. This is line *CD* or *DC*. It is written $\overleftrightarrow{CD}$ or $\overleftrightarrow{DC}$.

▶ **Intersecting** line segments or lines meet at a point.

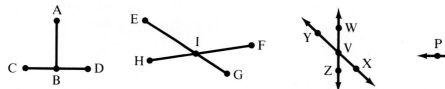

Here is another example of two lines that intersect.

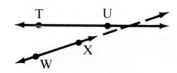

$\overleftrightarrow{WX}$ will intersect $\overleftrightarrow{TU}$ when $\overleftrightarrow{WX}$ is extended.

Remember, a line goes on forever.

▶ **Parallel** line segments or lines never cross or touch.

Study and Learn

A. Write two names for each.

1.

2.

3.

B. Tell whether each is intersecting or parallel.

4.

5.

6.

7.

8.

9.

Practice

Write two names for each.

1.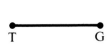

2.

3.

Tell whether each is intersecting or parallel.

4.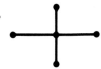

5.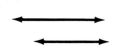

6.

7.

8.

9.

Draw each.

10. line segment *FG*   **11.** $\overleftrightarrow{BC}$ **12.** intersecting line segments

303

ANGLES

▶ A **ray** has one endpoint and goes on forever in one direction. This is ray AB or $\overrightarrow{AB}$.

A ●————————● B →

▶ An **angle** is two rays with the same endpoint. $\overrightarrow{AB}$ and $\overrightarrow{AC}$ intersect at point A. They form angle A. It is written $\angle A$.

Study and Learn

A. Which are angles? Write yes or no.

1. 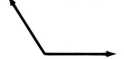   **2.** 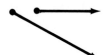   **3.**

B. Draw an angle. Here is how.

4. Draw $\overrightarrow{CD}$ and $\overrightarrow{CE}$ to form angle C.

5. Write the name of the angle.

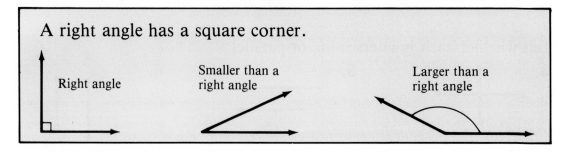

A right angle has a square corner.

Right angle   Smaller than a right angle   Larger than a right angle

C. Tell whether each is a right angle, smaller than a right angle, or larger than a right angle.

6.    **7.**    **8.**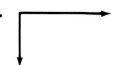

304

Practice

Write the name of each angle.

1.

2.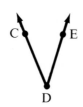

3.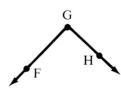

Tell whether each is a right angle, smaller than a right angle, or larger than a right angle.

4.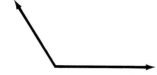

5.

6.

7.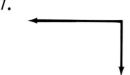

8.

9.

Draw each. Name each $\angle B$.

10. A right angle

11. An angle smaller than a right angle

12. An angle larger than a right angle

Something Extra
Non-Routine Problem

How many angles can you find?

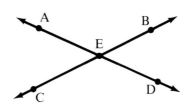

CIRCLES

This is a **circle.** Point A is the center of the circle.

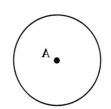

▶ All the points on a circle are the same distance from the center.

Study and Learn

A. Which are circles? Write yes or no.

1.
2.
3.
4.

▶ A **radius** is a line segment from the center of the circle to a point on the circle.

B. Look at the circle to the right.

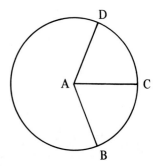

5. $\overline{AB}$ is a radius. Name 2 other radii. (Radii is the plural of radius.)

6. Name the center of the circle.

7. Measure each radius in centimeters. How do their lengths compare?

▶ A **diameter** is a line segment that connects two points on the circle and goes through the center of the circle.

C. Look at the circle to the right.

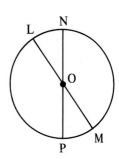

8. $\overline{LM}$ is a diameter. Name another diameter.

9. Measure each diameter. How do their measures compare?

306

Practice

Which are circles? Write yes or no.

1. 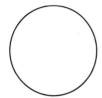 **2.**  **3.**  **4.**

Tell whether a radius, diameter, or neither is shown.

5.   **6.**   **7.**   **8.**

Look at the circle.

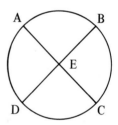

9. Name the center.

10. Name 4 radii.

11. Name 2 diameters.

★ **12.** If $\overline{AE}$ is 4 cm, how long is $\overline{AC}$?

Skills Review

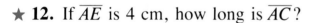

Divide.

1. 4)‾40‾ **2.** 7)‾700‾ **3.** 3)‾3,000‾
(207)

4. 6)‾360‾ **5.** 8)‾4,000‾ **6.** 5)‾3,500‾

7. 3)‾9‾ **8.** 7)‾35‾ **9.** 9)‾63‾
(126) *(132)*

10. 9)‾48‾ **11.** 4)‾30‾ **12.** 5)‾22‾ **13.** 6)‾53‾ **14.** 8)‾27‾
(208)

15. 4)‾893‾ **16.** 7)‾981‾ **17.** 9)‾3,284‾ **18.** 2)‾1,693‾ **19.** 9)‾7,478‾
(214) *(218)* *(216)* *(218)*

POLYGONS

These paths are called **curves**.

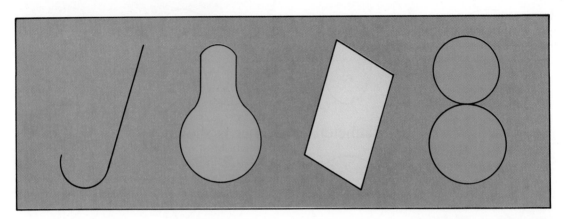

Study and Learn

A. Trace this curve with your finger.

    1. Does it end at the same point it started?

    2. Does it cross itself?

▶ A **closed curve** ends where it starts.

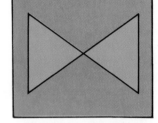

B. Trace this curve with your finger.

    3. Does it end at the same point it started?

    4. Does it cross itself?

▶ A **simple closed curve** ends where it starts and does not cross itself.

C. Which are simple closed curves? Write yes or no.

  5.   **6.**   **7.** 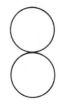   **8.**

▶ A **polygon** is a simple closed curve made of line segments.

D. Which are polygons? Write yes or no.

9. **10.** 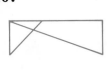 **11.**  **12.**

E. Draw each.

13. A polygon with three line segments

14. A polygon with four line segments

15. A polygon with eight line segments

Practice

Which are polygons? Write yes or no.

1. **2.** **3.** **4.**

5. **6.** **7.** **8.**

9. **10.** **11.** **12.**

13. Draw a polygon with six line segments.

TRIANGLES, RECTANGLES, AND SQUARES

Here are some special polygons.

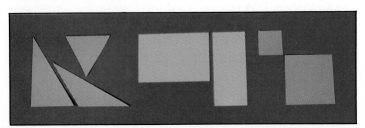

Study and Learn

▶ A **triangle** has three sides and three angles.

A. Which are triangles? Write yes or no.

1.   **2.**   **3.**   **4.**

▶ A **rectangle** has four sides and four right angles.

B. Which are rectangles? Write yes or no.

5.   **6.**   **7.**   **8.**

▶ A **square** is a special rectangle.
All four sides have the same length.

C. Which are squares? Write yes or no.

9.   **10.**   **11.**   **12.**

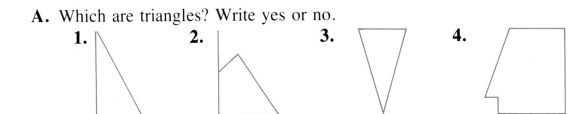

Practice

Write triangle, rectangle, square, or none.
If the rectangle is a square, just write square.

1.

2.

3.

4.

5.

6.

7.

8.

9.

10.

11.

12.

13.

14.

15.

16.

Look at this rectangle.

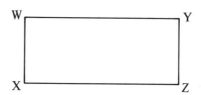

★ **17.** If $\overline{WX}$ is 22 cm, how long is $\overline{YZ}$?

★ **18.** If $\overline{WY}$ is 45 cm, how long is $\overline{XZ}$?

311

Midchapter Review

Write the name for each.

1.
(302)

2.
(302)

3.
(302)

4.
(304)

5.
(306)

6.
(310)

7.
(310)

8.
(310)

Draw each.

9. Point *A*
(302)

10. $\overleftrightarrow{AB}$
(302)

11. A pair of intersecting lines
(302)

12. An angle smaller than a right angle
(304)

Look at this circle. *(306)*

13. Name a radius.

14. Name a diameter.

Something Extra
Non-Routine Problems
These figures are called **slides, flips,** and **turns.**
The figures do not change shape or size.

Slide

Turn

Flip

Write slide, flip, or turn for each.

1.

2.

3.

COMPUTER—FLOWCHARTS

A flowchart shows the steps used to do something.
Programmers are people who use computer language. They
often use flowcharts to plan or check their programs.

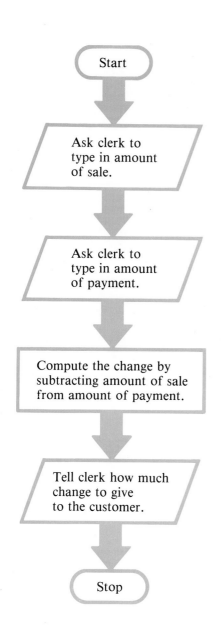

The flowchart shows how a
cash register finds the amount
of change to give a customer.

The commands that a cash
register computer follows are
shown below. Add the line
numbers to the program.

INPUT "AMOUNT OF SALE
$";S

LET C = P − S

END

PRINT "CORRECT CHANGE
IS $";C

INPUT "AMOUNT OF
PAYMENT $";P

SYMMETRY

These figures are symmetric. If each figure was folded on the line, the two parts would match.

 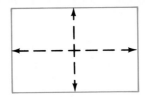 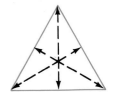

The dashed lines are lines of symmetry.

Study and Learn

A. Take a sheet of paper.

   1. Fold it in half.

   2. Draw an outline of a figure on the fold.

   3. Cut out the figure.

   4. Open it up. The figure is symmetric.

   5. Draw a line of symmetry on the fold.

   6. Fold to find another line of symmetry.

B. Trace each figure. Draw two lines of symmetry.

   7.

   8.

   9.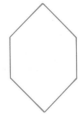

Practice

Which are symmetric? Write yes or no.

1.

2.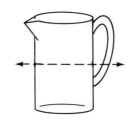

3.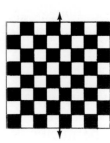

4.

5.

6.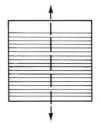

Trace each figure. Draw two lines of symmetry.

7.

8.

9.

10.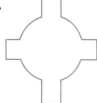

11.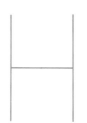

12.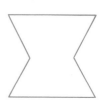

★ **13.** Trace this figure.
Draw as many lines of symmetry as you can.

315

PERIMETER

▶ The distance around a polygon is called the **perimeter.** The perimeter is found by adding the lengths of the sides.

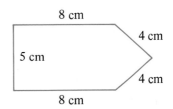

8 cm + 4 cm + 4 cm + 8 cm + 5 cm = 29 cm

The perimeter is 29 cm.

Study and Learn

A. Look at the triangle. Measure each side in centimeters.

  1. Add the lengths.
    2 cm + 3 cm + 3 cm = ___?___ cm

  2. What is the perimeter?

B. Find the perimeters.

  3.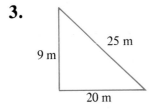

  4.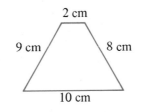

  5.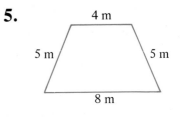

  6.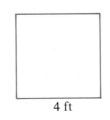

  7.

  8.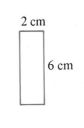

Practice

Measure each side in centimeters. Find the perimeters.

1.

2.

Find the perimeters.

3.

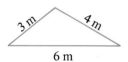

3 m   4 m

6 m

4.

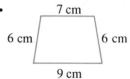

7 cm

6 cm   6 cm

9 cm

5.

9 m   9 m

8 m   8 m

10 m

6.

4 in.

7.

9 cm

15 cm

8.

3 m

9.

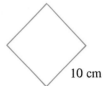

10 cm

10.

12 m

⭐ **11.**

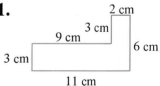

2 cm
3 cm
9 cm   6 cm
3 cm
11 cm

Something Extra
Calculator Activity

Add the lengths to find the perimeter.

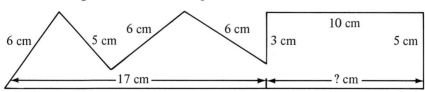

6 cm   5 cm   6 cm   6 cm   3 cm   10 cm   5 cm

←——— 17 cm ———→ ←—— ? cm ——→

317

ACTIVITIES WITH AREA

Units like this are used to measure length.

Units like this are used to measure **area.**
This is a square centimeter. Write 1 cm².

▶ Area is the number of square units that
will fit inside a figure.

The area of this rectangle is 6 cm².

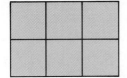

Study and Learn

Trace and cut out 15 square centimeters like the one above.
Use them for the problems below.

A. Look at the rectangle to the right.

    1. About how many square centimeters will it
take to cover the area of the rectangle?

    2. How many square centimeters
does it actually take to cover
the rectangle?

    3. What is the area?

B. Find the areas by counting the square centimeters.

    4.   **5.**   **6.**

 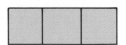 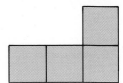

Practice

Find the areas by counting the square centimeters.

1. 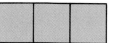   **2.**   **3.**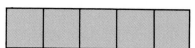

4. 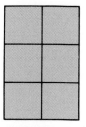   **5.** 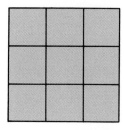   **6.**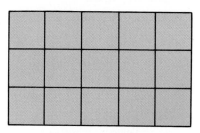

7. 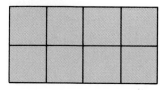   **8.**   **9.**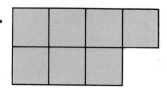

Skills Review

Add.

1.
(272)
$\frac{1}{4}$
$+ \frac{2}{4}$

2.
(276)
$\frac{2}{3}$
$+ \frac{1}{6}$

3.
$\frac{2}{4}$
$+ \frac{1}{8}$

4.
(278)
$1\frac{1}{3}$
$+ \frac{1}{3}$

5.
$2\frac{4}{6}$
$+ 1\frac{1}{6}$

6.
$3\frac{1}{3}$
$+ \frac{1}{3}$

7.
$14\frac{4}{8}$
$+ 11\frac{1}{8}$

8.
$6\frac{2}{5}$
$+ 1$

Subtract.

9.
(284)
$\frac{2}{3}$
$- \frac{1}{3}$

10.
$\frac{3}{4}$
$- \frac{2}{4}$

11.
(286)
$\frac{3}{8}$
$- \frac{1}{4}$

12.
$\frac{4}{9}$
$- \frac{1}{3}$

13.
$\frac{5}{6}$
$- \frac{3}{12}$

14.
(288)
$1\frac{4}{5}$
$- \frac{3}{5}$

15.
$12\frac{4}{6}$
$- \frac{1}{6}$

16.
$2\frac{1}{3}$
$- 1\frac{1}{3}$

17.
$6\frac{2}{8}$
$- 5\frac{2}{8}$

18.
$13\frac{3}{4}$
$- 8$

FINDING AREA BY MULTIPLYING

Count to find the area.
There are 20 tiles.

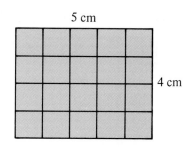

5 cm

4 cm

You can also multiply
to find the area.
Think: 4 rows of 5
    $4 \text{ cm} \times 5 \text{ cm} = 20 \text{ cm}^2$
So, the area is 20 cm².

▶ The area of a rectangle is found by
  multiplying length by width.

Study and Learn

A. Find the area of this rectangle.

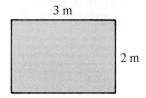

3 m

2 m

   1. Multiply. $2 \text{ m} \times 3 \text{ m} = \underline{\ ?\ } \text{ m}^2$

   2. What is the area?

B. Find the area of this square.

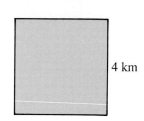

4 km

   3. Multiply. $4 \text{ km} \times 4 \text{ km} = \underline{\ ?\ } \text{ km}^2$

   4. What is the area?

C. Find the areas by multiplying.

   5. 2 cm

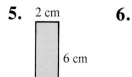

6 cm

   6. 9 cm

3 cm

   7.

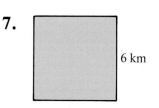

6 km

Practice

Find the areas by multiplying.

1.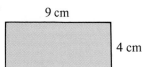
9 cm
4 cm

2.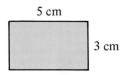
5 cm
3 cm

3.
5 m
5 m

4.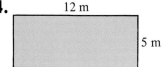
12 m
5 m

5.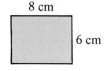
8 cm
6 cm

6.
3 cm
4 cm

7.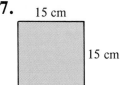
15 cm
15 cm

8.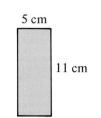
5 cm
11 cm

9.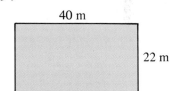
40 m
22 m

10.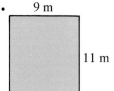
9 m
11 m

11.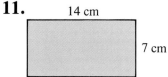
14 cm
7 cm

12.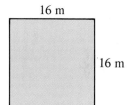
16 m
16 m

Solve Problems

13. The living-room floor is a rectangle 6 meters by 5 meters. How many square meters of carpet would be needed to cover it?

14. The workroom floor is a 7 meter square. How many square meters of tile would be needed to cover it?

● **15.** My neighbor is having a rectangular patio built. It will be 7 meters long and 6 meters wide. What is the perimeter of the patio?

★ **16.** Fred's backyard is 14 meters by 8 meters. Lynda's backyard is 15 meters by 7 meters. Who has the larger backyard?

Problem-Solving Skills
Using Pictures or Diagrams

Mr. Mark hired a fencing company to build a fence.
Mr. Mark's garden is 8 m long and 8 m wide. How much
fencing is needed for the garden?

> Sometimes drawing a picture can help you solve a problem.

PLAN   Step 1   Draw a picture.
           Step 2   What must you do
                    to solve the problem?

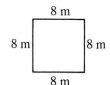

SOLVE   Perimeter = 8 m + 8 m + 8 m + 8 m
                    = 32 m

So, 32 m of fencing is needed.

Study and Learn

A. Solve. Draw a picture to help you.

1. Ms. Aaron drove 3.4 km to the fencing
   company. After work, she drove 4.5 km to
   the store. How far did she drive in all?

2. Mr. Stuart raked leaves on a lawn 25 m long
   and 20 m wide. What was the area of the lawn
   he raked?

Practice

Solve.

1. Miss Bunting mowed a lawn that was 40 m long and 35 m wide. How many square meters did she mow?

2. The Home Service is painting a wall 12 m long and 4 m high. What is the area of the wall?

3. Mrs. Turner is putting wallpaper on a wall that is 4 m long and 3 m high. How much wallpaper does she need?

4. Elaise made a picture. It is 9 inches long and 12 inches high. What is the perimeter of the picture?

5. Sam placed new tile on his kitchen floor. His kitchen is 8 feet by 14 feet. How many square feet of tile did he use?

6. Mrs. Steffen cleaned a square carpet that is 9 m on each side. She charged $0.75 a square meter. How much money did she get for cleaning the whole carpet?

★7. Donna's backyard is 7 m square. Steve's backyard is a rectangle that is 9 m wide and 7 m long. Whose yard has the larger perimeter?

★8. Mr. Hoffesfeld cleaned two windows. One was 3 m by 2 m. The other was 4 m by 2 m. What was the total area of both windows?

SOLID FIGURES

Some solid figures are related to rectangles.

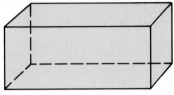

Rectangular prism

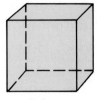

Cube

▶ A **rectangular prism** is made up of six rectangles.

▶ A **cube** is made up of six squares.

Study and Learn

A. Write the name for each.

1.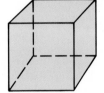
2.
3.
4.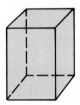

Some figures are related to circles.

Cylinder

Cone

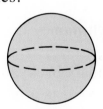

Sphere

B. Write the name for each.

5.
6.
7.
8.

Practice

Write the name for each.

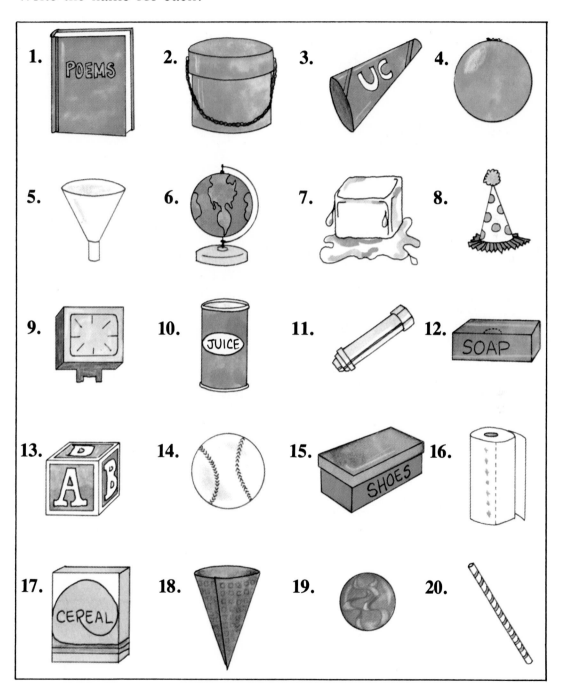

1. 
POEMS

2. 

3. 
UC

4. 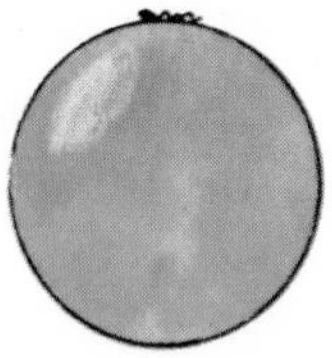

5. 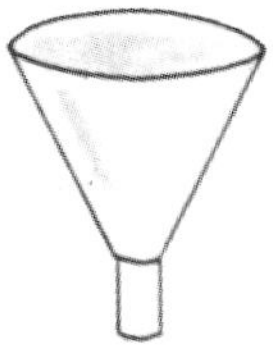

6. 

7. 

8. 

9. 

10. 
JUICE

11. 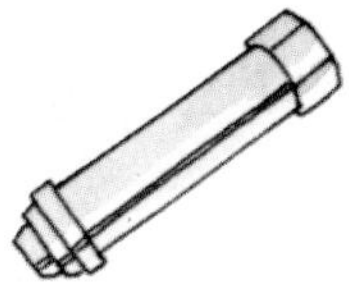

12. 
SOAP

13. 
D
A
B

14. 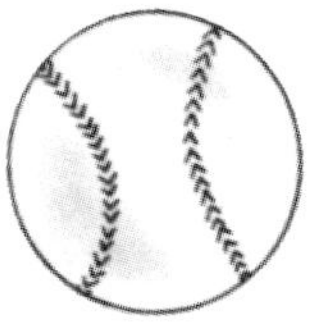

15. 
SHOES

16. 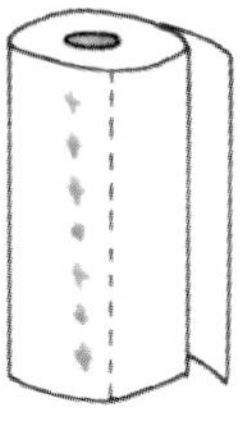

17. 
CEREAL

18. 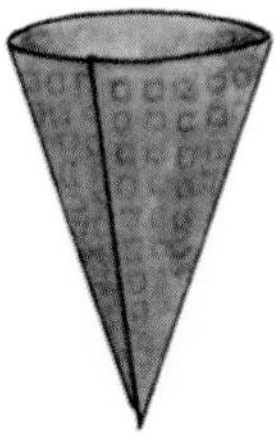

19. 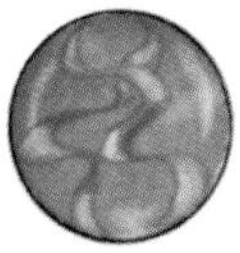

20. 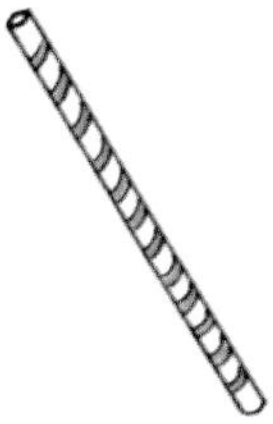

VOLUME

Square units are used to measure **area**.

1 square unit

▶ Volume is a measure of the space in a figure.

The volume of this figure is 6 cubic units.

Cubic units are used to measure **volume**.

1 cubic unit

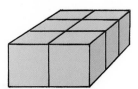

Study and Learn

A. Look at this figure.

    1. How many cubic units are there?

    2. What is the volume?

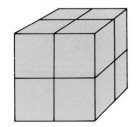

B. Find the volumes.

3.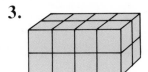

4.

5.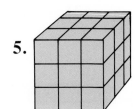

Practice

Find the volumes.

1.

2.

3.

4.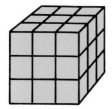

5.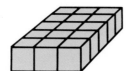

6.

7.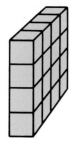

8.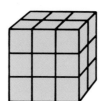

9.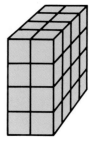

★**10.**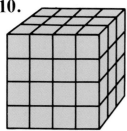

★**11.**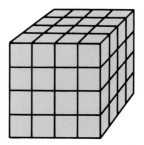

Problem-Solving Applications

Finding the Better Buy

Which is the better buy?
Lemons 2 for 28¢, or 3 for 39¢

$$2 \text{ for } 28¢ \text{ or } 2\overline{)28¢} \quad \frac{14¢}{} \text{ for each lemon}$$

$$3 \text{ for } 39¢ \text{ or } 3\overline{)39¢} \quad \frac{13¢}{} \text{ for each lemon}$$

$14 - 13 = 1¢$
1¢ is saved on each lemon.

So, 3 for 39¢ is the better buy.

Practice

Which is the better buy?

1. Bread   1 for 70¢, or
             2 for $1.42

2. Soap   2 for 50¢, or
            5 for $1.20

3. Soup   3 for 90¢, or
            6 for $1.86

4. Lettuce   1 for 88¢, or
               3 for $2.61

5. Peppers   2 for 72¢, or
                3 for $1.23

6. Corn   5 for 95¢, or
           10 for $1.80

Chapter Review

Write the name for each.

1.
(302)

X • ————— • Y

2.
(302)

◄——•——•——►
C   D

3.
(304)

4.
(306)

5.
(310)

6.
(310)

7.
(324)

8.
(324)

Tell whether each is intersecting or parallel. (302)

9.
(302)

10.
(302)

Look at this circle. (306)

11. Name a radius.

12. Name a diameter.

Find the perimeter. (316)

13.
7 in.
5 in.

14.
4 cm

Find the area. (320)

15.
2 cm
6 cm

16.
3 in.
3 in.

Find the volume. (326)

17.

Solve. (322)

18. Pam painted a wall 3 m by 4 m. What is the area of the wall?

Which is the better buy? (328)

19. Blouses 1 for $8.50, or 2 for $16.00

20. Blue jeans 1 for $12.95, or 2 for $26.00

Chapter Test

Write the name for each.

1.
(302)

2. F G
(302)

3. X Z Y
(304)

4. A
(306)

5.
(310)

6.
(310)

7.
(324)

8.
(324)

Tell whether each is intersecting or parallel. *(302)*

9.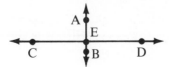

10.

Look at this circle. *(306)*

11. Name the radius.

12. Name a diameter.

Find the perimeter. *(316)*

13. 12 in. 8 in. 6 in.

14. 15 cm

Find the area. *(320)*

15. 3 km 9 km

16. 8 m 8 m

Find the volume. *(326)*

17.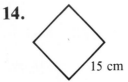

Solve. *(322)*

18. Tim tiled a floor 5 m by 4 m. What is the area of the floor?

Which is the better buy? *(328)*

19. Canned vegetables
1 can for 30¢,
or 3 for 99¢

20. Bread 1 loaf for 89¢,
or 2 for $1.76

Skills Check

1. Compare.

$$\frac{1}{4} \equiv \frac{1}{5}$$

A >   B <

C =   D +

2.

$\frac{1}{4}$ of 8 = ___?___

E $\frac{2}{8}$ F 2

G $\frac{4}{8}$ H 4

---

3. Complete.

$$\frac{1}{2} = \frac{?}{4}$$

A 1   B 2

C 3   D 4

---

4. What is line segment *AB*?

E radius   F diameter

G perimeter   H circle

---

5. What is the area?

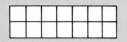

A 10 square
   units

B 14 square
   units

C 22 square
   units

D 26 square
   units

---

6. What is the volume?

E 9 cubic
   units

F 15 cubic
   units

G 12 cubic
   units

H 30 cubic
   units

---

7. What is the length of $\overline{GH}$ to the nearest centimeter?

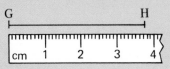

A 1 cm   B 2 cm

C 3 cm   D 4 cm

---

8. Which is a line segment?

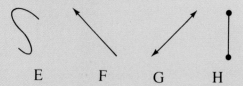

E   F   G   H

12 GRAPHS AND PROBABILITY

Flying in a Tiger Moth plane.

PICTOGRAPHS

You can arrange facts in a graph.
This pictograph shows how many students own cats.

Cats Owned by Students

Classes	Number of cats
Third grade	🐱
Fourth grade	🐱 🐱
Fifth grade	🐱 🐱 🐱

Each 🐱 represents 2 cats.

Study and Learn

A. Look at the pictograph above.

   1. Which class owns the fewest cats?

   2. How many more cats does the fifth grade class own than the fourth grade class?

   3. How would 14 cats be shown?

In the pictograph below, each symbol represents 2 birds.
Each half symbol represents 1 bird.

Birds Owned by Students

Classes	Number of birds
Third Grade	🐦
Fourth Grade	🐦 🐦
Fifth Grade	🐦 ⸯ

Each 🐦 represents 2 birds.

B. Look at the pictograph above.

   4. How many birds does the third grade own?

   5. Which grade owns the most birds?

   6. How many birds in all?

334

Practice

Use the pictographs to find the answers.

Students Who Owned Pets

Grade	Number of students
Third grade	人 人 ⌇
Fourth grade	人 人 人 人 人 人 人
Fifth grade	人 人 人

Each 人 represents 2 students.

1. How many students owned pets in each grade?

2. Which grade owned the most pets?

3. How would 18 students be shown on the pictograph?

Students Who Own Fish

Name	Number of fish
Enzo	🐟 🐟 🐟 🐟
Clyde	🐟 🐟 🐟
Alexis	🐟 🐟 🐟
Lesley	🐟 🐟

Each 🐟 represents 4 fish.

4. How many fish in all?

5. How would 20 fish be shown on this pictograph?

★ 6. Make a pictograph to show the number of pets in your class.

BAR GRAPHS

Bar graphs also organize facts.
Ms. Peters asked the students to vote for their favorite clubs.

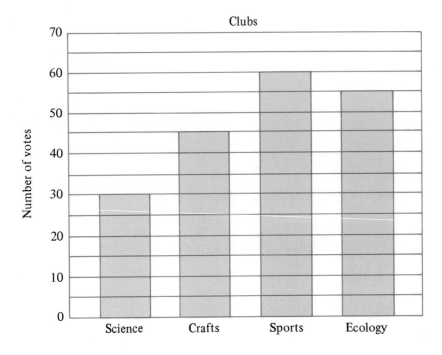

Study and Learn

A. Look at the bar graph above.

1. Which club received the most votes?

2. Which club received the least votes?

3. How many votes did the ecology club receive?

4. How many more students voted for the crafts club than for the science club?

5. How many more students voted for the sports club than for the ecology club?

Practice

Use the bar graphs to find the answers.

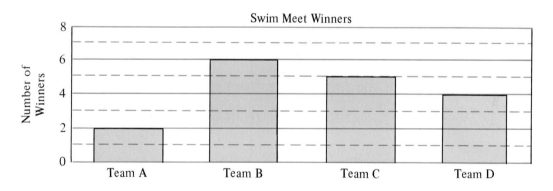

Number of Students on Teams

1. How many people are on the baseball team?

2. How many people are on the hockey team?

3. Which team has 18 members?

4. Which team has the most members?

Swim Meet Winners

5. How many winners on Team C?

6. Which team has the fewest winners?

7. Which team has 6 winners?

8. How many winners in all?

★ 9. Make a bar graph to show the number of people on teams in your class.

CIRCLE GRAPHS

The students held a carnival to raise funds for the hospital. This circle graph shows how they raised the funds.

Funds

Study and Learn

A. Look at the graph above.

1. $\frac{1}{8}$ of the funds were raised by entertainment. What part of the funds came from crafts?

2. What part of the funds came from rides?

3. What part of the funds came from games?

B. This graph shows what funds each game raised.

Funds Raised by Games

4. What part of the funds came from darts?

5. What part of the funds came from ring toss?

6. Which game raised the most funds?

Practice

Use the circle graphs to find the answers.

1. What part of the funds
   did the magic show raise?

2. What raised the most funds?

3. What part of the funds
   did the monster movie raise?

4. What part of the funds was raised
   by the puppet show?

5. What part of the funds was raised
   by the puppet and art shows altogether?

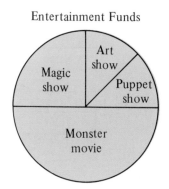

Entertainment Funds

6. Which ride raised $\frac{1}{4}$
   of the funds?

7. Which ride raised the
   most funds?

8. What part of the funds did
   the roller coaster raise?

9. Which rides raised the least funds?

10. What part of the funds
    did the bumper cars raise?

11. What part of the funds was raised
    by the roller coaster and haunted
    house altogether?

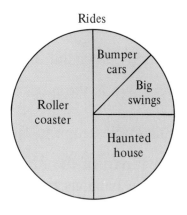

Rides

339

Midchapter Review

Use this pictograph to find the answers. *(334)*

Seashell Collection

Name	Number of sea shells
Lori	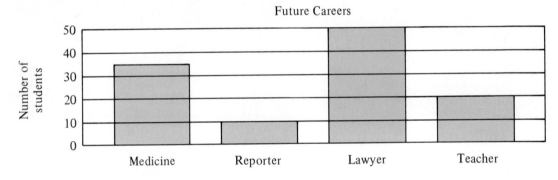
Donna	
John	

Each 🐚 represents 4 seashells.

1. How many seashells does Lori own?

2. Who owns the most seashells? How many?

Use this bar graph to find the answers. *(336)*

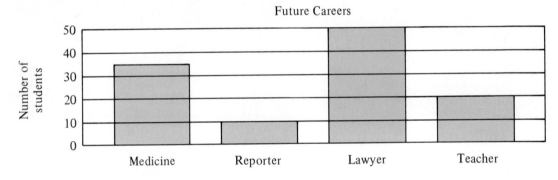

3. Which was the least favorite career?

4. Which career did 35 students select?

5. Which was the most popular career? How many chose it?

Use this circle graph to find the answers. *(338)*

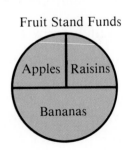

Fruit Stand Funds

6. What part of the funds did selling bananas raise?

7. What part of the funds did selling apples raise?

Skills Review

Add.

1. (54)
```
   6
   4
   9
 + 2
```

2. (56)
```
  86
  25
  38
+ 27
```

3. (58)
```
  376
  297
  486
+ 395
```

4. (62)
```
  6,284
  9,648
+ 7,587
```

5. (272) $\dfrac{3}{10} + \dfrac{4}{10}$

6. (274) $\dfrac{7}{8} + \dfrac{3}{8}$

7. (276) $\dfrac{1}{3} + \dfrac{2}{9}$

8. $\dfrac{1}{2} + \dfrac{2}{5}$

9. (278) $9\dfrac{3}{7} + 6\dfrac{1}{7}$

Subtract.

10. (82)
```
  86
 − 9
```

11.
```
  73
 − 16
```

12. (84)
```
  479
 − 384
```

13. (86)
```
  79,276
 − 18,498
```

14. (95)
```
$ 10.00
 − 1.76
```

15. (284) $\dfrac{7}{9} - \dfrac{3}{9}$

16. $\dfrac{11}{12} - \dfrac{3}{12}$

17. (286) $\dfrac{1}{2} - \dfrac{1}{4}$

18. $\dfrac{2}{3} - \dfrac{1}{4}$

19. (288) $12\dfrac{7}{11} - 9\dfrac{3}{11}$

Multiply.

20. (178)
```
  86
 × 7
```

21. (180)
```
  426
 × 3
```

22. (184)
```
$73.98
 × 9
```

23. (194)
```
  427
 × 40
```

24. (196)
```
  68
 × 27
```

Divide.

25. (130) $4\overline{)36}$

26. (208) $8\overline{)43}$

27. (216) $6\overline{)3,941}$

28. (228) $20\overline{)785}$

29. (230) $5\overline{)\$14.80}$

Something Extra
Non-Routine Problems

Put the numbers in order from largest to smallest.

1. 3,286   234   6,247   1,236,142   8

2. 26   4,927   624   56,302   162

3. 112   276,318   6,247,386   444   3,978

Problem-Solving Skills
Is There Enough Information?

Study and Learn

A. Look at the yogurt label above.
A box of raisins is next to the container of yogurt.
How many more calories are in the yogurt?

    1. How many calories are in the yogurt?

    2. How many calories are in the raisins?

    3. What does the problem ask?

    4. Can you solve the problem? Why or why not?

> Some problems do not have enough information to solve them.

B. Tell if there is enough information. Solve if you can.

    5. Sasha bought 6 containers of yogurt. She gave the cashier $5.00. How much change did she receive?

    6. Franklin mixed granola with his yogurt. How many calories in all?

Practice

Tell if there is enough information. Solve if you can.

1. Tania bought 2 cans of soup and 1 container of milk. What is the total cost?

2. Edward bought a loaf of bread for 92 cents. How much change should he receive from $5.00?

3. Mr. Carmichal bought 2 cans of tomato soup and 2 cans of vegetable soup with chicken. How much did it cost?

4. Jessica bought 7 oranges one week. The next week she bought twice as many oranges. How many did she buy in 2 weeks?

5. Marjorie bought a pound of cheese for $2.36. How much was the change?

6. Roger eats 3 bananas every week. How many bananas does he eat in 5 weeks?

GRAPHING ORDERED PAIRS

The park is at 2nd Street and 5th Avenue. Another way
to say this is (2, 5). To find the park, you must move 2
to the right and up 5.

▶  (2, 5) is called an **ordered pair** of numbers.

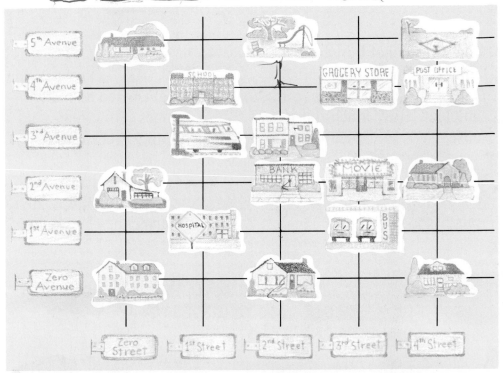

Study and Learn

A. What is located at each ordered pair?

  1. (1, 1)   **2.** (3, 4)   **3.** (4, 5)

  4. (3, 1)   **5.** (1, 4)

B. Write the ordered pair for each.

  6. Bus Station   **7.** Bank   **8.** Post Office

  9. Baseball Field   **10.** Grocery Store

344

Practice

Use the graphs to solve.

Ms. Peterson made
this graph of
library books.

	Row 1	Row 2	Row 3
Aisle 5	Art	Languages	Animal
Aisle 4	Music	History	Ecology
Aisle 3	Non-fiction	Sports	Science
Aisle 2	Fiction	Hobbies	Math
Aisle 1	Mystery	Geography	Chemistry

What kind of book is located at each ordered pair?

1. (2, 4) **2.** (1, 5) **3.** (1, 3) **4.** (2, 5) **5.** (3, 3)

Write the ordered pair for each book.

6. Music **7.** Animal **8.** Hobbies **9.** Math **10.** Sports

	Section 1	Section 2	Section 3
Counter 4	Rock	Opera	Ethnic
Counter 3	Disco	Classical	Spiritual
Counter 2	Western	Jazz	Soul
Counter 1	Folk	Country rock	Pop

What kind of record is located at each ordered pair?

11. (3, 1) **12.** (2, 2) **13.** (1, 3) **14.** (1, 1) **15.** (3, 3)

Write the ordered pair for each record.

16. Rock **17.** Soul **18.** Opera **19.** Western **20.** Classical

PROBABILITY

Look at the spinner.
What is the probability that the arrow will stop on red?

2 possible **outcomes** are
that the arrow will
stop on red or blue.

The **probability** is 1 out of 2 that the
arrow will stop on red.

Study and Learn

A. Look at the spinner. Complete.

    1. What are the possible outcomes?

    2. The probability that the arrow
    will stop on blue is __?__ out
    of __?__ .

    3. What is the probability that
    the arrow will stop on red?

    4. What is the probability that
    the arrow will stop on purple?

B. Think of flipping a coin.

    5. What are the possible outcomes?

    6. What is the probability
    of getting heads?

    7. What is the probability
    of getting tails?

C. Complete.

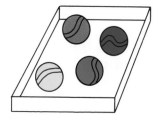

    8. How many marbles are green?

    9. How many possible outcomes are there?

    10. Think of closing your eyes and picking a marble. What is the probability of picking a green marble?

Practice

What is the probability of the arrow stopping on red?

1.   **2.**   **3.**

What is the probability of picking a red marble?

4. 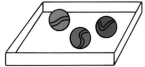 **5.** 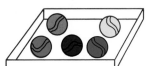 **6.**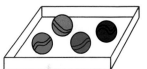

Solve.

★ **7.** Denise had 4 white socks and 4 red socks in a drawer. She closed her eyes and picked a sock. What is the probability that Denise picked a red sock?

Something Extra
Calculator Activity

If 3 shirt buttons are equal to 1 gram, how many buttons are there in 1 metric ton?

> Remember that 1,000 grams = 1 kilogram and 1,000 kilograms = 1 metric ton.

MORE PROBABILITY

Look at the spinner.
What is the probability that the arrow will stop on blue?

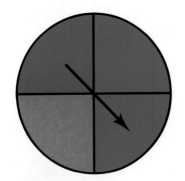

There are 3 possible outcomes for blue.

There are 4 possible outcomes in all.

The probability is 3 out of 4 that the arrow will stop on blue.

Study and Learn

A. Look at the spinner. Complete.

   1. How many possible outcomes are there for red?

   2. How many possible outcomes are there in all?

   3. The probability that the arrow will stop on red is __?__ out of __?__ .

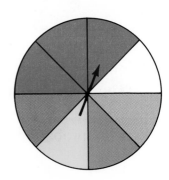

B. Complete.

   4. How many possible outcomes for red?

   5. How many possible outcomes in all?

   6. If you close your eyes, what would be the probability of picking a red marble?

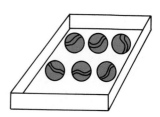

Practice

What is the probability of the arrow stopping on blue?

1.
2.
3.

What is the probability of picking a green marble?

4.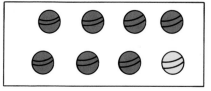
5.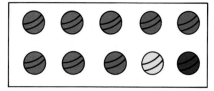

6.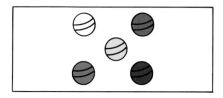
7.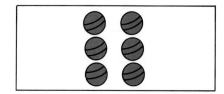

★ Write the probabilities in two ways.

8. There are 3 oranges, 2 pears, and 1 banana in a fruit bowl. What is the probability of picking a pear from the bowl?

9. Kate had 2 blue crayons, 4 red crayons, 1 green crayon, and 1 purple crayon in a box. She closed her eyes to pick a crayon. What is the probability that Kate will pick a red crayon?

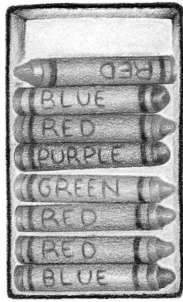

10. There are 2 red socks and 2 blue socks in a drawer. What is the probability of picking a red sock?

Problem-Solving Applications

Customary Measure

12 inches = 1 foot
3 feet = 1 yard
5,280 feet = 1 mile
16 ounces = 1 pint
2 pints = 1 quart
4 quarts = 1 gallon

Look at the chart above to solve.

1. The Sears Tower in Chicago is the tallest office building in the world. The total height is about 1,560 feet. How many yards is that?
   [Hint: $1,560 \div 3 = \underline{\ ?\ }$]

2. Peter Dowdeswell holds the record for drinking about one quart of milk in $3\frac{2}{10}$ seconds. How many ounces is that?

3. The largest wing span of a bird is 10 feet 4 inches. How many inches is that?

4. Cassandra and her friends drank 1 gallon of juice. How many pints is that?

5. The tallest cactus in the world is 78 feet. How many yards is that?

★ 6. The Great Wall of China is the longest wall in the world. The total length is 3,930 miles. How many feet is that?

Chapter Review

Look at the pictograph. *(334)*

Name	Number of ribbons won
Harry	★ ★ ★ ★
Mary	★ ★
Terry	★ ★ ★ ★

Track ribbons

Each ★ represents 2 ribbons

1. How many ribbons were won by Harry?

2. How many more ribbons did Terry have than Mary?

3. How many ribbons did they win altogether?

Look at the circle graph. *(338)*

Drink choices

Juice | Water
Milk

4. What part chose milk?

5. What part chose milk and juice altogether?

Write the ordered pair for each. *(344)*

6. Jane   **7.** Tom

8. Ron   **9.** Helen

	Row 1	Row 2
Seat 3	Ellen	Tom
Seat 2	Jane	Inez
Seat 1	Ron	Helen

10. What is the probability of
(346) picking a red marble?

Tell if there is enough information. Solve if you can. *(342)*

11. May had 8 apples. She ate some. How many apples were left?

Solve. *(350)*

12. The Verrazano-Narrows Bridge is the longest suspension bridge in the world. It measures 6,690 feet long. How many yards is that?

Chapter Test

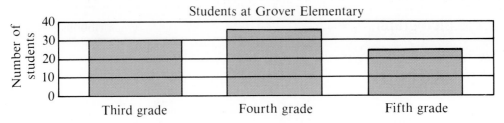

Students at Grover Elementary

Number of students

40
30
20
10
0

Third grade   Fourth grade   Fifth grade

1. How many students are in the fourth grade? *(336)*

2. How many more students are in the third grade than the fifth grade? *(336)*

3. How many students are there in the third, fourth, and fifth grades altogether? *(336)*

Look at the circle graph. *(338)*

Fruit

Apples

Oranges

Pears

4. What part is oranges?

5. What part is pears?

Write the ordered pair for each. *(344)*

	Row 1	Row 2
Aisle 2	Betty's desk	Lionel's desk
Aisle 1	Frank's desk	Jean's desk

6. Jean's desk   7. Lionel's desk

8. Frank's desk   9. Betty's desk

10. What is the probability of *(346)* picking a blue marble?

Tell if there is enough information. Solve if you can. *(342)*

11. John caught 12 fish. He gave 8 away. How many were left?

Solve. *(350)*

12. Sandy Allen holds the record for being the tallest woman. She is about 8 feet tall. How many inches is that?

Skills Check

1. It took 12 months to build a school. How many years is that?

   A 1 year   B 2 years

   C 3 years   D 4 years

2. Roberto was paid $1.25 an hour to clean up the yard. He worked for three hours. How much did he earn?

   E $3.75   F $4.25

   G $4.75   H $5.00

3. Sache bought 4 pints of milk and put them into quart bottles. How many quarts did she have?

   A 2 quarts   B 3 quarts

   C 8 quarts   D 12 quarts

4. What is the perimeter?

   12 cm

   3 cm   3 cm

   12 cm

   E 15 cm   F 24 cm

   G 30 cm   H 36 cm

5. Which unit would you use to measure the mass of a car?

   A milliliter   B gram

   C liter   D kilogram

6.

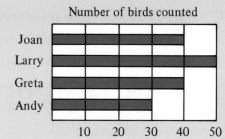

Number of birds counted

Who counted the least number of birds?

   E Joan   F Greta

   G Larry   H Andy

THE KEYBOARD AND ARITHMETIC

A. Turn on your computer. The blinking light tells you the computer is ready. It is called a **cursor**.

1. Does your computer have a key like this? 🔲
If it doesn't, skip to number 4.

2. Press the 🔲 key. What shows on the screen?

3. Hold the SHIFT key down and press 🔲
What shows on the screen?

4. Make these signs show on the screen.
* ( ) > < " % $ = !

B. The space bar is the longest key 🔲
Use it to put in spaces between words.

5. Type: **THIS COMPUTER LIKES ME!** RETURN
Did the word ERROR show on the screen? It's correct if it did. Just go on.

C. The RETURN key tells the computer to get to work.
You told the computer to get to work, but you didn't tell it what to do. So you got an ERROR message.

6. Type: **PRINT "THIS COMPUTER LIKES ME!"** RETURN

input

output

There's no error message now because you told the computer to PRINT.

D. PRINT is a command. When it is used with " ",
what is inside the " " shows on the screen.

Type this input. Write the output.

7. PRINT "A COMPUTER IS A TOOL." `RETURN`

8. PRINT "IT MUST BE TOLD WHAT TO DO!" `RETURN`

E. PRINT without " " can make the computer do arithmetic.
Type each input. Write each output.

9. PRINT 18 + 27 `RETURN` **10. PRINT 45 − 18** `RETURN`

11. PRINT 12 * 12 `RETURN` **12. PRINT 144/12** `RETURN`

▶ A computer uses an * for multiplying and a / for dividing.

F. The input below makes the computer show the problem, then the answer.
Type this input. Write the output.

13. PRINT "18 + 27 = "18 + 27 `RETURN`

14. PRINT "45 − 18 = "45 − 18 `RETURN`

15. PRINT "12 * 12 = "12 * 12 `RETURN`

16. PRINT "144 / 12 = "144 / 12 `RETURN`

G. A computer does not use commas in numbers.
Type this input. Write the output.

17. PRINT "8562 + 3986 = "8562 + 3986 `RETURN`

18. PRINT "1498 * 1359 = "1498 * 1359 `RETURN`

Type the input that will make the computer do each exercise.

19. $4,398 + 2,612$ **20.** $843 \div 3$

21. 98×112 **22.** $58,212 - 38,898$

23. $95,820 \div 15$ **24.** $43 \times 75,060$

25. $9,876 - 4,002$ **26.** $9,427 \div 11$

27. $6,427 \times 13$

COMPUTER COMMANDS

A computer cannot do anything by itself. You must give it commands.

A. You already know the PRINT command.

Type this input.	You get this output.
PRINT 8 * 6 [RETURN] .	48
PRINT "8 × 6 = "8 * 6 [RETURN] .	8 × 6 = 48

A ? may be used in place of PRINT.
Type the input above, using ? for PRINT.

Enter commands into the computer by pressing [RETURN] .

B. The **LET** command makes the computer store numbers.

Type: **LET X = 12** [RETURN] .

Type: **PRINT X** [RETURN] . Did 12 show on the screen?

LET X = 12 puts 12 into storage place X in the computer's memory.

C. The NEW command erases numbers from the computer's memory.

Type: **NEW** [RETURN] .

Type: **PRINT X** [RETURN] . Did 0 show on the screen?

When a storage place has no other number in it, the computer holds a zero there.

D. The HOME command clears the screen of print.

Type: **HOME** [RETURN] . Is the screen clear?

Most of the other commands can only be used in or with a program. These are covered in the next lessons.

ENTERING A PROGRAM

A program is a numbered list of commands. Each numbered command is a program line.

The computer carries out the commands in the order of their line numbers. The smallest line number is carried out first.

This program uses some commands you already know.

10 LET A = 12 ——— tells the computer to store 12 in A.

20 PRINT "THE NUMBER IN A IS " A ——— prints all words in quotes, then prints the number in A.

Here are more commands the computer uses.

A. Programs are stored in the computer's memory. Before you enter a program, you should type NEW. This erases any previous programs or numbers in the memory.

Type: **NEW** [RETURN] .

B. Now you can enter the program above into the computer's memory. Do this by typing in each program line and pressing [RETURN] after each.

C. Type: **LIST** [RETURN] to make the computer show the program stored in its memory. Is the program listed on the screen?

D. Type: **RUN** [RETURN] to make the computer carry out the program. Output is what shows on the screen afterwards. Write the output of this program.

PROGRAM DEBUGGING

A bug is an error. Fixing the bugs in a program is called debugging.

A. The ← key makes the cursor move left.

1. Type: **PRINT "ARITHMATIC"**. Do *not* press RETURN . ARITHMATIC is misspelled; it should be ARITHMETIC.

2. Press the ← key. What happens?

3. Keep pressing ← until the cursor is over the A.

4. Type an E. Now, type out the rest, TIC", and press RETURN . Write the output.

If you find a bug before pressing RETURN you can use the ← key to fix it.

B. Type NEW and enter this program. Copy it *exactly*.

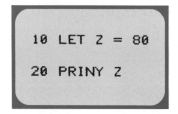

```
10 LET Z = 80
20 PRINY Z
```

PRINT is purposely misspelled.

5. Make the program run by typing: **RUN** RETURN . Which line has an error in it?

6. List the program by typing: **LIST** RETURN . What is wrong in line 20?

7. Type: **20 PRINT Z** RETURN . List the program again. Has line 20 been changed?

▶ To change a line, retype it. Then press RETURN .

C. Did you notice that line numbers are skipped in the program in section **B**? This is done in case we want to add lines between lines that are already typed.

   8. <u>Type</u>: **15 PRINT "THE NUMBER IN Z IS"** [RETURN]

   9. List the program. Is line 15 in the list?

   10. Run this new program. Write the output.

   ▶ To add a line in a program, give it a line number to put it where it should go in the program. Then type the line and press [RETURN] .

D. It is easy to erase a line of a program.

   11. <u>Type</u>: 20 [RETURN] .

   12. List the program. Is line 20 gone?

   13. Run the program with the changes. Write the output.

   ▶ To erase a line of a program: Type the line number. Press [RETURN] .

E. Type NEW. Enter and run. Write the output.

```
10 LET A = 512

20 LET B = 64

30 PRINT "TWO NUMBERS ARE "; A;" AND ";B

40 PRINT "THEIR SUM IS "; A + B

50 PRINT "THEIR PRODUCT IS "; A X B

60 PRINT "THEIR DIFFERENCE IS ";A - B
```

THE INPUT COMMAND

A. Type NEW and enter and run this program.

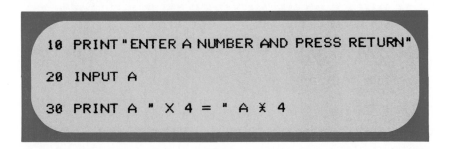

```
10  PRINT"ENTER A NUMBER AND PRESS RETURN"

20  INPUT A

30  PRINT A " X 4 = " A X 4
```

B. The INPUT command in line 20 makes the computer wait for a number to be entered. The number will be stored in A.

   1. <u>Type</u>: 5 [RETURN] . Write the output.

   2. Run the program again. <u>Type</u>: **TWELVE** [RETURN] . Did **REENTER** show on the screen? That's because the computer was told to wait for a number and got a word instead! Now INPUT 12. Write the output.

C. PRINT and INPUT may be combined into one program line by using INPUT with " " marks followed by a semicolon.

   3. Enter and run this program. (First enter NEW).

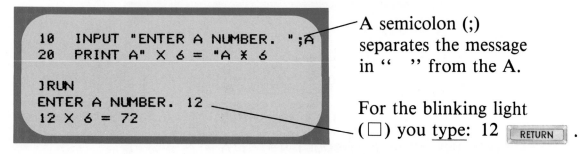

```
10   INPUT "ENTER A NUMBER.  ";A
20   PRINT A" X 6 = "A X 6

JRUN
ENTER A NUMBER. 12
12 X 6 = 72
```

A semicolon (;) separates the message in " " from the A.

For the blinking light (□) you <u>type</u>: 12 [RETURN] .

360

D. Enter and run this program.

```
10 PRINT"ENTER YOUR NAME AND PRESS RETURN"

20 INPUT N$

30 PRINT N$ ", YOU ARE A STAR!"
```

E. The INPUT command in line 20 makes the computer wait for a "string" of letters or words. These will be stored in N$. N$ is read "N string."

Type: (your name) and press ⬚RETURN⬚ . Write the output.

F. Type NEW. Enter and run this program.

```
10 INPUT "WHAT IS YOUR NAME ? " ; N$

20 INPUT "HOW OLD ARE YOU ? " ; A

30 PRINT N$ ", YOU WILL BE"

40 PRINT A + 1 " ON YOUR NEXT BIRTHDAY!"
```

G. Add these lines to the program and then run it.

```
50 INPUT "WHAT YEAR IS THIS ? "; B

60 PRINT "YOU WILL BE 100 YEARS OLD,"

70 PRINT N$ ", IN " ; B - A + 100
```

THE GOTO COMMAND

The GOTO Command makes the computer go to the line whose number follows GOTO. Here is a program that uses GOTO.

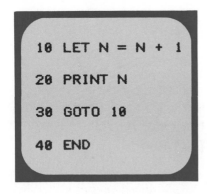

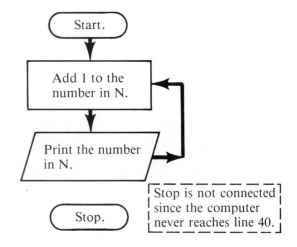

Stop is not connected since the computer never reaches line 40.

Compare this program to the flowchart shown.

1. Copy the flowchart and write the line number that goes with each part.

2. Enter and run this program. Describe the output.

3. Stop the program by holding CONTROL down and pressing C . What is the last number shown on the screen?

4. Change line 10 to count by 3's.

5. Run this new program and then stop the run. Check the output. Is it a list of numbers that are multiples of 3? It should be.

6. Write a flowchart to go with this program.

★7. Write a program to print the multiples of 5.

SCRAMBLED PROGRAMS

Remember that a computer program is a numbered list
of commands. The computer carries out the program in
the order of the line numbers.

1. Write the output of this program.

```
10 GOTO 60
20 PRINT "THE COMPUTER GO"
30 GOTO 80
40 PRINT "IN A COMPUTER PROGRAM"
50 GOTO 100
60 PRINT "THE GOTO COMMAND MAKES"
70 GOTO 20
80 PRINT "FROM ONE LINE TO ANOTHER"
90 GOTO 40
100 PRINT "GOTO CAN ALSO CREATE A LOOP"
110 GOTO 100
```

2. Make up a flowchart for this program.

3. Rewrite the program, using only one GOTO
command.

4. Write a flowchart to go with this program.

THE IF/THEN COMMAND

The IF/THEN command is a two-part command.

A. THEN may be followed by a line number. The computer goes to that line if the IF part is true.

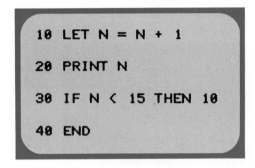

```
10 LET N = N + 1

20 PRINT N

30 IF N < 15 THEN 10

40 END
```

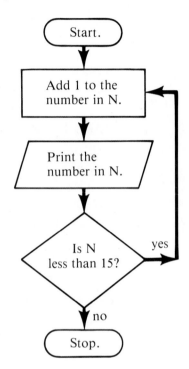

1. Copy the flowchart and write the line number that goes with each part.

2. Enter and run the program. Write the output.

B. THEN may be followed by a command. The computer does the command if the IF part is true.

3. Enter NEW. Run this program. Write the output.

```
10 LET N = N + 1

20 PRINT N

30 IF N = 15 THEN END

40 GOTO 10
```

C. IF/THEN may be used to check the computer user's answer to an INPUT command. Enter NEW. Now enter this program.

```
10 INPUT "DO YOU LIKE COMPUTERS ? (YES OR NO)";A$

20 IF A$ = "YES" THEN PRINT "ME TOO!"

30 IF A$ = "NO" THEN PRINT "SORRY!"

40 PRINT "GOODBYE!"
```

4. INPUT in line 10 makes the computer wait for the answer.

5. The IF in line 20 makes the computer check the word stored in A$. If it is "YES," the THEN is carried out, and ME TOO! is printed.

6. Run the program and answer the computer.

D. Use IF/THEN commands to do the following:

7. Write a program to count to 95 by 5's.

8. Write a program to print all multiples of 4 that are less than 19.

E. Enter this program. What is the output?

```
10 INPUT "HAVE YOU READ A COMPUTER BOOK ?";A$

20 IF A$ = "YES" THEN PRINT "GOOD"

30 IF A$ = "NO" THEN PRINT "TRY THE LIBRARY"

40 PRINT "HAPPY COMPUTING"
```

THE ADDITION TABLE

+	0	1	2	3	4	5	6	7	8	9
0	0	1	2	3	4	5	6	7	8	9
1	1	2	3	4	5	6	7	8	9	10
2	2	3	4	5	6	7	8	9	10	11
3	3	4	5	6	7	8	9	10	11	12
4	4	5	6	7	8	9	10	11	12	13
5	5	6	7	8	9	10	11	12	13	14
6	6	7	8	9	10	11	12	13	14	15
7	7	8	9	10	11	12	13	14	15	16
8	8	9	10	11	12	13	14	15	16	17
9	9	10	11	12	13	14	15	16	17	18

THE MULTIPLICATION TABLE

X	0	1	2	3	4	5	6	7	8	9
0	0	0	0	0	0	0	0	0	0	0
1	0	1	2	3	4	5	6	7	8	9
2	0	2	4	6	8	10	12	14	16	18
3	0	3	6	9	12	15	18	21	24	27
4	0	4	8	12	16	20	24	28	32	36
5	0	5	10	15	20	25	30	35	40	45
6	0	6	12	18	24	30	36	42	48	54
7	0	7	14	21	28	35	42	49	56	63
8	0	8	16	24	32	40	48	56	64	72
9	0	9	18	27	36	45	54	63	72	81

EXTRA PRACTICE

Add. *(Use with page 2.)*

1. 6 + 8	**2.** 9 + 3	**3.** 0 + 9	**4.** 6 + 4	**5.** 1 + 2	**6.** 5 + 8	**7.** 2 + 2
8. 2 + 9	**9.** 8 + 9	**10.** 9 + 9	**11.** 9 + 6	**12.** 7 + 6	**13.** 8 + 8	**14.** 4 + 1
15. 0 + 8	**16.** 2 + 6	**17.** 2 + 7	**18.** 6 + 0	**19.** 9 + 5	**20.** 7 + 9	**21.** 8 + 4
22. 2 + 8	**23.** 3 + 6	**24.** 5 + 7	**25.** 7 + 0	**26.** 5 + 5	**27.** 6 + 6	**28.** 3 + 2

★ Show how many ways you can write each of these as the sum of two numbers. Each number must be less than 10.

> *Example*   17   9 + 8, 8 + 9

29. 13   **30.** 16   **31.** 9

Subtract. *(Use with page 8.)*

1. 8 − 2	**2.** 14 − 6	**3.** 14 − 7	**4.** 6 − 3	**5.** 5 − 3	**6.** 11 − 2	**7.** 10 − 6
8. 8 − 4	**9.** 13 − 6	**10.** 13 − 9	**11.** 16 − 7	**12.** 15 − 7	**13.** 7 − 3	**14.** 10 − 9
15. 17 − 9	**16.** 9 − 4	**17.** 12 − 5	**18.** 12 − 9	**19.** 12 − 4	**20.** 12 − 6	**21.** 15 − 9
22. 6 − 2	**23.** 10 − 3	**24.** 7 − 7	**25.** 8 − 7	**26.** 7 − 2	**27.** 9 − 7	**28.** 9 − 3

★ Show how many ways you can write each of these as the difference of two numbers. Each number must be less than 15.

29. 9   **30.** 6   **31.** 7

Which operation would you use? Write + or − .
(Use with page 12.)

1. 6 girls
4 boys
How many in all?

2. 3 easy books
5 hard books
How many books?

3. 9 cats
2 dogs
How many more cats?

4. Have 7 cents
Earn 9 cents
How much now?

5. 7 apples
Ate 3
How many left?

6. 8 forks
3 knives
How many more forks?

7. 13 plates to clean
7 done
How many more to do?

8. 9 red balloons
8 blue balloons
How many in all?

9. 9 pens
7 pencils
How many in all?

10. 6 books to read
3 read
How many to read?

★ Make up stories to go with these facts.

11. 13 − 8

12. 9 + 6

Add. *(Use with page 21.)*

| **1.** 9 $+0$ | **2.** 6 $+3$ | **3.** 7 $+4$ | **4.** 8 $+9$ | **5.** 6 $+4$ | **6.** 8 $+8$ | **7.** 3 $+9$ |

| **8.** 8 $+4$ | **9.** 7 $+3$ | **10.** 6 $+5$ | **11.** 7 $+8$ | **12.** 4 $+9$ | **13.** 8 $+1$ | **14.** 9 $+4$ |

Subtract.

| **15.** 9 -4 | **16.** 7 -0 | **17.** 8 -8 | **18.** 12 -5 | **19.** 10 -4 | **20.** 11 -8 | **21.** 13 -8 |

| **22.** 18 -9 | **23.** 17 -8 | **24.** 15 -7 | **25.** 12 -6 | **26.** 16 -9 | **27.** 14 -5 | **28.** 11 -2 |

Write standard numerals. *(Use with page 26.)*

1. 20 + 6

2. 4 tens and 7 ones

3. 3 hundreds, 6 tens, and 5 ones

4. 800 + 50 + 6

5. 9 thousands, 2 hundreds, 6 tens, and 3 ones

6. 4,000 + 700 + 80 + 3

7. Thirteen

8. Eighty-nine

9. Six hundred fifty-one

10. Five thousand, twenty-two

★ **11.** Eighteen hundred

★ **12.** Forty thousand

★ **13.** Seven hundred thousand

★ **14.** Eighty thousand, eight hundred

What is the value of each underlined digit? *(Use with page 30.)*

1. 43,794

2. 26,874

3. 198,175

4. 64,107

5. 86,490

6. 187,164

7. 395,593

8. 67,487

9. 307,591

10. 625,185

11. 49,874

12. 276,149

13. 91,281

14. 427,129

15. 679,189

Write standard numerals.

16. 40,000 + 8,000 + 500 + 70 + 5

17. 600,000 + 70,000 + 9,000 + 400 + 80 + 1

18. 300,000 + 40,000 + 0 + 0 + 0 + 9

19. 76 thousand, 376

20. 900 thousand, 36

21. 46 thousand, 3

22. 304 thousand, 697

23. 63 thousand, 502

24. 276 thousand, 40

Which number sentence fits the story? *(Use with page 38.)*

1. 6 apples
7 pears
How many more pears?
$6 + 7 =$ ___?___
$6 - 7 =$ ___?___
$7 - 6 =$ ___?___

2. 7 red pencils
9 blue pencils
How many pencils?
$7 + 9 =$ ___?___
$7 - 9 =$ ___?___
$9 - 7 =$ ___?___

3. 74 horses
68 mules
How many animals?
$74 + 68 =$ ___?___
$74 - 68 =$ ___?___
$68 - 74 =$ ___?___

4. 42 boys
53 girls
How many children?
$53 - 42 =$ ___?___
$42 - 53 -$ ___?___
$42 + 53 =$ ___?___

5. 39 cats
42 dogs
How many more dogs?
$39 + 42 =$ ___?___
$42 + 39 =$ ___?___
$42 - 39 =$ ___?___

6. 12 dollars
Spent 7 dollars
How much left?
$12 + 7 =$ ___?___
$12 - 7 =$ ___?___
$7 + 12 =$ ___?___

★**7.** 50 questions
Finished some
How many more to do?
$50 + ? =$ ___?___
$50 - ? =$ ___?___
$? - 50 =$ ___?___

★**8.** Had 7 dollars
Earned some more
How much now?
$7 + ? =$ ___?___
$7 - ? =$ ___?___
$? - 7 =$ ___?___

Compare. Use $>$ or $<$. *(Use with page 40.)*

1. $47 \equiv 74$

2. $169 \equiv 170$

3. $987 \equiv 789$

4. $3,478 \equiv 3,748$

5. $4,295 \equiv 4,286$

6. $26,749 \equiv 26,857$

7. $849 \equiv 850$

8. $4,500 \equiv 4,487$

9. $92,470 \equiv 86,704$

10. $39,865 \equiv 40,000$

11. $86,700 \equiv 86,687$

12. $24,844 \equiv 25,414$

★**13.** $685,427 \equiv 684,949$

★**14.** $728,681 \equiv 731,148$

Round each to the nearest ten. *(Use with page 42.)*

1. 12　　　**2.** 19　　　**3.** 28　　　**4.** 35　　　**5.** 64

6. 87　　　**7.** 91　　　**8.** 45　　　★**9.** 463　　　★**10.** 7,768

Round each to the nearest hundred or dollar.

11. 715　　**12.** 297　　**13.** 364　　**14.** 928　　**15.** 849

16. 645　　**17.** $8.97　　**18.** $4.50　　**19.** $9.19　　**20.** $8.75

21. $4.48　　**22.** $5.62　　★**23.** 9,874　　★**24.** $26.87　　★**25.** $249.87

Round each to the nearest thousand. *(Use with page 44.)*

1. 7,386　　**2.** 4,947　　**3.** 6,849　　**4.** 1,348　　**5.** 7,500

6. 9,099　　**7.** 8,947　　**8.** 2,501　　**9.** 3,499　　**10.** 8,901

11. 3,500　　**12.** 7,498　　★**13.** 27,849　　★**14.** 68,149　　★**15.** 49,800

Add. *(Use with page 54.)*

1.　3
　　　8
　　+ 7

2.　6
　　　4
　　+ 9

3.　8
　　　8
　　+ 3

4.　4
　　　2
　　　6
　　+ 8

5.　9
　　　4
　　　7
　　+ 5

6.　8
　　　9
　　　7
　　+ 6

7.　2
　　　3
　　　5
　　　7
　　+ 9

8.　4
　　　8
　　　2
　　　6
　　+ 9

9.　3
　　　9
　　　8
　　　2
　　+ 4

10.　6
　　　6
　　　5
　　　5
　　+ 4

11.　8
　　　7
　　　6
　　　5
　　+ 1

12.　2
　　　9
　　　3
　　　8
　　+ 5

13.　7
　　　3
　　+ 9

14.　8
　　　6
　　　8
　　+ 2

15.　9
　　　7
　　　4
　　　8
　　+ 2

16.　8
　　　6
　　　4
　　　9
　　+ 4

17.　9
　　　4
　　　8
　　+ 6

18.　3
　　　9
　　+ 9

★**19.** 7 + 8 + 9 + 4 + 9 + 3

★**20.** 4 + 2 + 7 + 6 + 4 + 8 + 2

Add. *(Use with page 56.)*

1. 47
+ 32

2. 86
+ 74

3. 98
+ 64

4. 39
+ 11

5. 63
+ 85

6. 64
97
+ 26

7. 38
27
+ 42

8. 86
29
+ 48

9. 99
88
+ 77

10. 64
29
+ 78

11. 98
47
63
+ 24

12. 86
27
49
+ 19

13. 78
27
69
+ 48

14. 73
95
18
+ 9

15. 86
95
9
+ 8

16. 63
27
49
+ 82

17. 89
98
+ 19

★ **18.** 27
36
47
58
+ 27

★ **19.** 84
36
98
27
+ 9

★ **20.** 13
19
27
8
+ 4

Solve.

★ **21.** $36 + 29 + \square = 87$

★ **22.** $18 + \square + 46 = 93$

Add. *(Use with page 58.)*

1. 832
+ 165

2. 471
+ 296

3. 479
+ 954

4. 684
+ 99

5. 275
+ 8

6. 427
684
+ 195

7. 876
107
+ 340

8. 976
287
+ 484

9. 782
976
+ 49

10. 285
98
+ 7

11. 684
297
648
+ 209

12. 976
289
426
+ 878

13. 187
294
642
+ 98

14. 684
297
188
+ 9

15. 768
248
49
+ 7

★ **16.** 3,378
1,296
4,186
+ 353

★ **17.** 6,874
9,198
487
+ 3,146

★ **18.** 3,498
2,876
974
+ 888

★ **19.** 7,294
8,649
9,876
+ 7,006

★ **20.** 4,298
8,649
7,664
+ 978

Add. *(Use with page 60.)*

1. 4,014 + 3,742	**2.** 7,791 + 2,108	**3.** 3,764 + 9,319	**4.** 2,376 + 4,298
5. 7,894 + 6,387	**6.** 2,911 + 3,789	**7.** 33,798 + 28,973	**8.** 19,762 + 53,791
9. 62,775 + 85,884	**10.** 26,421 + 33,107	**11.** 36,291 + 42,786	**12.** 74,218 + 91,084
★ **13.** 337,649 + 118,747	★ **14.** 372,099 + 218,927	★ **15.** 564,684 + 679,856	★ **16.** 896,408 + 187,149

Add. *(Use with page 62.)*

1. 3,045 6,111 + 1,421	**2.** 7,298 8,764 + 9,407	**3.** 4,291 6,487 + 7,286	**4.** 9,444 6,271 + 5,148	**5.** 6,291 7,302 + 413
6. 1,246 2,357 + 3,468	**7.** 5,997 886 + 3,675	**8.** 2,871 1,762 + 3,873	**9.** 7,248 359 + 460	**10.** 2,773 3,894 + 4,905
11. 6,250 149 + 361	**12.** 2,743 854 + 2	★ **13.** 37,483 16,572 + 48,594	★ **14.** 63,707 14,606 + 32,994	★ **15.** 96,784 67,648 + 78,468

Write the number sentence that fits the problem. *(Use with page 66.)*

1. Ilse went to school 21 days in May and 11 days in June. How many days did she go in all?

2. Janell had 569 baseball cards. José had 735. How many baseball cards did they have altogether?

3. Sheila got 18 votes in an election and Charles got 13 votes. How many votes were there in all?

4. There were 307 boys and 299 girls at the school. How many more boys were there than girls?

5. Andy had 135 baseball cards. He gave 86 to Jeffrey. How many did Andy have left?

★ **6.** Jeri had $5.75. She earned $6.50 more. She spent $2.95. How much does she have now?

Add. *(Use with page 70.)*

1. $ 0.15
   + 0.43

2. $ 0.87
   + 0.86

3. $ 3.75
   + 2.98

4. $ 0.49
   + 1.87

5. $ 8.76
   + 9.48

6. $ 14.26
   + 27.39

7. $ 86.84
   + 49.50

8. $ 76.42
   + 89.48

9. $ 0.18
   0.19
   + 0.76

10. $ 1.75
   2.88
   + 9.75

11. $ 18.75
   36.14
   + 94.10

12. $ 68.14
   7.86
   + 0.74

★ **13.** $ 350.76
   + 189.74

★ **14.** $ 198.78
   + 532.97

★ **15.** $ 458.19
   + 0.75

★ **16.** $ 724.16
   + 9.48

Estimate the sums. Round to the nearest ten. *(Use with page 72.)*

1. 29
   + 48

2. 91
   + 82

3. 86
   + 29

4. 49
   + 52

5. 68
   + 23

6. 87
   29
   + 48

7. 63
   29
   + 44

8. 82
   93
   + 29

9. 28
   29
   + 27

10. 69
   72
   + 84

11. 26
   + 49

12. 87
   + 26

★ **13.** 376
   + 291

★ **14.** 488
   + 375

★ **15.** 498
   + 695

Estimate the sums. Round to the nearest hundred or dollar.

16. 278
   + 694

17. 821
   + 735

18. 398
   + 601

19. 279
   + 386

20. $ 7.85
   + 3.88

21. $ 9.18
   + 7.07

22. $ 9.08
   + 3.98

23. $ 8.47
   + 8.54

24. 376
   498
   + 287

25. 742
   752
   + 601

26. 829
   475
   + 850

27. $ 9.42
   6.85
   + 2.75

28. $ 9.15
   7.85
   + 6.42

29. $ 2.95
   4.10
   + 6.25

★ **30.** 3,784
   + 2,649

★ **31.** $ 91.85
   + 87.04

Add. *(Use with page 75.)*

1.	**2.**	**3.**	**4.**
39 + 9	6 4 + 3	9 2 7 + 4	87 + 48

5.	**6.**	**7.**	**8.**
749 + 684	6,284 + 9,618	47,296 + 82,147	87,498 + 25,697

9.	**10.**	**11.**	**12.**
74 26 + 49	827 906 + 754	3,948 4,059 + 2,837	6,211 9,488 + 748

13.	**14.**	**15.**	**16.**
$ 0.28 + 0.11	$ 1.86 + 2.97	$ 86.74 + 99.48	$ 37.40 26.75 + 8.77

Subtract. *(Use with page 82.)*

1.	**2.**	**3.**	**4.**	**5.**
74 − 2	87 − 7	64 − 5	71 − 6	82 − 7

6.	**7.**	**8.**	**9.**	**10.**
49 − 23	68 − 38	79 − 24	65 − 37	86 − 29

11.	**12.**	★ **13.**	★ **14.**	★ **15.**
48 − 19	40 − 12	73 − ?? 46	41 − ?? 27	86 − ?? 38

Subtract. *(Use with page 84.)*

1.	**2.**	**3.**	**4.**	**5.**
748 − 307	265 − 164	498 − 54	675 − 175	847 − 3

6.	**7.**	**8.**	**9.**	**10.**
276 − 118	427 − 196	842 − 659	420 − 146	759 − 389

11.	**12.**	★ **13.**	★ **14.**	★ **15.**
427 − 38	871 − 7	942 − ??? 275	888 − ??? 359	729 − ??? 76

Subtract. *(Use with page 86.)*

1.	9,875 − 4,014	**2.**	6,948 − 3,644	**3.**	7,248 − 3,914	**4.**	9,871 − 6,960
5.	8,276 − 391	**6.**	2,148 − 1,054	**7.**	7,281 − 6,019	**8.**	3,475 − 66
9.	87,428 − 14,203	**10.**	96,784 − 27,649	**11.**	39,184 − 27,879	**12.**	42,420 − 19,388
13.	49,872 − 16,985	**14.**	73,421 − 69,878	**15.**	42,819 − 19,428	**16.**	64,728 − 59,989
17.	2,784 − 988	**18.**	56,274 − 9,385	**19.**	32,198 − 899	**20.**	1,248 − 97
★ **21.**	642,745 − 381,696	★ **22.**	724,168 − 198,249	★ **23.**	486,280 − 198,267	★ **24.**	649,187 − ??? ??? 98,889

Subtract. *(Use with page 88.)*

1.	700 − 268	**2.**	300 − 297	**3.**	401 − 207	**4.**	807 − 129
5.	6,000 − 3,212	**6.**	9,000 − 4,281	**7.**	6,003 − 1,234	**8.**	8,004 − 296
9.	4,040 − 5	**10.**	7,010 − 6,481	**11.**	36,300 − 12,876	**12.**	49,074 − 26,185
13.	20,308 − 19,279	**14.**	24,000 − 12,413	**15.**	70,000 − 64,297	**16.**	36,003 − 18,121
17.	9,400 − 8,674	**18.**	904 − 876	**19.**	96,050 − 18,596	**20.**	7,010 − 247
★ **21.**	300,000 − 197,268	★ **22.**	400,005 − 396,487	★ **23.**	450,000 − 198,274	★ **24.**	407,301 − ??? ??? 128,816

Use the four steps to solve. *(Use with page 92.)*

1. Al sold 43 pens. Ann sold 29 pens. How many were sold in all?

2. Joe had 136 marbles. He lost 39 of them. How many are left?

3. Mike sold 387 papers in May and 426 papers in June. How many more papers did he sell in June?

4. Mr. Ortez sold 16,700 liters of gas in April and 17,400 liters in May. How much did he sell in all?

5. There were 287 boys and 317 girls at a show. How many children were there?

6. Ms. Allen drove 2,808 miles and Ms. Atler drove 1,989 miles. How much farther did Ms. Allen drive?

Subtract. *(Use with page 95.)*

1. $\begin{array}{r}\$\,0.47\\-\,0.18\end{array}$	**2.** $\begin{array}{r}\$\,0.80\\-\,0.37\end{array}$	**3.** $\begin{array}{r}\$\,1.97\\-\,0.34\end{array}$	**4.** $\begin{array}{r}\$\,8.26\\-\,1.74\end{array}$
5. $\begin{array}{r}\$\,25.64\\-\,19.48\end{array}$	**6.** $\begin{array}{r}\$\,37.40\\-\,18.75\end{array}$	**7.** $\begin{array}{r}\$\,42.70\\-\,9.86\end{array}$	**8.** $\begin{array}{r}\$\,9.00\\-\,1.46\end{array}$
9. $\begin{array}{r}\$\,10.00\\-\,4.85\end{array}$	**10.** $\begin{array}{r}\$\,5.00\\-\,0.49\end{array}$	**11.** $\begin{array}{r}\$\,26.50\\-\,19.95\end{array}$	**12.** $\begin{array}{r}\$\,80.07\\-\,39.84\end{array}$
13. $\begin{array}{r}\$\,347.85\\-\,210.96\end{array}$	**14.** $\begin{array}{r}\$\,268.74\\-\,190.69\end{array}$	★ **15.** $\begin{array}{r}\$\,4,297.49\\-\,1,486.54\end{array}$	★ **16.** $\begin{array}{r}\$\,6,000.00\\-\,5,897.48\end{array}$

Estimate the differences. Round to the nearest ten. *(Use with page 98.)*

1. $\begin{array}{r}48\\-\,29\end{array}$	**2.** $\begin{array}{r}47\\-\,28\end{array}$	**3.** $\begin{array}{r}74\\-\,33\end{array}$	**4.** $\begin{array}{r}91\\-\,32\end{array}$	**5.** $\begin{array}{r}86\\-\,47\end{array}$	**6.** $\begin{array}{r}42\\-\,33\end{array}$
7. $\begin{array}{r}58\\-\,47\end{array}$	**8.** $\begin{array}{r}81\\-\,33\end{array}$	**9.** $\begin{array}{r}88\\-\,59\end{array}$	**10.** $\begin{array}{r}79\\-\,38\end{array}$	★ **11.** $\begin{array}{r}875\\-\,39\end{array}$	★ **12.** $\begin{array}{r}784\\-\,198\end{array}$

Estimate the differences. Round to the nearest hundred or dollar.

13. $\begin{array}{r}427\\-\,134\end{array}$	**14.** $\begin{array}{r}788\\-\,290\end{array}$	**15.** $\begin{array}{r}550\\-\,361\end{array}$	**16.** $\begin{array}{r}912\\-\,399\end{array}$	**17.** $\begin{array}{r}\$\,8.04\\-\,1.88\end{array}$

Subtract. *(Use with page 101.)*

1.	86 − 9	2.	47 − 8	3.	62 − 27	4.	44 − 19	5.	60 − 15
6.	723 − 118	7.	287 − 195	8.	383 − 144	9.	760 − 287	10.	388 − 199
11.	7,241 − 4,101	12.	8,257 − 6,148	13.	9,628 − 4,809	14.	7,214 − 6,675		
15.	76,218 − 49,019	16.	48,679 − 39,884	17.	19,287 − 9,478	18.	500 − 168		
19.	8,000 − 1,256	20.	94,000 − 28,387	21.	$ 19.86 − 9.97	22.	$ 40.00 − 19.45		

Multiply. *(Use with page 112.)*

1.	5 × 2	2.	1 × 6	3.	7 × 3	4.	7 × 4	5.	0 × 4	6.	4 × 2	7.	4 × 8
8.	9 × 2	9.	5 × 3	10.	2 × 3	11.	1 × 3	12.	1 × 9	13.	8 × 2	14.	4 × 4

Write the missing factors.

★ **15.** $\underline{\ ?\ } \times \underline{\ ?\ } = 12$ ★ **16.** $\underline{\ ?\ } \times \underline{\ ?\ } = 16$ ★ **17.** $\underline{\ ?\ } \times \underline{\ ?\ } = 18$

Multiply. *(Use with page 119.)*

1.	6 × 6	2.	7 × 6	3.	6 × 8	4.	9 × 6	5.	7 × 7	6.	7 × 8	7.	9 × 5
8.	6 × 4	9.	9 × 7	10.	7 × 9	11.	8 × 8	12.	8 × 9	13.	8 × 6	14.	8 × 7
15.	9 × 8	16.	9 × 9	17.	6 × 5	18.	5 × 5	19.	8 × 3	20.	4 × 6	21.	6 × 9

Estimate. Is the answer reasonable? *(Use with page 122.)*

1. Mr. Hanson plowed 215 acres in March and 198 acres in April. How many acres did he plow in all?
Answer: 303 acres

2. Ms. Hernandez paid $8.98 for food and $8.89 for gas. How much did she spend in all?
Answer: $17.87

3. Mr. Hart drove 212 kilometers one week and 198 kilometers the next week. How far did he drive in the 2 weeks?
Answer: 300 kilometers

4. Bill scored 19, 21, and 32 points in three basketball games. How many points did he score in the three games?
Answer: 62 points

5. Linda scored 111, 172, and 113 for three bowling games. What was her total score?
Answer: 396

★ 6. Mr. Ting bought meat for $7.85 and fish for $4.10. He gave the clerk $20.00. How much change should he get?
Answer: $7.05

Divide. *(Use with page 130.)*

1. $6\overline{)24}$ 2. $1\overline{)0}$ 3. $1\overline{)2}$ 4. $3\overline{)12}$ 5. $2\overline{)6}$ 6. $4\overline{)20}$

7. $2\overline{)2}$ 8. $4\overline{)32}$ 9. $3\overline{)9}$ 10. $6\overline{)30}$ 11. $3\overline{)24}$ 12. $6\overline{)6}$

13. $6\overline{)36}$ 14. $1\overline{)6}$ 15. $4\overline{)8}$ 16. $5\overline{)40}$ 17. $3\overline{)18}$ 18. $5\overline{)15}$

★ Complete.

19. $30 \div \underline{\ ?\ } = 6$ 20. $36 \div \underline{\ ?\ } = 4$ 21. $40 \div \underline{\ ?\ } = 5$

Divide. *(Use with page 132.)*

1. $7\overline{)56}$ 2. $9\overline{)81}$ 3. $7\overline{)28}$ 4. $8\overline{)48}$ 5. $9\overline{)63}$ 6. $9\overline{)27}$

7. $7\overline{)7}$ 8. $8\overline{)40}$ 9. $8\overline{)56}$ 10. $9\overline{)54}$ 11. $9\overline{)9}$ 12. $7\overline{)49}$

13. $8\overline{)16}$ 14. $8\overline{)64}$ 15. $9\overline{)45}$ 16. $7\overline{)21}$ 17. $8\overline{)32}$ 18. $9\overline{)72}$

19. $7\overline{)63}$ 20. $9\overline{)0}$ 21. $8\overline{)72}$ 22. $7\overline{)42}$ 23. $7\overline{)35}$ 24. $9\overline{)36}$

EXTRA PRACTICE

Multiply. *(Use with page 137.)*

1. 0 ×5	**2.** 7 ×0	**3.** 8 ×1	**4.** 1 ×7	**5.** 2 ×5	**6.** 9 ×2	**7.** 8 ×2
8. 2 ×6	**9.** 4 ×2	**10.** 3 ×9	**11.** 8 ×3	**12.** 4 ×8	**13.** 6 ×4	**14.** 5 ×5
15. 5 ×6	**16.** 4 ×5	**17.** 6 ×8	**18.** 9 ×6	**19.** 8 ×7	**20.** 7 ×5	**21.** 7 ×4
22. 8 ×6	**23.** 8 ×8	**24.** 8 ×9	**25.** 9 ×4	**26.** 5 ×9	**27.** 7 ×9	**28.** 3 ×9

Divide.

29. $1\overline{)8}$ **30.** $3\overline{)3}$ **31.** $2\overline{)16}$ **32.** $3\overline{)6}$ **33.** $3\overline{)18}$ **34.** $3\overline{)12}$

35. $4\overline{)20}$ **36.** $4\overline{)36}$ **37.** $5\overline{)40}$ **38.** $6\overline{)36}$ **39.** $5\overline{)15}$ **40.** $6\overline{)54}$

41. $5\overline{)20}$ **42.** $6\overline{)42}$ **43.** $6\overline{)18}$ **44.** $7\overline{)49}$ **45.** $7\overline{)35}$ **46.** $8\overline{)64}$

47. $9\overline{)72}$ **48.** $8\overline{)48}$ **49.** $7\overline{)63}$ **50.** $9\overline{)18}$ **51.** $8\overline{)32}$ **52.** $9\overline{)81}$

Write the number sentence that fits the problem. *(Use with page 156.)*

1. David baked 6 batches of cookies. There were 8 cookies in each batch. How many cookies did he bake?

2. A farmer planted 45 tomato plants in 5 equal rows. How many plants were in each row?

3. Josh has 12 problems to do. He can do 3 a minute. How long will it take him to do the problems?

4. Laurie can do 8 problems a minute. How many can she do in 5 minutes?

5. Pam has 3 pages of stamps. There are 9 stamps on each page. How many stamps does she have in all?

6. There are 48 cans with 6 cans in a box. How many boxes are there?

★ **7.** Pencils are 10 cents each. How much will 2 dozen cost?

★ **8.** There are 3 dozen bottles with 6 bottles in a case. How many cases are there?

Multiply. *(Use with page 178.)*

1. 41 ×2	**2.** 63 ×3	**3.** 82 ×4	**4.** 70 ×6	**5.** 91 ×8	**6.** 74 ×3
7. 96 ×7	**8.** 47 ×8	**9.** 63 ×9	**10.** 87 ×4	**11.** 36 ×3	**12.** 51 ×8
13. 93 ×3	**14.** 85 ×5	**15.** 49 ×7	★ **16.** 31 ×? ——— 93	★ **17.** 42 ×? ——— 252	★ **18.** 78 ×? ——— 624

Multiply. *(Use with page 180.)*

1. 122 ×3	**2.** 212 ×4	**3.** 611 ×8	**4.** 323 ×3	**5.** 710 ×9	**6.** 827 ×2
7. 628 ×3	**8.** 906 ×5	**9.** 841 ×7	**10.** 692 ×9	**11.** 936 ×8	**12.** 801 ×6
13. 543 ×2	**14.** 876 ×9	**15.** 808 ×7	★ **16.** 411 ×? ——— 822	★ **17.** 673 ×? ——— 2,692	★ **18.** 899 ×? ——— 3,596

Multiply. *(Use with page 182.)*

1. 3,122 ×2	**2.** 6,210 ×4	**3.** 8,001 ×3	**4.** 4,183 ×3	**5.** 5,641 ×2
6. 6,234 ×3	**7.** 3,941 ×8	**8.** 6,204 ×5	**9.** 9,186 ×5	**10.** 4,279 ×3
11. 6,849 ×9	**12.** 8,423 ×6	**13.** 9,376 ×8	**14.** 3,149 ×7	**15.** 4,289 ×5
16. 7,481 ×6	**17.** 1,204 ×5	**18.** 6,789 ×2	**19.** 6,510 ×7	**20.** 2,461 ×3
★ **21.** 18,642 ×7	★ **22.** 39,753 ×8	★ **23.** 26,495 ×3	★ **24.** 68,149 ×5	

Multiply. *(Use with page 184.)*

1. $0.37
   × 2

2. $0.56
   × 4

3. $0.78
   × 6

4. $4.95
   × 5

5. $8.47
   × 3

6. $3.68
   × 5

7. $5.75
   × 8

8. $14.33
   × 7

9. $38.46
   × 8

10. $36.24
    × 4

11. $10.98
    × 5

12. $0.65
    × 2

13. $7.04
    × 6

14. $0.40
    × 9

15. $56.47
    × 5

★16. $216.18
     × 6

★17. $395.99
     × 8

★18. $189.75
     × 2

★19. $387.50
     × 8

Which number sentence fits the problem? *(Use with page 188.)*

1. A baseball glove costs $18.79. A uniform costs $24.25. How much do they cost together?
   $18.79 + $24.25 = __?__
   $24.25 − $18.78 = __?__
   $18.79 × $24.25 = __?__

2. A car gets 28 miles per gallon of gas. How many miles can it go on 24 gallons?
   28 − 24 = __?__
   28 + 24 = __?__
   28 × 24 = __?__

3. There are 42 bottles packed 6 to a box. How many boxes are there?
   42 × 6 = __?__
   42 + 6 = __?__
   42 ÷ 6 = __?__

4. Sue jogs 2 miles a day. In how many days will she jog 10 miles?
   10 × 2 = __?__
   10 ÷ 2 = __?__
   10 + 2 = __?__

5. Ken bought a radio for $12.95. He gave the clerk $20.00. How much change did he get?
   $20.00 − $12.95 = __?__
   $20.00 + $12.95 = __?__
   $20.00 × $12.95 = __?__

6. Sara has 15 coins on each of 12 pages. How many coins does she have on the 12 pages?
   15 − 12 = __?__
   15 × 12 = __?__
   15 ÷ 12 = __?__

★7. Pencils cost 9 cents each. What is the cost of 2 dozen pencils?
   2 × 9 = __?__
   2 × 12 × 9 = __?__
   2 × 12 ÷ 9 = __?__

★8. Bill had 3 dozen cookies. He ate 8. How many are left?
   3 × 8 = __?__
   3 × 12 + 8 = __?__
   3 × 12 − 8 = __?__

Estimate each product. Round the greater factor to the nearest ten or ten cents. *(Use with page 190.)*

1. 68	**2.** 22	**3.** 85	**4.** $0.63	**5.** $0.45
× 9	× 8	× 4	× 7	× 8

6. $0.51	**7.** 78	**8.** 49	**9.** $0.86	**10.** $0.43
× 2	× 6	× 5	× 9	× 4

11. 73	**12.** $0.18	★ **13.** 392	★ **14.** 197	★ **15.** $3.46
× 3	× 6	× 4	× 8	× 5

Estimate each product. Round the greater factor to the nearest hundred or dollar.

16. 398	**17.** 612	**18.** $8.50	**19.** $9.03	**20.** 888
× 5	× 6	× 3	× 8	× 8

21. $1.98	**22.** 303	**23.** $7.50	**24.** $9.14	**25.** 897
× 6	× 4	× 5	× 5	× 7

26. 447	**27.** $2.89	★ **28.** 997	★ **29.** $12.34	★ **30.** $59.79
× 6	× 7	× 4	× 8	× 5

Multiply. *(Use with page 194.)*

1. 37	**2.** 35	**3.** 84	**4.** 76	**5.** 49
× 30	× 20	× 90	× 30	× 40

6. 386	**7.** 475	**8.** 563	**9.** 349	**10.** $8.87
× 50	× 80	× 70	× 50	× 40

11. $0.83	**12.** $7.47	**13.** $6.95	**14.** $9.65	**15.** 549
× 70	× 80	× 50	× 70	× 60

16. 29	**17.** 75	**18.** 870	**19.** 248	**20.** $9.46
× 40	× 60	× 90	× 20	× 30

★ **21.** 1,387	★ **22.** 9,364	★ **23.** 4,248	★ **24.** $86.75	★ **25.** $19.46
× 50	× 80	× 20	× 60	× 30

EXTRA PRACTICE

Multiply. *(Use with page 196.)*

1.	2.	3.	4.	5.
48 $\times$ 12	54 $\times$ 36	97 $\times$ 25	48 $\times$ 39	75 $\times$ 43

6.	7.	8.	9.	10.
$0.86 $\times$ 58	$0.51 $\times$ 63	$0.75 $\times$ 84	$0.87 $\times$ 92	86 $\times$ 77

11.	12.	13.	14.	15.
48 $\times$ 23	87 $\times$ 58	$0.65 $\times$ 65	15 $\times$ 15	$0.25 $\times$ 25

★Complete.

16. $34 \times 2\underline{?} = 816$ **17.** $53 \times \underline{?}8 = 3{,}604$ **18.** $72 \times \underline{?}6 = 2{,}592$

Multiply. *(Use with page 198.)*

1.	2.	3.	4.	5.
763 $\times$ 41	297 $\times$ 65	583 $\times$ 74	342 $\times$ 29	468 $\times$ 63

6.	7.	8.	9.	10.
$5.39 $\times$ 88	$4.53 $\times$ 89	$9.21 $\times$ 23	$1.29 $\times$ 32	$3.67 $\times$ 49

11.	12.	13.	14.	15.
895 $\times$ 67	$9.42 $\times$ 15	$4.50 $\times$ 22	123 $\times$ 45	678 $\times$ 91

★16.	★17.	★18.	★19.	★20.
1,298 $\times$ 37	3,846 $\times$ 34	$15.35 $\times$ 84	$37.98 $\times$ 55	7,891 $\times$ 79

Multiply. *(Use with page 201.)*

1.	2.	3.	4.	5.
10 $\times$ 8	1,000 $\times$ 7	63 $\times$ 3	69 $\times$ 7	137 $\times$ 9

6.	7.	8.	9.	10.
682 $\times$ 4	3,906 $\times$ 8	3,704 $\times$ 2	$6.75 $\times$ 3	$86.92 $\times$ 8

11.	12.	13.	14.	15.
300 $\times$ 8	90 $\times$ 60	83 $\times$ 70	462 $\times$ 60	68 $\times$ 35

16.	17.	18.	19.	20.
$0.85 $\times$ 50	78 $\times$ 21	367 $\times$ 48	213 $\times$ 41	$7.89 $\times$ 36

Divide. *(Use with page 208.)*

1. 3)10   **2.** 9)40   **3.** 6)25   **4.** 7)50   **5.** 8)61   **6.** 3)7

7. 4)15   **8.** 5)22   **9.** 6)23   **10.** 7)45   **11.** 8)57   **12.** 9)70

                                   1 r 3   5 r 1   5 r 1   7 r 3

13. 7)41   **14.** 8)50 ★**15.** 9)?? ★**16.** 7)? ★**17.** 2)? ★**18.** 6)?

Divide. *(Use with page 210.)*

1. 2)42   **2.** 3)42   **3.** 4)87   **4.** 5)57   **5.** 6)84   **6.** 7)84

7. 8)98   **8.** 2)98   **9.** 8)99   **10.** 7)77   **11.** 6)87   **12.** 5)75

13. 4)98   **14.** 3)98   **15.** 2)94   **16.** 4)96   **17.** 3)96   **18.** 2)96

                                  12 r 1   31   12   12 r 3

19. 5)96   **20.** 6)96 ★**21.** 7)?? ★**22.** 3)?? ★**23.** 4)?? ★**24.** 5)??

Divide. *(Use with page 212.)*

1. 3)126   **2.** 4)126   **3.** 5)259   **4.** 6)429   **5.** 8)568

6. 2)138   **7.** 9)488   **8.** 3)254   **9.** 8)424   **10.** 4)288

11. 7)504   **12.** 5)386   **13.** 6)205   **14.** 5)422   **15.** 9)621

      82   55   93 r 6   63   72 r 2

★**16.** 5)??? ★**17.** 6)??? ★**18.** 8)??? ★**19.** 2)??? ★**20.** 3)???

Divide. *(Use with page 214.)*

1. 2)846   **2.** 3)687   **3.** 3)789   **4.** 4)968   **5.** 2)568

6. 3)986   **7.** 4)844   **8.** 5)617   **9.** 6)738   **10.** 7)784

11. 8)892   **12.** 7)922   **13.** 6)777   **14.** 5)945   **15.** 4)765

★**16.** $345 \div 3 = \underline{\ ?\ }$ ★**17.** $748 \div 2 = \underline{\ ?\ }$ ★**18.** $876 \div 6 = \underline{\ ?\ }$ ★**19.** $944 \div 8 = \underline{\ ?\ }$

Divide. *(Use with page 216.)*

1. $6\overline{)3,186}$
2. $7\overline{)3,186}$
3. $9\overline{)6,579}$
4. $6\overline{)2,796}$
5. $8\overline{)2,569}$

6. $6\overline{)2,250}$
7. $3\overline{)1,147}$
8. $4\overline{)1,764}$
9. $5\overline{)2,408}$
10. $7\overline{)4,312}$

11. $8\overline{)3,048}$
12. $4\overline{)2,579}$
13. $9\overline{)6,426}$
14. $8\overline{)6,526}$
15. $7\overline{)4,076}$

16. $6\overline{)1,696}$
17. $5\overline{)1,234}$
★ 18. $4\overline{)12,745}$
★ 19. $3\overline{)22,463}$
★ 20. $4\overline{)34,187}$

Divide. *(Use with page 218.)*

1. $7\overline{)75}$
2. $8\overline{)84}$
3. $9\overline{)93}$
4. $7\overline{)74}$
5. $4\overline{)41}$

6. $6\overline{)364}$
7. $9\overline{)728}$
8. $8\overline{)643}$
9. $3\overline{)901}$
10. $4\overline{)1,403}$

11. $3\overline{)1,204}$
12. $4\overline{)1,608}$
13. $3\overline{)1,201}$
14. $5\overline{)3,004}$
15. $8\overline{)1,683}$

16. $7\overline{)2,174}$
17. $4\overline{)3,680}$
★ 18. $3\overline{)6,092}$
★ 19. $7\overline{)8,421}$
★ 20. $4\overline{)24,007}$

Solve. *(Use with page 224.)*

1. Francisca bought 3 notebooks for $0.89 each and 1 pen for $1.49. How much did she spend in all?

2. Mr. Ritt brought 3 bags of apples to school. Each bag had 15 apples. The class ate 28 of the apples. How many apples were left?

3. Seth bought a book for $4.98 and paints for $3.95. He gave the clerk $10.00. How much change did he receive?

4. There were 523 passengers on the train. At a stop 146 passengers got off and 82 got on. How many passengers were on the train then?

5. Mrs. Whigham's class had 6 rows of seats with 5 children in a row. One day 7 children were absent. How many were present?

6. Kathy jogs 2 kilometers a day, Monday through Friday. On Saturday she jogs 5 kilometers. How many kilometers does she jog these 6 days?

Divide. *(Use with page 226.)*

1. $10\overline{)80}$ **2.** $30\overline{)90}$ **3.** $10\overline{)70}$ **4.** $20\overline{)40}$ **5.** $50\overline{)50}$

6. $40\overline{)200}$ **7.** $60\overline{)420}$ **8.** $90\overline{)450}$ **9.** $70\overline{)350}$ **10.** $80\overline{)560}$

11. $30\overline{)70}$ **12.** $50\overline{)90}$ **13.** $40\overline{)70}$ **14.** $20\overline{)30}$ **15.** $60\overline{)80}$

16. $30\overline{)260}$ **17.** $60\overline{)370}$ **18.** $90\overline{)850}$ **19.** $70\overline{)460}$ **20.** $40\overline{)270}$

★ Solve.

21. $120 \div \square = 4$ **22.** $360 \div \square = 7\,r\,10$ **23.** $620 \div \square = 7\,r\,60$

Divide. *(Use with page 228.)*

1. $10\overline{)280}$ **2.** $20\overline{)660}$ **3.** $30\overline{)660}$ **4.** $40\overline{)840}$ **5.** $30\overline{)930}$

6. $10\overline{)177}$ **7.** $20\overline{)746}$ **8.** $30\overline{)746}$ **9.** $40\overline{)964}$ **10.** $50\overline{)875}$

11. $50\overline{)750}$ **12.** $40\overline{)920}$ **13.** $30\overline{)820}$ **14.** $20\overline{)920}$ **15.** $10\overline{)920}$

16. $10\overline{)170}$ **17.** $10\overline{)289}$ **18.** $20\overline{)740}$ **19.** $30\overline{)780}$ **20.** $40\overline{)600}$

21. $60\overline{)960}$ **22.** $70\overline{)960}$ **23.** $80\overline{)960}$ ★ **24.** $40\overline{)7,875}$ ★ **25.** $50\overline{)9,875}$

★ Solve.

26. $360 \div \square = 20$ **27.** $927 \div \square = 15\,r\,27$ **28.** $756 \div \square = 18\,r\,36$

Divide. *(Use with page 230.)*

1. $2\overline{)\$0.12}$ **2.** $3\overline{)\$0.12}$ **3.** $4\overline{)\$0.12}$ **4.** $5\overline{)\$0.75}$ **5.** $5\overline{)\$0.80}$

6. $6\overline{)\$0.96}$ **7.** $7\overline{)\$1.05}$ **8.** $8\overline{)\$1.20}$ **9.** $9\overline{)\$1.80}$ **10.** $8\overline{)\$9.84}$

11. $7\overline{)\$16.45}$ **12.** $6\overline{)\$20.70}$ **13.** $5\overline{)\$19.85}$ **14.** $4\overline{)\$25.44}$

15. $2\overline{)\$15.44}$ **16.** $3\overline{)\$28.95}$ **17.** $4\overline{)\$23.92}$ **18.** $5\overline{)\$41.75}$

★ **19.** $9\overline{)\$128.25}$ ★ **20.** $4\overline{)\$385.28}$ ★ **21.** $9\overline{)\$209.25}$ ★ **22.** $8\overline{)\$293.68}$

Divide. *(Use with page 237.)*

1. $2\overline{)80}$
2. $3\overline{)1,200}$
3. $4\overline{)2,800}$
4. $3\overline{)10}$
5. $4\overline{)17}$

6. $5\overline{)44}$
7. $2\overline{)68}$
8. $3\overline{)98}$
9. $4\overline{)98}$
10. $2\overline{)168}$

11. $4\overline{)208}$
12. $5\overline{)145}$
13. $3\overline{)936}$
14. $7\overline{)819}$
15. $6\overline{)948}$

16. $4\overline{)2,864}$
17. $6\overline{)3,727}$
18. $5\overline{)2,734}$
19. $4\overline{)408}$

20. $7\overline{)4,902}$
21. $3\overline{)2,712}$
22. $20\overline{)80}$
23. $30\overline{)210}$

24. $50\overline{)176}$
25. $70\overline{)95}$
26. $10\overline{)247}$
27. $30\overline{)480}$

28. $50\overline{)756}$
29. $5\overline{)\$0.35}$
30. $6\overline{)\$1.92}$
31. $7\overline{)\$16.52}$

Solve. *(Use with page 254.)*

1. The coach had 2 dozen softballs. She gave 5 softballs to a class for a game. How many does she have left?

2. Mr. Olson reads 15 minutes twice a day. How many minutes does he read in a week?

3. Your heart beats 72 times a minute. How many times will it beat in 3 hours?

4. Tom picked 5 dozen ears of corn. He put them in sacks with 6 to a sack. How many sacks did he have?

5. A clock chimes 2 times an hour. How many times will it chime in 3 days?

6. Ms. Green has a 2-week vacation in the spring and a 3-week vacation in the fall. How many days of vacation does she have?

7. Jimmy bought 3 dozen eggs. He ate 4 of them. How many eggs were left?

8. Mrs. Higgins bought 1 kilogram of meat. Her 4 children shared it equally. How much meat did each child get?

★ 9. Betsy did 2 dozen jumping jacks twice a day for a week. How many jumping jacks did she do in all?

★ 10. Matt read 2 hours every day in May and June. How many hours did he read in those two months?

Add. *(Use with page 272.)*

1. $\frac{6}{8}$ $+\frac{1}{8}$ 2. $\frac{3}{9}$ $+\frac{4}{9}$ 3. $\frac{1}{4}$ $+\frac{2}{4}$ 4. $\frac{1}{8}$ $+\frac{2}{8}$ 5. $\frac{3}{7}$ $+\frac{2}{7}$ 6. $\frac{3}{5}$ $+\frac{1}{5}$

7. $\frac{1}{3}$ $+\frac{1}{3}$ 8. $\frac{1}{6}$ $+\frac{4}{6}$ 9. $\frac{4}{7}$ $+\frac{2}{7}$ 10. $\frac{5}{10}$ $+\frac{2}{10}$ 11. $\frac{3}{12}$ $+\frac{5}{12}$ 12. $\frac{4}{9}$ $+\frac{2}{9}$

13. $\frac{5}{8}$ $+\frac{1}{8}$ 14. $\frac{2}{9}$ $+\frac{2}{9}$ 15. $\frac{1}{10}$ $+\frac{2}{10}$ 16. $\frac{1}{12}$ $+\frac{4}{12}$ 17. $\frac{1}{9}$ $+\frac{3}{9}$ 18. $\frac{3}{10}$ $+\frac{2}{10}$

19. $\frac{4}{7} + \frac{1}{7}$ 20. $\frac{1}{5} + \frac{1}{5}$ 21. $\frac{1}{5} + \frac{2}{5}$

★22. $\frac{3}{9} + \frac{1}{9} + \frac{2}{9}$ ★23. $\frac{3}{10} + \frac{3}{10} + \frac{3}{10}$ ★24. $\frac{1}{6} + \frac{0}{6} + \frac{2}{6}$

Add. Change the sum to a whole or mixed number.
(Use with page 274.)

1. $\frac{3}{4}$ $+\frac{1}{4}$ 2. $\frac{7}{8}$ $+\frac{5}{8}$ 3. $\frac{3}{4}$ $+\frac{3}{4}$ 4. $\frac{3}{5}$ $+\frac{2}{5}$ 5. $\frac{7}{10}$ $+\frac{3}{10}$ 6. $\frac{4}{5}$ $+\frac{4}{5}$

7. $\frac{1}{2}$ $+\frac{1}{2}$ 8. $\frac{2}{3}$ $+\frac{2}{3}$ 9. $\frac{5}{6}$ $+\frac{2}{6}$ 10. $\frac{7}{9}$ $+\frac{2}{9}$ 11. $\frac{7}{9}$ $+\frac{6}{9}$ 12. $\frac{4}{7}$ $+\frac{3}{7}$

13. $\frac{3}{6}$ $+\frac{3}{6}$ 14. $\frac{4}{7}$ $+\frac{4}{7}$ 15. $\frac{5}{8}$ $+\frac{6}{8}$ 16. $\frac{7}{10}$ $+\frac{6}{10}$ 17. $\frac{7}{12}$ $+\frac{5}{12}$ 18. $\frac{5}{9}$ $+\frac{6}{9}$

19. $\frac{6}{7} + \frac{5}{7}$ 20. $\frac{8}{9} + \frac{7}{9}$ 21. $\frac{5}{6} + \frac{4}{6}$

★22. $\frac{3}{8} + \frac{2}{8} + \frac{3}{8}$ ★23. $\frac{2}{3} + \frac{2}{3} + \frac{2}{3}$ ★24. $\frac{4}{6} + \frac{3}{6} + \frac{1}{6}$

★25. $\frac{4}{9} + \frac{5}{9} + \frac{3}{9}$ ★26. $\frac{3}{7} + \frac{4}{7} + \frac{2}{7}$ ★27. $\frac{3}{4} + \frac{3}{4} + \frac{3}{4}$

EXTRA PRACTICE

Add. *(Use with page 276.)*

1. $\frac{1}{2}$ $+\frac{1}{4}$ **2.** $\frac{1}{3}$ $+\frac{1}{4}$ **3.** $\frac{3}{8}$ $+\frac{1}{4}$ **4.** $\frac{1}{4}$ $+\frac{1}{8}$ **5.** $\frac{3}{10}$ $+\frac{1}{5}$ **6.** $\frac{4}{9}$ $+\frac{1}{3}$

7. $\frac{1}{2}$ $+\frac{1}{5}$ **8.** $\frac{2}{3}$ $+\frac{1}{12}$ **9.** $\frac{1}{3}$ $+\frac{2}{9}$ **10.** $\frac{3}{4}$ $+\frac{3}{16}$ **11.** $\frac{1}{2}$ $+\frac{2}{3}$ **12.** $\frac{5}{6}$ $+\frac{2}{3}$

13. $\frac{1}{2} + \frac{7}{12}$ **14.** $\frac{2}{3} + \frac{3}{4}$ **15.** $\frac{7}{8} + \frac{1}{4}$ **16.** $\frac{1}{2} + \frac{3}{6}$

17. $\frac{3}{4} + \frac{3}{8}$ **18.** $\frac{4}{5} + \frac{7}{10}$ **19.** $\frac{2}{3} + \frac{4}{5}$ **20.** $\frac{7}{8} + \frac{2}{4}$

★ **21.** $\frac{1}{3} + \frac{4}{6} + \frac{1}{2}$ ★ **22.** $\frac{1}{2} + \frac{4}{5} + \frac{3}{10}$ ★ **23.** $\frac{3}{8} + \frac{2}{4} + \frac{1}{2}$

★ **24.** $\frac{1}{2} + \frac{2}{3} + \frac{2}{3}$ ★ **25.** $\frac{1}{3} + \frac{3}{4} + \frac{5}{6}$ ★ **26.** $\frac{1}{2} + \frac{4}{5} + \frac{3}{4}$

Add. *(Use with page 278.)*

1. $2\frac{1}{3}$ $+ 3\frac{1}{3}$ **2.** $6\frac{1}{7}$ $+ 7\frac{3}{7}$ **3.** $9\frac{2}{10}$ $+ 8\frac{3}{10}$ **4.** $7\frac{3}{12}$ $+ 8\frac{4}{12}$ **5.** $6\frac{1}{9}$ $+ 7\frac{2}{9}$

6. $8\frac{1}{3}$ $+ 6$ **7.** $7\frac{1}{2}$ $+ 8$ **8.** 9 $+ 6\frac{2}{3}$ **9.** $8\frac{3}{10}$ $+ \frac{5}{10}$ **10.** $9\frac{3}{8}$ $+ \frac{2}{8}$

11. $27\frac{1}{4}$ $+ 38\frac{2}{4}$ **12.** $79\frac{1}{3}$ $+ 26\frac{1}{3}$ **13.** $27\frac{7}{12}$ $+ 48\frac{1}{12}$ **14.** $65\frac{3}{10}$ $+ 74\frac{4}{10}$ **15.** $89\frac{6}{10}$ $+ 26$

16. $78\frac{3}{4}$ $+ 29$ **17.** $86\frac{1}{6}$ $+ 7\frac{2}{6}$ **18.** $37\frac{1}{2}$ $+ 6$ **19.** $3\frac{3}{4}$ $+ 4$ **20.** $7\frac{7}{10}$ $+ 8\frac{2}{10}$

★ **21.** $3\frac{4}{5} + 2\frac{2}{5}$ ★ **22.** $6\frac{5}{6} + 3\frac{1}{6}$ ★ **23.** $15\frac{5}{9} + 24\frac{6}{9}$

Subtract. *(Use with page 284.)*

1. $\dfrac{7}{8}$
$-\dfrac{1}{8}$

2. $\dfrac{3}{4}$
$-\dfrac{1}{4}$

3. $\dfrac{7}{12}$
$-\dfrac{2}{12}$

4. $\dfrac{9}{11}$
$-\dfrac{9}{11}$

5. $\dfrac{8}{10}$
$-\dfrac{3}{10}$

6. $\dfrac{7}{10}$
$-\dfrac{1}{10}$

7. $\dfrac{3}{9}$
$-\dfrac{1}{9}$

8. $\dfrac{4}{7}$
$-\dfrac{3}{7}$

9. $\dfrac{9}{12}$
$-\dfrac{5}{12}$

10. $\dfrac{5}{6}$
$-\dfrac{5}{6}$

11. $\dfrac{8}{9}$
$-\dfrac{1}{9}$

12. $\dfrac{8}{12}$
$-\dfrac{5}{12}$

13. $\dfrac{11}{12} - \dfrac{6}{12}$

14. $\dfrac{3}{7} - \dfrac{1}{7}$

15. $\dfrac{4}{10} - \dfrac{3}{10}$

16. $\dfrac{7}{9} - \dfrac{1}{9}$

17. $\dfrac{5}{6} - \dfrac{1}{6}$

18. $\dfrac{3}{12} - \dfrac{3}{12}$

19. $\dfrac{7}{8} - \dfrac{2}{8}$

20. $\dfrac{4}{6} - \dfrac{1}{6}$

★ **21.** $\dfrac{8}{10} - \dfrac{?}{10} = \dfrac{5}{10}$

★ **22.** $\dfrac{7}{9} - \dfrac{?}{9} = \dfrac{3}{9}$

★ **23.** $\dfrac{11}{12} - \dfrac{?}{12} = \dfrac{3}{12}$

★ **24.** $\dfrac{?}{9} - \dfrac{4}{9} = \dfrac{3}{9}$

★ **25.** $\dfrac{?}{8} - \dfrac{3}{8} = \dfrac{4}{8}$

★ **26.** $\dfrac{?}{10} - \dfrac{3}{10} = \dfrac{6}{10}$

Subtract. *(Use with page 286.)*

1. $\dfrac{1}{2}$
$-\dfrac{2}{5}$

2. $\dfrac{2}{5}$
$-\dfrac{1}{10}$

3. $\dfrac{7}{10}$
$-\dfrac{1}{2}$

4. $\dfrac{1}{2}$
$-\dfrac{1}{4}$

5. $\dfrac{2}{3}$
$-\dfrac{1}{6}$

6. $\dfrac{7}{8}$
$-\dfrac{3}{4}$

7. $\dfrac{1}{3}$
$-\dfrac{1}{9}$

8. $\dfrac{3}{5}$
$-\dfrac{1}{2}$

9. $\dfrac{7}{10}$
$-\dfrac{2}{5}$

10. $\dfrac{1}{3}$
$-\dfrac{2}{9}$

11. $\dfrac{7}{12}$
$-\dfrac{1}{3}$

12. $\dfrac{7}{10}$
$-\dfrac{3}{5}$

13. $\dfrac{11}{12}$
$-\dfrac{3}{4}$

14. $\dfrac{2}{3}$
$-\dfrac{2}{9}$

15. $\dfrac{9}{10}$
$-\dfrac{2}{5}$

16. $\dfrac{7}{12}$
$-\dfrac{1}{4}$

17. $\dfrac{2}{3}$
$-\dfrac{5}{9}$

18. $\dfrac{11}{12}$
$-\dfrac{1}{4}$

19. $\dfrac{3}{4} - \dfrac{1}{3}$

20. $\dfrac{5}{6} - \dfrac{1}{3}$

21. $\dfrac{7}{8} - \dfrac{2}{4}$

★ **22.** $\dfrac{7}{8} - \dfrac{?}{4} = \dfrac{1}{8}$

★ **23.** $\dfrac{2}{3} - \dfrac{?}{12} = \dfrac{1}{3}$

★ **24.** $\dfrac{5}{6} - \dfrac{?}{2} = \dfrac{2}{6}$

★ **25.** $\dfrac{?}{9} - \dfrac{2}{3} = \dfrac{1}{9}$

★ **26.** $\dfrac{?}{8} - \dfrac{1}{2} = \dfrac{3}{8}$

★ **27.** $\dfrac{?}{4} - \dfrac{3}{8} = \dfrac{1}{8}$

Subtract. *(Use with page 288.)*

1. $7\frac{7}{8}$
  $-1\frac{3}{8}$

2. $6\frac{4}{7}$
  $-3\frac{1}{7}$

3. $8\frac{9}{10}$
  $-7\frac{3}{10}$

4. $9\frac{2}{3}$
  $-9\frac{1}{3}$

5. $8\frac{7}{8}$
  -3

6. $7\frac{5}{10}$
  $-\frac{3}{10}$

7. $6\frac{4}{5}$
  $-\frac{4}{5}$

8. $5\frac{7}{9}$
  $-5\frac{3}{9}$

9. $7\frac{4}{11}$
  $-\frac{4}{11}$

10. $6\frac{2}{3}$
  -1

11. $8\frac{1}{2}$
  $-6\frac{1}{2}$

12. $38\frac{2}{3}$
  $-15\frac{1}{3}$

13. $47\frac{7}{8}$
  $-19\frac{1}{8}$

14. $67\frac{7}{10}$
  $-59\frac{7}{10}$

15. $36\frac{2}{5}$
  -19

16. $42\frac{7}{12}$
  $-36\frac{1}{12}$

17. $12\frac{5}{8}$
  $-9\frac{5}{8}$

18. $87\frac{1}{3}$
  -29

19. $9\frac{9}{10}$
  $-6\frac{3}{10}$

20. $7\frac{7}{8}$
  -1

★ **21.** 4
  $-2\frac{1}{2}$

★ **22.** $3\frac{5}{6}$
  $-1\frac{1}{2}$

★ **23.** $8\frac{3}{5}$
  $-2\frac{1}{2}$

★ **24.** $15\frac{5}{9}$
  $-8\frac{1}{3}$

★ **25.** $37\frac{3}{4}$
  $-18\frac{1}{5}$

Add or subtract. *(Use with page 297.)*

1. $\frac{5}{8}$
  $+\frac{3}{8}$

2. $\frac{7}{10}$
  $+\frac{5}{10}$

3. $\frac{2}{3}$
  $+\frac{5}{6}$

4. $19\frac{7}{10}$
  $+8\frac{2}{10}$

5. $36\frac{1}{5}$
  $+49$

6. $\frac{7}{8}$
  $-\frac{3}{8}$

7. $\frac{7}{12}$
  $-\frac{7}{12}$

8. $\frac{2}{3}$
  $-\frac{1}{6}$

9. $6\frac{5}{9}$
  $-2\frac{2}{9}$

10. $25\frac{3}{10}$
  -5

Add or subtract.

11. 7.5
  $+2.5$

12. 26.3
  $+19.8$

13. 79.62
  $+15.39$

14. 13.4
  -6.7

15. 93.45
  -32.18

TABLE OF MEASURES

METRIC

Length

1 centimeter (cm) = 10 millimeters (mm)
1 meter (m) = 100 centimeters
1 kilometer (km) = 1,000 meters

Mass/Weight

1 kilogram (kg) = 1,000 grams (g)
1 metric ton (t) = 1,000 kilograms

Liquid

1 liter (L) = 1,000 milliliters (mL)

CUSTOMARY

Length

1 foot (ft) = 12 inches (in.)
1 yard (yd) = 3 feet
1 yard = 36 inches
1 mile (mi) = 5,280 feet
1 mile = 1,760 yards

Mass/Weight

1 pound (lb) = 16 ounces (oz)
1 ton = 2,000 pounds

Liquid

1 pint (pt) = 2 cups
1 quart (qt) = 2 pints
1 gallon (gal) = 4 quarts

TIME

1 minute (min) = 60 seconds (s)
1 hour (h) = 60 minutes
1 day = 24 hours
1 week = 7 days
12 months = 1 year
1 decade = 10 years
1 century = 100 years

GLOSSARY

This glossary contains an example, an illustration, or a brief description of important terms used in this book.

Addends   Numbers that are added.
Example   5 + 6 = 11
                    5 and 6 are addends.

Angle   This is ∠ A.

Area   The number of square units contained in a surface. The area of this figure is 10 square units.

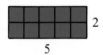

Average   The result of dividing the sum of several addends by the number of addends.
Example   The average of 2, 7, and 9 is 6.
                    2 + 7 + 9 = 18, and
                    18 ÷ 3 = 6

Bar graph   A graph that shows number information. It uses bars of different lengths.

BASIC   A computer language used by almost all school and home computers.

Circle   A simple closed curve with all points the same distance from the center.

Closed curve   A curve that ends where it starts.

Compass   A tool used to draw circles.

Cone   A figure in space of this shape.

Counting numbers   The numbers 1, 2, 3, and so on.

Cube   A figure in space of this shape. Each of its 6 faces is a square.

Cubic unit   The measure used for finding the volume or the number of cubes that will fit inside a figure.

Cylinder   A figure in space of this shape.

Debug   To fix the problems in a computer program so that it will do what you want it to do.

Decimal   A number such as 0.3 or 3.8.

Denominator In $\frac{2}{5}$, 5 is the denominator.

Diameter A line segment going through the center of a circle with both endpoints on the circle. $\overline{CD}$ is a diameter.

Difference The answer in subtraction.
Example $7 - 4 = 3$
3 is the difference.

Digit Any one of the ten basic numerals: 0, 1, 2, 3, 4, 5, 6, 7, 8, 9.

Dividend The number that is to be divided.
Example $35 \div 7$
35 is the dividend.

Divisor The number that is used to divide by.
Example $35 \div 7$
7 is the divisor.

Equal fractions Two or more names for the same fraction.
Example $\frac{2}{3} = \frac{6}{9}$

Equation A number sentence with an equals sign, = .
Example $7 + 5 = 12$

Estimate An answer that is found by using rounded numbers.
Example $32 + 59 = ?$
$30 + 60 = 90$
90 is an estimate of the sum.

Even number A whole number that has 2 as a factor. 8 is even because $2 \times 4 = 8$.

Expanded numeral A name for a number that shows the value of the digits.
Example $398 = 300 + 90 + 8$

Factors Numbers to be multiplied.
Example $3 \times 4 = 12$
3 and 4 are factors.

Flip This is an example of a flip. The figure does not change size or shape.

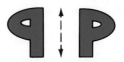

Flowchart A picture that shows the steps used to do something.

Fraction A number named by such numerals as $\frac{2}{3}, \frac{1}{2}, \frac{5}{1}$.

GOTO A computer command that tells a computer to go to the line number which follows.
Example   GOTO 40 makes a computer go to line 40.

Graph Information shown by use of pictures, dots, or bars.

Grouping property of addition The grouping of numbers added does not change the sum.
Example $(2 + 5) + 3 = 2 + (5 + 3)$

Grouping property of multiplication The grouping of numbers multiplied does not change the product.
Example $(3 \times 2) \times 4 = 3 \times (2 \times 4)$

Intersect For figures to cross or touch.

Line A straight path that goes forever in both directions. This line is called $\overleftrightarrow{CD}$ or $\overleftrightarrow{DC}$.

Line of symmetry A line of folding so that the two halves of a figure match.

Line segment A straight path with two endpoints. This line segment is called $\overline{GH}$ or $\overline{HG}$.

Mixed number A whole number and a fraction, such as $1\frac{1}{2}$ and $2\frac{3}{4}$.

Multiple The product of a number and any whole number.
Example Multiples of 3: 3, 6, 9, and so on, because $3 \times 1 = 3$; $3 \times 2 = 6$; $3 \times 3 = 9$.

Multiplication-addition property A factor may be distributed over two or more addends.
Example $3 \times (2 + 4) = (3 \times 2) + (3 \times 4)$

NEW A command that tells a computer to erase its memory.

Number sentence A number sentence tells about numbers.
Examples $4 + 3 = 7$ $7 - 4 = 3$

Numeral A name for a number.

Numerator In $\frac{3}{4}$, 3 is the numerator.

Odd number A whole number that is not even. 9 is an odd number.

Order property of addition The order of numbers added does not change the sum.
Example $4 + 3 = 3 + 4$

Order property of multiplication The order of numbers multiplied does not change the product.
Example $6 \times 2 = 2 \times 6$

Ordered pair A pair of numbers where order is important.

Parallel lines Lines are parallel if they will never intersect.

Parentheses These marks, ( ). They tell us to work inside them first.
Example $7 + (6 + 3) = 7 + 9$

Perimeter The distance around a geometric figure. The perimeter of this figure is 15 units $(3 + 4 + 1 + 7)$.

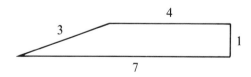

Periods in numerals   The groups of three digits in a numeral set off by commas.

Pictograph   A graph that uses pictures to show information.

Point   An exact location in space.

Polygon   A simple closed curve made of line segments.

PRINT   A command that tells a computer to print on a screen or paper.

Probability   The chance of something happening.

Product   The answer in multiplication.
Example $7 \times 3 = 21$
                21 is the product.

Quotient   The answer in division.
Example $21 \div 3 = 7$
                7 is the quotient.

Radius   Any line segment from the center of a circle to a point on the circle. $\overline{AB}$ is a radius.

Rectangle   A figure formed by four line segments. It has four right angles.

Rectangular prism   A figure in space of this shape. Each of its six faces is a rectangle.

Related sentences   Related sentences use the same numbers and the same or opposite operations.

Remainder   In the division $14 \div 3$, the quotient is 4 and the remainder is 2.

Right angle   An angle that looks like a square corner.

RUN   A command that tells a computer to carry out the commands in a program.

Simple closed curve   A curve that begins and ends at the same point. It does not intersect itself.

Slide   This is an example of a slide. The figure does not change size or shape.

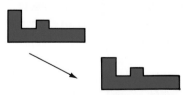

Sphere   A figure in space of this shape.

Square   A rectangle whose four sides have the same length.

Standard numeral   The usual or common name for a number. The standard numeral for fifteen is 15.

Sum   The answer in addition.
Example $4 + 7 = 11$
                      11 is the sum.

Symmetric   If the parts match when a figure is folded on a line, the figure is symmetric.

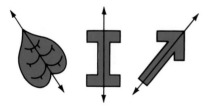

Triangle   A polygon with three sides.

Turn   This is an example of a turn. The figure does not change size or shape.

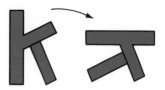

Volume   The measure of the inside of a space figure. The volume of this box is 10 cubic units.

Whole numbers   The numbers 0, 1, 2, 3, and so on.

LIST OF SYMBOLS

		Page
=	equals or is equal to	2
>	is greater than	40
<	is less than	40
60°	60 degrees	150
$\overline{AB}$	line segment from A to B	302
$\overleftrightarrow{AB}$	line through A and B	302
$\angle A$	angle A	304

399

◼ ANSWERS TO THE LEARNING STAGE ◼

ANSWERS TO THE
LEARNING STAGE

CHAPTER 1

PAGE 2
A. 2. 11 3. 5 and 6 4. 11
B. 6. 11
C. 7. 9;9 8. 10;10 9. 7;7

PAGE 4
A. 1. 9 2. 15 3. 11 4. 14 5. 16
B. 6. 11 7. 11 8. 11 9. 12 10. 12
C. 11. 17 12. 15 13. 12 14. 14
   15. 11

PAGE 8
A. 1. 6 2. 3 3. 3 4. 3
B. 5. 6 6. 8 7. 8 8. 3 9. 3
   10. 4 11. 9 12. 5 13. 9
   14. 8 15. 5 16. 8 17. 9
   18. 7 19. 9

PAGE 10
A. 1. 4 2. 8 3. 6 4. 1 5. 9
   6. 2
B. 7. yes 8. yes 9. yes
   10. yes 11. no 12. yes

PAGE 12
A. 1. How many more?
   2. subtract
B. 3. + 4. −

PAGE 15
A. 1. $9 + 6 = 15$ $6 + 9 = \underline{15}$
   $15 - 6 = \underline{9}$ $15 - \underline{9} = 6$
   2. $13 - 6 = 7$ $\underline{7} + 6 = \underline{13}$
   $\underline{13} - 7 = \underline{6}$ $6 + \underline{7} = \underline{13}$
   3. $7 + 8 = \underline{15}$ $8 + \underline{7} = \underline{15}$
   $15 - \underline{8} = 7$ $\underline{15} - \underline{7} = 8$
B. 4. The order may vary.
   $3 + 7 = 10$ $7 + 3 = 10$
   $10 - 7 = 3$ $10 - 3 = 7$
   5. $7 + 9 = 16$ $9 + 7 = 16$
   $16 - 9 = 7$ $16 - 7 = 9$
   6. $8 + 0 = 8$ $0 + 8 = 8$
   $8 - 8 = 0$ $8 - 0 = 8$
   7. $3 + 4 = 7$ $4 + 3 = 7$
   $7 - 4 = 3$ $7 - 3 = 4$

PAGE 16
A. 1. $16 - 9 = \square$;7 2. $17 - 8 = \square$;9
B. 3. 6 4. 6 5. 1 6. 7 7. 9 8. 8

PAGE 17
A. 1. PRINT 6 + 7; 13
   2. PRINT 9 + 5; 14
   3. PRINT 8 + 3; 11
   4. PRINT 4 + 7; 11
B. 5. PRINT 18 − 9; 9
   6. PRINT 16 − 7; 9
   7. PRINT 17 − 8; 9
   8. PRINT 15 − 6; 9
C. 9. PRINT 2304 + 4293; 6597
   10. PRINT 8385 − 5052; 3333
   11. PRINT 1312 + 2434 + 4121;
      7867
   12. PRINT 4938 − 1924; 3014

PAGE 18
A. 1. subtract 5 2. 8, 2, 3, 9
B. 3. increasing 4. 3
   5. 16, 19, 22, 25, 28, 31

CHAPTER 2

PAGE 26
A. 1. 48 2. 576 3. 721
   4. 8,970 5. 8,604
B. 6. 76 7. 90 8. 634 9. 512
   10. 5,654 11. 8,808
C. 12. thirty-three 13. eighty
   14. seven hundred sixty-seven
   15. four thousand, five hundred
   16. one thousand, two hundred one

PAGE 28
A. 1. 3 2. 7
B. 3. tens 4. hundreds 5. ones
   6. tens 7. ones 8. ones
   9. thousands 10. tens
   11. hundreds 12. thousands
C. 13. 200 14. 800 15. 7 16. 400
   17. 30 18. 9 19. 8,000
   20. 500 21. 40 22. 9

PAGES 30–31
A. 1. 800,000 2. 2,000
B. 3. 90,000 4. 7,000 5. 60
   6. 20,000 7. 700,000 8. 900
C. 9. 359,647 10. 54,870
D. 11. 47,276 12. 705,670
   13. 38,000 14. 706,007

PAGE 32
A. 1. 1 millions 2. 10 millions
3. 100 millions
B. 4. 76 million, 285 thousand, 101
5. 497 million, 286 thousand, 105
6. 8 million, 764 thousand, 491
C. 7. 29,348,768 8. 900,000,000
9. 9,009,009 10. 42,000,750

PAGE 35
1. The order may vary.
$5 + 4, 14 - 5, 10 - 1, 8 + 1,$
$16 - 7, 12 - 3, 2 + 7,$
$13 - 4, 9 + 0$
2. $6 + 2, 16 - 8, 4 + 4, 5 + 3,$
$12 - 4, 15 - 7, 11 - 3,$
$10 - 2$
3. $12 - 5, 15 - 8, 4 + 3, 6 + 1,$
$10 - 3, 11 - 4$
4. $9 - 3, 10 - 4, 2 + 4, 15 - 9$

PAGES 36–37
A. 1. 7 2. 27 3. 16 4. 166
B. 5. 9 6. 90
C. 7. 29 8. 47 9. 49 10. 394
D. 11. LXXV 12. XLIII
13. CCXXXIX 14. CCCXLIV

PAGES 38–39
A. 1. How many more meters is the Tyrannosaurus?
2. Tyrannosaurus is 15 meters, Stegosaurus is 6 meters.
3. subtract
4. $15 - 6 = \underline{\quad ? \quad}$
B. 5. $9 + 8 = \underline{\quad ? \quad}$
6. $75 - 48 = \underline{\quad ? \quad}$

PAGES 40–41
A. 1. > 2. < 3. = 4. >
5. <
B. 6. yes 7. yes 8. no
9. <, <
C. 10. < 11. > 12. > 13. <

PAGES 42–43
A. 1. 20 2. 40 3. 70 4. 10
5. 90
B. 6. 300 7. 500 8. 900
9. 300 10. 900

C. 11. $4.00 12. $5.00 13. $9.00
14. $4.00 15. $8.00

PAGE 44
A. 1. 7,000 2. 6,000 3. 4,000
4. 2,000 5. 9,000 6. 1,000
7. 3,000 8. 4,000 9. 6,000
10. 8,000

CHAPTER 3

PAGE 52
D. 4. 72 5. 85 6. 204 7. 9,001

PAGE 53
A. 1. 79 2. 38 3. 91 4. 26
5. 30

PAGE 54
A. 1. 16 2. 16 3. 16
B. 4. 15 5. 17 6. 20
C. 7. 12 8. 19 9. 23 10. 13
11. 21 12. 23

PAGE 56
A. 1. 24
2. 4 in the ones place and 2 over the tens place
3. 21 4. 214
B. 5. 58 6. 92 7. 154 8. 149
9. 190

PAGE 58
A. 1. 869 2. 1,197 3. 767
4. 503 5. 954
B. 6. 16 7. 21 8. 15 9. 1,516
C. 10. 879 11. 950 12. 996
13. 2,818 14. 1,059

PAGE 60
A. 1. 15,739 2. 8,976 3. 13,864
4. 12,328
B. 5. 11 6. 14 7. 6 8. 65,641
C. 9. 132,218 10. 45,742
11. 72,251 12. 92,332

PAGE 62
A. 1. 15 2. 24 3. 6 4. 19
B. 5. 16,687 6. 19,168
7. 23,331 8. 13,569

PAGE 65
A. 1. 7 2. 6 3. >
B. 4. = 5. < 6. > 7. =

PAGE 66

A. 1. How many in all?
2. 738 letters on Monday
85 letters on Tuesday
24 letters on Wednesday
3. add
4. 738 + 85 + 24 = ___?___
B. 5. 85 − 15 = ___?___
6. 362 + 138 = ___?___

PAGE 68

A. 1. 44¢; $0.44   2. 12¢; $0.12
3. 50¢; $0.50   4. 1¢; $0.01
5. $10; $10.00   6. $2; $2.00
7. $65; $65.00   8. $99; $99.00
B. 9. $5.81   10. $29.06
11. $70.70   12. $10.01
C. 13. eighty-two cents
14. fourteen cents
15. ninety cents
16. forty-four dollars
17. thirty-two dollars and ten
cents

PAGE 70

A. 1. $0.66   2. $13.67   3. $10.52
4. $13.05
B. 5. $1.83   6. $46.78   7. $47.41
8. $9.50

PAGE 72

A. 1. 70   2. 130   3. 120   4. 170
5. 190
B. 6. 700   7. 400   8. 300   9. 1,400
C. 10. $9.00   11. $6.00   12. $15.00
D. 13. 180   14. 1,000   15. $9.00
16. 2,000   17. $14.00

CHAPTER 4

PAGE 80

D. LET A = 14, LET B = 7
1. 14   2. 8   3. 7

PAGE 81

A. 1. 7;   7   2. 0;   0   3. 7;   7
$$\frac{+3}{10}\qquad\frac{+8}{8}\qquad\frac{+7}{14}$$

4. 7;   7   5. 5;   5   6. 8;   8
$$\frac{+6}{13}\qquad\frac{+0}{5}\qquad\frac{+8}{16}$$

PAGE 82

A. 1. 1   2. 5   3. 51
B. 4. 90   5. 27   6.
$$\begin{array}{r} 4\ \ 17\\ \cancel{5}\ \cancel{7}\\ -\ \ 8\\ \hline 4\ 9 \end{array}$$

7.
$$\begin{array}{r} 8\ \ 10\\ \cancel{9}\ \cancel{0}\\ -1\ 4\\ \hline 7\ 6 \end{array}$$
8.
$$\begin{array}{r} 3\ \ 12\\ \cancel{4}\ \cancel{2}\\ -2\ 6\\ \hline 1\ 6 \end{array}$$

C. 9. 22   10. 61   11. 19   12. 58
13. 19

PAGE 84

A. 1. 6   2. 4   3. 3   4. 346
B. 5. 317   6. 706

7.
$$\begin{array}{r} 11\\ 3\ \cancel{1}\ 16\\ \cancel{4}\ \cancel{2}\ \cancel{6}\\ -1\ 8\ 9\\ \hline 2\ 3\ 7 \end{array}$$
8.
$$\begin{array}{r} 6\ \ 16\\ 3\ 7\ \cancel{6}\\ -3\ 6\ 9\\ \hline 7 \end{array}$$

9.
$$\begin{array}{r} 11\\ 8\ \cancel{1}\ 14\\ \cancel{9}\ \cancel{2}\ \cancel{4}\\ -\ \ 7\ 9\\ \hline 8\ 4\ 5 \end{array}$$

C. 10. 593   11. 429   12. 317
13. 7   14. 67

PAGE 86

A. 1. 1,222   2. 5,385

3.
$$\begin{array}{r} 8\ \ 11\\ \cancel{9},\ \cancel{1}\ 9\ 8\\ -6,\ 6\ 8\ 4\\ \hline 2,\ 5\ 1\ 4 \end{array}$$

4.
$$\begin{array}{r} 11\ \ 13\\ 3\ \ \cancel{1}\ \cancel{3}\ 11\\ \cancel{4},\ \cancel{2}\ \cancel{4}\ \cancel{1}\\ -2,\ 3\ 8\ 5\\ \hline 1,\ 8\ 5\ 6 \end{array}$$

Continued on page 403

Page 86 (continued)
   B. **5.** 5 **6.** 1 **7.** 4

                  16
           2 6 12 8 11
   8.   3 7, 2 9 1
        − 1 9, 8 7 6
         1 7, 4 1 5

   C. **9.** 31,582 **10.** 60,287
      11. 40,869 **12.** 504

PAGE 88
   A. **1.** 18 **2.** 467

         9   9
        4 10 10   5 10 18
   3.   5 0 0 **4.**   6 0 8
      − 1 3 7   − 3 1 9
        3 6 3   2 8 9

         9
      7 10 17
   5.   8 0 7
      − 2 4 8
        5 5 9

   B. **6.** 602 **7.** 4,417 **8.** 1,092
      9. 4,937 **10.** 43,853
    11. 13,102 **12.** 20,757 **13.** 8,157

PAGE 91
   A. **1.** rectangle **2.** subtract again
   B.

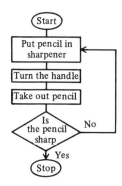

PAGE 92
   A. **1.** How many were not wearing hats?
      2. 126 − 78 = ___?___
      3. 48 students
      4. 78 + 48 = 126
   B. **5.** How many in all?

      6. 16 + 18 = ___?___
      7. 34 trees
      8. 34 − 18 = 16 or
          34 − 16 = 18

PAGE 95
   A. **1.** $1.65 **2.** $0.05 **3.** $16.36
                 16
          2 6 15 5 14
      4. $3 7 5 .6 4
        − 2 7 8 .4 7
         $9 7 .1 7
   B. **5.** $2.24 **6.** $18.46 **7.** $30.49
      8. $189.24

PAGE 96
   A. **1.** one-dollar bills
      2. five-dollar bill
   B. **3.** 2 pennies; 2 one-dollar bills

PAGE 98
   A. **1.** 50 **2.** 20 **3.** 50
      4. 20 **5.** 40
   B. **6.** 900 **7.** 400 **8.** 500
   C. **9.** $7.00 **10.** $3.00 **11.** $4.00
   D. **12.** $6.00 **13.** $100 **14.** $5.00
     15. $200 **16.** $5.00

CHAPTER 5
PAGES 106–107
   A. **1.** 7,6 **2.** 8,8 **3.** 7,8 **4.** 5,7
         42   64   56   35
   B. **5.** 2 × 9 = 18 **6.** 5 × 6 = 30
      7. 3 × 8 = 24 **8.** 4 × 2 = 8
   C. **9.** 2 + 2 + 2 = 6
     10. 3 + 3 + 3 + 3 = 12
     11. 5 + 5 = 10 **12.** 4 + 4 = 8
     13. 6 + 6 + 6 = 18
     14. 0 + 0 = 0

                            ...
   D. **15.**   5 .....   **16.**   3 ...
           × 3 .....   × 5 ...
           15 .....   15 ...
                            ...
    17.   4 ....   **18.**   9 ....
         × 6 ....   × 6 ....
        24 ....   54 ....
            ....
            ....
            ....

PAGE 108

A. **1.** yes **2.** 0

B. **3.** 0 **4.** 0 **5.** 0 **6.** 0

7. 0 **8.** 0

PAGE 109

A. **1.** yes

2. It is the other factor.

B. **3.** 5 **4.** 5 **5.** 6 **6.** 7

7. 8 **8.** 9

PAGE 110

A. **1.** 2, 4, 6, 8, 10,
12, 14, 16, 18

2. 2, 4, 6, 8, 10,
12, 14, 16, 18

3. increase by 2

B. **4.** 6; 6 **5.** 14; 14 **6.** 16; 16

PAGE 111

A. **1.** 22, 24, 26, 28, 30 **2.** even

B. **3.** 23, 25, 27, 29, 31 **4.** odd

C. **5.** E **6.** O **7.** O **8.** E **9.** O

PAGE 112

A. **1.** 3, 6, 9, 12, 15,
18, 21, 24, 27

2. 3, 6, 9, 12, 15,
18, 21, 24, 27

3. increase by 3

B. **4.** 4, 8, 12, 16, 20,
24, 28, 32, 36

5. 4, 8, 12, 16, 20,
24, 28, 32, 36

6. increase by 4

C. **7.** 12 **8.** 15 **9.** 24 **10.** 21

11. 32 **12.** 16

PAGE 114

A. **1.** 5, 10, 15, 20, 25,
30, 35, 40, 45

2. 5, 10, 15, 20, 25,
30, 35, 40, 45

3. increase by 5

B. **4.** 6, 12, 18, 24, 30,
36, 42, 48, 54

5. 6, 12, 18, 24, 30,
36, 42, 48, 54

6. increase by 6

C. **7.** 35 **8.** 42 **9.** 30 **10.** 40

11. 48 **12.** 54

PAGE 116

A. **1.** 7, 14, 21, 28, 35, 42, 49, 56, 63

B. **2.** 8, 16, 24, 32, 40, 48, 56, 64, 72

C. **3.** 56 **4.** 49 **5.** 72 **6.** 64

7. 63 **8.** 72

PAGE 117

A. **1.** 9, 18, 27, 36, 45,
54, 63, 72, 81

B. **2.** 18 **3.** 36 **4.** 54 **5.** 72

6. 81 **7.** 63

PAGE 120

A. **1.** 18, 18 **2.** 24, 24 **3.** 4 **4.** 1

PAGE 121

A. **1.** 18, 48 **2.** 24, 24, 48

3. $5 + 3, 4 + 4$ **4.** yes

B. **5.** 3 **6.** 6, 1 **7.** 7, 2

8. 4, 7, 3 **9.** 3, 5, 3, 2

10. 8, 9, 1

PAGE 122

A. **1.** 600 **2.** yes **3.** yes

B. **4.** no

PAGES 124–125

A. **1.** 8 **2.** 2 **3.** 4

B. **4.** 2 **5.** 3

C. **6.** 2 **7.** 3 **8.** 3

PAGE 126

A. **1.** 6 **2.** 7 **3.** 4 **4.** 6

B. **5.** 4 **6.** 7 **7.** 6 **8.** 5

9. 4 **10.** 1 **11.** 7 **12.** 0

13. 1 **14.** 1

PAGE 128

A. **1.** $1 \times 9 = 9$ $9 \times 1 = 9$
$9 \div 1 = 9$ $9 \div 9 = 1$

2. $2 \times 3 = 6$ $3 \times 2 = 6$
$6 \div 3 = 2$ $6 \div 2 = 3$

3. $3 \times 8 = 24$ $8 \times 3 = 24$
$24 \div 8 = 3$ $24 \div 3 = 8$

4. $2 \times 8 = 16$ $8 \times 2 = 16$
$16 \div 2 = 8$ $16 \div 8 = 2$

B. **5.** $\square \times 1 = 6$ **6.** $\square \times 3 = 15$

7. $\square \times 2 = 8$

C. **8.** 5 **9.** 7 **10.** 7 **11.** 6 **12.** 4

PAGE 130

A. **1.** 3 **2.** 3

Continued on page 405

Page 130 (continued)

B. **3.** 6 **4.** 5 **5.** 7 **6.** 0 **7.** 1
   8. 5
C. **9.** 2 **10.** 2 **11.** 4 **12.** 8
   13. 3 **14.** 0 **15.** 1 **16.** 3
   17. 9 **18.** 9

PAGE 132

A. **1.** 2 **2.** 4 **3.** 7 **4.** 6 **5.** 1
   6. 0
B. **7.** 6 **8.** 8 **9.** 2 **10.** 0
   11. 2 **12.** 5 **13.** 5 **14.** 9
   15. 8 **16.** 9

PAGE 134

A. **1.** 1, 2, 3, 4, 5
   2. 2, 4, 6, 8, 10
   3. 6, 12, 18, 24, 30
   4. 8, 16, 24, 32, 40
B. **5.** yes **6.** yes **7.** no **8.** no
C. **9.** 1, 2 **10.** 1, 2, 3, 6
   11. 1, 3, 9 **12.** 1, 2, 4, 8, 16
   13. 1, 17

CHAPTER 6

PAGE 142

A. **1.** 4 cm **2.** 4 cm
B. **3.** 5 cm **4.** 2 cm **5.** 12 cm

PAGE 144

A. **1.** 12 m
B. **2.** 6 km
C. **3.** cm **4.** m **5.** m **6.** km

PAGE 146

A. **1.** 300 **2.** 2 **3.** 400 **4.** 6
B. **5.** 2,000 **6.** 3 **7.** 5,000 **8.** 8

PAGE 147

A. **1.** 3,000 **2.** 2 **3.** 6,000 **4.** 9
B. **5.** mL **6.** L

PAGE 148

A. **1.** 3,000 **2.** 2 **3.** 4,000 **4.** 3
B. **5.** 3,000 **6.** 2 **7.** 4,000 **8.** 6
C. **9.** t **10.** g **11.** kg

PAGES 150–151

A. **1.** 100 °C **2.** 0 °C **3.** 100 °C
B. **4.** 33 °C **5.** 48 °C
   6. 16 °C below zero **7.** 55 °C
C. **8.** 30 °C **9.** 37 °C **10.** 26 °C

PAGE 156

A. **1.** How many teams?
   2. 36 hockey players, 6
      players on each team
   3. divide **4.** $36 \div 6 = \underline{?}$
B. **5.** $12 \times 8 = \underline{?}$ **6.** $72 \div 9 = \underline{?}$

PAGES 158–159

A. **1.** 3:25; 25 minutes after 3
   2. 7:40; 20 minutes to 8
   3. 11:19; 19 minutes after 11
B. **4.** 7:26; 26 minutes after 7
   5. 12:45; quarter to 1;
      15 minutes to 1
   6. 10:30; half past 10;
      30 minutes after 10

PAGES 160–161

A. **1.** am **2.** pm **3.** pm
B. **4.** 10 hours 52 minutes
   5. 4 hours 40 minutes
C. **6.** 6 hours 35 minutes
   7. 6 hours 37 minutes
D. **8.** 2:30 **9.** 2:55 **10.** 4:30
   11. 6:42 **12.** 2:10 **13.** 1:05

PAGE 162

   1. 10/21/76 **2.** June 16, 1977
   3. 1/20/84 **4.** January 13, 1985
   5. 3/10/86 **6.** March 25, 1986
   7. 6 days

PAGE 164

A. **1.** $1\frac{1}{2}$ in.
B. **2.** $1\frac{3}{4}$ in. **3.** $1\frac{1}{4}$ in.
C. **4.** $1\frac{3}{8}$ in.

PAGE 166

A. **1.** 36 in. **2.** 6 ft **3.** 108 in.
   4. 10,560 ft
B. **5.** in. **6.** yd or ft **7.** yd

PAGE 167

A. **1.** 4 **2.** 6 **3.** 12
B. **4.** cup **5.** gal

PAGE 168

A. **1.** 32 **2.** 6,000
B. **3.** oz **4.** lb

PAGE 169

A. **1.** 32 °F **2.** 212 °F
B. **3.** 78 °F **4.** 15 °F
   5. 5 °F below zero **6.** 34 °F **7.** 37 °F

CHAPTER 7

PAGE 177
  A. **1.** 2 **2.** 24 **3.** 2,400
  B. **4.** 120 **5.** 300 **6.** 6,000
     7. 1,600

PAGE 178
  A. **1.** 56
     2. 6 in the ones place and 5
        over the tens place
     3. 28; 33 **4.** 336
  B. **5.** 84 **6.** 729 **7.** 344
     8. 539 **9.** 520

PAGE 180
  A. **1.** 56
     2. 6 in the ones place and 5
    over the tens place
     3. 32; 37 **4.** 5,176
  B. **5.** 928 **6.** 638 **7.** 1,416
     8. 2,992
  C. **9.** 1,233 **10.** 2,472 **11.** 5,467
     12. 4,832

PAGE 182
  A. **1.** 12 **2.** 8; 9 **3.** 4 **4.** 36,492
  B. **5.** 8,246 **6.** 28,492 **7.** 26,564
     8. 56,244
  C. **9.** 3,690 **10.** 12,854
     11. 53,406 **12.** 38,742

PAGE 184
  A. **1.** $0.35 **2.** $15.95 **3.** $74.55
     4. $777.60
  B. **5.** $3.90 **6.** $21.84 **7.** $34.52
     8. $790.20
  C. **9.** $1.84 **10.** $47.40
     11. $27.63 **12.** $390.00

PAGE 188
  A. **1.** subtraction
     2. $1,450 - 344 = \underline{\ \ ?\ \ }$
  B. **3.** $15,000 \div 3 = \underline{\ \ ?\ \ }$

PAGE 190
  A. **1.** 540 **2.** $2.80
  B. **3.** 420 **4.** $3.00 **5.** $3.50
     6. 270
  C. **7.** 1,600 **8.** $40.00
  D. **9.** 3,600 **10.** $40.00
     11. 2,400 **12.** $36.00

     13. $54.00 **14.** 2,100
     15. $25.00 **16.** 2,100

PAGE 192
  A. **1.** 60 **2.** 600 **3.** 40 **4.** 400
     5. 4,000
  B. **6.** 3 **7.** 24,000
  C. **8.** 350 **9.** 3,500 **10.** 270
     11. 2,700 **12.** 27,000
     13. 20,000 **14.** 2,100
     15. 4,000 **16.** 1,400 **17.** 25,000

PAGE 194
  A. **1.** in the ones place
     2. 1,076 **3.** 10,760
  B. **4.** 2,340 **5.** $499.20
     6. 3,200 **7.** $785.70
     8. 22,960
  C. **9.** 5,220 **10.** 2,820
     11. 17,440 **12.** $379.20
     13. $332.00 **14.** $47.40
     15. 21,840 **16.** $269.40
     17. 1,950 **18.** $55.80

PAGE 196
  A. **1.** 141 **2.** 2,820 **3.** 2,961
  B. **4.** 1,702 **5.**

$$\begin{array}{r} 96 \\ \times\ 34 \\ \hline 384 \\ 2880 \\ \hline 3,264 \end{array}$$

    6.
$$\begin{array}{r} 87 \\ \times\ 56 \\ \hline 522 \\ 4350 \\ \hline 4,872 \end{array}$$
  7.
$$\begin{array}{r} \$0.35 \\ \times\ 79 \\ \hline 315 \\ 2450 \\ \hline \$27.65 \end{array}$$

    8.
$$\begin{array}{r} \$0.46 \\ \times\ 33 \\ \hline 138 \\ 1380 \\ \hline \$15.18 \end{array}$$

  C. **9.** 252 **10.** 1,875 **11.** 1,026
     12. $2.88 **13.** $19.36

PAGE 198
  A. **1.** 615 **2.** 4,920 **3.** 5,535

Continued on page 407

Page 198 (continued)

B. **4.** 23,136 **5.**
$$\begin{array}{r} 478 \\ \times\ 21 \\ \hline 478 \\ 9560 \\ \hline 10,038 \end{array}$$

6.
$$\begin{array}{r} 735 \\ \times\ 15 \\ \hline 3675 \\ 7350 \\ \hline 11,025 \end{array}$$
7.
$$\begin{array}{r} \$4.82 \\ \times\ 37 \\ \hline 3374 \\ 14460 \\ \hline \$178.34 \end{array}$$

C. **8.** 13,536 **9.** 15,204
  10. 39,555 **11.** \$466.32

CHAPTER 8
PAGE 206

1. Light up a horizontal row of blocks from column 0 to column 39 in row 25.
2. Light up a vertical column of blocks from row 0 to row 39 in column 25.
3. 35 HLIN 4, 6 AT 3

PAGE 207

A. **1.** 8 **2.** 2 **3.** 4,000
B. **4.** 300 **5.** 60 **6.** 600 **7.** 500

PAGE 208

A. **1.** 2r2;
$$\begin{array}{r} 2 \\ \times\ 3 \\ \hline 6 \\ +2 \\ \hline 8 \end{array}$$
2. 2r3;
$$\begin{array}{r} 2 \\ \times\ 8 \\ \hline 16 \\ +3 \\ \hline 19 \end{array}$$

3. 2r5;
$$\begin{array}{r} 2 \\ \times\ 6 \\ \hline 12 \\ +5 \\ \hline 17 \end{array}$$
4. 6r3;
$$\begin{array}{r} 6 \\ \times\ 4 \\ \hline 24 \\ +3 \\ \hline 27 \end{array}$$

5. 5r4;
$$\begin{array}{r} 5 \\ \times\ 8 \\ \hline 40 \\ +4 \\ \hline 44 \end{array}$$

B. **6.** 7r1 **7.** 5r6 **8.** 8 **9.** 8r3

PAGE 210

A. **1.**
$$\begin{array}{r} 22 \\ 3\overline{)66} \\ \underline{6} \\ 6 \\ \underline{6} \\ 0 \end{array}$$
2.
$$\begin{array}{r} 14r1 \\ 4\overline{)57} \\ \underline{4} \\ 17 \\ \underline{16} \\ 1 \end{array}$$

3.
$$\begin{array}{r} 24r1 \\ 2\overline{)49} \\ \underline{4} \\ 9 \\ \underline{8} \\ 1 \end{array}$$
4.
$$\begin{array}{r} 11r4 \\ 5\overline{)59} \\ \underline{5} \\ 9 \\ \underline{5} \\ 4 \end{array}$$

5.
$$\begin{array}{r} 14 \\ 6\overline{)84} \\ \underline{6} \\ 24 \\ \underline{24} \\ 0 \end{array}$$

B. **6.** 12 **7.** 12r2 **8.** 11r2
  9. 22r2 **10.** 48r1

PAGE 212

A. **1.** 0; 8 **2.** 24 **3.**
$$\begin{array}{r} 89r2 \\ 3\overline{)269} \\ \underline{24} \\ 29 \\ \underline{27} \\ 2 \end{array}$$

4. 89 × 3 = 267;
   267 + 2 = 269
B. **5.** 42 **6.** 84 **7.** 31r3
  8. 44r2

PAGE 214

A. **1.**
$$\begin{array}{r} 132 \\ 3\overline{)396} \\ \underline{3} \\ 9 \\ \underline{9} \\ 6 \\ \underline{6} \\ 0 \end{array}$$
2.
$$\begin{array}{r} 184 \\ 4\overline{)736} \\ \underline{4} \\ 33 \\ \underline{32} \\ 16 \\ \underline{16} \\ 0 \end{array}$$

Continued on page 408

Page 214 (continued)

```
        153r3              117r2
3. 6 ) 921       4. 5 ) 587
        6                  5
        32                 8
        30                 5
        21                 37
        18                 35
         3                  2
```

B. **5.** 114 **6.** 211r2 **7.** 119r3
8. 131r1

PAGE 216

```
         388r1               923r1
A. 1. 3 ) 1,165    2. 2 ) 1,847
         9                   1 8
         26                  4
         24                  4
         25                  7
         24                  6
          1                  1
```

```
         612r3               877r2
3. 6 ) 3,675       4. 5 ) 4,387
        3 6                 4 0
         7                  38
         6                  35
         15                 37
         12                 35
          3                  2
```

B. **5.** 921r3 **6.** 711r2 **7.** 738
8. 534r4

PAGE 218

A. **1.** 1 **2.** 1 **3.** none; 0

```
        102r5
4. 7 ) 719
        7
        1
        0
        19
        14
         5
```

```
       10r3              70r6
B. 5. 7 ) 73     6. 7 ) 496
        7                49
        3                6
        0                0
        3                6
```

```
      100r7               303r3
7. 8 ) 807       8. 7 ) 2,124
       8                 2 1
       0                 2
       0                 0
       7                 24
       0                 21
       7                  3
```

PAGE 222

A. **1.** 35 **2.** 15 **3.** 100 **4.** 4
5. 25
B. **6.** 8 **7.** 40 **8.** 262

PAGE 224

A. **1.** $3.94 **2.** $6.69 **3.** $6.69

PAGE 226

A. **1.** 5 **2.** 150 **3.** 5 **4.** 10
B. **5.** 2 **6.** 3 **7.** 5 **8.** 7
9. 3r10 **10.** 2r10 **11.** 7r10
12. 1r10 **13.** 9 **14.** 6
15. 6r30 **16.** 5r50

PAGE 228

```
        17r6                24r27
A. 1. 10 ) 176    2. 40 ) 987
        10                 80
        76                 187
        70                 160
         6                 27
```

```
        15r24               11r9
3. 60 ) 924       4. 90 ) 999
       60                  90
       324                 99
       300                 90
        24                  9
```

B. **5.** 34 **6.** 24r27 **7.** 15r24
8. 13r4

PAGE 230

A. **1.** $\begin{array}{r} \$0.10 \\ 8\,\overline{)\,\$0.80} \\ 8 \\ \hline 0 \end{array}$ **2.** $\begin{array}{r} \$0.13 \\ 6\,\overline{)\,\$0.78} \\ 6 \\ \hline 18 \\ 18 \\ \hline 0 \end{array}$

3. $\begin{array}{r} \$1.16 \\ 2\,\overline{)\,\$2.32} \\ 2 \\ \hline 3 \\ 2 \\ \hline 12 \\ 12 \\ \hline 0 \end{array}$ **4.** $2.44

B. **5.** $0.12 **6.** $0.75 **7.** $0.32 **8.** $0.70

PAGE 232

A. **1.** 60 **2.** 60 **3.** 420

B. **4.** 180 **5.** 96 **6.** 42 **7.** 156 **8.** 730 **9.** 300

C. **10.** 1 **11.** 60 **12.** 8

D. **13.** 2 **14.** 5

PAGE 234

A. **1.** 5 **2.** 375

3. $\begin{array}{r} 5r4 \\ 75\,\overline{)\,379} \\ 375 \\ \hline 4 \end{array}$ **4.** $\begin{array}{r} 2r9 \\ 43\,\overline{)\,95} \\ 86 \\ \hline 9 \end{array}$

5. $\begin{array}{r} 4 \\ 24\,\overline{)\,96} \\ 96 \\ \hline 0 \end{array}$ **6.** $\begin{array}{r} 6r1 \\ 73\,\overline{)\,439} \\ 438 \\ \hline 1 \end{array}$

7. $\begin{array}{r} 4r8 \\ 82\,\overline{)\,336} \\ 328 \\ \hline 8 \end{array}$

C. **8.** 3r1 **9.** 7r10 **10.** 4r9 **11.** 8r4

CHAPTER 9

PAGE 242

A. **1.** two halves **2.** one third **3.** four sixths **4.** two fourths **5.** three fifths

B. **6.** 2 **7.** 1 **8.** 5 **9.** 1 **10.** 3

C. 3; 4; 4; 2; 6

D. **11.** $\frac{7}{8}$ **12.** $\frac{5}{6}$ **13.** $\frac{3}{4}$

E. **14.** $\frac{1}{3}$ **15.** $\frac{4}{4}$ **16.** $\frac{3}{5}$

PAGE 244

A. **1.** no **2.** no **3.** yes

C. **8.** yes **9.** no **10.** no

PAGE 246

A. **1.** $\frac{2}{6}$ and $\frac{1}{3}$ **2.** $\frac{4}{6}$ and $\frac{2}{3}$

3. $\frac{3}{4}$ and $\frac{6}{8}$

B. **4.** $\frac{4}{8}, \frac{1}{2}$ **5.** $\frac{1}{2}, \frac{3}{6}$

6. $\frac{4}{10}, \frac{2}{5}$

PAGE 248

A. **1.** Each is one more than the one before.

2. Each is three more than the one before.

3. $\frac{5}{15}, \frac{6}{18}, \frac{7}{21}$

B. **4.** $\frac{5}{20}, \frac{6}{24}, \frac{7}{28}$

5. $\frac{10}{15}, \frac{12}{18}, \frac{14}{21}$

C. **6.** 4, 6, $\frac{9}{12}, \frac{12}{16}$

7. $\frac{3}{4}, \frac{6}{8}, \frac{9}{12}, \frac{12}{16}$

D. **8.** $\frac{1}{5}, \frac{2}{10}, \frac{3}{15}, \frac{4}{20}$

9. $\frac{2}{5}, \frac{4}{10}, \frac{6}{15}, \frac{8}{20}$

10. $\frac{1}{6}, \frac{2}{12}, \frac{3}{18}, \frac{4}{24}$

11. $\frac{2}{3}, \frac{4}{6}, \frac{6}{9}, \frac{8}{12}$

12. $\frac{2}{4}, \frac{4}{8}, \frac{6}{12}, \frac{8}{16}$

PAGE 250

A **1.** $\frac{2}{3}, \frac{4}{6}, \frac{6}{9}, \frac{8}{12}, \ldots$

2. $\frac{8}{12}$

3. 8

B. **4.** 3 **5.** 9 **6.** 4 **7.** 6

Continued on page 410

Page 250 (continued)

C. 8. $\frac{1}{2}$, $\frac{2}{4}$, $\frac{3}{6}$, $\frac{4}{8}$, $\frac{5}{10}$, $\frac{6}{12}$

9. $\frac{6}{12}$ 10. 12

D. 11. 4   12. 9   13. 6   14. 12

PAGE 253
A. 1. 16, 18   2. no   3. no
B. 4. yes   5. no   6. no   7. yes

PAGE 254
A. 1. 12, 48   2. 20   3. 20
B. 4. 1,750g   5. 3:00 pm

PAGE 256
A. 1. 2   2. 2
B. 3. 2   4. 4   5. 5

PAGE 257
A. 1. $\frac{4}{3}$

2. 3 to 4 or $\frac{3}{4}$

B. 3. 4 to 5 or $\frac{4}{5}$

4. 5 to 4 or $\frac{5}{4}$

PAGE 259
A. 1. yes   2. >   3. >
B. 4. >   5. >   6. <   7. >
PAGE 260
A. 1. no

2. $\frac{1}{2}$, $\frac{2}{4}$, $\frac{3}{6}$, $\frac{4}{8}$
$\frac{3}{4}$, $\frac{6}{8}$, $\frac{9}{12}$, $\frac{12}{16}$

3. $\frac{4}{8}$, $\frac{6}{8}$; $\frac{2}{4}$, $\frac{3}{4}$ 4. $\frac{1}{2} < \frac{3}{4}$

B. 5. >   6. <   7. =   8. >
PAGE 262
A. 1. <   2. =   3. >
PAGE 263
A. 1. $3\overline{)2}$ 2. $8\overline{)5}$ 3. $1\overline{)7}$
4. $6\overline{)6}$

B. 5. $\frac{4}{5}$ 6. $\frac{5}{4}$ 7. $\frac{8}{1}$ 8. $\frac{1}{8}$

410

PAGES 264–265
A. 1. 5   2. $\frac{5}{3}$ 3. 1   4. $\frac{2}{3}$

5. $1\frac{2}{3}$

B. 6. $\frac{3}{2}$ 7. $\frac{10}{8}$

C. $1\frac{1}{2}$; $1\frac{2}{8}$

D. 8. $1\frac{1}{2}$ 9. 1   10. $1\frac{2}{7}$

11. $1\frac{1}{3}$ 12. $1\frac{1}{5}$

CHAPTER 10
PAGE 272
A. 1. yes   2. $\frac{2}{3}$ 3. $\frac{2}{3}$
B. 4. $\frac{2}{4}$ 5. $\frac{5}{7}$ 6. $\frac{7}{9}$ 7. $\frac{4}{10}$
PAGE 274
A. 1. $\frac{8}{8}$; 1   2. $\frac{6}{6}$; 1   3. $\frac{10}{10}$; 1

4. $\frac{4}{4}$; 1

B. 5. $\frac{13}{9}$; $1\frac{4}{9}$ 6. $\frac{4}{3}$; $1\frac{1}{3}$

7. $\frac{11}{10}$; $1\frac{1}{10}$ 8. $\frac{12}{8}$; $1\frac{4}{8}$

PAGE 276
A. 1. no

2. $\frac{1}{3}$, $\frac{2}{6}$, $\frac{3}{9}$, $\frac{4}{12}$, $\cdots$
$\frac{1}{4}$, $\frac{2}{8}$, $\frac{3}{12}$, $\frac{4}{16}$, $\cdots$

3. 4, 3   4. $\frac{7}{12}$

B. 5. $\frac{3}{4}$ 6. $\frac{3}{6}$ 7. $\frac{9}{10}$ 8. $\frac{7}{8}$
PAGE 278

A. 1. $\frac{7}{8}$ 2. 9   3. $9\frac{7}{8}$

B. 4. $6\frac{2}{3}$ 5. $11\frac{4}{5}$

6. $123\frac{5}{7}$ 7. $62\frac{1}{10}$
PAGE 282
A. 1. The fence is 5,532 kilometers. It is 6 times longer than the distance from Los Angeles to the Grand Canyon.

Continued on page 411

Page 282 (continued)

      2. The fence is 2 meters high.

      3. $5,532 \div 6 = 922$ kilometers

B. **4.** 98 years; Her book was published in 1971.

      5. 237 feet; The largest jellyfish was found in Massachusetts in 1865.

PAGE 284

A. **1.** yes **2.** $\frac{1}{3}$ **3.** $\frac{1}{3}$

B. **4.** $\frac{2}{4}$ **5.** $\frac{5}{9}$ **6.** $\frac{6}{8}$ **7.** $\frac{8}{10}$

PAGE 286

A. **1.** no

      2. $\frac{1}{3}, \frac{2}{6}, \frac{3}{9}, \frac{4}{12}$

          $\frac{1}{4}, \frac{2}{8}, \frac{3}{12}, \frac{4}{16}$

      3. 4, 3 **4.** $\frac{1}{12}$

B. **5.** $\frac{1}{4}$ **6.** $\frac{3}{6}$ **7.** $\frac{1}{6}$ **8.** $\frac{1}{8}$

PAGE 288

A. **1.** $\frac{4}{8}$ **2.** 3 **3.** $3\frac{4}{8}$

B. **4.** $3\frac{1}{5}$ **5.** 3 **6.** $\frac{2}{7}$

      7. $12\frac{2}{3}$

PAGE 290

A. **1.** one tenth

      2. nine tenths

      3. one and eight tenths

      4. nine and seven tenths

      5. thirty-six and four tenths

B. **6.** 0.7 **7.** 0.2 **8.** 3.6 **9.** 8.1

     10. 21.4

C. **11.** $\frac{2}{10}$ **12.** $\frac{4}{10}$ **13.** $3\frac{5}{10}$

     14. $7\frac{7}{10}$ **15.** $46\frac{9}{10}$

PAGE 292–293

A. **1.** 0.06 **2.** 0.56 **3.** 1.75

B. **4.** seven hundredths

      5. eighty hundredths

      6. twenty-nine hundredths

      7. four and five hundredths

      8. twenty-six and seventy-eight hundredths

C. **9.** $\frac{5}{100}$ **10.** $\frac{10}{100}$

   11. $\frac{44}{100}$ **12.** $7\frac{15}{100}$

   13. $46\frac{7}{100}$

D. **14.** 3.04 **15.** 17.99 **16.** 0.08

   17. 0.64 **18.** 7.09 **19.** 58.92

PAGE 294

A. **1.** 0.9 **2.** 5.6 **3.** 12.5

     4. 44.5 **5.** 165.4

B. **6.** 0.23 **7.** 22.46 **8.** 42.08

     9. 62.13 **10.** 391.41

PAGE 295

A. **1.** 0.5 **2.** 6.8 **3.** 8.6

     4. 0.3 **5.** 87.9

B. **6.** 0.67 **7.** 0.75 **8.** 15.14

     9. 14.83 **10.** 202.61

CHAPTER 11

PAGE 303

A. **1.** $\overleftrightarrow{EF}$ or $\overleftrightarrow{FE}$ **2.** $\overline{LM}$ or $\overline{ML}$

      3. $\overrightarrow{ST}$ or $\overrightarrow{TS}$

B. **4.** intersecting **5.** parallel

      6. intersecting **7.** parallel

      8. intersecting **9.** parallel

PAGE 304

A. **1.** yes **2.** no **3.** yes

B. **4.**

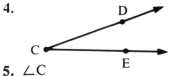

      5. ∠C

C. **6.** larger **7.** smaller **8.** right

PAGE 306

A. **1.** no **2.** no **3.** no **4.** yes

B. **5.** $\overline{AC}$, $\overline{AD}$ **6.** point A

      7. The lengths are the same.

C. **8.** $\overline{NP}$

      9. Their measures are the same.

PAGES 308–309

A. **1.** yes **2.** yes

B. **3.** yes **4.** no

C. **5.** no **6.** yes **7.** no **8.** yes

D. **9.** yes **10.** no **11.** no **12.** yes

PAGE 310

A. **1.** yes **2.** no **3.** yes **4.** no
B. **5.** yes **6.** no **7.** no **8.** yes
C. **9.** yes **10.** yes **11.** no
    12. yes

PAGE 314

7.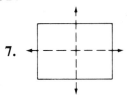

8.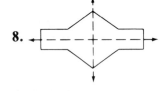

9.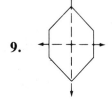

PAGE 316

A. **1.** 8 **2.** 8 cm
B. **3.** 54 m **4.** 29 cm **5.** 22 m
    6. 18 in. **7.** 16 ft **8.** 16 cm

PAGE 318

A. **1.** 12 cm² **2.** 12 cm²
    3. 12 cm²
B. **4.** 4 cm² **5.** 3 cm²
    6. 4 cm²

PAGE 320

A. **1.** 6 **2.** 6 m²
B. **3.** 16 **4.** 16 km²
C. **5.** 12 cm² **6.** 27 cm²
    7. 36 cm²

PAGE 322

A. **1.** 7.9 km **2.** 500m²

PAGE 324

A. **1.** cube **2.** rectangular prism
    3. cube **4.** rectangular prism
B. **5.** cone **6.** cylinder
    7. sphere **8.** cone

PAGE 326

A. **1.** 8 cubic units
    2. 8 cubic units
B. **3.** 16 cubic units
    4. 24 cubic units
    5. 27 cubic units

CHAPTER 12

PAGE 334

A. **1.** third grade **2.** 2
    3. 7 symbols
B. **4.** 2 **5.** fourth **6.** 9

PAGE 336

A. **1.** Sports **2.** Science
    3. 55 **4.** 15 **5.** 5

PAGE 338

A. **1.** $\frac{1}{8}$ **2.** $\frac{1}{4}$ **3.** $\frac{1}{4}$
B. **4.** $\frac{1}{2}$ **5.** $\frac{1}{4}$ **6.** darts

PAGE 342

A. **1.** 260 **2.** not known
    3. How many more calories is
    the yogurt?
    4. no; not enough information
B. **5.** not enough information
    6. not enough information

PAGE 344

A. **1.** hospital **2.** grocery store
    3. baseball field
    4. bus station **5.** school
B. **6.** (3, 1) **7.** (2, 2) **8.** (4, 4)
    9. (4, 5) **10.** (3, 4)

PAGES 346–347

A. **1.** red, blue, purple **2.** 1; 3
    3. 1 out of 3 **4.** 1 out of 3
B. **5.** heads and tails
    6. 1 out of 2 **7.** 1 out of 2
C. **8.** 1
    9. 4; red, green, yellow, blue
    10. 1 out of 4

PAGE 348

A. **1.** 3 **2.** 8 **3.** 3; 8
B. **4.** 5 **5.** 6 **6.** 5 out of 6

412

INDEX

A

Activity
  with areas, 318–319
  division and zero, 135
  making a bar graph, 337
  making a pictograph, 335
  names for numbers, 35
Addends, 2
  rounding, 72–73
Addition
  basic facts, *see* Addition
    facts
  checking subtraction by, 81
  column, 54–59, 62–63
  of decimals, 294
  estimating sums, 72–73
  if 4-digit and 5-digit
    numbers, 60–63
  of fractions, 272–277
  grouping property of, 54
  of mixed numbers, 278–279
  with money notation, 70
  multiplication-addition
    property, 121
  of 9's, 4
  of 1-digit and 2-digit
    numbers, 53
  order property of, 2
  Skills Review, 14, 29, 45,
    94, 187, 231, 319, 341
  of 3-digit numbers, 58–59
  with time notation, 160–161
  of 2-digit numbers, 56–57
  zeros in, 2
Addition facts, 2–5
Addition sentences
  related to subtraction
    sentences, 15–17
  for multiplication, 106–107
am time, 160–161
Angle(s), 304–305
  of triangles, rectangles,
    and squares, 310
Area:
  activity with, 318–319
  finding by multiplication,
    320–321

  measurement of, 318–321
  units used to measure,
    318, 326
Arrays
  products found by
    drawing, 107
  quotients found by
    drawing, 124
Averages, finding, 222–223

B

Bar graphs, 336–337
Better buy, finding the, 328
Bright Ideas, 4–5

C

Calculator, computer as, 17
Calculator Activity, 6, 64,
    133, 186, 280, 317, 347
Calendar, 162
Career
  air controllers, 20
  announcers, 266
  barbers, 200
  lunchroom managers, 136
  pharmacists, 74
Celsius (°C) temperature
    scale, 150–151
Centimeter (cm), 142–146
  square, 318–321, 326
Century, 233
Chapter Review, 21, 47, 75,
    101, 137, 171, 201, 237,
    267, 297, 329, 351
Chapter Test, 22, 48, 76, 102,
    138, 172, 202, 238, 268,
    298, 330, 352
Charts, 46, *see also* Graphs
  solving problems using,
    350
Circle, 306–307
Circle graphs, 338–339
Clock, *see* **Time**
Closed curve, 308–309
Column addition, 54–59,
    62–63

Comparing
  fractions, 259–262
  sums and differences, 65
  whole numbers, 40–41
Computation skills
  with decimals: addition
    and subtraction, 294–295
  with fractions: addition,
    272–277; subtraction,
    284–287
  with mixed numbers:
    addition, 278–279,
    subtraction, 288–289
  with whole numbers:
    addition, 53–63, 70, 72–
    73; addition facts, 2–5;
    division, 207–219, 226–
    230, 234–235; division
    facts, 124–133;
    multiplication, 177–185,
    190–199; multiplication
    facts, 106–117;
    subtraction, 81–89, 95–
    99; subtraction facts, 8–11
Computer
  BASIC language, 154
  as a calculator, 17
  commands, 80, 354–357,
    360–362, 364–365
  debugging, 358–359
  decimals from fractions on
    the, 291
  division on the, 127, 235
  early, 52
  entering a program on the,
    357
  error messages, 354
  finding averages on the,
    223
  flow chart, 313, 362, 364
  fractions to decimals on
    the, 291
  GOTO command, 362–363
  graphics, 206
  Hands On, 17, 80, 118,
    127, 155, 206, 223, 235,
    291
  HOME command, 356

413

how it works, 7
IF/THEN command, 154–155, 364–365
input, 7
INPUT command, 80, 354, 360–361
keyboard, 354–355
language, 154
LET command, 80
LIST command, 154
math, 118, 127, 235, 355
multiplication on the, 118
NEW command, 357
output, 7, 354
Pascaline, 52
PRINT command, 17, 354–356, 360–361
program, 154–155, 357
robot, 176
RUN command, 154
storing information in the, 80
Cone, 324–325
Consumer Skills
computing with money, 70, 95, 184–185, 230
finding the better buy, 328
making change, 96–97
saving energy, 236
Cube, 324–325
Cubes of whole numbers, 186
Cubic unit, 326–327
Cup, 167
Curves, 308
Customary system, 164–169
cup, 167
Fahrenheit (°F) scale, 169
foot (ft), 166
gallon (gal), 167
inch (in.), 164–166
mile (mi), 166
ounce (oz), 168
pint (pt), 167
pound (lb), 168
problem-solving with, 350
quart (qt), 167
ton, 168
yard (yd), 166
Cylinder, 324–325

D

Dates, 162
Days, 232–233

Decade, 233
Decimal point, 294–295
Decimals, 290, 292
addition of, 294
and fractions on the computer, 291
subtraction of, 295
writing fractions or mixed numbers from, 290, 292–293
Degree (°), 150–151, 169
Denominator, 242–243
Diameter, 306–307
Differences, 8, 82, 84, 86, 258
estimating, 98–100
Digit, 28
Dividend, 124
4-digit, 216–217
3-digit, 212–213, 214–215, 228–229
2-digit, 210–211
zeros in, 207, 226–229
Division
basic facts, *see* Division facts
checking by multiplication, 126, 208
on the computer, 127, 235
finding averages by using, 222–223
fractions as, 263
with money notation, 230
by multiples of 10: with 1-digit quotients, 226–227; with 2-digit quotients, 228–229
with remainders, 208–219 226–229
Skills Review, 163, 258, 307, 341
with 3-digit quotients (1-digit divisor): with 3-digit dividends, 214–215; with 4-digit dividends, 216–217
with 2-digit divisors, 234–235
with 2-digit quotients (1-digit divisor): with 2-digit dividends, 210–211; with 3-digit dividends, 212–213
with zeros in dividend, 207, 226–229

with zeros in quotient, 207, 218–219, 226–227
Division facts, 124–133
for 1, 2, and 3, 126–127
for 4, 5, and 6, 130–131
for 7, 8, and 9, 132–133
Division sentences related to multiplication sentences, 128–129
Division by zero, 135
Divisor, 124
remainders less than, 208
2-digit, 234–235
Dollar sign, *see* **Money notation**

E

Eighth inch, 164–165
Equal fractions, 246–251
checking for, 253
finding, 250–251
lists of, 248–249, 276, 286
multiplication and, 248–249
Equal to (=), 40–41, 65, 260–262
Estimating
differences, 98–100
products, 190–191, 200
sums, 72–74
Evaluation, *see* **Chapter Test**
Even number, 111
Expanded numeral, through 9,999, 26–27
Extra information
solving problems with, 282–283

F

Fact Tricks, for subtraction, 10–11
Factor(s), 106, 134–135
0, 108
1, 109
2, 110
3 and 4, 112–113
5 and 6, 114–115
7 and 8, 116
9, 117
zeros in, 177, 192–193

Fahrenheit (°F) temperature scale, 169
Figures
  slides, turns, and flips of, 312
  symmetric, 314–315
Flips of figures, 312
Flow chart, 91
  computer, 313
Foot (ft), 166
Fortnight, 233
Fraction(s), 242–253, 256–257, 259–266
  addition of, 272–277; with different denominators, 276–277; sums greater than 1, 274–275
  comparing, 259–262
  to decimals on the computer, 291
  as division, 263
  equal, *see* Equal fractions
  finding, of whole numbers, 256
  meaning of, 242
  mixed numbers and, 264–265
  on a number line, 262, 284
  as parts of a group, 244–245
  as parts of a whole, 244–245
  ratios as, 257
  Skills Review, 319, 341
  subtraction of, 284–287; with different denominators, 286–287
  whole numbers and, 264–265
  writing, from decimals, 290, 292–293

G

Gallon (gal), 167

Geometric shapes
  identifying, 306–311, 324–325
  patterns in, 119, 187
Geometry
  angle, 304–305, right, 304–305
  area, 318–321
  circle, 306–307
  closed curve, 308
  cone, 324–325
  cube, 324–325
  curve, 308
  cylinder, 324–325
  diameter, 306–307
  intersecting lines, 302–303
  line, 302–303, 314–315
  line segment, 302–303
  parallel lines, 302–303
  perimeter of a polygon, 316–317
  point, 302
  polygons, 308–311
  radius, 306–307
  ray, 304
  rectangle, 310–311
  rectangular prism, 324–325
  simple closed curve, 308
  solid figures, 324–325
  sphere, 324–325
  square, 310–311
  symmetry, 314–315
  triangle, 310–311
  volume, 326–327
Gram (g), 148–149
Graph, 334–339
  bar, 336–337
  circle, 338–339
  pictograph, 334–335
Graphing ordered pairs, 344–345
Greater than ($>$), 40–41, 65, 259–262
Group, fractions as part of a, 244–245
Grouping property of addition, 54
Grouping property of multiplication, 120

H

Half hour, 158
Half inch, 164–165
Hands On, 17, 80, 118, 127, 155, 206, 223, 235, 291
Hour hand, 158; *see also* Time
Hours, 160–161, 232–233

I

Inch (in.), 164–166
Inequality, 40–41, 65, 259–262
Intersecting lines, 302–303
Inverse operations, 81, 208

K

Kilogram (kg), 148–149
Kilometer (km), 144–146
  square, 320

L

Less than ($<$), 40–41, 65, 259–262
Line segment(s), 302–303
  drawing polygons with, 309
Linear measurement, 142–146 164–166, 318
Line(s), 302–303
  intersecting, 302–303
  parallel, 302–303
  of symmetry, 314–315
Liquid measurement, 147, 167
Liter (L), 147

M

Maintenance, *see* Skills Check; Skills Review
Making
  a bar graph, 337
  a pictograph, 335
Mass measurement, 148–149
Measurement, 142–172
  area, 318–321
  customary, *see* Customary system

dates, 162
linear, 142–146, 164–166, 318
liquid, 147, 167
mass, 148–149
metric, *see* Metric system
Skills Review, 281
temperature, 150–151
time, 158–162, 232–233
weight, 168
Meter (m), 144–146
square, 320–321
Metric system
area measurement, 318–321
Celsius (°C) scale, 150–151
centimeter (cm), 142–146
changing, 146–149
cubic units, 326–327
gram (g), 148–149
kilogram (kg), 148–149
kilometer (km), 144–146
liter (L), 147
meter (m), 144–146
metric ton (t), 148–149
milliliter (mL), 147
square units, 318–321
Metric ton (t), 148–149
Midchapter Review, 6, 34, 64, 90, 119, 152, 186, 220, 252, 280, 312, 340
Mile (mi), 166
Milliliter (mL), 147
Minute hand, 158; *see also* Time
Minutes, 158–161, 232–233
Missing information, problems with, 342–343
Mixed numbers, 264
addition of, 278–279
fractions and, 264–265
subtraction of, 288–289
sums of fractions as, 274–277
writing, from a decimal, 290, 292–293
Money notation, 68–69
addition with, 70
division with, 230
estimating: differences with, 98–99; products

with, 190–191
making change with, 96–97
multiplication with, 184–185
rounding with, 43
Skills Review, 231
subtraction with, 95
word names for, 68–69
Month/day/year form, 162
Multiple, 134–135
Multiplication
basic facts, *see* Multiplication facts
checking division by, 126, 208
on the computer, 118
equal fractions and, 248–249
estimating products, 190–191
finding area by, 320–321
grouping property of, 120
with money notation, 184–185
with multiples of 10, 194–195
multiplication-addition property, 121
of a 1-digit number: by a 2-digit number, 178–179; by a 3-digit number, 180–181; by a 4-digit number, 182–183
order property of, 110
patterns in, 177, 192–193
Skills Review, 129, 153, 221, 231, 341
of tens, hundreds, and thousands, 177, 192–193
of a 2-digit number: by a 2-digit number, 196–197; by a 3-digit number, 198–199
Multiplication-addition property, 121
Multiplication facts, 106–117
drawing an array, 107
with 0 as a factor, 108
with 1 as a factor, 109
with 2 as a factor, 110
with 3 and 4 as factors, 112–113

with 5 and 6 as factors, 114–115
with 7 and 8 as factors, 116
with 9 as a factor, 117
Multiplication sentences, 106–107
related to division sentences, 128–129

N

Non-Routine Problems, 14, 37, 71, 90, 94, 119, 152, 163, 187, 195, 221, 258, 281, 305, 312, 341
Number line, fractions on a, 262, 284
Number sentences
choosing, 38–39 (+, −), 188–189 (+, −, ×, ÷)
comparing, 65
related, *see* Related sentences
writing, 15 (+, −), 66–67 (+, −), 128–129 (×, ÷), 156–157 (×, ÷)
Numbers/Numeration
completing patterns, *see* Patterns
even, 111
mixed, *see* Mixed numbers
names for, 35
odd, 111
ordered pairs, 344–345
place value, 28–33, 293
puzzle, 258
Skills Review, 71, 187
whole, *see* Whole numbers
Numeral(s)
expanded, writing, 26–27, 30–31
Roman, 36–37
writing standard: through 9,999, 26–27; through 999,999, 30–31; through 999,999,999, 32–33
Numerator, 242–243

O

Odd number, 111
Order property of addition, 2

Order property of
multiplication, 110
Ordered pairs, graphing,
344–345
Ordering whole numbers, 341
Ounce (oz), 168
Outcomes, possible, 346–349

P

Parallel lines, 302–303
Parentheses, 120–121
Pascaline, 52
Patterns
  completing in a sequence:
  of fractions, 248–249,
  281; of geometric
  shapes, 119, 187; of
  letters and numbers, 37;
  of numbers, 18–19, 71
  in multiplication, 177
  192–193
  in quotients, 207
  in subtraction, 90
Perimeter, 316–317
Periods in numerals, 32
Pictographs, 334–335
Pictures, solving problems by
  drawing, 322–323
Pint (pt), 167
Place value, 28–33, 293
Pm time, 160–161
Points, 302
Polygons, 308–311
  perimeters of, 316–317
Possible outcomes, 346–349
Pound (lb), 168
Probability, 346–349
Problem Formulation, 1, 24–
  25, 50–51, 78–79, 104–
  105, 140–141, 174–175,
  204–205, 240–241, 270–
  271, 300–301, 332–333
Problem-Solving Application
  careers, 20, 74, 136, 200,
  266
  estimating differences, 100

finding the better buy, 328
Non-Routine Problems,
  14, 37, 71, 90, 94, 119,
  152, 163, 187, 195, 221,
  258, 281, 305, 312, 341
solving problems involving
  fractions and decimals,
  296
using customary measure,
  350
using information in a
  chart, 46, 350
using metric measures,
  321–323
using multiplication or
  division to solve, 170, 236
Problem-Solving Skill
choosing correct
  operations, 12–13
choosing number
  sentences, 38–39
  (+, −), 188–189
  (+, −, ×, ÷)
determining if problems
  have enough
  information, 342–343
estimating for checking
  reasonable answers, 122–
  123
solving problems by
  drawing pictures, 322–
  323
solving problems using
  four steps, 92–93
solving problems with extra
  information, 282–283
solving problems with
  hidden steps, 254–255
solving two-step problems,
  224–225
writing number sentences,
  66–67 (+, −), 156–157
  (×, ÷)
Products, 106
  estimating, 190–191
  found by drawing arrays,
  107
  zeros in, 177, 192–193
Programming computer, see
  Computer
Puzzle, number, 258

Q

Quart (qt), 167
Quarter hour, 158
Quarter inch, 164–165
Quotients, 124
  as a mixed number, 265
  found by drawing arrays,
  124
  found by using
  subtraction, 125
  found using related facts,
  128–133
  1-digit, 208–209, 226–227,
  234–235
  patterns in, 207
  3-digit, 214–217
  2-digit, 210–213, 228–229
  zeros in, 207, 218–219
  228–229

R

Radius, 306–307
Ratios, 257
Ray, 304
Reasoning, see also Patterns
  flow charts, 91, 313, 362–
  364
  identifying geometric
  shapes, 119, 187, 306–
  311, 324–325
  recognizing slides, flips,
  and turns, 312
  time relations, time before
  and after, 160–162
Rectangle, 310–311
Rectangular prism, 324–325
Related sentences
  addition and subtraction,
  15–16
  division and multiplication,
  128–129
Remainders
  as a fraction, 265
  division with, 208–219,
  226–229, 234–235
  less than divisors, 208
Renaming in subtraction, 82–
  89

Right angles, 304–305
Roman numerals, 36–37
Rounding
  addends, 72–73
  to estimate differences,
    98–99
  factors, 190–191
  numbers, 42–44
  Skills Review, 71, 187

S

Seconds, 232–233
Sequences, 37, 119, 187, 281
  see also Patterns
**Sides of triangles, rectangles,
  and squares,** 310
Simple closed curve, 308
Skills Check
  applications, 77, 173, 269,
    353
  computation, 23, 103, 203,
    299
  concepts, 49, 139, 239, 331
Skills Review
  addition, 14, 29, 45, 94,
    187, 231, 319, 341
  division, 163, 258, 307, 341
  facts, 14, 29, 34, 45, 129,
    153, 163
  fractions, 319, 341
  measurement, 281
  mixed addition and
    subtraction drill, 45
  money notation, 94, 118,
    187, 221, 231, 341
  multiplication, 129, 153,
    221, 231, 341
  numeration, 71
  rounding, 71, 187
  subtraction, 14, 34, 45,
    118, 187, 231, 319, 341
  time, 281
Slides of figures, 312
Solid figures, 324–325
Something Extra
  Activity, 135
  Calculator Activity, 6, 64,
    133, 186, 280, 317, 347

Non-Routine Problems,
  14, 37, 71, 90, 94, 119,
  152, 163, 187, 195, 221,
  258, 281, 305, 312, 341
Special Topic
  checking equal fractions,
    253
  comparing sums and
    differences, 65
  flowcharts, 91
  multiples and factors, 134–
    135
  multiplication-addition
    property, 121
  names for numbers, 35
  symmetry, 314–315
  using related sentences,
    16
Sphere, 324–325
Square, 310–311
Square centimeter, 318–321
Square kilometer, 320
Square meter, 320–321
Squares of whole numbers,
  186
Standard numeral, 26–27,
  30–33
Subtraction
  basic facts, *see* Subtraction
    facts
  checking, by addition, 81, 91
  of decimals, 295
  estimating differences, 98–
    100
  of 4-digit numbers, 86–87
  of fractions, 284–287
  making change, 96–97
  of mixed numbers,
    288–289
  with money notation, 95
  of 9's, 10
  patterns in, 90
  quotients found by using,
    125
  Skills Review, 14, 34, 45,
    118, 187, 231, 319, 341
  of 3-digit numbers, 84–85
  with time notation, 160–
    161

  of 2-digit numbers, 82–83
  zeros in, 88–89
Subtraction facts, 8–11
**Subtraction sentences related
  to addition sentences,**
  15–16
Sums, 2, 54, 56, 58, 94
  estimating, 72–73
  of fractions, 1 or greater,
    274–275
Symbols in pictographs, 334–
  335
Symmetry, 314–315

T

Temperature measurement,
  150–151, 169
  Celsius (°C), 150–151
  Fahrenheit (°F), 169
Thermometer, 150–151, 169
Time, 158–162
  addition with, 160–161
  am and pm, 160–161
  calendar, 162
  converting unit of, 232–233
  reading a clock, 158–159
  Skills Review, 281
  subtraction with, 160–161
Ton, 168
Triangle, 310–311
Turns of figures, 312

V

Volume, 326–327

W

Week, 232–233
Weight measurement, 168
Whole number(s), *see also*
  **Computation skills with
  whole numbers**
  comparing, 40–41
  cubed, 186

factors of, 134–135
finding fractions of, 256
fractions and, 265
multiples of, 134–135
ordering, 341
rounding, 42–44
squared, 186
sums of fractions as, 274–275
word names for, 26–27, 31, 33
writing, *see* Numerals, writing standard

Word names
for decimals, 290, 292
for money, 68–69
for whole numbers, 26–27, 31, 33
Word problems, *see* **Problem-Solving Application; Problem-Solving Skill**

Y

Yard (yd), 166

Year, 232–233

Z

Zeros
as a divisor, 135
in addition, 2
in factors and products, 177, 192–193
in multiplication, 108
in quotients, 207, 218–219, 228–229
in subtraction, 88–89

INDEX

ART CREDITS

Eulala Connor: pp. 4, 6, 12, 33, 43, 54, 69, 73, 100, 107, 108, 112, 114, 146, 147, 167, 182, 191, 217, 219, 230, 253, 257

Alice Coxe: pp. 28, 40, 53, 56, 82, 160, 178, 208, 272, 274, 278, 284, 288, 292, 293, 326

Ebet Dudley: pp. All "HANDS ON" and "SKILLS REVIEW" feature art

Elizabeth Frenchman: pp. 184, 334

Jean Helmer: pp. 10, 27, 31, 36, 38, 62, 70, 99, 110, 116, 124, 125, 128, 130, 132, 145, 168, 169, 177, 185, 192, 194, 226, 233, 243, 244, 245, 256, 286, 296, 323, 344, 349

Yee Chea Lin: p. 154

Patti Perleberg: pp. 2, 18, 19, 64, 92, 96, 97, 106, 134, 142, 144, 148, 150, 162, 188, 211, 225, 250, 277, 311, 316, 328, 338, 342

Katherine Schwan: p. 120

Jerry Smath: p. 7

Vantage Art Inc.: pp. 7, 42, 44, 52, 171, 172, 206, 243, 267, 268, 302, 303, 304, 305, 312, 313, 329, 330, 340, 348, 351, 352, 362, 364

PHOTO CREDITS

HRW photos by **Russell Dian** appear on the following pages: 42, 131, 280, 308, 310.

HRW photos by **Yoav Levy** appear on the following pages: 147, 224, 229, 285.

HRW photos by **Daniel Quat** appear on the following pages: 8, 118, 346.

Chapter 1: p. vi/1, © Frank J. Miller/Photo Researchers; p. 5, Alan Pitcairn/Grant Heilman; p. 13, M. Skott/Image Bank; p. 15, Grafton Smith/Image Bank; p. 20, Larry Downing/Woodfin Camp. **Chapter 2:** p. 24/25, Gabe Palmer/Image Bank; p. 35, Michael Salas/Image Bank; p. 39, Stephen J. Kraseman/Peter Arnold; p. 46, NASA. **Chapter 3:** p. 50/51, John Lewis Stage/Image Bank; p. 52, Courtesy of IBM; p. 67, Bill Grimes/Black Star; p. 73, D. & J. Heaton/The Stock Shop; p. 74, Charles Harbutt/Archive Pictures. **Chapter 4:** p. 78/79, Reinhart Wolf/© *Geo Magazine*; p. 87, Robert Frerck/Woodfin Camp; p. 93, Timothy Eagan/Woodfin Camp. **Chapter 5:** p. 104/105, Tom Stringer/Image Vendors; p. 111, HRW by Don Huntstein; p. 113, Christopher Springman; p. 123, H.M. Edwards/The Stock Market; p. 136, J. Barry o'Rourke/The Stock Market. **Chapter 6:** p. 140/141, Larry Smith/Black Star; p. 149, Frank Siteman/Stock Boston; p. 156 (top) Wally McNamee/Woodfin Camp, (bottom) Focus on Sports; p. 157, Chuck Mullstock/Focus on Sports; p. 170, Paul Slaughter/Image Bank. **Chapter 7:** p. 174/175, Peter Vadnai; p. 176 (top), Jet Propulsion Lab, California Institute of Technology, (bottom), Bill Gallery/Stock Boston; p. 180, NASA; p. 189, Harvey Lloyd/Image Bank; p. 190, HRW by Bill Hubbell; p. 196, Dan McCoy/Rainbow; p. 198, Barry Rourke/Stock Market; p. 200, Richard Hutchings/Photo Researchers. **Chapter 8:** p. 204/205, Joseph F. Viesti; p. 207, HRW by Ken Lax; p. 215, Craig Aurness/West Light; p. 236, John Neubauer/International Stock Photo. **Chapter 9:** p. 240/241, Bob Stern/International Stock Photo; p. 249, Wayne Sproul/International Stock Photo; p. 254, Paul Fusco/Magnum; p. 255, Carl Wolinsky/Stock Boston; p. 265, Clyde H. Smith/Peter Arnold; p. 266, Bill Stanton/The Stock Market. **Chapter 10:** p. 270/271, Ted Horowitz/Image Bank; p. 276, Chattanooga/Times; p. 283, Shostal Associates. **Chapter 11:** p. 300/301, Michael Heron, 1980; p. 320, Joe Munroe/Photo Researchers; p. 322, Steve Allen/Peter Arnold; p. 326, Junebug Clark/Photo Researchers. **Chapter 12:** p. 332/333, James A. Sugar/Black Star; p. 339, Omni Photo Communications © Lea; p. 343, HRW by Bruce Buck.